SUBSCRIPTION NOTICE

This Wiley product is updated on a periodic basis with supplements to reflect important changes in the subject matter. If you purchased this product directly from John Wiley & Sons, Inc., we have already recorded your subscription for this update service.

If, however, you purchased this product from a bookstore and wish to receive (1) the current update at no additional charge, and (2) future updates and revised or related volumes billed separately with a 30-day examination review, please send your name, company name (if applicable), address, and the title of the product to:

Supplement Department
John Wiley & Sons, Inc.
One Wiley Drive
Somerset, NJ 08875
1-(800)-225-5945

Real Estate Valuation

Real Estate Valuation

Guide to Investment Strategies

TERRY VAUGHN GRISSOM

JULIAN DIAZ III

JOHN WILEY & SONS, INC.

New York • Chichester • Brisbane • Toronto • Singapore

Library of Congress Cataloging-in-Publication Data

Grissom, Terry V. (Terry Vaughn)
Real estate valuation: guide to investment strategies / Terry Vaughn Grissom and Julian Diaz III.
p. cm.—(Real estate practice library)
Includes index.
ISBN 0-471-60087-3 (alk. paper)
1. Real property—Valuation. 2. Real estate investment. 3. Tax assessment. 4. Real property and taxation. I. Title. II. Series.
HD1387.G75 1991
333.33′2—dc20 91-10657
CIP

Printed in the United States of America

10 9 8 7 6 5 4 3 2 1

The authors would like to dedicate this book to their families, both immediate and extended, for their aid and support over the years. They also dedicate this book to their mentors, James A. Graaskamp, PhD, SREA, CRE; Richard B. Andrews, PhD; William "Tubby" Grissom, MAI; Julian Diaz, Jr., JD, SREA, MAI; and Frank Newman, MAI.

The authors would also like to thank the Director, Richard Floyd, PhD; Senior Research Economist, Ted C. Jones, PhD; Secretary, Lois Carter; and the staff at the Real Estate Center, Texas A&M University, for their help and encouragement.

Preface

Several years ago, a regionally noted real estate analyst was engaged by a large corporation to analyze a specific property that the corporation owned. He conducted the analysis and submitted a bill for $3,000. The corporation returned the bill to him and asked for an itemized bill instead.

His response was:

- $ 200 for research and data gathering
  $ 100 for assembling the report
  $2,700 for settin' and thinkin'.

This story addresses the essence of understanding real estate properties as economic goods. Much of the difficulty in integrating real estate into standard business decisions arises from a dichotomy in how real estate is viewed. One perception is that real estate is a unique good or investment that requires different, specialized knowledge. The other perception is that real estate is only another form of capital.

The appropriate approach seems to be somewhere in between the two perceptions. Detailed and informed insight is needed, however, given the problems that have been experienced in real estate in the recent past and those that loom for the immediate and long-term future. The quest of this book is to identify a process for appropriately analyzing real estate.

Bertrand Russell wrote that understanding causal relationships is an abstract matter; the abstraction creates more powerful thoughts. The application of this power-thought abstraction process to real estate is illustrated by the following situation. A real estate property's physical nature is best understood by the property manager, who knows every corner of the building and its functional capacity. Yet, the property manager makes relatively little money compared to the professionals who view real estate more abstractly.

For example, a real estate agent who may be retained to sell the property operated by the manager may view the realty as a product to be bought and/or sold. The agent's perception of the property is slightly more abstract than the property manager's, but is often associated with more income in relation to the property.

At the most abstract level is the stock exchange manipulator, a professional who has never seen the property and knows it only as a purely abstract realty that may go up or down in value. Of all those concerned, the offeror may make the most money from the property and may have the most control over it. By operating on a higher level of abstraction, the offeror sees the problem—or the asset or situation—from a perspective that can break through the institutional setting and the burden of specifics that often divert decisions. Making the appropriate decisions is often linked to experience and the ability to sit and think about the problem.

This book offers a process of investigating the dimensions of real estate, real estate problems, and real estate decisions. Novices will gain from this process insights that may otherwise be gained only from experience. Those experienced in real estate decision making will find identification and articulation of the steps they intuitively take in solving specific problems and applying their experience in the context of a changing economic environment.

No book can guarantee wealth and power from following its process or advice. The goals here are to give insights into the causal relationships in real estate, to offer an opportunity of exposure to techniques and models for making real estate decisions, to investigate the fundamentals of physical real estate as they relate to the abstract behavior of markets, and, consequently, to develop readers' potential for innovative insights and alternative perceptions of real estate.

Alternative perspectives on the familiar enable the development of power thought, which is the essential ingredient in sophisticated decision making. The development of power-thought skills, when combined with an understanding of real estate fundamentals, markets, and economics, far outdistances the pretensions of power and hints of important connections that must be endured so often at power lunches.

Bryan/College Station, Texas
August 1991

TERRY VAUGHN GRISSOM
JULIAN DIAZ III

Contents

Introduction

In simpler times, real estate was "the land and everything attached to it." This definition still serves to describe a farm, but does little to capture the nature of a condominium on the 69th floor of the John Hancock Tower or a time-share interest in a condo in Lake Tahoe. The creation of new physical and financial products has crippled the old definition of real estate and made real estate investment analysis a dangerous enterprise. If the nature of a product is not understood, the analysis of the product will be confused. If the old definition leads to confusion, a new definition is needed.

What is the common element in a farm, a condominium in a downtown business district, and a time-share interest in a popular resort area? James Graaskamp identified this common element as space to be used over time.[1] Real estate, whether in fee (owned) or leased, is a space–time product that is subject to external forces. This realization leads to the following formal definition:

> Real estate is artificially delineated space that has a fourth dimension, time, referenced to some point on the surface of the earth. This delineated space, created to house some economic activity, is subject to cultural preference and is constrained by public infrastructure.[2]

[1] James A. Graaskamp, *A Guide to Feasibility Analysis* (Chicago: Society of Real Estate Appraisers, 1973).

[2] Terry V. Grissom, "Real Estate Analysis with an International Perspective," *International Real Estate Journal,* 7:1 (1984): 18–23.

This definition introduces the basic business elements of real estate: physical or economic space that can be used over time; the use of the space, which forms the basis of a property's financial return; and the amount of financial return received over time.

SPACE–TIME CHARACTERISTICS

The space–time element is central not only to a meaningful definition of real estate but also to a fruitful analysis of real estate. An overquoted axiom, that the three most important factors in analyzing real estate are location, location, and location, is only partly true. Only when the concept of location is expanded to encompass the dimension of time can the essence of real estate value be fully comprehended. The space–time characteristic of any given piece of real estate is a function of social, legal, political, economic, and physical forces. These forces become attributes of the real estate, expanding the physical characteristic of location into a social, legal, political, economic, and physical characteristic: space–time. Because real estate analysis involves units of comparison and measurements of revenue, the space–time characteristics of a property provide the focus of analysis.

The heart of any analysis, however, is the methods employed. The methods or models of real estate investment analysis can be classified into three groups, according to the decision criterion each method uses: value, solvency, or rates. These models are fully examined in Chapter 1.

REAL ESTATE CONCERNS

To buy or to sell is the classic real estate decision, but real estate analysts face numerous other problem contexts or environments. A partial list includes:

1. Acquisition/disposition of ownership or change of control
2. Extension of credit or the pledge of real estate as security
3. Indemnification or compensation for loss
4. Taxation
5. Development or redevelopment
6. Portfolio management.

Any decision to acquire or dispose of real property ownership involves an estimate of appropriate price and timing. Change of control decisions—trading of property, reorganization of ownership, estate distribution, or merger—require similar estimates, often as mandated by law. Generally, value models are preferred, but investors who are concerned about the return and the risk of a prospective acquisition should focus on solvency by examining cash flow patterns, levels of financial risk, and competitive potential.

When money is borrowed and credit is extended, the concerns of the creditor are cash flow and collateral. A property that is a single-family residence generates no cash flow; the lender will then focus on the cash flow of the borrower. If a property is income-producing real estate, the lender's focus shifts to the income productivity of the property. Solvency models are used, and the analysis of solvency issues is of primary concern in this decision environment. Because the collateral is the lender's second line of defense, the analysis of market value through the use of value models is also necessary.

When destruction of property occurs, indemnification or equitable compensation to the property owner for the loss in property value may be appropriate. A loss in property value is often termed an involuntary conversion, which simply means a loss of control over an asset. The property owner no longer controls the factors that would have determined the best timing for a conversion of the property to cash. Involuntary conversion can result from the accidental destruction of property (an insurable loss) or from the exercise of the public right of eminent domain (condemnation). Both types of involuntary conversion require an analysis of value, but the values—and hence the analysis—can be very different. For an insurable loss, the value estimate generally is defined within the insurance policy; for condemnation, a just and adequate compensation based on market value is required.

The estimation of tax is an important analytical problem in real estate. Even when the purpose of analysis is not expressly tax determination, taxes cast a large shadow. Most taxes (property, gift, or estate) are based on a measure of value, that is, they are *ad valorem*. The major concern in calculating property tax is consistency in application, or tax equity. With consistent application, similar properties are equally assessed in relation to their market value. Income tax is based not only on the income generated by the property, but also on the difference between the property's value at the time of purchase and its value at resale. Both solvency and value, therefore, are issues of analysis for purposes of tax estimation.

Development or redevelopment is a form of real estate "manufacturing"; investment value, or the value of the asset to the specific owner, and is its primary concern. If a property is placed on the open market, the focus shifts to the market value or exchange value of the asset. Value may be the developers' primary concern, but they must also be aware of solvency and rate-of-return issues. Liquidity is developers' most common problem and any developer who ignores issues of solvency will soon face a liquidity crisis.

Investment management, whether of a single piece of real estate or a portfolio of real property, requires monitoring asset productivity. The heart of single-asset or portfolio management is rate analysis and the risk/return trade-off. Against this background of rate analysis value and cash flow, forecasts become especially critical because of the paucity of data generated by the thin trading that is typical of real estate markets. Risk can lead to variations in cash flow and therefore in value; with little or no historical information, variation in value must be tied to the variability of cash flow estimates.

THE MARKET AS A FRAMEWORK

Armed with a fundamental definition of real estate, basic tools for analysis, and an understanding of the problem environments in which the tools are likely to be used, an analyst needs a framework for the systematic solution of any real estate problem. The definition of real estate describes a complex entity that is both a durable and a financial good and is defined by physical forces as well as by social, legal, and economic factors. To understand a real estate asset, more than a delineation of its physical characteristics is needed; its market must also be understood. An analyst seeking to understand a real estate market must investigate supply and demand, the structure and growth of the neighborhood, city, and region, and expectations of change over time. All these forces must be brought together in an ordered process, to improve the quality of real estate decisions.

THE APPRAISAL PROCESS

The most systematic approach for analyzing real estate, the appraisal process, has developed within the appraisal industry. Like scientific methods and other systematic problem-solving methodologies, the appraisal process begins with the identification of the problem. Within the traditional appraisal process, the identification of the problem has been reduced to the following steps:

1. Identification of the real property (e.g., a street address)
2. Identification of the appropriate property rights (e.g., fee simple, leasehold, or leased fee)
3. Date of value estimate
4. Objective of assignment
5. Definition of value.

In addition to defining the problem to be addressed, these steps delimit the relevance and usefulness of the outputs of analysis. Consequently, they delimit the professional liability of the analyst and discourage inappropriate use of his or her work.

Identification of the Problem

Steps 1 and 3 define the space–time characteristics of the property being appraised. Only within the space–time envelope does the concept of real estate value hold any meaning. A specific parcel of real estate does not maintain the same value over time, nor are different parcels of real estate likely to have identical values at any point in time.

Even when the geography and time of analysis are set, the appropriate property rights must be specified (step 2). Is the entire bundle of rights (fee simple estate) to be valued, or only the rights specified in a 20-year lease (leasehold estate), or the rights remaining to the fee holder who has leased out the property for 20 years (leased fee estate), or the right to airspace 20 feet above the ground? Each of these property rights represents a distinct and separable interest within a parcel of real estate, and each may enjoy a very different value. The specific rights to be analyzed must be identified.

The objective or purpose of the appraisal (step 4) is to determine the type or concept of value being estimated. Market value (value in exchange) is the value concept used in most appraisal problems, but it is not always appropriate. Investment value, an entirely different value concept, may be more proper than market value for a given analysis. A failure to specify the type of value being estimated makes the appraisal misleading and invites abuse and liability. The function of the appraisal is the use to which the analysis will be put by the client, and, while not synonymous with the appraisal purpose, the intended use helps to identify the appropriate value concept. The function of an appraisal is often omitted from appraisal reports, to underscore the analyst's objectivity, but contemplation of the client's reason for seeking an appraisal can yield the most important clue to the correct value concept.

Closely related to the objective of the assignment is definition of the appropriate value concept (step 5). Much like the hypothesis in scientific method, the value definition drives the appraisal analysis. In scientific method, the hypothesis contains the question to be investigated and thus directs the scientific investigation. In the appraisal process, the value definition contains the problem to be solved and thus directs the search for data, the techniques of analysis, and the conclusions drawn. Unfortunately, there is no standardization of value definitions. The presence of many regulators and decision makers, each with a potentially different set of concerns, has spawned a proliferation of value definitions. Each definition carries the parameters and presumptions of its specific decision maker.[3] Because the value definition drives the valuation analysis, different definitions for the same value concept can lead to different estimates.

The Planning Stage

After the five-step problem definition, the traditional appraisal process proceeds to a planning stage in which the work necessary to conduct and complete the analysis is envisioned and scheduled. The gathering of data commences in this stage. The data needed will vary from one analysis to the next, depending on the appraisal objective. The range of data will include aspects of the general economy, the specific market, the real property, and even the relevant decision makers. The gathering process is deductive—its focus attenuates from the most general economic data to the most specific property data. Not all desired data will be available; data poverty is a reality faced by all real estate analysts. The data gathered are synthesized in the analysis of highest and best use, which leads into the three approaches to valuation: the cost approach, the market or sales comparison approach, and the income approach (see Chapter 1). This triumvirate of methods is the heart of

[3] Terry V. Grissom, "Value Definition: Its Place in the Appraisal Process," *The Appraisal Journal*, 53:2 (April 1985): 217–225.

the traditional valuation analysis and yields three separate value indications that must be reconciled into a final value estimate.

The Classification System

The analysis of real estate will always be ad hoc: many different objectives are possible, available data vary from assignment to assignment, and every parcel of real property is unique. Nonetheless, the traditional appraisal process provides a structure, through its system of classifications. The system defines the problem itself by defining and grouping the data needs, the data availability, the appropriate techniques, and the preliminary findings. From the classifications flow the descriptive analyses required when objectives need to be revealed, when good data are not always available, when property uniqueness needs to be explained, and when various regulating authorities must be satisfied.

Analysis by Analogy

Comparisons between the subject property being analyzed and various comparable or competitive properties are central to all three approaches to valuation. The process of making such comparisons and contrasts is analysis by analogy. Statistical analysis techniques, with their data-rich requirements, are currently not a significant part of the traditional appraisal process—one of its unfortunate and important weaknesses. Other weaknesses have led to the development of alternative solution processes.

Alternatives to the Appraisal Process

Any solution process applied to real estate concerns must aim toward framing the analytical problem in terms of the structure laid out by professional standards, governmental regulations, financial institutions, economic conditions, and client objectives. These constraints of the problem shape the form of its analysis. The primary tasks of the analyst, then, are to identify the constraints and to conform the analysis and solution so that the constraints are satisfied. The quest for appropriate forms has led to the development of alternative models. The traditional appraisal process, illustrated in Figure A, is not sacrosanct,

Figure A The Valuation Process

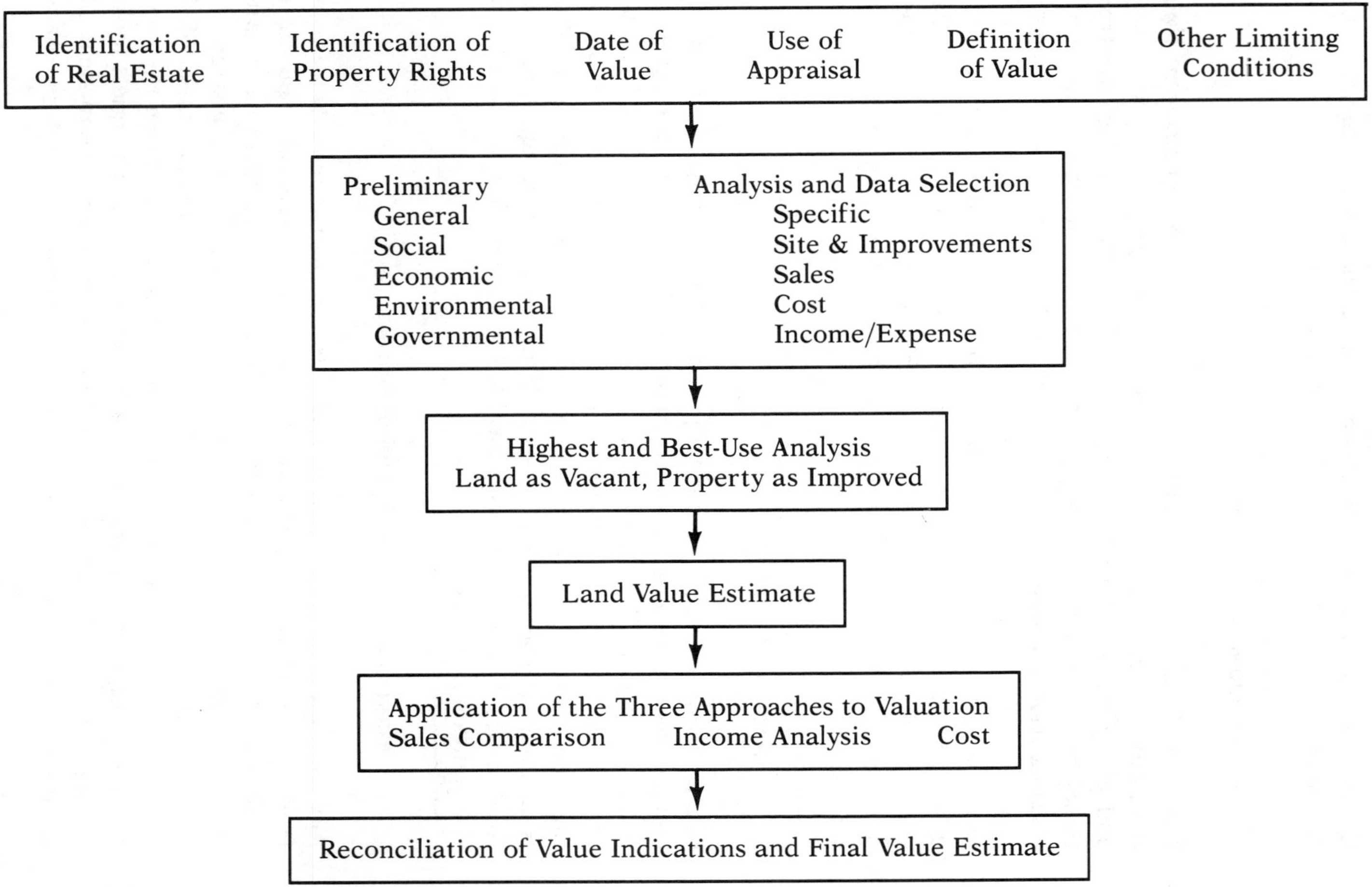

as some professionals would suggest. There is even evidence that appraisers do not routinely follow it.[4]

Wendt's alternative model proposed in 1956, represented the first significant challenge to the traditional appraisal process.[5] Wendt's model required limited detail in problem delineation but recognized the importance of legal attributes by prescribing a separate position to them. The valuation techniques were emphasized in Wendt's model, but the market comparison approach was its heart. The final value estimate was depicted as a judgment.

A second model was proposed by Wendt in 1974.[6] Like his first model, the enhanced model envisioned only a limited problem delineation; unlike the earlier model, it emphasized the role of value definition in driving the solution process. Two value concepts were specifically identified: most probable selling price, and investment value. Traditional valuation techniques were again included, but the second model also formally incorporated cash flow analysis and multiple regression.

A model offered by Case in 1976 expanded the process of defining the problem.[7] The solution process itself became structured on location and on market dimensions of the product. Case defined a real estate market to incorporate Keynesian parameters of individuals, firms, governments, and the economy, and he integrated contemporary issues that have developed since the neoclassic economics that underlies the traditional appraisal process. This innovative yet little known model anticipated Federal Home Loan Bank memoranda that expressed concern for a direct statement of the structure of the market in terms of speculation, degree of activity, supply, demand, absorption, and the impact of financing on actual transaction prices.

In 1972, Smith developed the model shown in Figure B.[8] Immediately after the problem definition, the process moves to the valuation methods. In addition to external economic conditions, the model injects risk

[4] Julian Diaz III, "How Appraisers Do Their Work: A Test of the Appraisal Process and the Development of a Descriptive Model," *The Journal of Real Estate Research,* 5:1 (Spring 1990): 1–16.

[5] Paul F. Wendt, *Real Estate Appraisal—A Critical Analysis of Theory and Practice* (New York: Holt, 1956).

[6] Paul F. Wendt, *Real Estate Appraisal: Review and Outlook* (Athens: University of Georgia Press, 1974).

[7] Fred E. Case, "The Theory of Valuation," in *Recent Perspectives in Urban Land Economics,* Edited by Michael Goldberg (Vancouver: The University of British Columbia Press, 1976).

[8] Halbert C. Smith, *Real Estate Appraisal* (Columbus, OH: Grid, 1976).

Figure B The Appraisal Process

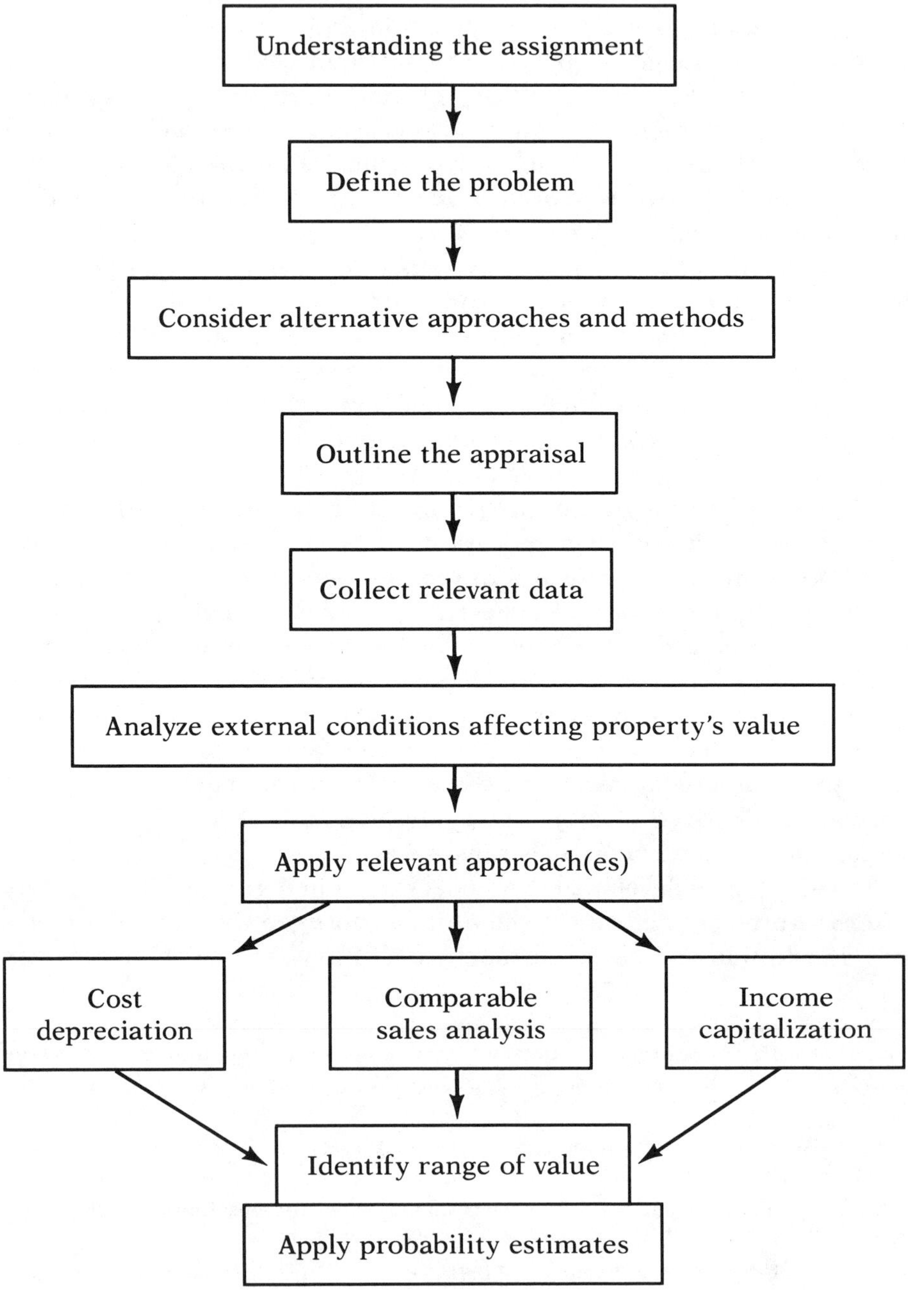

Source: Halbert C. Smith, *Real Estate Appraisal* (Columbus, OH: Grid 1976).

considerations into the process of valuation by introducing probability and interval estimates.

A model introduced by Smith and Racster in 1969 had shared many of the properties of the previously discussed processes.[9] The Smith–Racster process, much like Wendt's 1956 model, had centered on value issues, on an analysis of the market, and on the market comparison approach. Unlike Wendt's early model, the Smith–Racster process suggested a property residual approach; however, like the subsequent Wendt model, investment value and most probable sales price were the integral value concepts. Smith's 1972 model (Figure B) uses probability estimates to inject risk considerations into the analysis, a feature of the Smith–Racster process.

Figure C illustrates the Ratcliff–Graaskamp model,[10] which deviates from others by flowing directly from the purpose into an analysis of the attributes of the property. Directed by the property attributes, alternative uses are examined and the most probable use is identified. The identification of the most probable use drives an investigation into supply and demand and the construction of a probable buyer profile. The probable buyer profile, in turn, directs the selection and application of the most suitable valuation techniques, that is, the techniques that most accurately reflect the motivation of the most probable buyer. The process is inductive (from specific to general) rather than deductive. (Other processes, including the traditional appraisal process, are deductive.)

The dynamics of recent real estate markets have suggested the need for change in the traditional appraisal process. It can neither capture nor reflect the psychological movements that characterize today's investment and market environment. Because it cannot lead to an understanding of all current market situations, it cannot by itself provide a reliable framework for analyzing many of today's real estate problems. There is some promise in the alternative models. The Ratcliff–Graaskamp model, because of (1) the efficiency of its inductive orientation and (2) its focus on the psychological processes of most probable buyers, is adopted as the basis of the process proposed in this book. The investment fundamentals and probable selling price orientation of the 1974 Wendt model, the value theory issues developed by Case and

[9] Halbert Smith and Ronald Racster, "Should the Traditional Appraisal Process Be Restructured?" *The Real Estate Appraiser*, November–December, 1970.

[10] James A. Graaskamp, *The Appraisal of 25 North Pinckney: A Demonstration Case for Contemporary Appraisal Methods* (Madison, WI: Landmark Research, Inc., 1977).

Figure C The Ratcliff-Graaskamp Appraisal Model

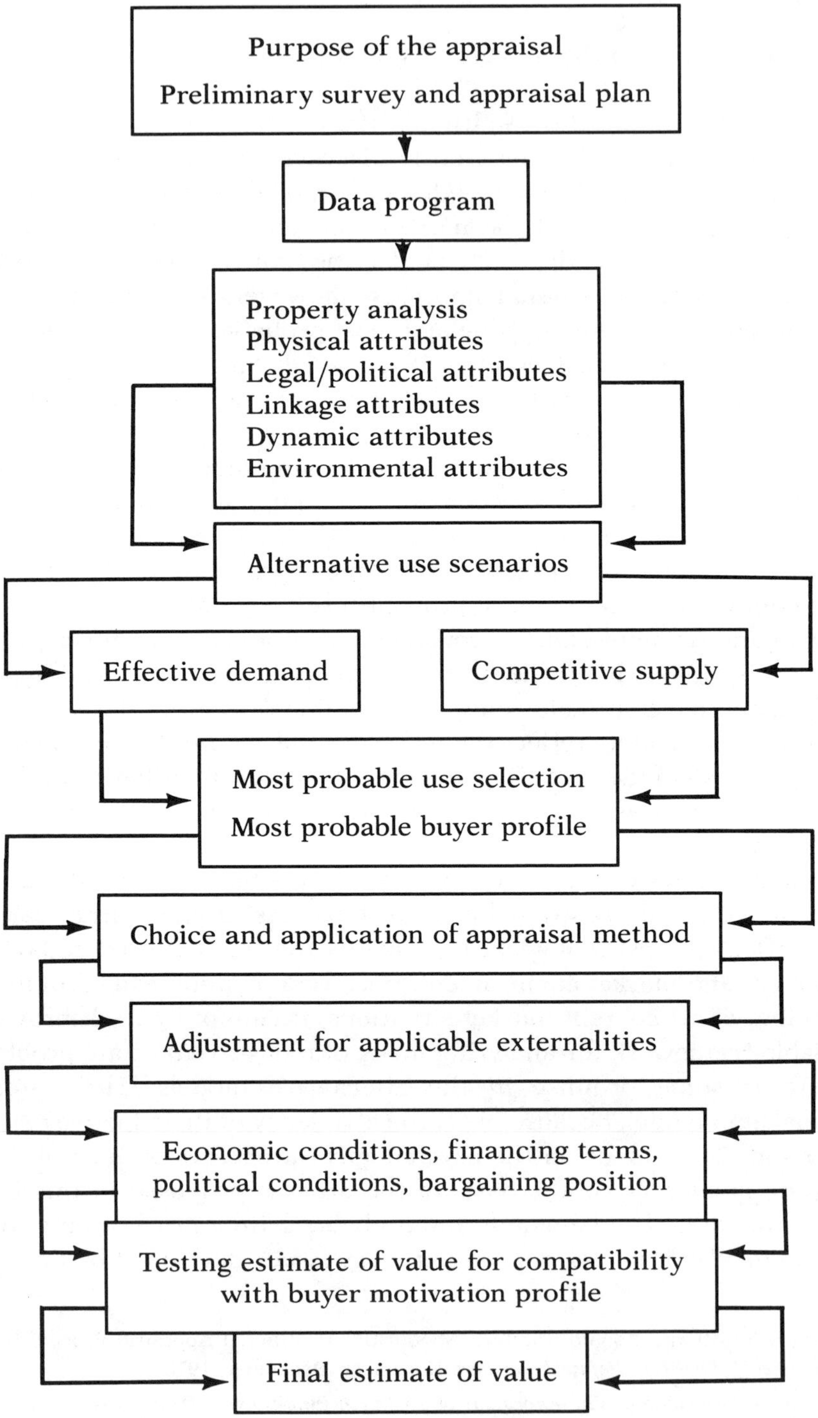

Source: James A. Graaskamp, *The Appraisal of 25 North Pinckney: A Demonstration Case for Contemporary Appraisal Methods* (Madison, WI: Landmark Research, 1977).

by Smith and Racster, and the economic theory introduced by Case will all be integrated into the evolving analytical processes.

ANALYSIS AS A PROCESS

This book views overall real estate analysis as a process, thus taking a broader perspective than is taken in the appraisal process, which limits its analytical conclusions to a value estimation. Figure D shows both the general process proposed in this book and the details involved in the overall analysis. However, the depiction in the figure is only one scenario of application. This particular scenario was selected to appear here because it is the application that is most similar to the appraisal process. Like the Ratcliff–Graaskamp appraisal model, the method progresses from the site to the market and the valuation approaches, using an inductive format. If real estate is unique because of its real asset attributes, then the site poses the major constraints on asset use. Unlike many other products or assets, the use and employment of real estate must be determined. The use then directs the product to the appropriate market and the measurement of return or value. Again, this inductive process is only one scenario. Other real estate problems—such as a market in search of a site, or the consideration of real estate as an alternative investment—require a deductive format or at least, a different emphasis of the model's parts. (These different scenarios are discussed in detail in Chapter 8.)

Section III of Figure D, Decision Models Investment Analysis, encompasses investment analysis models, valuation techniques, discounted cash flow, risk analysis, and numerous other approaches promulgated by commercial investment brokers and real estate counselors (designated, respectively, by the National Association of Realtors as CCIMs and CREs). An expanded discussion of the process and its various scenarios appear in Chapter 8, a more general approach. The third section of Figure D will be adaptable, depending on the problem situations.

OVERVIEW

The overall format of the book follows the process scenario of Figure D. Part One, Chapter 1 puts the process into a behavioral context by developing the array of decision models available. The chapter also

Figure D The Real Estate Process

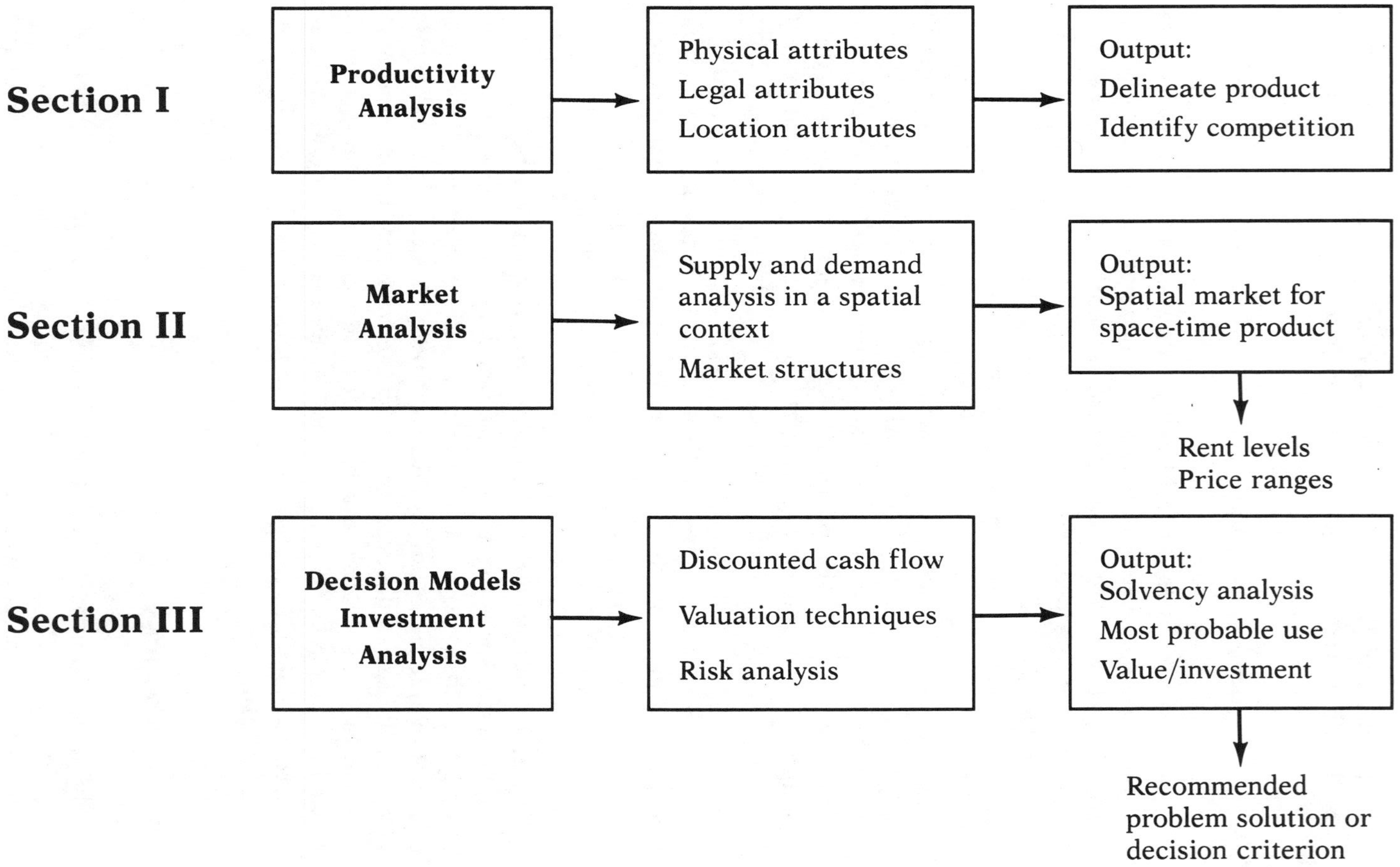

links the models to problem situations. Chapters 2 and 3 address the productivity analysis of the property, investigating the physical, legal, and location dimensions of real estate as they may impact various decision needs. Chapter 4 illustrates the space–time equation that links the productivity attributes to the discounted cash flow (DCF) model.

The classification of alternative income models is addressed in Chapter 5. Two popular and distinct classes of models are discussed in Chapters 6 and 7. Chapter 6 looks at the history of direct capitalization and ratio models. This historical perspective documents the appropriate situations in which these techniques can be employed. Chapter 7 discusses the alternative yield models and their application, and links direct capitalization to discounted cash flow models.

Chapter 8 expands on the analytical process initiated in this Introduction, by illustrating the array of problem solution scenarios. These scenarios then link the property attributes to the market and to the various decision models available. The emphasis of the relationship among product, market, and decision models varies with the problem context.

Part Two of the book investigates the contemporary market in the context of the decision process proposed in Part One. Real estate securitization, appraising/decision making with a lack of comparable sales, asset management and decision making in a down market, and the estimation of property taxes with limited information of the property's value are among the issues investigated. The array of problem situations in Part Two is intended to show the flexibility of the process and how it can span the concerns of several trade and professional areas.

Part One

The Process of Analysis and Decision Making

Chapters 1 through 8 discuss a real estate decision process. The process links the productive attributes of real estate (the physical, legal, and locational dimensions) to the market structure and then to the appropriate decision technique. The decision techniques include valuation models, solvency analysis, and rate analysis.

Three alternative scenarios are proposed within the process to link the productivity, market, and decision methods, but in different orders. The order of the methods and the emphasis of the scenarios vary with the problem situation that the decision makers may face.

The scenario offered as the process in Chapters 2 through 7 emphasizes the site-to-market orientation. This scenario best matches the traditional appraisal approach and is used for its comparative potential in allowing alternative presentations of the methods.

One

Alternative Decision Models: Value, Solvency, and Rates

§ 1.1 INTRODUCTION

Decision making in real estate centers around an investment or a consumption calculation. The choice of calculation is dependent on the nature of the real estate and on related problems.

The consumption calculation is predominant when the real estate is residential or recreational and is to be used for housing, leisure, or esthetic purposes. The investment calculation is the decision process used when the property is an income-producing property or commodity, a factor of production, or a resource. The basis for judging an investment must be the tradeoff of the money coming in versus the money going out, because the cash flows are associated with control of the property.

The consumption of real estate can be considered in an investment format, if the satisfactions of home ownership or the pleasure of recreation can be thought of as psychic income. Therefore, the investment calculation need not be limited to the tradeoff of income and capital gains received versus purchase price; it can be expanded to include the comparison of benefits received versus the intense effort expended in controlling specific parcels of property.

The generalized investment process helps to identify the basic categories of techniques used in real estate decisions. Figure 1.1 illustrates the general models used, grouped under the three broad criteria for decisions: value, solvency/income, and rate analysis. Under each of these categories is a broad array of analytic techniques.

Figure 1.1 Real Estate Decision Models

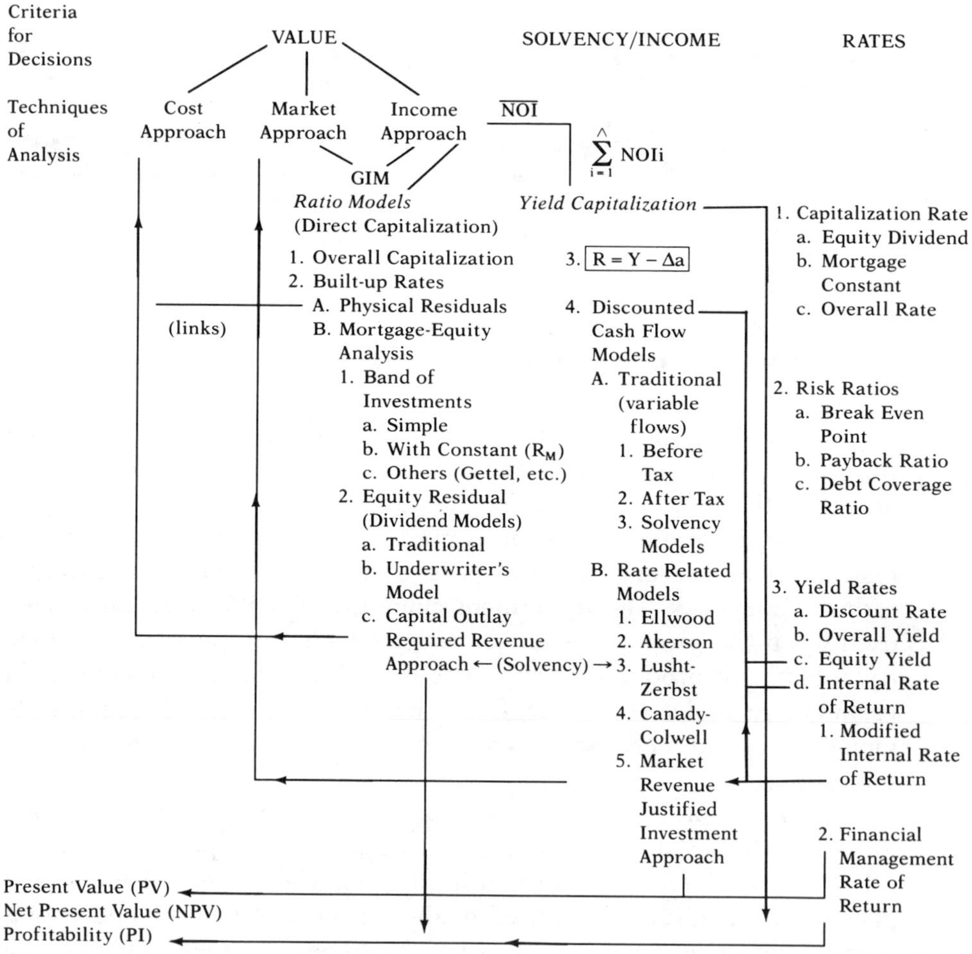

Source: Real Estate Center at Texas A&M University

§ 1.2 VALUE

The traditional and most popular criterion is value. The focus on value in real estate appeared in early texts[1] and is documented by the number of appraisal organizations that exist today.[2] The plethora of appraisal organizations suggests that there is a great demand, if not a national need, for value estimates.

The conceptual relevance of value as an economic criterion is based on its two theoretical foundations: value theory, and the range of valuation techniques available. Value theory identifies the worth of an object or property on the bases of its nature and the determinants of its future returns in the marketplace. The operative words are *future* and *marketplace.*

Concern with value requires a differentiation between value and price. Because common parlance tends to interchange the two terms, value is often estimated by analyzing transaction prices (actual prices that were paid). Price and value are not the same. Price is a historical fact, an actual occurrence that can be verified, and value is a potential price, a hypothetical event that has yet to occur.[3]

The *future* dimension of value emphasizes the principle of anticipation; value is the present worth of future anticipated benefits.[4] This orientation of anticipated returns supports the investment calculation involved in real estate decisions.

An actual decision to invest, however, cannot be limited to the personal situation of an individual investor. The decision is often constrained by the competitive context of the *marketplace.* Even in an analysis oriented toward the expectations, financial situation, and tax perspective of a given individual, the final *potential* price paid will probably reflect the competitive actions of others. These actions will depend on the supply of alternative (or substitutable) properties or on the number of people competing for a given site (or for similar properties).

[1] See, for example, Halbert Smith, Carl Tschappat, and Ronald Racster, *Real Estate and Urban Development* (Homewood, IL: Richard D. Irwin, Inc., 1973): 43–56.

[2] Ted C. Jones, "The Texas Real Estate Source Book," Real Estate Center, Texas A&M University, Austin, Technical Report, January 1988.

[3] Terry V. Grissom, "Appraisal Without Comparables," Real Estate Center, Texas A&M University, Austin, Technical Report, January 1989.

[4] American Institute of Real Estate Appraisers, *The Appraisal of Real Estate* (Chicago: AIREA, 1987): 32.

Value as a decision criterion, then, is important because value theory stresses the determinants that identify the productivity of an asset.

Two premises of value are value in use and value in exchange. Value in use addresses the fact that an asset has worth because it has or contributes to an overall function. The value of real estate may derive from its contribution to broader economic processes such as being a manufacturing site or housing specialized services. This perspective has often led to the notion that real estate is a resource to be rewarded, at best, with a residual return—an unearned profit resulting from ownership rather than effort.

A more contemporary view is that real estate, in the value-in-use context, is one of several factors of production that contribute value to the overall economic enterprise; as such, it is competing for returns and resources along with all other factors of production. When viewed as a productive factor, real estate has value because all economic undertakings require space and the comparative advantage of specific locations. These features, among other productive attributes, determine the worth of real estate as a factor of production.

Value in exchange is the aggregate notion that various economic enterprises compete for the ownership and/or use of real estate as a factor of production or as an asset to control. The issue of value in exchange is contingent not only on a use being provided but also upon the relative scarcity of the property type (the available supply) and the effective demand for the asset. These market forces establish the basis for the future price at which the realty may be transacted. Recognition of these transactions enables an actual dollar measure of the value.

§ 1.3 VALUATION

The second theoretical foundation recommending value as a decision tool is the range of valuation techniques available. Valuation theory is concerned with the tools or procedures by which value is estimated, measured, or predicted.[5] Value directs decision makers to identify both why a property has economic worth and how one can estimate that worth. As depicted in Figure 1.1, analytical techniques in valuation are traditionally grouped as the cost approach, the market approach (or sales comparison approach), and the income approach.

[5] Terry V. Grissom, "Value Definition: Its Place in the Appraisal Process," *The Appraisal Journal*, 53:2 (April 1985): 217–225.

(a) COST APPROACH

The value premise behind the cost approach is the theory of substitution. Cost new is not value; cost is a proxy for value. Under the principle of substitution, the worth of an existing facility is theoretically the cost of building it. If comparable sales are not available to indicate a property's value, then it is worth the cost of reproducing it.

Reproducing, or the reproduction cost new, has a very precise meaning in appraisal. It means the cost of producing an exact replica of existing facilities. The cost approach is only a valuation model. The property is not physically reproduced, but the cost of the reproduction is estimated, as one way of calculating the basis of the value estimate.

An alternative cost model is replacement cost new. Reproduction cost new would build an exact replica, even of an older facility that is deficient under current building standards. Replacement cost new would build a building of similar utility—the building would supply similar functional capacity to the existing structure. Supplying similar capacity would entail having the same building size, number of rooms, services, and so on, but constructing with current building materials, standards, and quality. For example, an existing old building may have solid masonry walls (three layers of brick), but its replacement cost estimate may be based on a brick veneer wall.

With either the reproduction or the replacement model, a cost new is estimated. This cost is then reduced, by various measures of depreciation, to approximate a value estimate. The depreciation deductions are true economic losses linked to the physical deterioration of the property, as caused by its functional capacity and interior design, and/or to any possible market penalties attributed to exterior factors.

The depreciated cost of the facility is then added to the land value, to provide an estimate of the overall property value. The cost approach is a summation approach that follows an accounting format but is based on economic analysis.

Although a site can be manufactured, land value is traditionally calculated by gathering data on comparable tracts that have been sold in the current market environment. This same approach is applicable to the overall property.

The weakness of the cost approach is that it is very complex; physical examples must be used, to arrive at a hypothetical replacement for the basis of value. The model's actual physical measure and current building cost are then altered by depreciation adjustments. Both the estimate of cost new and the depreciation *measures* are discussed as tangible occurrences, but, in fact, they do not exist. For example, a functional and curable obsolescence loss may be phrased as a tax measure deficiency by comparing the difference between the simulated cost, assuming the deficiency had been included at the time of the original construction, versus the cost of including it in the estimate today.

The chief weakness of the cost approach is that it is highly normative; it is based on how things *ought to be* rather than on what actually exists.

(b) SALES COMPARISON/MARKET APPROACH

The traditional market approach uses sales comparison techniques. The valuation process is to compare transactions that are similar to the subject property. The techniques of comparison range in sophistication from a qualitative analogy to highly quantitative statistical models.

A simple analogy best identifies the philosophy of the techniques: the market approach is like an extensive shopping trip for durable goods. Comparison is key, because the shopping choices are between heterogeneous goods (if the physical and locational attributes are emphasized). In an economic sense, the "goods" become much more fungible if abstracted to their essence of space used over time.

The market or sales comparison approach is a direct reflection of the important effect of the marketplace on value and illustrates the immediate issue of value based on the principle of substitution and exchange. Gathering data on actual transactions enables insights to market actions in the distant past, the immediate past, and the current market. When interpretation of these transactions is reflected across broad economic and market data, short-term, limited forecasting becomes possible.

The timing phase covered in the sales comparison approach varies with the technique employed. The traditional grid method best represents the current market, because it allows a basis for estimating value and explaining the variation in the prices paid in the observed transactions.

Various statistical techniques, such as price–quality regression and multiple regression, enable market inference and descriptive analysis that can establish overall market patterns.

Another important aspect of the sales comparison approach is that it identifies alternative units of comparison. The units of comparison allow a basis for comparing actual transactions to the subject property. The units can be separated into spatial or geometric units, or ratios. Examples of spatial or geometric units are sales price per unit per square foot, or sales price per apartment unit per acre, or price per linear foot or front foot. Examples of ratios are capitalization rates or gross income multipliers (GIMs). GIMs have been approached in the literature as units of comparison in the market approach, as an income model, and as a separate approach.[6] Because of its unique perception as being an income valuation technique and a market unit of comparison, the GIM is identified as a linking subsection of the market and income approaches in Figure 1.1.

The sales comparison approach is the easiest valuation technique to comprehend and employ in estimating market value. It appears to be preferred by many decision makers and has been encouraged via court decisions and litigation. However, a realization that real estate markets are cyclical pops up periodically, usually in a down market. Active markets (at the time) are perceived to continue forever. The fact that down markets occur means that transactions are not available to estimate value. Yet, the need to make a decision concerning real estate is often most intense when data are limited. The fact that price is not value is often lost in the heat of an up market; prices may not significantly indicate or support the legal and economic definitions of value. This conflict between decision standards and the simplest valuation method is revealed in the market value definition used by the Federal Home Loan Bank Board in its memoranda R-41b and c.[7] The definition implied a need to be aware of undue stimuli on market activities. These stimuli, such as duress or speculative pressure, could bias prices to the high side or low side of what might be a property's *future potential price* (value).

The weaknesses of the sales comparison approach are that the comparable sales are not identical to the subject property. This creates

[6] Richard U. Ratcliff, "Don't Underrate the Gross Income Multiplier," *The Appraisal Journal*, 39:2 (April 1971): 264–271.

[7] R-41b and c were memoranda developed by the Federal Home Loan Bank Board (FHLBB; now dissolved because of financial trouble from the loan reinsurance). The FHLBB has been replaced by the Office of Thrift Supervision (OTS) under the Federal Deposit Insurance Corporation (FDIC). Several of the former FHLBB functions are carried out by the Resolution Trust Corporation (RTC). The objectives of R-41b and c were to ensure that an appraisal report was self-contained.

The regulatory memoranda altered the practice, procedure, and pricing of appraisals. The regulatory force of the memoranda waned, after litigation in Louisiana as to the proper use of an internal operating memorandum as a tool of regulation. However, enforcement of R-41b and c can be identified among the regulatory events (along with the savings and loan and banking crisis) that linked to major reforms in appraisal practice, if not in theory. The spirit of the memoranda can be related to the state and federal drive for certification of appraisers.

concern for the application of the traditional valuation technique and it forces a questioning of value as the sole decision criterion.

(c) INCOME APPROACH

The income approach is the final technique employed in traditional appraisal analysis. The underlying principle of the income approach is anticipation. Value is the present worth of future anticipated benefits. In a market context, the principle of substitution comes into play with the estimate of a market rent: What rent would the space in a building generate if the building were placed on the current market (rather than emphasizing the contract rent, or the actual rent that the property is now receiving)? The rental analysis is conducted by comparing the subject property to comparable properties and observing their rental levels. The market rental analysis is similar to the market approach's sales comparison.

The principle of substitution also functions in the selection or analysis of the cap rates and yield rates used to capitalize or convert the market income into a value estimate. The rates are identified by comparing the ratios of the various income levels—such as net operating income (NOI)—to the transaction price. The cap rates and yield rates reflect the substitution principle via the concept of opportunity cost. The essence of this theory is that, to acquire the benefits of a property (in the forms of income), benefits to other properties as well as the return on capital employed must be forgone. If $1,000 is tied up in one property, the $1,000 will not be available for other opportunities that come along.

Traditional income appraisal is akin to accrual accounting. The more common cash flow method has not been used until recently. The assumption of a stabilized income has been necessary in the ratio models, because the income input is only for one year (see Figure 1.1, where the bar is over NOI ($\overline{NOI}$). Because only one year's income was used, it is necessary to stabilize and reschedule or recalculate the income, to fit the traditional ratio models.

As seen in Figure 1.1, ratio models can be derived in many ways. The rates can be derived from the comparable market, using their NOI and sales prices (NOI/SP). The rates can also be built up by separating the physical, legal, and financial components of the property. These categories are depicted in Figure 1.1 as physical residuals and mortgage-equity analysis.

Traditional appraisal models have also been extended to include yield capitalization techniques. Previously, this yield concept was addressed as annuity capitalization. Yield or annuity capitalization dealt with constant income flow or graduated income (level income for a number of years, followed by a step up or down in the income for another series of years).

The yield capitalization techniques are the link between ratio capitalization and discounting (as used in the discounted cash flow (DCF) models). Figure 1.1 shows several rate-related discounted cash flow models. Each is a specialized case of the generic income analysis, which possesses characteristics of both accrual and cash accounting aspects. (The details of these models will be related later.)

The yield capitalization models are especially significant because they incorporate a time horizon other than perpetuity and they consider a future resale price. The value of the property is not based only on the income flow; the resale price at the end of the holding period is also forecast.

The combination of the time period and resale potential with the linkage of discounting to capitalization is illustrated in the equation $R = Y - \Delta a$ as shown in Figure 1.1.

The equation, called the universal cap rate formula,[8] includes consideration of:

R = cap rate

Y = overall yield or discount rate

Δ = change in value over holding period

a = annualizer (to convert the expected change in property value over the holding period to an annual amount).

The annualizer illustrates the relationship of ratio capitalization to yield capitalization. The ratio is depicted as a single year. Yield capitalization is concerned with numerous years—the holding period.

The weakness of the income approach is that much data and many assumptions have to be employed to apply it to a given property. The decision maker must be concerned not only with the quantity and quality of data (as in the cost and market approaches) but also with the duration of the data.

The time issue expands the analysis of income from a valuation technique to an alternative decision model (to value). Income analysis enables a year-by-year or periodic investigation of a property. This periodic insight varies from value, which can deal with a long-term time frame but collapses the decision criterion to the current period (that is, the present worth of future benefits).

[8] Charles Akerson, *Capitalization: Theory and Techniques* (Chicago: AIREA, 1985): 100.

The periodic analysis of income can be addressed on a cash basis with an independent analysis of impacts for each period. These shifts of emphasis enable a decision criterion based on projected assets or investment solvency.

§ 1.4 CONCLUSIONS ON VALUE

Despite its popularity as a decision tool, value suffers from many problems when it is used to make decisions. Technically, it has a very precise meaning: value at a given time represents the monetary worth of property, goods, or services to buyers and sellers. Value is a concept, not a historical fact like a transaction price. Because it is a concept, professional appraisers, to avoid confusion, do not use the word value alone. For example, they qualify value with adjectives, or create terms such as "market value," or designate other *specific* kinds of value.[9]

A list of alternative values on the same site might suggest that, rather than having many or multiple values, the property has a variety of problems that may arise and require decisions to be made. The need for qualifiers shows the "ambiguity" (or subjectivity) in value as a standard for decisions. The plethora of "value definitions" that guide the analysis (in appraisals) is not concerned only with the economic issues of exchange, wealth transfer, and wealth storage; it also includes elements of institutional policy.[10] The policy elements are derived from the administrative initiatives of many institutions as they attempt to direct economic activities. The institutions' desired objectives may not fit the economic criteria needed by specific decision makers who are concerned with a given parcel of realty. Yet, it is not unusual to see those individuals relying on an appraisal that incorporates a value definition as canned information that may be totally inappropriate for the problem at hand.

The prime example is the generic market value definition, that is delivered from condemnation litigation. This definition establishes a value premise of a perfectly competitive market environment in which all participants have freedom of choice, no constraints on resources, equal bargaining positions, full knowledge of the market and all options, and the context of a very active market. The definition exists because condemnation typically involves a forced market, with

[9] AIREA, *supra* note 4, at 16–20.
[10] Grissom, *supra* note 5, at 220.

unequal bargaining positions between an unwilling seller and a monopsonistic buyer and with both parties under duress to act.

At best, value is a benchmark enabling decision makers to orient themselves in an uncertain environment. Rather than attempting to manage risk and uncertainty, valuation, at present, assumes away uncertainty or risk.

Alternative decision tools that allow for increased objectivity and the potential for risk management must be considered by persons making real estate decisions.

§ 1.5 SOLVENCY

Value is a fluid concept requiring many qualifiers. By contrast, the standard of solvency in solving real estate problems is very straightforward. Solvency is the ability to pay all legal debts. In a more generalized perspective, it is a comparison of the money coming in and the money going out, in the operation of a property. If more money comes in than goes out, a profit or return is made and the enterprise is a success. The prospect of positive solvency is a basis of value, given the principle of anticipation.

When the concerns of money-in are compared to those of money-out, the analysis of real estate can be viewed in the context of cash accounting via the discounted cash flow rather than the accrual accounting concepts used in traditional appraisal.

The cash accounting format requires that cash returns to real estate be identified. These various returns are important to understanding discounted cash flow analysis. In the traditional appraisal income models, two types of return were identified: (1) the periodic income return derived from the operation of the property, and (2) the reversion received at the resale of the property. Many of the mortgage-equity techniques allowed for the periodic build-up of equity through mortgage amortization; unfortunately, this is not an accurate manner in which to receive an equity build-up return. Cash accounting is necessary to appropriately measure the benefits of amortization as a return.

The possible cash returns to real estate are:

1. *Positive* cash generated by the operation of the property
2. Potential tax savings on other income, generated by the application of the tax law to the ownership of the real estate
3. Cash gain at the resale of the property

4. Cash received in the refinancing of a project over and above the existing debt.

In each of these situations, solvency (or positive cash) is not generated until all debt obligations are satisfied.

The solvency issue links directly to the productivity of the real estate. Following the format of the cash flow program, the analysis begins with the potential gross income (PGI). Deductions are taken for vacancy and for fixed and variable expenses; the result is the net operating income, as in the following restatement:

Potential gross income – Vacancy and credit losses = Effective gross income.

Effective gross income – Operating expenses (both fixed and variable) = Net operating income.

The net operating income (NOI) is the measure of the economic productivity of the property. Because it represents the cash return to the operation of the property, NOI is much like the return to the efficient operation of a business enterprise. If no debt financing is used, it is the overall cash return to the owner or investors. Regardless of financing, NOI is a measure of cash return to the real estate and the labor and management involved in the operation of the property.

If debt financing is involved, the solvency analysis must be extended. The net operating income must be divided between the lender and the equity owners, as follows:

Net operating income – Debt service (principal and interest) = Cash flow to equity.

Much of the cash flow jargon is consistent throughout the debt service deduction. The cash return to the equity position, however, has many names. Among them are:

1. Cash on cash return
2. Equity dividend
3. Before-tax cash flow
4. Cash throw-off.

The cash flow to equity is the measure of return to the owner after considering the operation of the property (expressed as the NOI) and the ability of the owner(s) to negotiate financing. The financing capacity for income property is based on the strengths or perception of the property's business worth and marketability as collateral. For single-family or owner-occupied residential property, the emphasis is on the salary level of the borrower. For both types of property, the negotiating ability and personality of the borrower are key factors.

Given the emphasis on the negotiating capacity of the borrower and the economic position of the lender, the equity return can be seen to be concerned with more than only the productivity of the real estate. Financial markets and personality are the economic issues introduced. Therefore, NOI is the major measure of real estate productivity. The income returns calculated after NOI are based on factors and conditions outside of the real estate productivity.

The strength of property productivity in relation to financial capacity is illustrated by a measure of solvency that is important to lenders: the debt coverage ratio (DCR) or debt service coverage ratio (DSCR). The DCR is a risk management technique that relates the debt service (DS) to the NOI. The formula is:

$$\frac{\text{Net operating income (NOI)}}{\text{Debt service (DS)}} = \text{DCR}$$

Assuming NOI of \$10,000 and DS of \$8,000, the result is:

$$\frac{\$10{,}000}{\$8{,}000} = 1.25$$

The lender in this example is seeking a 25 percent buffer between the debt on a property and the income it generates. The use of a DCR is a risk management attempt to ensure solvency. The uncertainty is whether that NOI may be forthcoming (at least predicted).

The above formula illustrates the calculation of the DCR. The policy implication is that lenders establish an acceptable DCR and then determine the debt service, given the actual income or its forecast. Therefore, in the same example:

$$\frac{\text{NOI}}{\text{DCR}} = \text{DS}$$

$$\frac{\$10{,}000}{1.25} = \$8{,}000$$

The DS (in this case, $8,000) can be capitalized into a value by using the mortgage constant. (This process is indicated in § 1.6.)

With this technique, loans can be determined without the need for estimating a value (as in the loan-to-value model).

After a solvency analysis of financial debt, the legal obligation of income tax can be assessed in a solvency context.

(a) TAX SAVINGS ON OTHER INCOME

The idea of tax savings on other income is often overemphasized or not recognized as a cash return associated with the control of a parcel of real estate.

A cash return can be generated by the ownership (or control) of real estate in conjunction with the federal income tax laws. The cash return is not produced by the real estate, but is the result of legislation initiated to encourage investment in long-term capital assets. The cash return results from a legal benefit that allows investors to deduct *book* depreciation and interest from the productivity measure (expressed as the NOI) of the property. The equation is:

NOI – Depreciation and interest = Taxable income

Adding $11,000 assumed depreciation and $9,000 assumed interest to the earlier example yields:

$10,000 – ($11,000) – ($9,000) = ($10,000)

If the depreciation allowance and interest exceed the net operating income, then the taxable income is negative. In the above example, the $20,000 write-off (depreciation plus interest) exceeds the NOI of the property and creates a negative $10,000 taxable income. The investor's marginal tax rate of 28 percent is applied to the negative taxable income and results in a $2,800 shelter on income that the investor has made outside of or in addition to the low income on the subject real estate.

The current tax law limits the income to which this shelter ($2,800) can be applied. The law now identifies income as active, passive, or portfolio income. Most real estate returns are identified as passive returns, especially if the investor is involved as a limited partner or has a similar status that connotes limited participation in the management of the property. The qualification of the income source is important, because a passive income shelter can only offset passive income (currently).

The assets identified as passive income sources generally are real estate projects. Therefore, to take advantage of the shelter potential of a real estate investment, investors often are involved in other real estate investments that are generating a positive income flow.

Although the above discussion oversimplifies the impact of the current tax law, it enables the identification of three concerns:

1. The ownership of real estate can help generate cash returns outside of the property's productivity.
2. These outside returns are subject to different risk than the property returns (because of tax law changes), because they are only tertiarily related to the property.
3. The returns generated via the tax shelter are not tied to the economics of the property but are linked to tax legislation and the financing terms.

The implication of tax savings on other income as a cash return to real estate is that, if a property is insolvent before taxes, it will be insolvent after taxes. Currently, tax savings may be a source of income only to the wealthy or to others who are heavily invested in real estate.

The cash potential from real estate investment broadens the analysis process to a portfolio perspective, expanding decision-making concerns from the traditional project basis. To have an economic impact, the cash potential of tax savings must be linked to passive income generated by other investments. These investments, as defined by law, are often other real estate enterprises. The solvency standard expands the decision issues relevant to real estate analysis because solvency enables consideration of more than a project-by-project basis. A portfolio perspective of combining real estate with other assets can be introduced.

(b) GAINS ON SALE

The cash received at the time of sale can be considered on a before- and an after-tax basis and from the perspective of alternative financing positions.

Initially, the gain is simply the surplus of cash received at resale (net of the sales commission), over and above the purchase price of the property. This difference is illustrated in section A of Figure 1.2.

If financing is used, the cash received includes the equity build-up that results from the periodic amortization of the loan. On a cash flow

Figure 1.2 Components of Gain on Sale

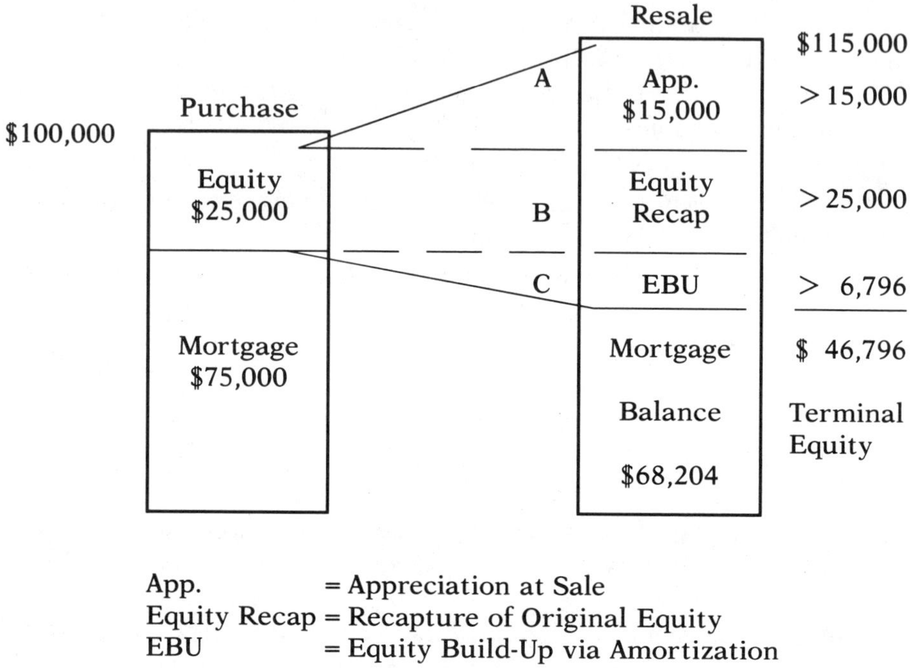

basis, the recapture of debt financing as a return can be more accurately estimated than the periodic recapture allowance built into the Ellwood mortgage-equity model or other traditional appraisal methods. (See § 5.2(c) for detailed discussion.)

The truth of the situation is that a periodic return is not the issue. The ability to pull out the equity build-up as cash does not occur until resale (or refinancing, as discussed below). The cash component of amortization at resale is depicted as section B in Figure 1.2.

The segmentation of the cash components is useful in understanding rate analysis. Figure 1.2 shows that the cash to the equity position is composed of section A, the gain or appreciation received at the sale, section B, the equity build-up through loan amortization, and section C, the return of the original investment. The classification of these cash returns establishes the basis of delineating returns *on* and *of* an investment. The return of the original invested capital definitely represents a return *of* the capital. The gain on sale is a return *on*. The return from equity build-up is a return both *on* and *of*. It is a return *of*, given that the principal of the loan is the same as adding more equity to the investment. It is a return *on*, because positive leverage has occurred: the equity return or overall return is greater than the cost of capital.

Assigning numbers to sections A, B, and C will illustrate. The property was originally purchased for $100,000. The loan-to-value ratio was 75 percent. Therefore, $25,000 in equity was put up by the investor and $75,000 was borrowed from a lender. The loan was for 30 years at 10 percent interest, with monthly payments.

The property was held by the investor for 10 years. It was sold at the end of the 10th year for $115,000 (net of brokerage and other sales and transfer fees). The cash from the gain at sale was $15,000. During this period, 9.062 percent, or $6,796.49, of the loan was paid off.

The cash going to the owner at the time of sale is:

A	$15,000.00
B	6,796.49
C	25,000.00
Total gain	$46,796.49

Without considering the cash flow from operation of the project, on the benefits of the tax shelter, the return at sale is $46,796.49 on a $25,000 investment. This return is 187.18 percent greater than the *original* investment and represents a return on the sale of 6.47 percent over a 10-year period.[11]

Part of the reason for isolating the gain on sale as a cash return and calculating the investment rate is to illustrate that investment mechanics

[11] The formula and calculation of the annual growth rate are:

$$Y_o = \sqrt[n]{\frac{FV}{PV}} - 1$$

$$= \sqrt[n]{\frac{46{,}796.49}{25{,}000}} - 1$$

$$= \sqrt[10]{1.8718} - 1$$

$$= .0647$$

where:

Y_o = overall return

n = 10-year term

FV = future value (at resale)

PV = present value

can be applied to a single residence that is not purchased primarily as an investment. However, solvency can still be the decision criterion. The analysis of a home purchase must consider a purchase price, a holding (or dwelling) period, and a resale price. These are the components involved in the analysis above. Although the income problem above assumed away the cash flow as covering the periodic debt service, this is not the case in a residence. In an economic sense, because the decision maker must live somewhere, the rental cost for similar facilities can be compared to the debt service (DS). The capitalized difference between the DS and the rent can be deducted from the present value of the gain at sale, to arrive at the overall return of the residence. This return can then be compared to the return on like-kind investments. Investments comparable to a residence may require a mental stretch. An argument can be made that shelter, privacy, and the other services supplied by a house are basic requirements and any return is a bonus; appropriate comparable returns might then be the returns on passbook savings accounts, money markets, or interest on checking accounts, with a loading for limited liquidity.

(c) REFINANCING

Liquidity is the problem many investors perceive as the greatest constraint in real estate investment. The potential for overcoming this constraint lies in refinancing, the fourth form of cash return to real estate. Refinancing is the process by which the built-up equity in real estate can be converted to cash without selling the property. Although it is a solvency concept, refinancing is based on issues of both solvency and value, as shown in the following examples.

The first example deals with an income property. The potential for refinancing can be observed in the increasing strength of the income stream. The property's potential gross income (PGI) has been increasing by 5 percent per year for the past 5 years. This increase rate is expected to continue over the next 5 years, given the economic climate of the area and city. The effective gross income (EGI), or the amount remaining after deducting vacancy from PGI, is calculated on that assumption. The initial rental income is $10,000 (per year). The PGI in the fifth year of operation is $12,155.06. The total operating expenses (OE) are 22 percent of the EGI and are increasing at 8 percent per year. These relationships are indicated in the cash flow statement shown in Table 1.1.

Table 1.1 Example of Cash Flow Statement

	Year				
	1	2	3	4	5
PGI	$10,000	$10,500	$11,025	$11,576	$12,155
Vacancy	500	525	551	579	608
EGI	9,500	9,975	10,474	10,997	11,547
OE	2,090	2,194	2,304	2,419	2,540
NOI	$ 7,410	$ 7,781	$ 8,170	$ 8,578	$ 9,007
Divided by: DCR	1.20	1.20	1.20	1.20	1.20
Equals: DS	$ 6,175	$ 6,484	$ 6,808	$ 7,148	$ 7,505

After the net operating income (NOI) is calculated, the debt coverage ratio (DCR) is used to indicate the potential debt service (DS) that the income stream can support. The actual DS is the $6,175 indicated for year 1 (as per the mortgage contract). By year 5, the income can carry a DS of $7,505.

Even if the interest rate and mortgage terms remain the same, the property can now carry a larger mortgage. Using the mortgage constant of .105309 at 10 percent interest, 30-year term with monthly payments, the following mortgage is indicated for year 5:

$$\frac{DS}{R_M} = V_{M_n} \text{ or } \frac{\$7{,}505}{.105309} = \$71{,}266.74$$

where:

DS = debt service, the periodic income to the mortgage
R_M = the mortgage constant or capitalization rate of the mortgage
V_M = the original mortgage value or amount
V_{M_n} = the new mortgage amount at refinancing in year 5

The balance in year 5 of the original mortgage is $56,495.98. The difference in the two mortgages is received as cash to the owner:

V_{M_n}	$71,266.74
V_M	−56,495.98
Cash	$14,770.76

In the real world, the concern must be: Is the cash received worth the administrative and service cost and time expended to get a new loan? In this case, the net cash is $14,770.76. Had the interest rate been lower in the fifth year than in the first year, the cash received would have been greater, and if the scale of the project had been much larger, the cash potential would have been obvious.

This same general process can be applied to a single-family residence; this is the philosophical basis of shared equity investments. When the shared equity concept is applied to an individual residence, the issues of a gain as a source of cash and the basis of collateral for financing are put into action. The market for the shared equity comes about because individual consumers do not have the capital necessary for a down payment and cannot comply with the restrictions of lenders (loan-to-value ratios or the periodic debt coverage). Therefore, the down payment is borrowed from an investor or group of investors. The trade-off for the down payment loan is that the homeowner must give up part of the appreciation when the property is sold in the future. At the time of resale, the borrower repays the original amount of the down payment and splits the equity appreciation with the equity lender.

For example, a couple purchases a $175,000 home. An investor puts 10 percent ($17,500) down and the couple pays the closing costs and makes the payments on the $157,500 mortgage (9 percent interest, 30 years, payable monthly). This example assumes the house appreciates by 7 percent a year for 5 years, and then is sold. Calculations are as follows:

Resale of house after 5 years	$245,000.00
Less: Mortgage balance	151,011.00
Less: Sales cost (6%)	14,700.00
Total equity	79,289.00
Less: Investor's down payment	17,500.00
Total shared equity	61,789.00
(50–50% split)	30,894.50
Investor's profit	30,894.50
Return of investment	17,500.00
	$ 48,394.50
Rate of return	22.56%

The 22.56 percent return is based on the relationship of money-in to money-out. The solvency issue is then considered over time, to enable the calculation of the compounding rate. The rate is also a tool that can help with decisions of capital allocation. The investor helping the couple purchase the house can now consider the return of 22.56 percent over 5 years against the alternative options open for investment. These options must be considered in terms of the quantity of the return, the risk that is associated with the level of the return, and the duration for which a return is expected.

(d) SUMMARY OF SOLVENCY

Solvency is the ability of the property's cash returns to cover debt and other obligations. The concept of solvency expands the traditional measure of returns used in appraisal: basic returns are not limited to cash from productivity and resale. Cash returns are expanded to include tax savings on other income, and refinancing. Identification of these sources of return broadens the analysis of real estate from a narrow project-by-project basis to an approach that includes comparisons with other assets. The ability to compare real estate with other assets requires a recognition of time. Issues of time are addressed in the use of rates as a real estate decision tool.

§ 1.6 RATES

Rates, like the solvency models and income approaches in appraisal, can be divided into *ratio* or capitalization rates and *yield* rates. An additional category of *risk ratios* is also introduced. (See Figure 1.1.)

Emphasis on the appropriate rate has varied with the availability of technology. Investment decisions that emphasize ratio or capitalization rates can be linked to the convenience of the calculation (divide an income by a value or price), the availability of data (or inputs), and the simplicity of the concept.

(a) RATIO RATES

Ratio rates (also called dividend rates) are a result of dividing a reported or estimated income by a value or purchase price. Ratio rates are a general category of rates; several other names are used in describing this measure or level of return: the overall capitalization rate, the equity dividend or equity cap rate, or the cash on cash rate of return. The overall capitalization rate is derived from dividing the net operating income (NOI) by the sales price (or value). Examples of various rates as they relate to capital components of a property are illustrated in Table 1.2.

(b) CONCERNS WITH RATIOS

Complexities arise in determining the appropriateness of a measure of income. For example, when using the overall cap rate, there must be a determination as to what is being measured as the net operating income. Is it the first year's income or a stabilized income that represents several years' productivity? Is the appropriate income the actual income, a market derived income, or a stabilized (market or property based) income?

The decision on the appropriate income to use is contingent on the problem situation. If the objective is a market value, as is often the

Table 1.2 Ratio Rates

Rate	Component of Value	Formula	Rate Symbol
Overall capitalization rate	Total property	$\frac{NOI}{V_o}$	R_o
Mortgage constant	Original loan amount	$\frac{DS}{V_M}$	R_M
Equity dividend rate	Original equity amount	$\frac{CTO}{V_E}$	R_E

where:

NOI = net operating income
V_o = overall property value or purchase price
DS = debt service
V_M = original mortgage value
CTO = cash throw-off (the same income return as the before-tax cash flow or the equity dividend = CF_E)
V_E = original equity investment or cash down

purpose in an appraisal, then the income used is a stabilized market rental. Appraisers have also been known to use the first year's income. Use of stabilized market rental is a traditional application, in appraisal analysis, of the accrual accounting standard.

Investors may use the cap rate, because of a lack of other information. Cap rate data are available from sources such as the American Council of Life Insurance (ACLI) and Real Estate Research Corporation (RERC) publications. As the universal cap rate formulation has shown, discount rates and expectations of growth or decline can be abstracted from ratio rate information.

Investors can also use the cap rate in conjunction with discounted cash flow analysis. Using the cash flow example presented in § 1.5(c), the following net operating incomes are projected (or experienced over time):

	Year				
	1	2	3	4	5
NOI	$ 7,410	$ 7,781	$ 8,170	$ 8,578	$ 9,007
Market value	78,000	81,900	85,995	90,295	94,810
Cap rate	.095	.095	.095	.095	.095

From a management or investors' perspective, the relationship shown between NOI and value is desirable because a constant (or frozen) cap rate is maintained. The ratio of the net operating income (the asset's productivity) to the asset's worth, as perceived in the market, should remain constant; otherwise, a changing value pattern can occur, which may not be consistent with market comparables. For example, if the cap rate had dropped in year 3 (or any year) and began to show a declining pattern—a 9 percent rate in year 3, 8.5 percent in year 4 and so on—the cap rate would be indicating that the sales price (market value) is growing at a faster rate than the income return. This pattern would suggest that the investor's expectations of the property's value (based on the potential for increasing future rents or other returns) are not evident in the current rental contracts. A comparison of the property's leases to market activity might support the need to renegotiate leases as they turn over and to increase the rent for any new tenants. A marketing effort for new tenants might be emphasized; or, it may be an opportune period to sell the property.

If the cap rate begins to increase, opposite conditions are suggested. The market expectations are declining and the strength of the property lies in the current income streams. Management or investors should strive to protect the income return, to control property expenses, and to keep current tenants satisfied. If rental returns are sufficient, the owners may want to avoid exposing the property to the market until cap rates drop into a rational range. If they drop significantly, it is possible that a speculative market exists and an oversupplied market may follow.

(c) MORTGAGE-EQUITY DIVIDENDS

Value and income can be divided into debt and equity components (the mortgage value and equity value, and the debt service and equity cash flow, respectively), and so can the cap rate. The cap rate to the mortgage, called the mortgage constant, is the ratio of the debt service to the original mortgage amount, using the formula in Table 1.2. The debt service is the calculated payment, based on the term of the loan. The payment obtains a periodic repayment and interest payment. The amount of the debt service and the mortgage constant are affected by the frequency of payment (monthly, quarterly, annually, or at any other agreed-on time intervals).

The mortgage constant is useful in situations where the value (and/or mortgage) is known and terms of the loan are available. Such information helps decision makers in estimating overall returns and solvency. If value is unknown, then knowledge of the financing terms, such as the amortization period, interest rate, frequency of payment of the loan, and any other lender requirements, can be used to make decisions based on value or solvency. The connection of financing terms to value and solvency is made with the loan-to-value ratio and debt coverage ratio.

The mortgage constant, in combination with the overall cap rate, is a key factor in making leverage decisions.

Again using the example of the refinancing cash flow, and considering the original mortgage amount as $75,000, Table 1.3 shows a calculation of mortgage constants.

It is *important to note* that, with traditional fixed rate financing, the mortgage constant of .105556 would be used throughout the 30-year mortgage term and/or the 5- to 10-year investment period. The varying rates are illustrated to show the impact of an increasing income stream on leverage potential, to illustrate that the concept of a mortgage

Table 1.3 Example of Mortgage Constants

	Year				
	1	2	3	4	5
Debt service (DS)	\$ 6,175	\$ 6,484	\$ 6,808	\$ 7,148	\$ 7,505
Original mortgage $(V_M) = V_o \times M$ or \$58,500 = \$78,000 × .75	\$58,500	\$58,500	\$58,500	\$58,500	\$58,500
Annual mortgage constant $R_M = \frac{DS}{V_M}$	.105556*	.110838	.116376	.122188	.128291

*Mortgage constant based on DS calculated from DCR. Had interest terms been used, then DS = \$6,160 and $R_M = .105309$ (see earlier calculations).

constant is still used in variable rate mortgages as well as fixed rate mortgages, and to show that financing can impact the value estimate of a property.

(d) EQUITY DIVIDEND RATE/EQUITY CASH FLOW RATE

The equity dividend rate is the ratio rate that represents the relationship of the equity cash flow to the original equity investment (see Table 1.2). The two elements of greatest confusion, in relation to this rate, are that it has many names and it is not the same concept as the equity yield rate.

The equity dividend rate, the equity cash flow rate, the cash on cash rate of return, the before-tax rate of return, and the cash throw-off rate of return are alternate names for the equity ratio rate. The particular name used often varies with the name given to the income flow that the return rate is capitalizing, with industry segments, and with geographical areas of the country. The Appraisal Institute is pushing for a consensus on "equity cash flow rate."

In traditional appraisal analysis, given the use of a stabilized NOI measure, a constant equity dividend rate (R_E) is used. The information from the previous cash flow example would allow an appraiser to develop an overall cap rate using (ratio) mortgage-equity analysis, as follows:

$$M \times R_M = .75 \times .105556 = .079167$$

$$(1 - M) \times R_E = .25 \times .06333 = .01583$$

$$R_o = .095$$

where:

M = loan-to-value ratio of 75 percent of the value
R_M = mortgage constant of .105556 (calculated above)
$(1 - M)$ = equity contribution of 25 percent or $(1 - .75)$
R_E = equity dividend rate of 6.33 percent
R_o = overall cap rate (as shown above)

The equity cash flow rate can also be considered in the changing context of the cash flow model, as shown in Table 1.4.

The equity dividend rate, when used in conjunction with cash flow projection, enables a periodic measure of equity solvency in relation to the initial investment. The increasing equity dividend rate illustrated in the example indicates that the cash flow–equity relationship is improving. A decline in the equity dividend rate would suggest a

Table 1.4 Example of Equity Cash Flow

	Year				
	1	2	3	4	5
NOI	\$ 7,410	\$ 7,781	\$ 8,170	\$ 8,578	\$ 9,007
Less: DS	−6,175	−6,484	−6,808	−7,148	−7,505
Equity cash flow	1,235	1,297	1,362	1,430	1,502
Original equity value	\$19,500	\$19,500	\$19,500	\$19,500	\$19,500
Equity cash flow rate $CF/V_E = R_E$	.06333*	.066513	.069846	.0733	.077026

*Note that the first year's equity dividend is the same as the R_E used in the ratio mortgage equity capitalization model. However, as the cash flow analysis above illustrates, the equity dividend rate can change over time, because of the varying equity cash flow stream. The base of the ratio, the original equity amount invested, remains the same—\$19,500, the difference between the original market value (purchase price) of \$78,000 and the original mortgage of \$58,500.

decreasing project solvency. The equity dividend, like the mortgage constant, can also indicate the leverage position of an investment.

(e) LEVERAGE

Leverage is the use of borrowed funds to increase (or decrease) the amount of the equity return on the invested portion, free and clear. Leverage analysis considers a comparison and a combination of rates. The combination of debt and equity dollars results in the overall cost of capital to the investment.

The objective of leverage is to combine the lower-cost debt dollars with the more costly equity dollars. Besides the cost of debt, investors are concerned with the procurement of funds to augment their limited capital and to shelter their limited dollars from exposure to market risks. Therefore, leverage is a risk management technique and a measure of return analysis that can be decided based on rate comparison.

Given the objectives of leverage, decision makers will find ratio rate comparison helpful. The status of leverage can be classified as positive, neutral, or negative. Positive leverage occurs when the cost of debt funds is less than the overall cap rate, implying that the dividend return on equity is higher than the overall rate and the debt service rate. (See Table 1.5.)

Neutral leverage indicates that the overall rate, the mortgage constant, and the equity dividend are all the same rate. (See Table 1.5.) If this occurs, the economic advantages of using other people's money are limited to offsetting a lack of available funds, and the difference between debt and equity is then more of a legal difference than an economic issue. The legal difference identifies variances in the priority

Table 1.5 Classes of Leverage and Decision Rules

Class of Leverage	Decision Rule	Mortgage–Equity Relationships
Positive	$R_o > R_M$	$R_M < R_o < R_E$
Neutral	$R_o = R_M$	$R_M = R_o = R_E$
Negative	$R_o < R_M$	$R_M > R_o > R_E$

where:

R_o = overall cap rate
R_M = mortgage constant
R_E = equity cap rate (equity dividend rate, etc.)

of payments, control of and claims upon the asset, and ownership rights.

Negative leverage occurs when the mortgage constant exceeds the overall rate. (See Table 1.5.) This was the situation illustrated in the earlier mortgage-equity and cash flow example, where $R_M = .105556$ and $R_o = .095$ ($R_E = .0633$). In this situation, the investor is paying more to use the debt (or borrowed) capital (at a cost of \$.105 on each dollar) than is received on the equity (\$.063 on each dollar).

Why would an investor go into a deal using negative leverage? One rational answer is that the situation is expected to change to positive leverage through either an improved cash flow or a large gain at sale. Another reason may be that the investor has limited funds but still wants to buy into the deal. However, for this scenario to work, there must again be an expectation of change (to either positive cash flow or leverage and capital gains).

The relationship between the overall rate and the mortgage constant rate sets the basic decision rule. (This information can usually be procured from the market and/or financial institutions.) The equity dividend is often unknown (even by the investors). However, given the loan-to-value requirements of most lenders, the mortgage–equity relationships indicated in Table 1.5 will tend to hold. For R_o to exceed R_M, R_E must be greater than the overall and mortgage cap rates. In a neutral leverage position, all rates are equal; in a negative leverage situation, equity dollars are receiving a lower dividend than the debt dollars and the overall property. The overall property ratio (R_o) is simply a weighted artifact that depends on the capital structure of the deal. A great degree of knowledge can be gained from information on a property's cap rate and financing terms.

(f) SUMMARY OF RATIO

As the example of leverage illustrates, ratio rates can be useful decision-making tools. With further information, such as a possible holding period and future expectations of change, decision makers can develop additional insights to property performance. The additional information broadens investment analysis beyond the constraints of ratio analysis to an analytical format that considers more of the components discussed in solvency analysis, such as gain at sale and mortgage amortization. This additional information enables yield analysis. However, before the overall yield issues can be considered, the alternative forms of appreciation as a return rate must be introduced.

§ 1.7 APPRECIATION

Investment value is concerned with the present worth of future expected benefits. In real estate, these benefits can be considered in two general forms: (1) the cash flow and its pattern over time, and (2) the cash received from appreciation at the future resale price. Property purchased for investment is not limited to income properties; investment can be acquired solely for capital gain. This latter form of return may be the only type of compensation received from investment in single-family residential real estate and raw land. (With only a few exceptions, these are not the property types purchased by many institutions.)

The appreciation return for non-income-producing investment property must consider the potential negative cash flows—for example, property tax payments and debt service payments (if the property is encumbered with a loan). Given these concerns, an investment

Table 1.6 Appreciation Rates

Rate	Component of Value	Formula	Rate Symbol
Overall appreciation rate	Change in total property value	$\frac{V_1 - V_o}{V_o}$	Δ_o
Equity build-up rate	Decline in debt amount	$\frac{V_M - B}{V_M}$	P*
Equity appreciation rate	Change in equity amount	$\frac{V_{E_1} - V_E}{V_E}$	Δ_E

where:

V_1 = future resale price
V_o = original value (purchase price)
Δ_o = overall appreciation rate
V_M = value of mortgage
B = mortgage balance at time of resale
P = percentage of mortgage paid off over holding period
V_{E_1} = future equity value at time of resale
Δ_E = equity appreciation rate

*The percentage of the mortgage paid off during the holding period is the portion of value shifted from the debt side to the equity side. This is a build-up in the equity value at the time of sale. If this component exceeds a decline in the overall or equity value if the market falls, the investor may still receive a return on or an increasing yield to the investment.

decision regarding a non-income-producing property must be based on a comparison between the expected appreciation rate and the holding or waiting costs. Holding or waiting costs are composed of the opportunity cost of capital (the existing interest rate on the debt, or the returns that would be obtainable if investing in other investments of similar risk) and the property tax rate. The opportunity cost must include a factor for inflation. After the total holding cost is identified, the investment decision criterion for non-income-producing property is based on a comparison of the appreciation rate to the holding cost (stated as a rate). A decision proxy can be the point at which the appreciation rate is equal to or exceeds the opportunity cost of capital plus the tax rate.

The major concern with investment in real estate is that the purchaser is tied to a long position (gain can occur only if the future price is greater than the original price). Usually this happens only in a growth market or if the property has a unique or monopolistic position.

Appropriate leveraging can offset part of this exposure, if the equity build-up or pay-down (amortization) of the mortgage exceeds the decline in property value. Based on this insight, appreciation rates can be linked to a variety of property components, as were the ratio rates. (See Table 1.6.)

§ 1.8 YIELD RATES

Yield rates are concerned with total returns over time. Often, the time period is a known, finite term, and the term used is a typical investment holding period. An investment's total return, a decision criterion often sought in the analysis of investments, is a combination of the income component and the appreciation return. In securities analysis, the total return (for one period) is identified as the dividend and appreciation stated as a combined rate:

$$r = \frac{\mathrm{D}t + (\mathrm{P}_{t+1} - \mathrm{P}_t)}{\mathrm{P}_t}$$

where:

r = overall yield for the period
P_t = purchase price
P_{t+1} = future sales price
$\mathrm{D}t$ = dividend

In real estate, this same concept can be considered for the overall property or any of its component parts. The concept, using real estate symbols, is:

$$Y_o = \frac{NOI_1 + (V_1 - V_o)}{V_o}$$

$$Y_o = \frac{NOI_1}{V_o} + \frac{(V_1 - V_o)}{V_o}$$

$$Y_o = R_o + \Delta_o$$

where:

Y_o = yield to overall property based on effective cost of capital (this depends on the combination of debt and equity funds)

NOI_1 = net operating income in year 1

The above formula shows a one-period investment model. The yield concept is the sum of the income for each year of the holding period plus the gain at a future resale. As with the ratio rates and the appreciation rates, the total return can be allocated among the capital components of the property. (See Table 1.7.)

As Table 1.7 illustrates, there are various yield rates to consider. Several examples are discussed in the following subsections.

Table 1.7 Total Return Rates

Rates	Components of Value	Formula	Rate Symbol
Overall yield	Total property	$\sqrt[n]{\dfrac{\sum_{i-1}^{n} NOI_i + (V_1 - V_o)}{V_o}} - 1$	Y_o
Mortgage yield or effective interest rate	Original mortgage amount	$\sqrt[n]{\dfrac{\sum_{i=1}^{n} DS_i - (V_M - B)}{V_M}} - 1$	Y_M
Equity yield	Original equity amount	$\sqrt[n]{\dfrac{\sum_{i=1}^{n} CTO + (V_{E_1} - V_E)}{V_M}} - 1$	Y_E

(a) DISCOUNT RATE

The discount rate is a rate of return on capital; it is used to convert future payments or receipts into present value. The objective of the discount rate is to convert the income or solvency (or nonsolvency) measure of each period into a value on a common or given date.[12] The discount rate can work in a past or a future direction. If cash flow occurs before (earlier than) the common date, the cash flow is converted to a future value by compound accumulation or discounting. If cash flow occurs after the common date, it is discounted back to the designated date. In investment analysis, the designated date is often the current date (or year zero). The discount rate as a return is a yield rate. It can be an overall yield rate, a equity yield rate, or even the interest rate.

(b) INTEREST RATE

An interest rate is the yield on a mortgage. The interest rate does not allow for the repayment of invested capital (the mortgage). The symbols for interest rates are illustrated in Tables 1.7 and 1.10. The combination of the interest rate and the mortgage amortization as a percentage is a component of the mortgage constant.

(c) EQUITY YIELD RATE

The equity yield rate is the rate of return on equity capital. The yield is established by the opportunity cost involved in investment options available to the investor. Economic and investment decisions are choices; they are made in the context of time and are necessitated by the economic constraint of limited resources. The requirement to make choices establishes the behavioral basis of opportunity cost. For example, pleasure is derived from the accumulation of assets, the purchase of a house, or the receipt of income over and above expenses. The more quickly one receives the returns or benefits of ownership and investment, the greater is the satisfaction. The economic premise illustrating the association between time and satisfaction is that a dollar received

[12] C. Gordon Blackadar, "Dynamic Capitalization: An Income Approach in Real Dollars at Real Interest, Part 3: The Dynamics of Expectation," *The Appraisal Journal*, 58:3 (July 1989): 346.

today can be invested for return over the next year. If the return is 18 percent, the investor's wealth a year from now will be \$1.18.

If the payment of a dollar is deferred a year, the opportunity to invest the dollar and earn 18 percent is *foregone*. Because an opportunity is lost, the dollar promised a year from now is worth only *approximately* \$0.82 (\$1.00 – \$0.18 = \$0.82, or actually \$0.847, given compounding effects: \$1.00/1.18 = \$0.847).

The compounding effects of discounting are linked back to the behavior concepts of utility. A buyer or investor may achieve a 100 percent utility if a benefit is received or experienced today, but only 84.7 percent utility if the benefit is not received until a year from now. The ratio of the utility less one year indicates the discount rate:

$$U_1/U_2 - 1 = Y$$

where:

U_1 = current utility
U_2 = future utility
Y = discount rate, opportunity cost, or yield

Example:

$$(100/84.7 - 1) = 18\%$$

The issue of opportunity cost is not only the timing of receipts, but also the choices between options. An equity investor may have *sufficient funds* to invest in a duplex, a money market certificate, a commercial syndication, or a security investment. If the investor makes one choice, the possibilities of the others are foregone. The cost of making a decision when resources are limited is that the potential return from the other options is lost.

The time element links the equity yield measure to the discount rate. The alternative opportunities lost (because of making a decision among alternative investments) set the range of yields desired on equity dollars.

When comparing alternative investments, the investor must consider the certainty and duration of the benefits to be received, the pattern and flow of the benefits, and the timing of receipt of the returns. (The alternative forms of the benefits were discussed in § 1.5.) An example of the cash flow to equity (CFE) is given in Table 1.8.

Table 1.8 Example of Cash Flow to Equity

	Year				
	1	2	3	4	5
NOI	$ 7,410	$ 7,781	$ 8,170	$ 8,578	$ 9,007
−DS	−6,175	−6,484	−6,808	−7,148	−7,505
CFE	$ 1,235	$ 2,197	$ 1,362	$ 1,430	$ 1,502
Discounted @ 14.5%	$ 1,079	$ 989	$ 907	$ 832	$ 763
Cumulative value of equity: Income	$ 1,079	$ 2,968	$ 2,975	$ 3,807	$ 4,570
Market value	$78,000	$81,900	$85,995	$90,295	$94,810

Future sales price (net of commission) = $94,810
Loan balance = $6,496 (rounded)
Cash to equity = $38,314
Discounted @ 14.5% = $19,468
Value of equity = $4,570 + $19,468 = $24,038

In the example, the equity yield is used to estimate the present value, given information on a cash flow. The present value is based on a desired yield (or one directed by the market).

The emphasis of the decision maker could focus on the desired equity yield—in this case, 14.5 percent. This rate is based on the returns to equity funds in the current market (alternative investment options of a similar investor). The rate allows for the investor's required rate of return and considers opportunity cost, inflation, and certainty of payment (or risk).[13] The certainty of payment and the validity of receiving a 14.5 percent return in this example are contingent on the property's appreciating at 5 percent per year for a 5-year period, given the available financing of a 30-year loan at 10 percent, with monthly payments. If any of these variables or assumptions changes, the yield will change.

As Table 1.8 shows, the yield is for a flow of funds over a 5-year period; the market value shows the return from the gain at resale. The equity yield is different from the equity dividend—the ratio of that

[13] Stephen A. Pyhrr and James R. Cooper, *Real Estate Investment* (New York: John Wiley and Sons, Inc., 1982): 285.

year's equity cash flow to the original equity value. In the example used in Table 1.8, the equity dividend is 6.33 percent in year 1 and changes yearly, becoming 7.7 percent in year 5. This periodic dividend can be compared to a 14.5 percent equity yield throughout the 5-year period.

The relationships between the equity dividend rate (equity cap rate) and the equity yield is:

$$R_E = Y_E - D_{E_a}$$

where:

R_E = equity cap rate (dividend)

Y_E = equity yield rate

D_E = change in equity value (from initial equity to equity value at end of year 5)

a = annualizer

This relationship between cap rates and yield rates will be discussed in more detail in the discussion of overall yields in Chapter 7.

The impact of yields on decision making can be related to the initial purchase price. Given the forms of return identified above (such as income gain), the lower the price paid, the higher will be the yield. If a high yield is required, then income and future resale price must appreciate. The least risk and the greatest control occur in the negotiation of the initial price paid and the financing arrangement. Therefore, yield analysis cannot be limited to only the quantity of the yield.

Based on the capital structure and the productivity of the asset as constrained by the market, the income flowing to the equity comprises about 19 percent of the value ($4,570/$24,038). Therefore, 81 percent of the equity value is contingent on the assumption or expectations at the sale of the property.

(d) OVERALL YIELD RATE

The overall yield rate is conceptually and mathematically derived like the equity yield rate. (See Table 1.7.) The overall yield is derived from the net operating income line (unlike the equity yield which derives from the equity cash flow after debt).

Table 1.9 Example of Analysis of Overall Yield

	Year				
	1	2	3	4	5
NOI	$ 7,410	$ 7,781	$ 8,170	$ 8,578	$ 9,007
Discounted @ 11.14%	$ 6,667	$ 6,299	$ 5,951	$ 5,622	$ 5,312
Cumulative value of NOI	$ 6,667	$12,966	$18,917	$24,539	$29,851
Market value	$78,000	$81,900	$85,995	$90,295	$94,810

Future sales price (after commissions)	$94,810
Beginning value	−78,000
Cash at sale	$16,810

	Cash	Future Sales Price
Discounted @ 11.14%	$9,913	$55,912

Value of property = $29,851 + $55,912 = $85,762

The overall yield is not concerned with debt and equity allocations in the income stream and at resale. A cash flow analysis related to the overall yield is shown in Table 1.9.

The income flow to the property comprises about 35 percent of the value ($29,851/$85,762). The remainder (65 percent) is based on the resale of the property in 5 years. The greater the component of value represented by the income flow, the lower the business and market risk of the property. A comparison of the income productivity value of 35 percent to the equity cash flow of 19 percent of value illustrates the increased financial risk potential of negative leverage ($R_M > R_o$ or $.10556 > .095$).

The overall yield is based on a calculation of the property's overall cost of capital. As stated earlier, the property has a debt cost of 10 percent. The 10 percent is the yield on the debt capital, or an interest rate. This rate is charged to 75 percent of the project. The cost of the equity capital, as seen above, is 14.5 percent. The equity capital comprises 25 percent of the project. The combined or weighted rate is:

$$\begin{array}{lll} M \times Y_M & = .75 \times .10 & = .075 \\ + (1 - M) \times Y_E & = .25 \times .145 & = \underline{.03625} \\ \hline = Y_o & & = .11125 \end{array}$$

where:

M = loan-to-value ratio

Y_M = debt or mortgage yield, the interest rate of 10 percent

Y_E = equity yield of 14.5 percent

A more precise calculation is obtained by using the Akerson format for mortgage-equity analysis. (See § 5.2(c) for detailed discussion.) This format allows for the changing cost of capital as the debt structure considers the amortization of the loan over the 5-year holding period. The Akerson format combines the mortgage constant with the equity yield and hence has to deduct the equity build-up component within the rate structure. The overall rate developed by this method is 11.14 percent.

The significance of the overall yield rate is that it considers the productivity of the real estate asset, based on the net operating income and the gain or loss at resale. The equity yield analysis views the property from the position of the equity investor after the debt structure is in place. The comparison of the two rates enables insights to the levels of different risks the property is subject to and the relationships among solvency, leverage, and value. The relationships arise because the yields are used for investment comparisons and as discount rates for estimating present values.

(e) INTERNAL RATES OF RETURN

The internal rates of return as applied in real estate and presented in Figure 1.1 are identified as three types: the traditional internal rate of return, the modified internal rate of return, and the financial management rate of return. All three rates have the same basic premise: they equate the present value of expected cash flows to the purchase price or the initial capital invested. The internal rate of return, like the yield rate, can be applied to either the NOI or the equity cash flow. The application of the technique to the NOI gives an indication of the property's productivity in relation to the purchase price. The application of the technique to the equity cash flow as it relates to the initial equity capital enables investors to compare property performance (after debt or taxes) to alternative investments and to test whether desired yields are being achieved. The internal rate of return (IRR) may or may not be equal to the equity yield rate (or discount rate).

The IRR calculations are the end product of an analytical technique. When the yield analysis is typically used to arrive at a present value (PV), the IRR analysis compares (and contrasts) the initial capital outlay (or all capital outlays) to capital returns. This being the case, the following example, which indicates a cash flow of net operating income and a future sale after a 5-year period, would be compared to the current price of $78,000. Therefore, a rate of 13.65 percent would equate the period cash flow to $78,000, as follows:

	Year					
	1	2	3	4	5	Resale
NOI	$7,410	$7,781	$8,170	$8,578	$9,007	$94,810

The equation is:

$$\mathrm{IRR} = \sqrt[n]{\frac{\sum_{i=1}^{n} \mathrm{NOI}_i + \mathrm{Resale}}{\mathrm{PV}}} - 1$$

The 13.65 percent rate can be compared to the overall yield (the weighted cost of capital) to show that, despite the initial negative leverage position, the overall return based on the productivity of the project (including the assumptions of resale) exceeds the weighted cost of capital. The information further shows that the productivity of the property supports or more than justifies the original investment purchase price.

The IRR on the equity position compares the equity investment of $19,500 (in this case) to the cash flow to equity and gain over the same 5-year period. The equity flow is:

	Year					
	1	2	3	4	5	Resale
CFE	$1,235	$1,297	$1,362	$1,430	$1,502	$38,314

The IRR to the equity flow is 19.875 percent. This rate of return can be compared to the returns of alternative equity investments, enabling decision makers to compare between options. Additional information is necessary, such as the pattern and timing of the returns, risk expenses, and capital structure.

The equation for the equity IRR is:

$$IRR_E = \sqrt[n]{\frac{\sum_{i=1}^{n} CF_E + V_{E_1}}{V_E}} - 1$$

where:

IRR_E = equity IRR
CF_E = cash flow to equity
V_E = equity value
V_{E_1} = equity value in future

The central issue of the equity IRR is the same as with the overall IRR: a rate must be identified that equates the benefits of the investment with the initial price paid (or all cash outlays). The rate is then used for comparison between investment alternatives. Successful analysis then requires an understanding of the patterns and flows of the funds generated by the investment.

(f) MODIFIED INTERNAL RATE OF RETURN AND FINANCIAL MANAGEMENT RATE OF RETURN

The modified internal rate of return (MIRR) and the financial management rate of return (FMRR) are attempts to combine information on the flow of funds, reinvestment alternatives, and the pattern of cash flows within the IRR calculation. A key difference between the modified IRRs and the traditional IRR is that, because the traditional rate is used to equate all inflows to all outflows over time, a constant reinvestment rate is assumed. The implication is that, when a rental return is received, it is immediately reinvested at the IRR received on the project. Reinvestment is a necessary return, to address the common time issue required in discounting. The potential to receive the IRR rate as a reinvestment return, unfortunately, often assumes unlimited investment options are possible. Large corporations, for whom the IRR technique was developed, may have unlimited options, but most real estate investors do not. Both the MIRR and the FMRR have attempted to alter the traditional reinvestment assumptions.

The MIRR deals with the problem in the following manner:

1. All cash outflows are discounted at the desired yield rate (in this case, 14.5 percent), to reflect the opportunity cost of investment.
2. All cash inflows are compounded forward at the marginal investment rate available on all new investment options. For example, the subject investment may be a small office building earning 14.5 percent. The owners are in a small limited partnership and have limited capital. At best, they have the funds to buy a duplex or they are limited to a money market fund at, say, a 7 to 10 percent return. They do not have the capital for another office building (or any investment) generating a 14.5 percent return. To diversify their exposure and retain a level of liquidity, they opt for the money market fund at 7 percent. All rentals generated by the office facilities are compounded to the end of the holding period at the rate of 7 percent. The terminal value of the cash inflows at the end of the holding period can then be estimated.
3. The *n*th root or compound rate that equates the terminal value to the present value of the cash outflows is calculated.

The overall internal rate of return for the earlier subject property was 13.65%. The reinvestment rate is lower because of limited options. Therefore, the MIRR is 10.83%, as shown in Figure 1.3.

Like the MIRR, the FMRR addresses the "split" rate potential of investors because of limited options. However, unlike the MIRR, the FMIRR introduces an implicit concern for project solvency.

The FMRR model shown in Figure 1.4, like the MIRR model in Figure 1.3, considers the $10,000 cash outflow for roof repairs, occurring in year 3. The model first attempts to pay off the $10,000 repair with the $8,170 generated in year 3. This leaves a deficit of $1,830. The FMRR offsets the remainder of the outflow with the positive cash flows generated in years 1 and/or 2. In this case, the positive cash flows from year 1 (end of year) are compounded forward at 14.5 percent to the end of year 3. The income from year 1 ($7,410) compounded to the end of year 3 is $9,715. Deducting the $1,830 remaining roof cost from the $9,715 brought forward leaves $7,885. The $7,885 is then compounded to the end of year 5 (end of holding period). The

Figure 1.3 Example of MIRR Calculation

	End-of-Year Cash Flows				
	Year				
Investment	1	2	3	4	5
\$78,000	$7{,}410 \times (1.07)^4$ →				\$ 9,713 (end of year 5)
		$7{,}781 \times (1.07)^3$ →			9,532
6,661 ←			$\left(\frac{1}{1.145}\right)^3$ [10,000]		
			$8{,}170 \times (1.07)^2$ →		9,354
				$8{,}578^1 \times (1.07)$ →	9,178
					9,007 (at end of year 5)
					94,810 (2 at end of year 5)
\$84,661					\$141,594

1. $PV\,(1 + MIRR)^5 = FV$
2. $\$84{,}661(1 + MIRR)^5 = \$141{,}594$
3. $(1 + MIRR)^5 = \dfrac{\$141{,}594}{\$84{,}661}$
4. $(1 + MIRR) = \sqrt[5]{\dfrac{\$141{,}594}{\$84{,}661}}$
5. $MIRR = \sqrt[5]{\dfrac{\$141{,}594}{\$\ 84{,}661}} - 1$
6. $MIRR = \sqrt[n]{\dfrac{FV}{PV}} - 1$
7. $MIRR = \sqrt[5]{1.67} - 1$
8. $MIRR = 1.108338 - 1$
9. $MIRR = 10.83\%$*

*This rate is partially lower because of consideration given to the need to repair the roof in year 3 at a cost of \$10,000.

Figure 1.4 Example of FMRR Calculation

	End-of-Year Cash Flows				
	Year				
Investment	1	2	3	4	5
\$78,000	7,410 × (1.45)² →		+9,715		
		7,781 × (1.145)³ →			\$11,680
			+8,170		
			−[10,000]		
			7,885 × (1.145)² →		\$10,337
				8,578 × (1.145)¹ →	9,882
					9,007
					94,810
PV \$78,000					FV \$135,656

$$\text{PV}(1+\text{FMRR}) = \text{FV}$$
$$\$78{,}000(1+\text{FMRR})^5 = \$135{,}656$$
$$(1+\text{FMRR})^5 = \frac{\$135{,}656}{\$78{,}000}$$
$$\text{FMRR}^5 = \frac{\$135{,}656}{\$78{,}000} - 1$$
$$\text{FMRR} = \sqrt[5]{1.739179} - 1$$
$$\text{FMRR} = 1.117040 - 1$$
$$\text{FMRR} = 11.70\%$$

$7,885 compounded at 14.5 percent for two years (end of year 3 to end of year 5) equals $10,337. See Figure 1.4.

The FMRR also views the discounting problem with a perspective opposite to that of the MIRR. The FMRR perceives that the dollars tied up in the office building should be receiving a return of 14.5 percent and thus uses this rate to compound forward. Because the funds tied up in this project are not available for the reinvestment option, all cash outflows are discounted at the reinvestment rate (of 7 percent), as shown in Figure 1.4.

The variation in the rates is explained by the different recognition each technique gives to reinvestment assumption, the emphasis on income patterns, and solvency issues. A key revelation to decision makers is that, despite the emphasis on a yield or rate as a decision model, there is a link between issues of value and solvency.

The weakness of yield analysis in real estate is that data to calculate the yields are limited and a yield has little use without a comparative context.

§ 1.9 INTEGRATION OF DECISION TOOLS

As the IRR analysis infers, there is a relationship among values, income/solvency, and rates. To help in understanding this relationship, the symbols linking values, incomes, rates, and yields are presented in Table 1.10.

Table 1.10 synthesizes the relationships among specific value components and levels of the income streams. The rates (R_s) are ratios

Table 1.10 Related Values, Incomes, Rates, and Yields, and their Symbols

Values	Incomes	Rates	Yields
V_o	NOI	R_o	Y_o
V_M	DS	R_M	Y_M
V_E	CF_E	R_E	Y_E

where:

V = value
R = cap rate (or ratio)
Y = yields

Subscripts:

o = overall property
M = mortgage or debt
E = equity

calculated by dividing the income levels by the appropriate value component. The yields (Y_s) introduce a time element into the income–value relationship and also consider a change in income and value over the time period (see § 1.7). Table 1.10 and Figure 1.1 offer evidence of the relationship among the decision concepts of values, solvency, and rates.

Rates are related to yields, even though a timing element exists. (This was noted earlier, in the linkage of equity dividends to equity yields.) This relationship can be emphasized in the context of measuring the total return to an investment.

The correlation of the equity and mortgage ratios to their correspondent yields can be illustrated as:

$$Y_M = R_M + (-\Delta_M)a$$

where $\Delta_M = P$

$$Y_E = R_E + (\Delta_E)a$$

or, transposing:

$$R_M = Y_M - (-\Delta_M)a$$

$$R_E = Y_E - \Delta_{Ea}$$

The relationship between the cap rate and the yield rate can be expanded to broader decision issues. The cap rates link income flows to values; the yield rates, used in discounting, relate cash flows to present values. The relationships are illustrated in Figure 1.1 by the lines that link rates and incomes to present values and the value approaches.

The support of the interrelated decision tools can be seen when leverage and solvency are compared. The example used throughout this study has had negative leverage but cash solvency. The potential for varying states of existence is illustrated in the following example:

Positive Leverage and Solvency: $R_o > R_M$ and thus $R_E > R_o$

Therefore

$$\frac{NOI}{V_o} > \frac{DS}{V_E} \qquad \frac{CF_E}{V_E} > R_o$$

$$\frac{\$1{,}000}{\$10{,}000} > \frac{\$500}{\$7{,}000} \qquad \frac{\$500}{\$3{,}000} > R_o$$

$$.10 > .071 \qquad .16667 > .10$$

where:

$$\begin{aligned} NOI &= \$1{,}000 \\ V_o &= \$10{,}000 \\ V_M &= \$7{,}000 \\ DS &= \$500 \\ CF &= \$500 \\ V_E &= \$3{,}000 \end{aligned}$$

In the above example, positive leverage exists and the property is solvent. The debt service is covered and \$500 is directed to the equity position.

Neutral Leverage and Solvency: $R_o = R_M$; $R_E = R_o$

Therefore

$$\frac{NOI}{V_o} = \frac{DS}{V_M} = \frac{CF_E}{V_E}$$

$$\frac{\$1{,}000}{\$10{,}000} - \frac{\$800}{\$8{,}000} = \frac{\$200}{\$2{,}000}$$

$$.10 \qquad .10 \qquad .10$$

The cost of capital on debt and the equity dollars are equal. The project is solvent, but cash flow to equity has been reduced with the increased flow of cash to the debt component.

Negative Leverage and Solvency: $R_o < R_M$; $R_E < R_o$

Therefore

$$\frac{NOI}{V_o} < \frac{DS}{R_M} \qquad \frac{CF_E}{V_E} < \frac{NOI}{V_o}$$

$$\frac{\$1{,}000}{\$10{,}000} < \frac{\$900}{\$8{,}000} \qquad \frac{\$100}{\$2{,}000} < R_o$$

$$.10 < .1125 \qquad .05 < .10$$

In the last example, positive solvency occurs and $100 is disbursed to the equity position, even though the property is negatively leveraged. Negative leveraging is not the same as overpowering the property with debt and totally choking off cash flow. Leverage is concerned with the relative cost of capital, that is, debt capital versus equity capital. Leverage decisions are concerned with rates; solvency is concerned with cash flow.

However, as indicated in the three examples, as the leverage becomes negative, the mortgage constant increases and the cash flow to debt increases as the cash to equity declines.

The rate calculations are dependent on the income flows and purchase or stock prices. The values, in turn, are contingent on the income flows, because, as the leverage–solvency analysis shows, despite the financing level (leverage), property solvency is constrained by both the cash flowing out and the cash coming in. The cash inflow is contingent on the competitive strength of the property in relation to other properties. These solvency concerns, competitive constraints (or substitutability), and anticipation are the key issues in value estimation. The basis of value is a positive cash flow. Value is premised on solvency.

The concepts of value, rates, and solvency are interrelated. However, the emphasis on the decision tool must be related to the problem situations decision makers face.

For example, in a down market, value should not be the central decision premise. The appropriate concern is solvency. The issue is: Can all parties remain solvent, so that the asset is not placed on the market? If the property is listed in a down market, the previous value will almost surely be eroded.

In an inflationary or rapidly growing market, value is a key concern. The decision emphasis is on the present worth of future expectations. Rational behavior requires receiving those benefits as quickly as possible.

A negative amortizing mortgage is an example of a disregard for solvency and an emphasis on value. This vehicle is used when personal income (residential) or property rent (income/commercial) is not sufficient to cover debt service. The decision emphasis is on capturing future appreciation today (before it goes higher). The key concern for decision makers is whether the property appreciation exceeds the build-up of the negative equity.[14]

[14] Terry V. Grissom and Charles H. Wurtzebach, "A Proposed Underwriting Model for Negative Amortization Mortgages," *Appraisal Review Journal*, 7:2 (Fall 1984): 19–26.

In one situation, solvency is the key issue; in another, it is value. The emphasis can change with the problem, the property type, or the economic environment. It is important that decision makers recognize the interrelation between the methods and when to switch decision criteria.

Decision models must be selected to coincide with real estate cycles. Timing is important, and timing skills require a conscious investigation and knowledge of real estate markets. Property knowledge alone is not sufficient. When and where to emphasize the appropriate decision model is a skill needed for success.

Two

Productivity Analysis: The Basis of Market Analysis

§ 2.1 INTRODUCTION

Productivity analysis is concerned with the evaluation of a product's marketable capabilities for providing services and satisfactions. In real estate, the services and satisfactions are valued from the perspective of a property's ability to meet human needs, the needs of economic activities, and the needs of emotional satisfactions and amenities.

The attributes of a property establish the basis of its value for an economic use and are the reason for its market appeal, which directly links the property to the delineation of demand and identifies the competitive supply.

The worth of a property is not limited to tangible attributes such as soil, size, frontage, or the type of building material; the value of a site or improvement (as compared to other properties) may be the effect of a view, a babbling brook, or other pleasant features of the property. Value factors are not limited to the features of the property that have an impact on the purchase or selling price. Other value elements originate in the psychology of the people involved in the transaction. Psychological impact is the concern of market research and will be further investigated in § 2.8(b) and in Chapter 8. The point to be made over and over is that the market research process is recursive and has many interrelated parts. The concern at this phase of the process is to emphasize the fundamentals of a particular site.

To understand the fundamental productivity of a particular site, it is important to begin with the specifics of the site, not those of the market. This characteristics approach has its roots in the new approach to consumer theory proposed by Lancaster.[1] In general, the theory states that a particular commodity or good can best be comprehended in terms of a number of the characteristics or basic attributes of the good. For real estate, examples of the attributes would be features such as size, location, amenities, and other qualities to be identified in the appraisal process. As traditionally practiced, appraisal documents the value estimate of a site by analyzing its features and comparing them to features of similar sales or rentals. This book emphasizes using the property characteristics not only to estimate values but also to explain variation in the market and to more thoroughly understand the nature of assets and their existing and potential markets. This extension of the traditional appraisal function necessitates an alternative emphasis in the appraisal process.

Productivity analysis begins with the physical, legal, and locational attributes of a given parcel of land. The site-specific orientation is logical, for several reasons. It enables the identification of (1) attributes that prompt people to pay for the privilege of occupancy and use of a property, and (2) key components of a good that initiate market action. In investigating individual properties, real estate analysis compares and contrasts unique or heterogeneous assets and the attributes of those assets. A general model or single-decision model is therefore not appropriate for the problem situations that involve real estate. Because of the lack of a general model, both appraisal and market analysis are designed as processes.

Productivity analysis is an initial step in real estate market analysis because the use of realty is flexible and the nature of land markets is heterogeneous. For example, in a recent study of urban land markets, the spread in prices paid was compared to the mean of the prices in different market segments of the city. The study illustrated a greater price range in the suburban areas than in the central business district

[1] Kelvin J. Lancaster, "A New Approach to Consumer Theory," *Journal of Political Economy* (April 1966): 132–157.

(CBD). The CBD had a more constant range of alternate uses and a higher degree of certainty than the suburbs.[2]

The coefficient of variation (the ratio of the standard deviation to the mean) of the prices ranged from a low of 30 percent to a high of 206 percent in the markets outside the CBD. The CBD had a range of 4 percent to 13 percent. The large percentages of variation demonstrate the need for the appraisal/market analysis to support differences identified in the comparison of the heterogeneous properties. Finally, a process must be established that directly links the attributes creating the economic use of a property to the valuation techniques.

This link of property characteristics to market activity and valuations can be accomplished with the use of productivity analysis. The general categories of attributes that form the basis of productivity and lead to economic value because of their market appeal (or lack of it) are:

1. Physical attributes
2. Legal attributes
3. Locational attributes.

Physical and legal attributes are discussed in detail in this chapter. Location is the topic of Chapter 3.

§ 2.2 PHYSICAL ATTRIBUTES

Real estate's lack of physical flexibility contributes to the perception of its economic uniqueness. Real estate is a real asset. It is immobile. It can have many uses, despite its physical fixity. Overcoming a perception of the limitations of real estate is part of the objective of the market research that is integrated with the appraisal process. To aid the appraiser in handling the use flexibility of real estate, the market research is incorporated into the appraisal report in a section on highest and best use. The report's section on highest and best use begins with the analysis of the physical constraints.

Unlike many economic goods, real estate as a product must be identified. The attributes that make it desirable for any specific use must be

[2] Terry V. Grissom, "Urban Land Price Indices: Austin, Texas," Real Estate Center, Texas A&M University, College Station, TX, Technical Report; Summer 1989.

pointed out. Appraisers often treat a property's physical characteristics with a descriptive analysis rather than with an analytical investigation of the impact of this dimension on the final value. A good example of this situation is a recent appraisal that arrived at a $100 million value for an acreage tract. The value was based on its potential as a site for a planned mixed-use development, almost a new town concept or planned community. As in many situations, the project did not get off the ground. The lenders took it back and required a reappraisal. The new appraisal indicated a $1 million value, based on the discovery that the site was a former landfill. The site could not physically support the proposed use—or very many other possible development plans—because of the weakness of the underlying soil. Furthermore, market perceptions of the proximity of a landfill could prevent the potential of demand for the site or any future development in the area. The potential for use on the site was physically limited, and physical limitations lead to economic limitations.

§ 2.3 PROCESS OF PRODUCTIVITY ANALYSIS—PHYSICAL ATTRIBUTES

The objective of productivity analysis is to identify a property's physical potential in terms of its possibilities and its constraints. The constraints can be taken as limits to alternative development or uses. They are finite constraints, if it is not economically feasible to overcome any physical problems. A further concern of the analysis is to identify any variation from expectations. Therefore, as the physical attributes are identified, the potential for change must be evaluated. Value is the present worth of future expectations. In a valid productivity analysis, the changing expectations of the market in relation to the fundamental features of the property must be considered.

The process for conducting a productivity analysis would be to descriptively identify the physical attributes and constraints for the subject property and then to consider the possible variations that can physically occur over a given, proposed, or planned holding period. The expectations are then compared to actual occurrences, to calculate the variations and expenses involved in the proposed operation of a use or site.

Physical attributes can be subdivided into natural features and features produced by human endeavor. The natural or geological features are the dominant constraints on the use potential of any site.

The physical characteristics are the most constraining factors in a land use decision.

(a) NATURAL FEATURES AS PRODUCTIVE FACTORS IMPACTING VALUE

Natural physical features are considered to be influential factors in determining a site's productive capacity.

Topography

Change or consistency in the terrain is important to the variation often reflected in prices. The terrain can determine the presence of amenities such as scenic views, brooks, and other physical features that are desirable for residential use but can be relevant for commercial uses also. The hi-tech industry has promulgated a demand (and consequently, a marketing strategy by developers) for campuses at their new developments—pleasant environments that can encourage creative and productive thought. Supposedly, esthetic environments aid creative thought, which, in turn, encourages the development of ideas for new products and services and for problem-solving models.

The various elevations of the terrain influence the direction and speed of drainage and run-off. In addition to the cost of curing a drainage problem, the cost of potential litigation must be considered when alterations are made in existing drainage flows. The floodplain can greatly alter a land use plan, increasing costs and lowering revenues. Insolvency in development or abandonment of existing facilities can result. The specter of this cash flow dilemma can be avoided long before the proforma is forecast or material is purchased for the development. Many developments' up-front costs increase because of the necessary expense of channelizing a site in a floodplain area, in order to get approval to develop. They also face an additional cost for the flood insurance that would be incurred by building a development in such an area. The nature of the terrain often requires an increased on-site development cost. Physical conditions can create a comparative advantage for one property or can result in another property's having less market potential. Appropriate analysis of a site's productive potential is a necessary step in identifying an area's potential competitive supply of properties for specific uses.

Topsoil and Subsoils

Topsoil often results when an area has underlying bedrock and the elements of nature interact, clash, and deposit materials on its surface over a long period of time. For example, within a few miles of Austin, Texas, real estate developers must deal with impervious clay topsoils that are capable of expanding and contracting to such a degree that buildings, over time, suffer weakened superstructures. Limestone bedrock multiplies the high cost of installing the infrastructure—the utility lines, sewers, and road networks. The impervious clays cause difficulty in an area of several hundred square miles. In cities within the area, appraisers must always be aware of the shrink–swell potential of the soil and its impact on the structural integrity of the buildings. The problem results in increased costs of initial construction, increased operating maintenance over time, and possibly, a lower terminal value at resale (depending on market situations).

In a market framework, the soil conditions affect the level of potential supply by delineating the area that has acceptable structural support. The mere reporting of acreage available for sale or acceptably zoned will not give a clear description of the local market. In an area otherwise characterized by impervious clay soil, a site that lies on a major rock outcropping and that can support intensive development will have a monopoly position, with higher levels of demand than would exist for a standard site.

Productivity analysis can direct the interpretation of the market information. A well-constructed building that suffers no stress because of the soil conditions can bring a premium in the local market.

Information on the terrain can be gained by reading the contour lines of a map, by making a personal inspection, and by researching the soil literature available. The U.S. Department of Agriculture (USDA), through Agriculture Extension offices, distributes copies of county soil surveys that allow insights to the terrain. This product knowledge is useful to novice researchers or to those with limited experience.

On a larger scale, the impact of soil conditions in an area can mold the form of an urban structure and the direction of its growth in the future. This is important because the form of an urban structure directs the actions of the market in terms of land use and transaction prices. City planners in the Austin area, aware of the significance of natural terrain conditions, laid out the city's comprehensive plan so that consideration was given to the limestone on the west and the impervious clay on the east. Their plan resulted in a politically defined preferred growth corridor running north and south.

Knowledge of the physical form of the urban structure and of legal constraints is not enough. In Austin, despite the preferential treatment given development within the growth corridor, the market tended to grow to the southwest and northwest—toward the hill country in the west. Insights to market preferences must be developed in different areas. Despite the higher cost of development, the preferred direction for growth will be toward terrain that has amenities and, consequently, market premiums.

Ground Cover

Ground cover is another concern in the use potential and value of sites. For example, some plant life may be protected in different areas, and the level of the protection may prohibit development to the maximum potential. Disturbance of ground surface may be illegal in areas that otherwise have recreational and industrial potential. The combination of physical and legal constraints can totally control the marketability of a property.

Sites with trees often bring a premium in market transactions, even though the trees may have to be cut down to build the proposed development. In one case, in Denton, Texas, a shopping center was developed on a wooded area in a prime location within the community. To maximize the development, the entire outcropping of trees was razed. Community standards were so offended that the developer could not get enough tenants to successfully operate the property. Businesses that would ordinarily locate in the development feared that customers would not come. This type of market resistance may dissolve in the long run but, given the outstanding debt on the property, this developer has come to understand John Maynard Keynes's statement that, in the long run, we are all dead.

By using productivity analysis, the market potential for the shopping center site might have been better exploited; the monopoly potential of the site might have been recognized. To plan a structure that would have preserved the foliage of the Denton site would have cost more, but a unique center might have been developed. In Trammel Crow's Arboretum Center in Austin, the effort to preserve the trees in this prime location was carried to such an extreme that the parking facilities are curved and insufficient; yet the center was considered successful.

A key reason for discussing the relationship among physical features, community standards, and development plans is that, in valuation techniques and value theory, cost is not considered equal to value in most situations. Often, a clearing cost will be necessary before a given lot can be compared to a developable site, and the cost may or may not be recouped. Research of the market enables advance insight to these economic and hence value concerns.

Planning departments often furnish documentation of development restrictions or proposed plans that indicate the physical dimensions of the local terrain. These data are often available from local engineering companies, architectural firms, and landscape contractors.

Sun and Wind

A site's orientation to sun and wind can influence its value. The orientation can have an impact on use, desirability, or occupancy of a facility or site. If a major retail area runs north–south, the facilities on the east side of the street are exposed to the afternoon sun. In a southern community, because of the shade afforded by the buildings on the west side, most of the pedestrian traffic will occur on the west side of the street. The east side stores may experience more sun-faded inventory, higher utility and operating costs, and fewer customers. Passive investors, lenders, or review appraisers who must form opinions on value, vacancy, return, and rent must understand such unique physical, locational, and market situations. Locational issues can be linked to a physical characteristic that directly influences the marketability and worth of a building.

(b) DYNAMIC FEATURES

Geological features are more than static constraints. They are dynamic features that must be analyzed and dealt with. However, the dynamics may not be limited to market perceptions; the physical problems themselves may be dynamic issues. Californians are constantly exposed to the movement of geological features. Earthquakes are changing property relationships. The owner of a subject site that lay on the San Andreas fault wanted to develop a retail center on the parcel. Engineers came in with massive earth pounders and beat on the property until they felt it was solid enough to be capable of supporting the structure. As time went by and several earth movements occurred, the building began to shift toward the property line. Eventually, the building began to overlap on the adjoining property until about a third of the structure encroached on the neighbor's parcel. The neighbor began to rent his third out. Under the legal concept of encroachment, if a structure is built on other people's property, it is theirs.

The dynamics of plate tectonics not only alters legal rights of ownership, and thus value, but also can create and/or destroy value or increase the cost of ownership of property. As an example of dynamic land movement creating value, the Balcones escarpment in Austin created the delineation between the impervious clay topography and the limestone bedrock, discussed earlier. The higher land values to the west of the city can, in part, be attributed to the hilly terrain and its amenities.

Irregular, minor fault lines are an example of dynamics that can destroy housing and commercial value. These faults, unlike the San Andreas or Balcones, are small and run in intermittent angles. Their impact is not as traumatic to an entire section of a city but can be devastating to a building owner's return. Unplanned split-level office buildings are difficult to rent because of their unsightly appearance and the increased maintenance they incur. The importance of preengineering studies, core drilling, and knowledge of the physical dimension of real estate cannot be overlooked. Many of the valuation problems that analysts encounter can be linked to this element.

As will be observed later, awareness of both the physical constraints of any given site and its legal opportunities does much to establish the value of the site in relation to comparable properties. An understanding of the combination of these two elements enables analysts to identify the *natural* monopolistic capacity of a site in a market context and may help critics of the appraisal process to recognize the need for appraisal to deal with individual ad hoc situations.

§ 2.4 SITE IMPROVEMENTS AS CAPITAL EXPENDITURES CREATING VALUE

Market analysis and valuation are tools that aid in a complex decision process. Real estate is a complicated asset that takes on the characteristics of both land and capital. The land-versus-capital debate has a long tradition. Land is a necessary factor of production because of the physical need for space and situation for all activities and the productive requirements of agricultural activities. Capital is the result of savings, investment, or accumulation resulting from economic activities.

These distinctions are important in the context of market analysis and valuation. Regardless of how the asset came about, the return to the asset must be identified in order to appropriately employ the asset in an economic context.

Despite the common characteristics of the return criteria for land and capital, an important difference is that the tangible attributes of the realty asset control its productivity. As pointed out in § 2.3, the physical, legal, and locational dimensions of land are key determinants of its return. In some situations, physical attributes are significant to capital returns—on *real* capital; financial capital is basically defined by legal qualities. Rarely is capital identified by location factors, and it is especially unusual to have the return of a capital asset determined by spatial attributes.

The debate on capital in real estate can be extended to a concern as to whether real estate should be analyzed, managed, valued, or operated as a commodity or a resource. This debate is directly related to the valuation of real estate from an income approach rather than a sales comparison approach. A commodity is a good that is traded in a market context, subject to the short-term or spot market forces of immediate supply and demand. A resource is an asset that is intensively managed and allocated over time. The central themes of resource management are control, maintenance, and allocation over time. Productivity analysis of real estate has much to do with whether the economic decisions of real estate are made in the context of a resource or a commodity. The distinction between these two contexts will be important to the issues between value and price and the appropriate valuation techniques. The reliance on fundamentals or market movements and the explanation and documentation of the difference between these perspectives will be related to whether the real estate is identified as land or capital, a commodity or a resource. Productivity analysis guides the appraiser to the data-gathering process of market analysis and appraisal. Placing land in the context of a commodity or a resource also directs the emphasis toward short-term market activity capture rates or toward the concerns of absorption periods, forecasts of supply and demand over time, and discounts to reflect long- or short-term market risks.

(a) SITE IMPROVEMENTS

The physical dimension of real estate cannot be limited to the natural attributes of the property. The conflict between real estate as land or capital is complicated by the real capital improvements that are made to any given site. The improvements define the problems that often require specific decisions. Although improvements to a site and structure can be viewed as capital, an analysis must be made in the context of the site, the decision, and the problem. Improvements are usually intended to make the land more usable. They can be viewed in the categories of on-site and off-site improvements. On-site improvements, the most familiar capital additions that are contributed to the land, range from the general structure on the site (a house, apartment, office building, restaurant, or other construction) to development facilities and site improvements that directly alter the site. Among the latter improvements would be grading and leveling the site, terracing slopes, constructing retaining walls, and treating drainage problems. These improvements incur expenditures that must be accounted for in any cost analysis of a specific property, but are often neglected in the value estimation of a parcel. This cost/value consideration is often ignored for competitive sites that do not need these improvements, and it is not reflected in a market standard.

Other on-site improvements involve surfaced areas. Examples are driveways, walks, parking areas, landscaping, and plant coverage. An amazing array of underground improvements could impact on the capital value of the site. Among these subsurface improvements are utility connections such as sewer and water laterals, gas lines, and electrical wires.

Off-site improvements also contribute to the value of an urban site. Because off-site improvements are often improvements in common, they are considered in the location analysis of a site. Specific locational attributes are physical features that result in the economic product of an urban site.

Examples of off-site improvements are the street and road system, the public sewage system, water systems, disposal plants, pumping stations, sidewalks, and other capital/physical infrastructure facilities. Any of these factors might afford competitive advantages to a given parcel relative to comparable sites. Awareness of these factors is necessary to argue for (or defend against) income return differentials among competitive or substitutable properties.

An interesting aspect of off-site improvements that contribute to the value of a given site is that they can be installed by several sources—developers, an appropriate unit of government, or quasi-public agencies such as public utility companies. Because the source of installation can vary, so can the source of the payment. The capital outlay for off-site developments can range from a lot price that includes the improvements' cost to the developer, to a general property tax levied by the community. Intermediary stages of payment can consist of specific user fees, such as utility charges, or special assessments for public expenditures that may benefit only specific sites. Consumers—and hence, appraisers—must be aware of the fact that well-structured streets, curbs and gutters, or sidewalks are additional capital expenses in the development of residential or commercial lots, and those expenses must be recaptured in some manner. The mechanism of the capital recovery may be reflected in price differences and market preferences.

An interesting aspect of off-site improvements is that property values to owners are often created at public expense. In many ways, every parcel of real estate is a free rider. Many of the capital costs of every parcel of realty are often shifted to others. The productivity analyses linking to market aspects in this context might identify the properties or neighborhoods receiving preferential treatment from taxing authorities or determine whether the market is capitalizing these benefits into a value.

(b) BUILDING STRUCTURE

In addition to its importance in market analysis and valuation, analysis of the physical dimension of real estate contributes to an understanding of why certain assets command a higher price than other assets at specific times. Productivity analysis investigates the improved physical attributes of a property in terms of:

- Quality of the facilities
- Attractiveness of the facilities
- Functional efficiency of a property.

A key concern of the analysis of real estate's physical dimension is an understanding of the market's preference for an attractive project rather than a less desirable one.

The quality of the improvements on any site can contribute to a property's marketability and transaction price. Hough and Kratz have empirically shown that architecture contributes to a property's value.[3] Appraisers often consider structural variations and architectural

[3] D. E. Hough and C. G. Kratz, "Can 'Good' Architecture Meet the Market Test?," *Journal of Urban Economics* (August 1983): 40–54.

differences in a condition-of-property adjustment. The condition adjustment should represent the market's discounted price, which would reflect lower maintenance costs and decreased reserves for replacement of short-lived capital improvements.

More market research than usual is needed to understand quality differences in structures. For example, the possible premiums paid for quality are often reflected in the rents and prices paid for class A office space over and above class B and lower-quality space. The concern in appraisal, however, cannot be limited to the cost of quality or the rents demanded by landlords. Valuation is contingent on identifying the market for higher-quality goods. The relationship among users, based on market function, income levels, and activities or occupations, cannot be divorced from the product quality considerations in market analysis.

The attractiveness of a product cannot be easily uncoupled from the quality of the product. Quality has a special appeal to certain market segments; attractiveness must be addressed from the perspective of the market segment that, in essence, defines the standard of attractiveness. The appraiser must ask the question, "Attractive to whom?"

The productivity potential of the property's attributes, and the delineation of the attributes themselves, can do much to segment the actual market for the property and help the appraiser identify the potential demand profile for the property and the competitive supply. The linkage of the product to the market concerns of supply and demand is the essence of the market appeal identified in the reconciliation of productivity analysis.

The ratings of office buildings illustrate both the quality and the attractiveness with which productivity analysis is concerned. Decisions regarding quality or attractiveness are always of interest in the development process. The Seagram's Building is an interesting case in point. The Seagram's Building's exterior finish is constructed with bronze rather than steel. The reasons for using this material were the company's emphasis on amenities and the advertisement campaign contributing to the building's high profile. Bronze is the color of whiskey, a major product of the Seagram's organization.

Conflicts in valuation can result from use of nonstandard building materials. Conflict arose in valuation of the Seagram's Building, when a comparison of the cost analysis to the income or market sales comparison approach yielded a major value estimation difference. The cost estimate was declared to be too high. However, market analyses of rental rates and terms indicated that tenants would pay no more for space in the Seagram's Building than in other buildings, unless they were seeking benefits other than the occupancy of space. For example, a segment of the market was seeking the economic benefits of attractiveness, quality, prestige, or a combination of advertisement advantage, recognition, and space to house an enterprise. These prospective tenants were viewing the layout of the space from the perspective of identifying the property attributes that would serve their specific needs or functions.

The quality of a property's building materials, elevation, design, or layout is a major factor in market differentiation, over and above the spatial essence of improved real estate. Functional efficiency is based on real estate's being a three-dimensional space created to house a human or economic activity. The three dimensions are length, width and height. For any site, these dimensions are created by the combination of natural terrain and legal space as defined by surveys. The space created within buildings constructed on the site involves actual material development. The standards applicable to the space can vary with the attitudes and tastes of the users at any given time. The levels of the tastes and their rate of change are concerns of market analysis, which, at this stage, emphasizes linking consumer tastes to property attributes.

Functional efficiency analysis in appraisal addresses the concerns of the market participants regarding the property's physical attributes and layout. Real estate, like other products, is subject to changing market tastes. For example, central heating and air circulating systems have been standard in newer buildings for some time. Because these systems are lacking in older facilities, the newer facilities initially charged a premium for the new technology. As time went by, the premium became incorporated into the price, and older buildings became penalized. Examples of other functionally deficient facilities are office buildings that have restrooms on every other floor, retail facilities that lack parking even though they are not in a highly active pedestrian area, multistory retail facilities, and two-bedroom apartments with only one bathroom. The list of possible functionally deficient features is inexhaustible, and emphasizes the need for appraisers to link the tastes of markets to existing and future competitive properties. To appropriately investigate market trends, a property's productive attributes must be analyzed.

The physical elements of a parcel of real estate are important for the market comparisons that are made in the valuation context. The direct sales comparison approach requires information on the physical elements, to make comparative adjustments. Furthermore, the issues of productivity analysis that define the market's preferences should be reflected in the cost approach and should also be considered in the context of projecting revenue and estimating expenses in the income approach.

The basis for adjustments in each approach is linked to the market research that identifies the supply and demand and the use parameters of value theory. The productive capacity of the physical attributes is the first step in this linking process (if the problem relates to a site-specific assignment).

§ 2.5 SUMMARY OF PHYSICAL ATTRIBUTES

Physical attributes, one of the most restrictive aspects of the productivity of a parcel, are a primary determinant of real estate return. Physical attributes are a property's most static attributes. They are the most difficult to change, in terms of manual labor and economic expenditure, and they can be critical when full consideration is being given to competitive properties. Physical attributes create the three-dimensional nature of real estate, which supports the spatial or areal nature of the realty product. The product is used over time via temporary transfers of the space (leasehold estates) or permanent transfers of the space (freehold estates).

§ 2.6 LEGAL ATTRIBUTES

To understand the nature of productivity analysis in an economic context, it is appropriate to investigate the legal attributes of realty. The physical attributes of property must be transferred by legal means, to produce the economic issues that are of significance in a market, and the extension of the essence of a property (its three-dimensional space) is achieved in the legal context. The various estates in law introduce a fourth dimension, time, to real estate, because the key issue is use of the space over a defined period of time. Therefore, the combination of legal attributes with physical attributes creates the space–time product that is at the heart of the real estate market. The time dimension enables creation of alternative products and further segmented markets.

Attributes defined by law make possible the third and fourth dimensions of real property—height and time—and these dimensions generate the economic potential of real estate. Without the legal delineation of real estate, there is no product of space to be used over time. The three-dimensional space of the real estate product is often contingent on a legal description and delineated by a legal estate. Time, the fourth dimension, is essential to the worth of real estate and to the use and control of physical space. The legal concept of real estate enables users, owners, and investors to grasp the flexibility of a property. The ability to transfer more than the surface rights has led to claims of air rights, transfer of minerals, and the right to tunnel under properties.

Another byproduct has been complex investment strategies, such as Zuckendorf's Hawaiian technique: By introducing the fourth dimension of time into real estate, alternative property products can be created; these various leasehold estates can result in the sum of the leases' positions exceeding the fee simple estate.

When legal estates are created, financial interests can be expanded and additional markets for debt instruments or investment contracts can be created. For example, fee simple estates can be expanded with use of the fee simple condominium estate. The legal delineation is essential to understanding the value of a 900-square-foot condominium on the 69th floor of the John Hancock Tower. Another example of the legal potential for expanding real estate products is the time-share interest. A time share could exist in the John Hancock condominium. If there is a time share, the analyst must investigate the market and estimate a value for the right of use, for three months, of 900 square feet located 700 feet in the air. Another dimension is introduced.

§ 2.7 PRIVATE PROPERTY RIGHTS—THE BASIS OF PRODUCTIVITY AND VALUE

When legal actions create new or alternative products, those products enable the understanding and delineation of segmented markets. The segmented markets can be developed because three-dimensional space can be transferred into perpetuity or for an uncertain period by means of a freehold estate, or transferred for a stated period by means of a leasehold. The rights that can be transferred by various types of estates are subject to both private and public constraints. The property rights that create both the economic entity of property and the constraints on the ways in which the property is owned, possessed, transferred, and used can be separated into private rights and public rights.

The various types of estates transfer the quantity of rights that defines the real estate product. The quantity of rights in a transfer is important in the analysis of markets. The ability to identify the levels of competitive supply and effective demand can often be illustrated by an understanding of the quantity of rights describing a property's estate.

The legal aspects of real property are concerned with the quality as well as the quantity of property rights. The quantity of rights involved with most properties distinguishes them as freeholds or leaseholds; the general quality levels of properties are classified by warranties.

The quality of rights of a parcel of realty is identified by the warranties passing with the title. The types of warranties are: the general warranty, the special or specific warranty, and the quit claim deed. The general warranty protects the purchaser against all claims that might arise from clouds on the title, regardless of the source of a claim or action initiating the adversity. Under the special or specific warranty, the seller agrees only to protect the buyer against claims that might arise out of actions during the ownership of the seller (or the seller's estate).

The least level of quality in the ownership of property is represented by the quit claim deed, a procedure to protect against legal clouds on the property's title. In quit claim deeds, persons sign a statement that they forgo any interest that they may have in a property (if they even have a claim).

The categories of warranties, and the quality of rights they reflect in a property, stratify various levels of risk. The understanding of appropriate measures of risk is an important concern in market analysis. Both market risk and business risk must be addressed. The nature of the product and the potential for liability, loss, additional expenses, and variation from expectations associated with the productivity on the asset must be investigated in the valuation of the property.

If exposures to market risk exist because of a lack of quality in the title, then the property fundamentally should be expected to sell for less—that is, it should have a lower value. Support for the estimation of a lower value based on lesser quantities and qualities of rights in a property must be identified in the actions of the market. These actions are essentially issues of supply and demand for a product. A real estate product must be clearly delineated, to explain the prices paid and the variation in prices illustrated by the market participants.

Valuation should be possible after identification of the quantity and quality of estates in real property. The valuation process, however, must be tied to market activity.

The standards and practice regulations of the Appraisal Institute state that a property cannot be estimated by summing up the value of its component parts and addressing summation as the value of the entire property, nor can the value of its component parts be valued by taking percentages of the overall property. Highway departments often do the latter, but specifically identify the value as a contributory value, not a market value. It is important to identify the value of concern as a market value.

To estimate a market value of a component legal interest, it is necessary to find a sale of a partial interest and support the actions of that sale by further investigating the supply of competitive alternatives and the effective demand for the partial interest.

However, the market for freehold estates or partial interests does not exist in a vacuum. Regardless of the level of warranty attached to the transfer of a property, each parcel of property and the form of each transaction is subject to external forces. Real estate is a regulated market (and industry). The highest private property estate, even though it may be defined as a fee simple absolute estate, is, at best, only exclusionary, which means that the best the property owner can do is exclude others from the property.

All private property market activity is constrained by various levels of public rights. To understand the delineation of a market product, the public constraints on the property's productivity must be identified.

§ 2.8 PUBLIC PROPERTY RIGHTS—CONSTRAINTS ON PRODUCTIVITY AND VALUE

The restraints on productivity are represented by the *rights of the state,* a generic term for federal, state, local, and quasi-public agencies' rights to control, use, and acquire private property. As discussed earlier, fee simple absolute estates are not absolute, in the sense that the state, as defined generically, has certain rights in the use and distribution of realty. These rights may come in the form of eminent domain rights, police powers, taxation, and escheat.

Eminent domain is the right of the state to take private property for public use. The concept of public use is broad and subject to litigation. As shown later in this section, the delineation of eminent domain rights has evolved over time. The action of condemnation accompanies the state's right of eminent domain. Despite the right of the state, an owner does not have to meekly turn over a parcel of land. The Constitution states that, in order for the government to take private property, "just" compensation must be paid. Just compensation is identified as the market value of the property. If the offer from the state is not considered sufficient by the property owner and condemnation is instigated, then the owner's attorneys can initiate inverse condemnation proceedings. The net effect is that valuation becomes a matter of judicial review.

A second right of the state is its police powers, which allow the state controlling powers to protect the public welfare. Applied to real property, these powers come in the guise of zoning, subdivision development controls, building codes, and safety and sanitary regulations. Some people place environmental controls under the police powers; others perceive environmental constraints as a separate power. In either view, they are applied in a similar manner. The valuation issues related to the police powers are different from those of eminent domain. No compensation is usually paid. Compensation is not required by law. The state has preeminent property rights as compared to those of the individual. As such, the state can control the activities conducted in any given area of a community.

An example of this sovereign right is the direct impact of zoning. A city does not have to compensate an owner for a change in zoning, even if the zoning change alters land use potential and development rights, and thus value.

In another example, a city need not pay property owners if density is decrease. A decrease in density can reduce the number of units that can be placed on a particular parcel of land. The decrease in developable units can reduce the value based on overall units or based on the price per unit.

Appraisers must understand the impact of these powers on the market. As an example, in one city, there was a concentrated effort by condominium developers to get tracts on land zoned "O," an office–institutional zoning. A novice to the community might have wondered about the significance of this type of zoning to condos. Why were "O" zoned tracts bringing more per square foot on the market?

The reason was that the city zoning was a progressive, inclusive zoning. This type of zoning is like a pyramid, with the most restrictive, high-class, residential zone at the top (peak). As the land use types expanded from the peak of the pyramid to the base, the possible uses increased. Each zoning class below included all the uses of the zoning classes above it. Therefore, the office–institutional zoning allowed residential uses. The important feature was that, because it was less restrictive, the "O" zoning allowed a greater density of development. The cash flow proforma on a proposed project indicated that the land zoned "O" generated more return. Competition for this zoning type drove up the square-foot price as was justified by the revenue return.

The ultimate concern with the police powers is the "taking" issue. This issue basically asks: If you control a property to a great extent, have you in essence taken it? The perception of environmental controls as being separate from the police powers involves this issue. If the state prohibits development on a tract of land in order to enable a scenic view easement, has the state destroyed value? If value is the present worth of future anticipated benefits, and future development potential on the site is prohibited in order to create a public good of an esthetic view, has value been destroyed or transferred? Has the market potential of the site been altered? If use is the basis of value and a property cannot be improved in order to receive a market-indicated capital return under a possible highest and best use, could it be argued that value was destroyed? On the other hand, a loss of value may not be considered as a taking of property.

The interpretation of this issue is discussed later in this chapter. These points are significant to an understanding that the value of real estate is based on its productivity, and that productivity is based on certain general and numerous specific characteristics of property. Researchers' concern is to identify the appropriate market participant for a series of property attributes and the market participant's reaction to those attributes. The legal dimension of real estate is often an essential element of much market delineation.

The third right of the state restricting private productivity is taxation. This right ranges from the federal, state, and city taxation of income produced by real estate and attributed to an individual or legal taxable entity, to the taxation of real property by local levels of government. The latter type of taxation is the property right being considered here. The state or sovereignty has the first claim on a property's income stream and that claim or lien takes priority over the mortgage debt lien.

The local property tax can be thought of as a cover charge for a location within a community or jurisdiction. Each site does not bear the true or full cost of its development because of the off-site improvements discussed above. This situation raises a parallel question: If the tax flow from a property is the equity interest of the community in each and every parcel of real estate in a city, then are the community officials appropriately managing the assets in their care? This is a concern in estimating the highest and best use of a site, as defined in a community's objectives. It is also a key element in value theory and market analysis for appraisal.

The final right of the state, escheat, illustrates why the sovereignty has the prior claims to use, title, control, and possession on all property.

Escheat is brought into play when an individual property owner dies intestate (without a will). If no apparent heirs are identified to enable the laws of devise to be carried out, the property reverts to the state. The key word is reverts, which implies that the state owned the property previously. The underlying concept is that the right to hold private property is defined and given by the state. The state bequeathed certain rights to the private citizen but retained certain controls. These controls are the right of eminent domain if there is a need to take private property for a public use; the right to control property for the protection of the public welfare (or the preservation of the status quo); and the right to first claim of a site's productivity as a property tax.

(a) LEGAL RIGHTS AND MARKET DELINEATION

The emphasis of a community on the various public rights can often delineate a market. This is a possibility in a major metropolitan area where jurisdictions change within short distances. For example, the Atlanta metropolitan area extends over several counties. Two primary counties are Fulton and DeKalb. In the not too distant past, DeKalb County was "dry" (no alcoholic beverages were sold) and Fulton County was "wet." The land use market along major thoroughfares in east Fulton County was influenced by the demand for alcohol in DeKalb County. Accessibility to the market was important.

The alternative emphasis of different jurisdictions on public rights or on the enforcement of these rights is a method of delineating markets on a geographic basis. Collectively, legal attributes and concerns of location address the cultural concerns of a community, which can be a windfall or a wipe-out to individual property owners. Texas holds two extreme examples within 170 miles of each other. At one extreme is Houston, which currently has no zoning (an election on zoning is being discussed). Land use control is a judicial concern worked out by interpretation of restrictive covenants in the courts. The lack of zoning reflects the city's capitalist views (and laissez-faire attitude) toward property rights. Houston's development requirements are printed on both sides of one page. The city is pro-growth and eager for economic change. However, as recent years have shown, capitalism without failure is akin to religion without sin. Uncontrolled access to profits is also often coupled with limited safety nets on the downside.

At the other extreme is Austin, which has a comparatively attractive environment relative to many markets in Texas. The environment is an economic attraction. Much of the resident citizenry and the city hierarchy favor regulating land use and the market, to prevent uncontrolled exploitation of the countryside. The regulations include zoning, watershed ordinances, hill country ordinances, roadway ordinances, extensive extraterritorial jurisdiction controls, exactions, and dedications. Land use, a private contract–judicial process in Houston, is a matter of legislative and executive governmental action in Austin. The development regulations and ancillary literature require an encyclopedic knowledge. Local experts are available as consultants, just to get outside developers through the physical–legal dimensions of the development process.

Despite the regulated nature of its land markets, Austin has experienced economic cycles, although the phases have occurred in different patterns and at different times than those of the Houston market. The concern of appraisers is that the varying regulatory levels of the different communities influence the cost of producing products. Compared to Houston, Austin has a higher preliminary development cost. This cost has an impact on the quantity of supply available over time. The cultural orientation also influences the level of demand for different real estate products. As a general observation, a larger component of the Austin market is concerned with (natural) recreational properties.

The essence of the public rights dimension of real estate is that it is an integral part of the market activity for property. Failure to identify its components is a failure to fully recognize the product and its market structure.

(b) EVALUATING PREFERENCES AND MARKET STRUCTURE

A cultural preference for real estate is not a static geographic concern; it is constantly evolving. Changes in cultural preference can be identified from the changing legislation and litigation concerning land use.

Cultural perceptions of the community's or state's right to control private real estate have changed over time. Their cycles have alternated from a strong emphasis on the government's rights to a weaker enforcement of the public's rights. Communities have tended to lean toward property rights, only to change again and go in the opposite direction. As if the problem of complying with the unique physical heterogeneity of real estate were not enough, many of the decisions as to the enforcement of rights have been ad hoc in nature. The degree of fluctuation of the cultural preference cycle is determined by where one begins an investigation of the legal tendencies. The beginning is easily identified because the United States is a young nation. Thomas

Jefferson and some of his contemporaries originally perceived that it was beneficial to the well-being and growth of the country to enfranchise the individual with the right to property. This was not a unanimous decision, but it prevailed for numerous decades. Its prevalence is indicated by the land grants, land rushes, and manifest destiny policy encouraged by the government. This perspective predominated while the United States was basically a rural nation. As urbanization began, the potential for conflict in property rights increased. When people began to live in greater proximity to one another, the conflicts were not concerned only with rights to space, but with status or civil rights versus property rights.

As stated earlier, certain controls were retained by the state, partly to deal with the conflicting goals of a diverse society and with the changes that can occur over time.

Enforcement of the controls, the philosophy supporting the enforcement, and the perceptions of the government and the public as to the extent of the state's rights have ebbed and flowed. An understanding of the current perception of property rights and limitations is necessary, in order to evaluate the returns, risk, and expectations associated with markets for property ownership and investment. Often, the current level of rights can only be put in perspective by comparing them to the level of rights or the perception of rights in the past. This comparison explains some of the variation observed in the available data on prices paid over time and on yields. The same approach shows the impact on value of changes in zoning and density. Therefore, the broader cycle of the perception of property rights—what exactly is entailed in the fee simple estate and all other lesser estates—must be recognized.

The fluctuation in the perception of rights in property can be illustrated by a series of cases. Beginning in 1910, in *Hadacheck v. Sebastian,*[4] the legal conclusion was that the community had the right to zone an undesirable use out of existence. A brick yard, which preexisted the surrounding land uses, was deemed to be a nuisance because it was spreading dust over the residences and businesses in the area. The larger issue, beyond a nuisance matter between neighbors, was a test of the right of the city of Los Angeles to enforce zoning controls. The conclusions were that a city could zone out of existence a preexisting use and that state powers were sufficient to override private rights and hence totally destroy value without compensation.

[4] *Hadacheck v. Sebastian,* 239 U.S. 394 (1915).

In the 1920s, the cycle shifted in the other direction, as represented by *Pennsylvania Coal Co. v. Mahon.*[5] The Supreme Court overturned a lower court that had ruled that a mining company must cease operating in a manner that was causing the houses on the surfaces to collapse. The final decision was that the value of a property was in the anticipated returns from the operation. The Court's decision stated that to constrain the operation to the extent that it was not earning an appropriate return was equivalent to a taking of property. In essence, to destroy value is equivalent to taking property.

With this interpretation is observed a deemphasis of the state's police power to protect the general welfare—specifically, the welfare of the people living in the houses on the surface area of the mine, who were employees of the mine. Instead, individual or corporate property rights were favored. The key was that individual property rights could be expressed in spite of the public controls and this expression could be reflected in value estimation and market prices. Furthermore, the value of these rights was recognized as being subject to interpretation and to periodic changes that are often measured by market activity. The major insight from the *Mahon* case is that value and rights periodically equate and that value, even in litigation, is the present worth of future anticipated benefits.

The spirit of *Mahon* continued into the 1970s, when the taking issue began to receive more intensive attention. The taking issue basically deals with the question as to what degree of control the state can exercise until it has, in effect, taken a property.[6] One example of the controversy of the taking issue was addressed in *Just v. Marinette County.*[7] In that case, the judge delineated the issue of eminent domain and the police powers by pointing out that eminent domain involves the taking of private property for an affirmative public use. Alternatively, the police powers involve the control of the property to protect the general welfare and sustain the status quo. The nature of the issues and the context of the problem direct the need to estimate a value or dollar damage estimate in eminent domain and not in enforcement of the police powers.

[5] *Pennsylvania Coal Co. v. Mahon,* 260 U.S. 393 (1922).

[6] Fred P. Bosselman, David L. Callies, and John Banta, "The Taking Issue: A Study of the Constitutional Limits," *Management and Control of Growth,* Vol. 1, Edited by Randall Scott (Washington, DC: Urban Land Institute, 1975): 256–265.

[7] *Just v. Marinette County,* 201 N.W. 2d 761 (1972).

Based on the perception of the problem or the spirit of legal interpretation, different value estimates can be derived for a single parcel of property, as illustrated in the following *simplified* example.

Example

A vacant parcel of property has three acres. Comparable sales in the area, for vacant tracts of similar size, location, and all other factors of comparison, indicate a value of $60,000 per acre or a total value of $180,000.

The owner has permitted, filed, and approved plans to develop a 150-unit hotel on the three-acre site. For some reason, the state decides to prevent the development of the site as planned. Because of the inverse condemnation possibility, based on the proposed plan of use, the following value can be estimated:

150 units rentable 360 nights per year = 54,000 potential revenue units annually

54,000 potential revenue units annually @ $30.00 per unit = $1,620,000 potential revenue per year

The $1,620,000 represents the total potential annual revenue that can be produced if the proposed facilities are developed. The following value calculation is based on this potential annual income, plus the supportive market information concerning vacancy, expenses, and capitalization rates:

Potential gross income (PGI)	$1,620,000
Less: Vacancy at 15%	243,000
Effective gross income (EGI)	$1,377,000
Less: Expenses @ 40% (of EGI)	550,800
Net operating income (NOI)	$ 826,200

$$\text{NOI capitalized @ } 10\% = \frac{\text{NOI}}{R_0} = \frac{\$826{,}200}{.10} = \$8{,}262{,}000$$

The value range for the property is $180,000 to $8,262,000, depending on the legal interpretations of the basis of value, as indicated by the various cases. In a very simplistic extension of the findings, the following values would result:

Case	Value Award
Hadacheck v. Sebastian	$0
Pennsylvania Coal Co. v. Mahon	$8,262,000
Just v. Marinette County	Cannot be decided without determining why the state has taken action. Range: $0–$180,000–$8,262,000

Since the 1970s, there have been many cases concerning the private use of property and the state's right to take and/or control private land. Much of this litigation concerns the developers' right to develop and the city regulators' rights in terms of growth management, environmental concerns, and retention of the status quo. All of these issues are important when the premise of value is defined as the present worth of future benefits. Private property rights, as they interface with public rights, delineate the expected benefits, the right to those benefits, and the risk associated in receiving those benefits.

Recent court decisions suggest a preference for the preeminence of private rights and the recognition of the value of future benefits. In 1987, in *First English Evangelical Lutheran,*[8] a temporary administrative ordinance denied the church the right to reconstruct buildings destroyed in a flood. The church brought suit, seeking damages for the taking of the property's use. The conflict was between a prior use and the city's right of control (much like the *Hadacheck* conflict). An additional issue in the *First English* case was the principle of compensation applied to a temporary taking.

In *Nollan v. California Coastal Commission,*[9] the owner/developer's position was established as predominant to the public's rights.[10] Again, the conflict was one of development rights (as a product to market) versus public control, as in *Mahon*. The Coastal Commission required that a public access easement be dedicated along the water's edge, as a condition for allowing a new house to be built on the property. The court found that the relationship between a new house and the public's right to beach access was too tangential to the concept of safety via the

[8] *First English Evangelical Lutheran Church of Glendale v. County of Los Angeles,* 482 U.S. 304 (1987).

[9] *James Patrick Nollan, et ux., v. California Coastal Commission,* 483 U.S. 825 (1987).

[10] *See also* Joel G. Shapiro, "Potential Bonanza for Real Estate Owners," *Real Estate Outlook,* 11:1 (Spring 1988).

police powers. The easement requirement was held to be a taking, and the restriction was found to be discriminatory against Nollan. To be nondiscriminatory, the Coastal Commission would have to ensure access to the beach, with all residents bearing the cost.

§ 2.9 SUMMARY OF LEGAL ATTRIBUTES

The legal aspects of real estate influence not only the real estate product but the way in which business and real estate decisions are implemented. The enactment of real estate activities subject to legal constraints can result in a loss of real estate value and opportunity, or in windfalls such as the ownership of the only commercially zoned tract in an area, the creation of entitlements, and an increased certainty of expected benefits.

The concern of the general appraisal and market research processes is that all of the economic activity involving land is subject to cultural preference, which defines the product and delineates the market. Because cultural preference is an evolving concept, the past, the present, and the future perceptions of the rights to property, and the benefits that flow from those rights, must be considered in the market research and valuation process. The estates in land, the public constraints on those estates, the timing economies of those estates, the risk associated with the contractual agreements, and the enforcement of those agreements are the essentials of the value decision supported by market expectations.

The interaction of the legal and physical dimensions of real estate is directly related in the legal description of a property. Legal descriptions in the United States are in four general categories; they vary from region to region or state to state, according to the cultural heritage of a particular area. The English common law bequeathed the *metes and bounds system,* which is used in the states that were formerly the thirteen original colonies and in the states south of the Ohio River and east of the Mississippi, plus Texas, Louisiana, and Arkansas. This system of measures and distances relates to the directions of the compass. An older form of the metes and bounds system was called the monument system.

The expansion of the American frontier into the Northwest territories and the Louisiana Purchase necessitated a more generalized legal description system than the ad hoc approach of metes and bounds. The rectangular format of the *government survey system* was devised, to allow large-scale descriptions of remote territories. The government system, comprised of ranges and tiers or townships, resembles the grid patterns of latitude and longitude.

The Spanish heritage of the Southwest set the standards of community property that are linked to the *Spanish land grant system.* The Spanish system is an organized grid system similar to the government survey system used in the Midwest. Both systems were created to enable the legal and physical delineation of property in the expanding frontiers.

A more modern urban system is the *lot and block system,* a generalized process in which a subdivision or addition to the existing urban landscape is platted. The individual lots within the subdivision are often laid out with dimensions.

The significance of the legal descriptions is that they physically and legally delineate the estates in property. The delineated estates form the basis for the three-dimensional aspects of the space–time real estate product. This basis is then altered by the public controls on the delineated estates. The combination of the physical and legal dimensions is illustrated in § 2.10.

This discussion has not been intended as a discourse on real estate law or an exhaustive list of legal examples of property rights. It is an attempt to emphasize the importance of identifying (1) the legal dimensions of a generic parcel of real estate and (2) the relevant characteristics of the real estate product and its market. Knowledge of physical and legal attributes is necessary to identify the product, develop the basis of market analysis, and direct the analyst to the appropriate models to simulate and infer market behavior. The interaction of buyers and sellers will enable the estimation of value.

§ 2.10 BUILDING ENVELOPE—THE SPACE–TIME PRODUCT

The identification of real estate as essentially a space–time product may be alien both to those who are experienced and those who are inexperienced in real estate. However, a realization that real estate is space that is to be used over time to house economic activities or satisfy human needs is a necessary first step toward understanding the behavioral nature of value. Market actions may displace the problems linked to value's being considered inherent in physical objects. Acknowledgment of the error of the concept that value is inherent in physical objects may improve the documentation of market factors that can alter values over time.

To develop an understanding of market behavior for a product, real estate must be seen as a space–time product, and that perspective can be found in the interaction of legal and physical property attributes. The concluding section of the chapter gives a prime example of this interaction in the development of the building envelope on a specific property.

(a) EXAMPLE: POTENTIAL ONE-STORY RETAIL BUILDING

A lot measures 150 feet by 100 feet, or 15,000 square feet of basis lot, as defined in a lot-and-block or metes-and-bounds description. The lot is situated on a corner of two major streets and abuts a residential neighborhood. The zoning classification suggests the possibility of a one-story retail structure. Compared to several other possible uses, the retail facility would generate the greatest potential return to the site. The zoning classification requires a 5-foot setback on the side abutting the residential land. A 10-foot building line is required at the rear of the property (the building cannot be closer than 10 feet from the rear property line). However, the rear 10 feet can be used for parking; the 5 feet abutting the residential property cannot, because, by law, no improvements can be made on the land that lies near a different property use. Based on the zoning restrictions, the following land is usable:

Land basis (150 × 100)	15,000 sq. ft.
Less: setback (150 × 5)	750
Land available for use	14,250 sq. ft.

The development regulations in this area and zoning classification require that 300 square feet of parking be allotted for each 300 square feet net of building area (total area) that is planned. This calculation enables the calculation of the building foot print, which is the dimension of the building on the land's surface. The land use equation for the building foot print also allows the calculation of the building volume (if more than one story is possible). The planned building efficiency, based on the market trend and comparable structures, is 90 percent.

300 sq. ft./.90 = 333.33 sq. ft. of gross building = size of one parking unit (including parking stall and access area)

Each 300 square feet of net building area requires one parking unit; therefore, for the one-story retail facility, each 300 square feet of building foot print requires 300 square feet of parking on the ground.

This requirement sets up the basic land area calculation:

Building foot print	333.33 sq. ft.
Add: Surface parking	300.00
Total land used per unit	633.33 sq. ft.

$$\frac{\text{Land available for use}}{\text{Total land used per unit}} = \text{Land allocation units}$$

$$\frac{14{,}250 \text{ sq. ft.}}{633.33} = 22.50$$

Land use allocation	Sq. Ft. Gross	Sq. Ft. Net (90%)
Building area per floor: 333.33 sq. ft. × 22.50	7,499.96	6,749.96
Parking area: 300 sq. ft. × 22.50	6,750.03	—
Total restricted site	14,250.00 (rounded)	

The above calculations illustrate how the physical and legal components of real estate interact to produce the space that will be delivered in the market. Following is a general formula for developing the space–time envelope:

$$\frac{A - Sb}{\frac{Bu}{Er} + Pu(S) + O} = \text{Land allocation unit}$$

where:

A = gross area of lot
Sb = setbacks, if space cannot be built out
Bu = net building area based on zoning and/or parking requirements
Er = building efficiency ratio
Pu = parking unit size
S = number of stories
O = open space requirements (none, or zero, in this example)

Using the previous example:[11]

$$\frac{15{,}000 - 750}{\frac{300}{.90} + 300(1) + 0} = 22.50$$

The number of land allocation units (22.50) is then applied to the building and parking areas, to enable the check of the basic adjusted lot size.

The example illustrates that the physical and legal constraints are important to the delineation of the product, the projected income, and the estimation of value for a property. The building had (rounded) 7,500 square feet. At a cost of $45 per square foot, the total building cost was $337,500. The land was purchased for $100,000, so the total investment was $437,500.

The net floor area (rounded) was 6,750 square feet. This was the basis of the rental income. At a net rental of $8 per square foot per year, the total potential income to the property was $54,000. At a 10 percent cap rate from the market, the value was $540,000. This was $102,500 greater than the cost of constructing the property, which indicated that the market was paying a premium over and above the cost of construction for retail facilities in this area.

The fundamentals of a real property, combined with market activities, establish the productivity and value of the property. The fundamentals addressed in this chapter were the physical and legal dimensions. In the next chapter, a complex but essential element of understanding realty productivity and value is discussed—location.

[11] If a multiple-story (e.g., two stories) building and an open-space requirement of 100 feet for each net building area unit are assumed, then the land allocation unit would be:

$$\frac{15{,}000 - 750}{\frac{300}{.90} + 300(2) + 100} = 13.80$$

Three

Location: The Fundamentals of Real Estate

§ 3.1 OVERVIEW OF LOCATION

The three most important factors affecting real estate value are often said to be location, location, and location. As stated in the Introduction, location contributes to the valuation of real estate but is not the only factor. Chapter 2 has illustrated how important the physical and legal attributes of a property are to a site's marketability. Any in-depth discussion of location must be interrelated with physical and legal dimensions. For example, zoning has a spatial dimension that influences property value and impacts highest and best use.[1] Urban structures cannot be described without reference to the physical terrain, the infrastructure, and the skyline of the city.[2]

[1] Zoning is often presented in a map format, which best relates the spatial nature of land use restrictions and the effect of the legal constraints of zoning.

[2] A range of issues depicting urban structure appears in research by economists (urban and land), sociologists, geographers, and engineers. For insight to the eclectic extent of this topic, see the series of monographs by Richard B. Andrews, *Urban Structure Theory,* Parts I–V (Madison: Center for Urban Land Economics Research, Graduate School of Business, University of Wisconsin, 1984ff.).

Because traditional wisdom places a primary emphasis on location, this chapter investigates the attributes of location on three levels. The first level of location is the immediate surroundings and the internal space planning of the site. The second level is the relationship of the site to its surroundings. This is the land economics concept of *situs*. Situs is the relationship of the total urban environment to a specific land use on a specific land parcel as these factors function in a given period of time.[3]

The third level of location is the overall urban structure and the interrelationships of a community's land use pattern. A study of location at this level involves analysis of the community's economic base; the existing, past, and future land use pattern; and the magnitude and direction of expected growth.

Figure 3.1 gives the relationship of the three levels of location a biological analogy. The site can be thought of as a cell. In a living organism,

Figure 3.1 Analogy Between a Site and a Cell

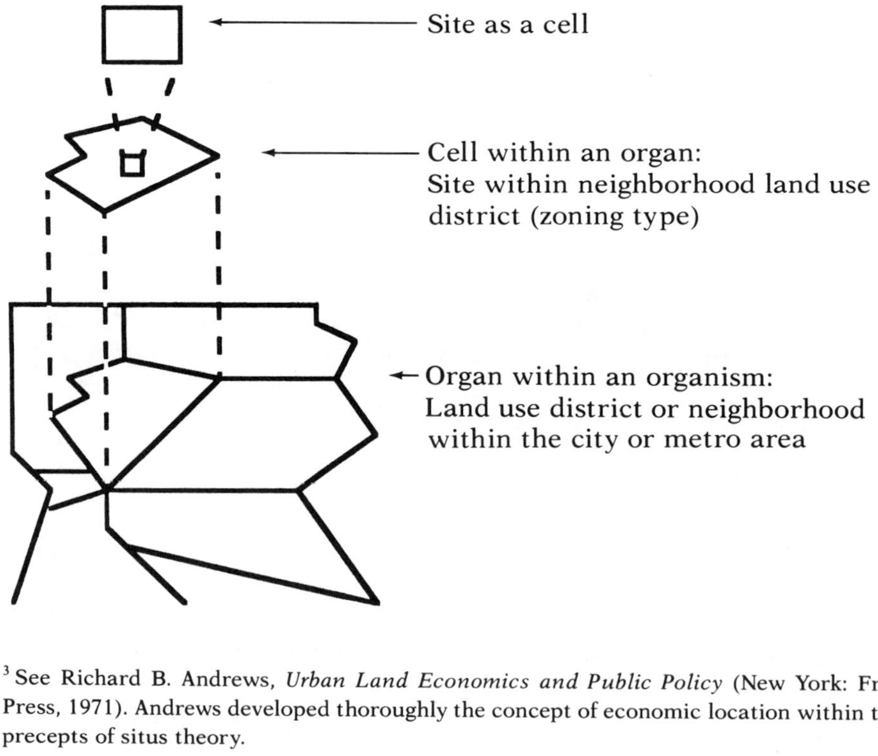

[3] See Richard B. Andrews, *Urban Land Economics and Public Policy* (New York: Free Press, 1971). Andrews developed thoroughly the concept of economic location within the precepts of situs theory.

each individual cell has a specialized function that operates in relation to the immediately surrounding cells—the organ to which it belongs—and the overall organism. Despite the cell's specialties, it shares many attributes in common with all other cells.

A site has this same interrelationship of the part to the whole. As the physical and legal analyses indicated in the previous chapter, any parcel of land has characteristics that are similar, if not identical, with other sites. However, given specific combinations of property characteristics, the unique socioeconomic functions that can be conducted on any given site are on a widespread range of possibilities.

The specialized functions of a cell are interdependent with those of the surrounding cells. The biological linkage of the cells within an organ is the functional concern of the analogy. This same situation exists for real estate. The "biological" link is between the site and the neighborhood (or land use district, or trade area). The situs concept allows analysis of the linkages of a site to urban environments. The concept can be applied as a process to the evaluation of a site's economic situation.

At the third level of Figure 3.1, the organ is linked into the overall organism. For the site, the overall organism is the city, community, statistic metropolitan area (SMA), or metropolitan area. Understanding of the overall community, its history, and its economic base allows insights in the spatial and market dynamics that are the concerns of market analysis. Urban economic analysis delineates the economic relationships of supply and demand that are the essence of real estate value.

The significance of the link of urban location to real estate value was established by Alfred Marshall, who not only established the foundations for the valuation approaches adopted by the American Institute of Real Estate Appraisers, as it was called in the 1930s, but also identified location as the essence of urban real estate. He termed it "urban situation value."[4]

The biological example enables a location analysis process. Through this process, a direct link between productivity analysis and market analysis (issues of supply and demand) is identified. The issues of supply and demand for real estate must be considered within a spatial context. Supply and demand forecasts must consider the alternative levels of location, to appropriately identify the magnitude of demand

[4] Alfred Marshall, *Principles of Economics* (New York: Maxwell Macmillan, 1979).

and the direction of movement of possible buyers, as well as to delineate existing and proposed competition.

Market analysis can be viewed as having three channeling agents or filters. The filters are: a location filter (combined with the other productivity attributes), a supply filter, and a demand filter. These filters remove the irrelevant data needed for market analysis and direct the focus of the analysis to the appropriate factors influencing a site's (or facilities') use and the related value estimate.

§ 3.2 LOCATION: SITE AND SITUS—LEVELS ONE AND TWO

This section begins an investigation of the first two levels of location analysis. Following tradition, the appraisal problem, in the context of market analysis, is seen as a site in search of a use or market. Location analysis, in an appraisal context, begins with a specific site. Appraisal/market analysis requires inspection of the site, because the appraiser/analyst is concerned with both the off-site locational characteristics and the locational attributes within the site. In this area of productivity analysis, location and physical or legal attributes are interrelated and often cross-categorized. All real estate, per its fourth dimension, has a spatial nature.

Location is concerned with the relative placement of spatial attributes and their links to specific functions. Analysis of location is difficult without being use-specific. Therefore, given that location analysis requires that the analysis be in the context of a specific use, then use analysis requires an investigation of location. The specification is only for *type* of use; the use need not exist in fact at the time of the analysis. For example, in the highest and best use analysis, various scenarios of use are considered as if the site were vacant. The property is valued from the perspective of one use (an office, for example) and found to be deficient because of a lack of supportive activities in the area. The same is true for retail and other possible alternative uses. Finally, a residential use is given a location scrutiny. The process can be compared to the screening function of a funnel or sieve; various uses are "shifted" and considered until one appropriate use finally passes through all of the filters in the funnel. The process of considering first an office, then a retail, then a residential or mixed use, can be carried out on a given property even though it is currently improved with a warehouse! Even generic location will be discussed here from the perspective of a fit to a specific land use.

§ 3.3 THE SITE—LEVEL ONE

The spatial layout of a site and the location of activity within the property must be related to the parcel's shape. A recursive link exists between the physical and locational concerns regarding the site. The shape of the property, or the number of sides on the site, often influences the placement of the structures on the site and the layout of yard improvements, parking facilities, and general maintenance requirements. Market preference or market appeal based on the shape can vary with alternative uses and market perspectives over time.

For example, the number of sides is linked to the exposure of the site or its potential for privacy. In a retail use, exposure would be desirable and may be heightened by the site's having many sides (assuming the accessibility is appropriate and the flow of traffic is manageable).

For a residential site, having many sides may be undesirable. Residential users often seek privacy. For example, a corner site in a subdivision links shape and location characteristics. In one neighborhood studied, corner lots sold at higher prices than other lots. Corner lots were especially desirable because they were often larger than midblock lots. As time passed, corner lots, in the same market and specific subdivisions, became less desirable. The survey showed a decline in desirability because street exposure and the difficulty of situating the structure on the sites had resulted in loss of privacy. The only way to achieve privacy was to place the house diagonal to the corner, a positioning that often resulted in a triangular rear yard. The market, studied over time, began to reflect a penalty in the pricing of corner lots.

The retail and/or industrial preference for exposure is important in the placing of buildings within the dimensions of a lot and in the procurement of sites that have exposure, if not direct access, to major thoroughfares.[5] The functional layout of a site or of the facilities on the site is often key to a site's marketability. The internal spacing of a site cannot be separated from the site's ease of ingress or egress, as it relates to various transportation linkages contingent or available to the site.

The ease of entering a site, the site's exposure in relation to the surrounding streets, its number of sides, its shape—all these and other locational factors are important to the development of a site or the success of any activity carried out on the property. The lack of friction in accessing a site is a measure of its linkage to the surrounding area.

[5] William Kinnard, *Industrial Real Estate* (Washington, DC: Society of Industrial Realtors, 1967): 64–67.

The ingress–egress potential of a site must be considered from the perspective of whether the major movement is inwardly or outwardly oriented. This orientation must also be coupled with whether goods, services, or people are being moved. The movement of people will need the highest level of convenience or the lowest cost of aggravation in approaching and entering the site. The movement of goods has needs that vary with the weight and bulk of the materials being moved. Service delivery requires a reasonable level of accessibility.

The overall lack of friction in the ingress or egress of a site is often neglected in the analysis of accessibility. Accessibility analysis, in many appraisals and market analyses, is conducted on a situs level. (See § 3.4.) However, the appraiser in productivity analysis must be concerned with gaining a better understanding of the product, and that understanding must begin with a study of the immediate accessibility of the site. The profitability of a given site is often established by comparing the subject site's ingress–egress level to that of other sites. Once this micro level analysis of accessibility and the accompanying anxiety associated with travel are identified, a link must be made to the situs level of accessibility.

Identification and evaluation of the access points to the site make it possible to delineate the paths of on-site traffic flow. An important location concern at the site level is the flow of people within the site. An example of the productivity effects of successful and unsuccessful people movements can be found in a comparison of flow patterns at Ghiradelli Square and the Cannery in San Francisco. The two developments are remodeled factories (canneries) that have been converted to specialty shopping centers. They are located between the same west–east streets, within two blocks of one another. Both developments are located on hillsides, and for both developments, the hillside location has created people and goods movement problems. Vertical movement costs more and people resist it.

Ghiradelli Square was more successful initially, partly because of the design of the site. People could wander uphill in moderate increments at a leisurely pace. This moderate movement was achieved by requiring an ascent of a limited number of steps and then a walk along a level plateau where shop windows were exposed to the viewers outside. The customers then traveled up a few more stairs to reach the next level of shops. The facilities were designed so that, in many sections, only a few steps had to be overcome in any given time segment. As the steps were encountered, part of the awareness of vertical movement was overcome with an arrangement of the shops that kept the customers' minds constantly occupied and distracted.

The Cannery, as a result of its original building design, required customers to move vertically on elevators and long, open escalators into enclosed hallways. The problem created by retaining much of the historical structure was a disjointed path of on-site traffic. In vertical movement, the ability to view the goal of a trip is not enough. The level of travel anxiety and the friction of movement must be offset with appropriate placement of facilities and design that has functional as well as esthetic appeal to the market (customers).[6]

(a) SPATIAL PORTFOLIO

Another concern linked to on-site location decisions is the design and management of a spatial use portfolio. The on-site location decisions possible on a given tract of land can involve the appropriate placement of structures and the relationship of uses. These decisions of use or tenant mix can be akin to the mix and management of a financial portfolio. Real estate is a real asset composed of space used in an economic context. A central issue of real estate decisions is how to link the spatial dimensions of a property to its financial return. On-site location decisions must be made, based on the site's portfolio of uses, or spatial portfolio.

The mix of uses or on-site tenants will vary with the property type. For example, in retail properties such as shopping centers, much consideration is given to the appropriate tenant mix. The right combinations of service/retail uses must be selected, and the nature of their aggregate associations must result in revenue benefits to the project. However, in terms of appropriate design and enterprise risk management, the appropriate placement of the activities is as relevant as the types of the activities considered.

For example, in a regional center or even in a theme park area, the major draws should be at a sufficient distance from the entrance, to encourage walking past other facilities and shopping comparatively along the way. Within this distance, the supportive uses (or ancillary uses) should be close to the major draws, to ensure the exposure of the

[6] For the relationship of movement to site layout, see Grady Clay, *Close-up: How to Read the American City* (Chicago: University of Chicago Press, 1971).

satellite activities and the increase of their potential revenues. In essence, related or competitive facilities should be placed near but not next to one another. Support and ancillary activities should be in proximity to the enterprises that draw people into the project.

Knowledge of the nature of the planned and actual activities and their associations is essential to all location decisions. The significance and degree of impact of activities and their spacing are covered in more detail in § 3.4. However, in a management decision process, the design and management of the spatial portfolio and of the situation of activities within a site are as important to risk and return levels as is the mix of uses in a given project.

(b) EXAMPLE OF ON-SITE SPATIAL ARRANGEMENT LINKED TO PHYSICAL AND LEGAL ATTRIBUTES

The combination of physical, legal, and locational spacing within a site is illustrated by the options available in cluster housing (zero-lot-line) residential developments. Zero-lot-line development is a marketing and production strategy that allows developers to boost the density of houses per acre by 50 to 100 percent. This physical–legal change in the basic single-family product is contingent on successful on-site spatial design, supported by reduced cost to the developer. The cost decreases are derived from using less land per unit and shorter street and utility runs.

The reduction of the lots' width by 20 to 40 percent (40 or 30 feet frontage instead of 50 feet) and the placement of the structure on the setback line on one side enable an increase in density per acre.

Creative planning that establishes easements can allow owners to use their neighbors' setbacks as space for their own yards. This combination of legal attributes with spatial arrangement can offer a more private product and a perception of outdoor roominess, without paying for two side yards. Figure 3.2 depicts the easement and zero-lot-line combination.

An alternative to the traditional zero-lot-line is the Z lot. The Z-lot concept intermixes the legal and physical dimension of the realty to develop a spatial arrangement that is totally different from the traditional single-family plot development.

In the Z-lot concept, the front and rear lots are spatially staggered because of the physical placement of privacy fences. This spatial–physical offset appears irregular, even though the legal description allows for a more traditional but narrow rectangular lot. The Z-lot

Figure 3.2 Zero-lot-line with Use Easement

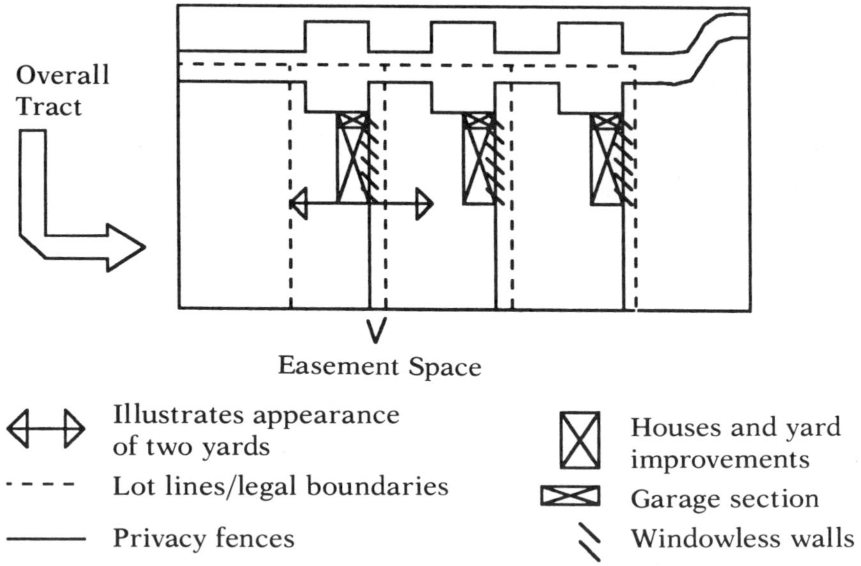

layout allows more creative design of the facilities and more panoramic views, as shown in Figure 3.3.

Another on-site location pattern is the shallow lot or wide-shallow lot. The shallow lot is narrow from the frontage to a rear property line that stretches lengthwise, parallel to the street. The spatial pattern of the shallow lots allows a variety of architectural styles, facades, and arrangements of the improvements. The layout also affords the option of wide side yards between the driveways. (See Figure 3.4.)

A problem of the shallow-lot plan is the possible increase in infrastructure cost. This plan is often appropriate only for narrow or irregular land parcels situated between existing road patterns. An advantage is that windowless walls used in many cluster developments are often not required.

A modification of the shallow-lot plan is the zipper plan illustrated in Figure 3.5. The zipper lot is a shallow lot that has a zig-zagging rear line jutting out in the vicinity of the living areas. The zig-zagging allows the perception of deeper back yards (at strategic points).

Cluster housing, often developed in planned unit developments (PUDs), is usually centered around a courtyard or cul-de-sac street, as shown in Figure 3.6. Because of the circular cluster-lot arrangements and the potential for spatially varying development, this approach

Figure 3.3 Z-lot Plans with Staggered Easements

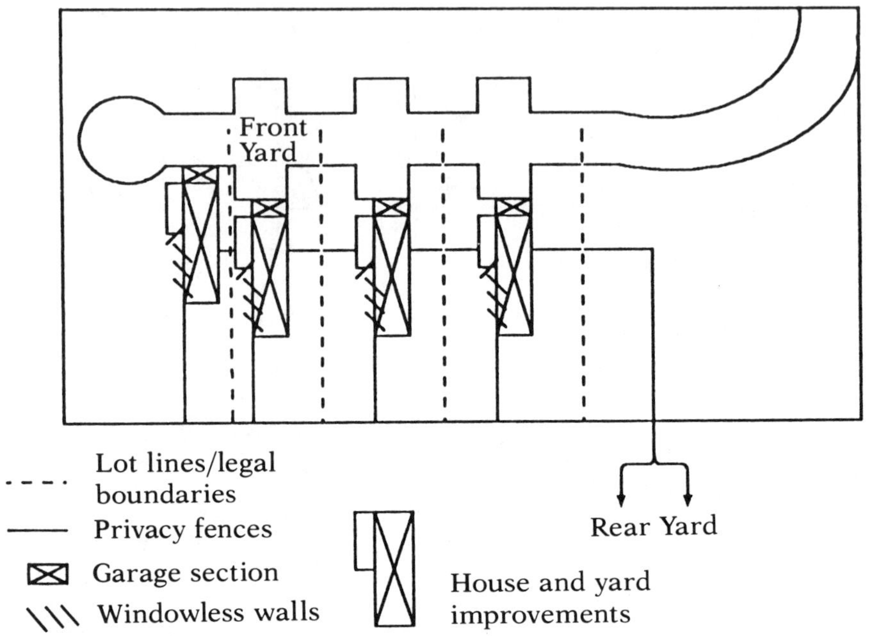

Figure 3.4 Shallow Lots

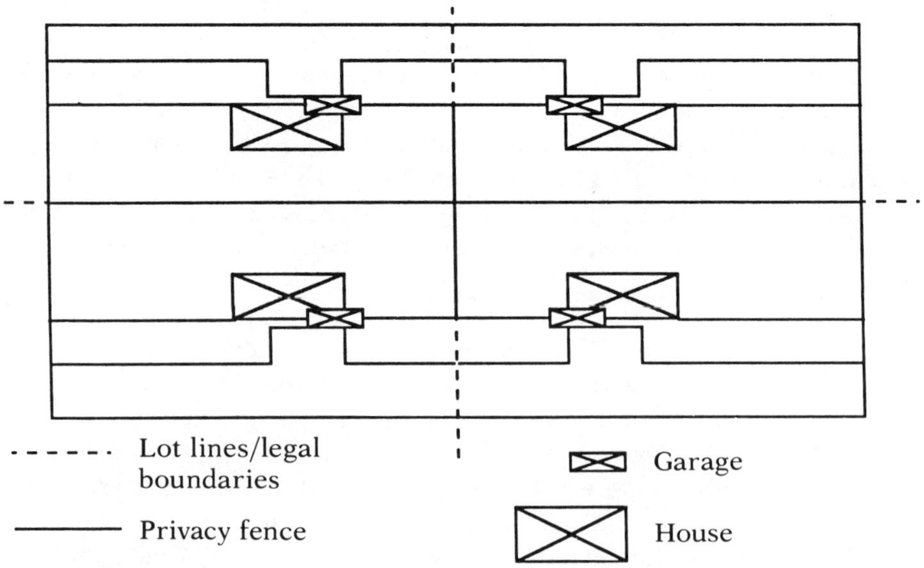

Figure 3.5 Zipper Lots

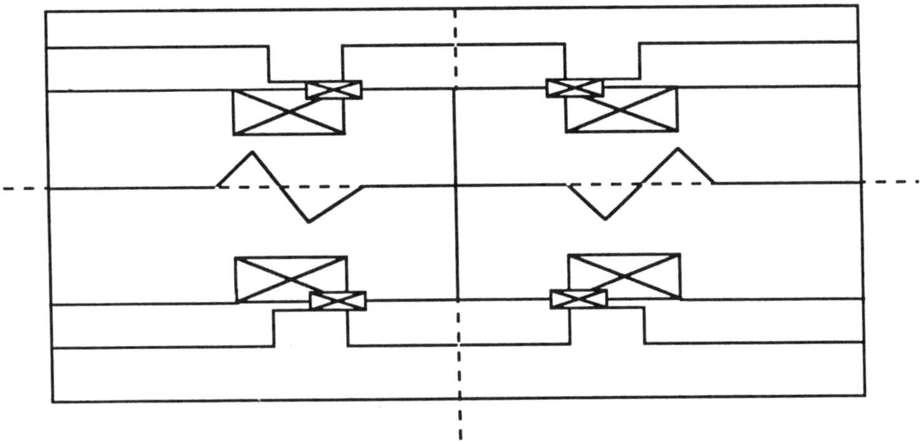

Figure 3.6 Cluster Plan PUD

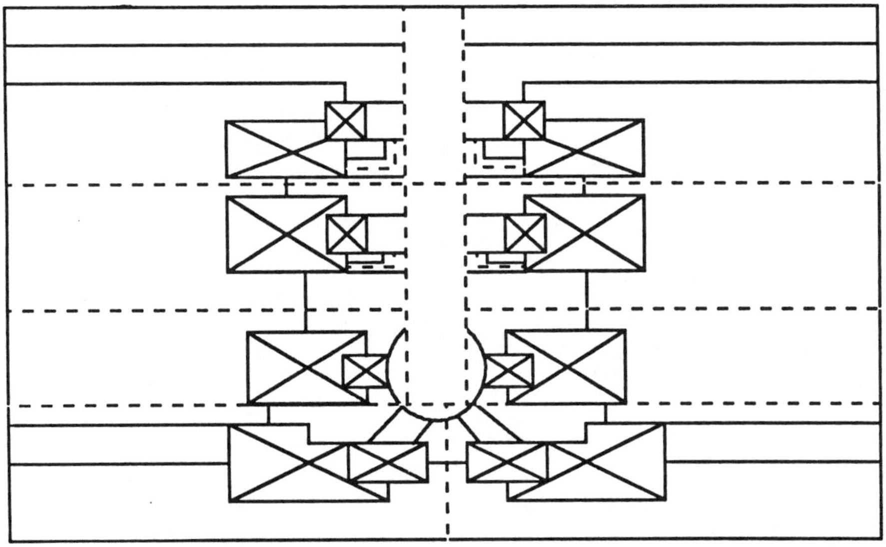

offers a mix of floor plans and elevations. A modification of the cluster pattern is the fan plan (Figure 3.7), which reduces the undesirable garage exposure by angling the door away from the street.

(c) VEHICULAR ACCESS

Besides the layout within a given site, the on-site location decision is affected by accessibility. The microaccessibility factor is important to vehicular as well as pedestrian traffic. A major concern in the analysis of a site and its accessibility to automobiles and other vehicles is the friction of movement involved in site ingress and egress. The site's shape, its frontage, and its visibility or exposure all influence a vehicle's ease of entering and leaving a site.

The desirability of a site's access and use is influenced by factors such as the turn ratio at a service station, the capacity for parking, and the ease of access at convenience stores or fast-food restaurants. At a service station, an industry standard allows a minimum of a 45° angle of turn-off from the main street.[7]

Figure 3.7 Fan Plan

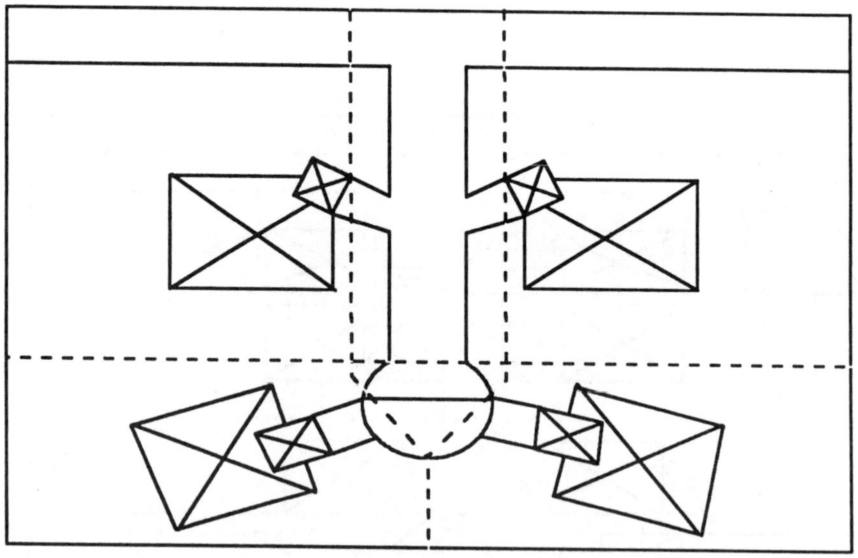

[7] R. James Claus and Walter G. Hardwick, *The Mobile Consumer* (Toronto: Collier-Macmillan, 1972): 8–10.

The accessibility of convenience services for mobile consumers is a productive feature that affects the level of the site's income and value. If a driver cannot easily access the site at a moderate speed, the site is at a competitive disadvantage with other convenience or drive-in facilities. This microaccess or site-specific disadvantage might override the property's location on the going-home or going-to-work side of the street. (Other contributing factors could be the nature of the business and the buying patterns of its specific clientele.)

The ease of access for convenience retail is enhanced if the site is located on the right-hand side of the major flow of traffic, just past an intersection with a traffic light. Even with this enhancement, aggravated ingress or egress can have adverse economic effects.

Coupled with concerns for aggravated ingress and egress to a site are concerns with circuity of travel. Circuity of travel may result when a site is located on a one-way street and can be accessed only from one direction. This site-specific factor can totally offset proximity to a major market area. Circuity of travel can also result from traffic islands, unmountable medians, or road dividers. A combination of dividers, one-way access, and linear frontage often occurs on the service roads of expressways or other linkages that would, on a larger location scale, be considered major accessibility advantages. The circuity of travel that often causes location or access problems can result from physical or legal constraints off the site. One-way streets, medians, traffic islands, and similar issues are the result of a city's police powers. The diminution (or loss) of a previous property right is not compensated, even when it can totally alter the use and the market for a given parcel of property.

Appropriate valuation of the locational potential of a given site is often tied to the property's physical and legal dimensions. Productivity analysis is key to the use and market potential of a site. With the site-specific orientation of appraisal market analysis and use analysis, the site's micro level location must be linked not only to the site but also to the immediately contiguous properties and the extended neighborhood. The link to these broader location concerns is addressed in the framework of situs analysis.

§ 3.4 SITUS—LEVEL TWO

Situs theory rests on the fact of use interdependence, on the relationship and intermovement of activities, and on the accessibility between the activities' physical and economic loci. Situs is defined as the total urban environment as it relates to a specific land use on a specific land parcel over a period of time.[8] This definition points out several important elements in appraisal and market analysis. The first element is that the concept of land use and the use of a given parcel are separated. Any given site can have a range of possible uses that can legally, physically, and locationally fit the site. The site is physically fixed in space, but it is economically flexible in use and location. Therefore, economic location is the key concern in market delineation and valuation. However, in everyday jargon and in professional analysis, it is difficult to separate economic location from physical notions of location. Physical location is based on the relative loci of one parcel to those of another. Proximity and accessibility are often interused with physical location. In this chapter, the common concept of location is extended to include the economic issues that affect appraisal and real estate market analysis. The extension results in segmentation of the general concepts of location, proximity, and accessibility into distinct technical perspectives that are necessary for a thorough development of the product and market in a spatial context.

The situs definition also shows that the relationship of uses is a function of time as well as space. As forces external to the parcel of land change use relationships, the activities conducted on the site, and the economic nature of the site itself, begins to change. For the appraiser, this means that the location analysis of a site cannot be separated from the life cycle of a neighborhood. The concept of situs is the building block that ties all of these economic issues together.

(a) SITUS PROCESS

Situs can be presented as a practical process for analysis, not just a theory that ties an individual site to the immediate neighborhood and the overall urban environment. In gathering, classifying, and analyzing information, the situs process can be set up as four steps, as follows:

1. Identify activities in the area
2. Establish the nature of associations among the activities
3. Identify and analyze the accessibility of the site to the surrounding area

[8] See Andrews, *supra* note 3, Chapter 2.

4. Identify and evaluate the total environmental impact of the area on the site use.

The application of situs theory is a process linking the data and the issues generated by the data into an overall synthesis of location, land use, and market analysis.

To assist in the identification of activities and the analysis of associations, the spatial boundaries of the subject neighborhood or trade area must first be established. The spatial nature of real estate and real estate markets is an analytical aid to appraisers and analysts, because it enables an enclosed, physical delineation of the market. Natural and physically identifiable boundaries can be established for the potential market—a luxury that does not often exist for many consumer goods or commodities. The boundaries of other goods' markets are often constrained by the productive capacity of the manufacturer or the distributive strength of the marketing or warehousing firm.

The locational or spatial dimension of a property is a key determinant of the product. This complicates the productivity analysis but benefits the delineation of the market.

(b) MARKET BOUNDARIES

The productivity of real estate is influenced by economic and physical location. Economic locational analysis is more than simply identifying the physical position of one property in relation to another.[9] Locational analysis begins with identifying the economic activities in the neighborhood or market trade area by physical, geographical, political, and socioeconomic boundaries or economic time–distance delineation.

A real estate market can be identified by its location. An appraiser ascertains a market for a particular property by delineating the surrounding physical or political boundaries within which related economic decisions are made. This market area should be separated, in terms of time and distance, from common destinations and origins, as identified in the urban structure discussion in § 3.5.

A property can have an international, national, regional, statewide, urban, rural, district, and neighborhood market. When appraising a large industrial plant, an appraiser might study its national, or even its international, market. The real estate or space involved, the price level

[9] Terry V. Grissom, "A Feasibility Process: The Benefits of Land Economics and Risk Management," *The Appraisal Journal* (July 1984).

or price range of the properties, and the current or intended use of the space help determine the geographical extent of the market for that property. For example, the geographical extent of the market for office buildings in major commercial cities frequently is broader than that for single-family residences in rural communities.

The boundaries can be established by the use of alternative segmentation criteria. Boundaries to neighborhoods and trade areas can be established by geographical features such as lakes, rivers, hills, mountains, bogs, and any other natural topographical feature that prevents development of or easy transport between sections of a community. The boundaries can be the result of human endeavor as well as natural phenomena. Examples are expressways (raised or surface), divided highways, one-way streets, walls, building bulk lines, lakes, bridges, parks, infrastructures, and other constructed environmental features. Market boundaries can be established by political or legal jurisdictions. The change from one incorporated community to another within the same metropolitan area can result in having a variety of community services and legal restrictions confront any development or land use. The location of a subdivision within an incorporated community's limits rather than in an extraterritorial jurisdiction can alter the cost of maintenance and the lot prices that are prevalent in the market. The location can also determine the services available to any given real estate product. The combination of cost and available services can help delineate the competition and market for any particular facility.

A major economic determinant of a market trade area or boundary is the time–distance variable. The cost of transport from a facility to specific other locales must be considered in the context of the cost to access competitive sites. The economic and psychological dimensions of a market area are often defined by the effort or cost of travel between one location and another. The limits of commutation often set the boundaries of a neighborhood. (This issue is addressed further in §§ 3.4(e) and 3.7(f).)

Because the neighborhood within these boundaries is in part established by the homogeneity or compatibility of the land uses, the next step in the overall location analysis is to identify the major neighborhood characteristics.

(c) ACTIVITIES

The identification of activities in an area can range from a simple survey or observation of existing land uses to a major economics based study. The key activities or features to identify when characterizing a neighborhood are those that attract, draw, or otherwise motivate people to come to a specific location. These activities function like economic magnets. They may be major employers, recreational activities, institutions, services, or physical features such as rivers and roads. They generate even more activities in an area, and function like the major draws of a shopping center. They attract people from other neighborhoods into the subject area.

These primary activities often define the character of the areas or neighborhoods. The enterprises' impact on an area helps to form the basis of the neighborhood's economy. In a general example, the central business district of most communities is typified by high-rise office buildings. The nature of the activities of the office tenants determines the overall character of the area. Manhattan offers a comparison, in the different uses or tenant types that occupy the office facilities on Madison Avenue and on Wall Street. The office needs and character of ancillary and surrounding land uses and tenants are different because Madison Avenue has marketing/advertising activities and Wall Street has financial concerns. Both areas are dominated by business enterprises, but the associated activities in close proximity can vary. Identification of the primary activities on a city-wide basis is the idea behind economic base analysis. The concept should not vary for a more specifically defined trade area or neighborhood.

The significance of situs to office facilities was identified in the following actual market analysis. The assignment was to identify the market demand and feasibility of a multistory, class A office building in the central business district (CBD) of Austin, Texas, during the active market period of the early 1980s. At that time, office demand exceeded a limited supply; the supply was insufficient to meet the desired space requirements, suggesting ample market opportunity. However, despite the developers' expertise in intercity office construction, the approach and marketing plan were not an appropriate fit to the subject area.

The developers were out of Denver. They had had success in the mid-1970s and early 1980s, renting out their facilities to oil industry tenants. Their market approach was to lease 60,000 square feet to a single tenant. This information, in the context of the traditional market analysis approach, which emphasizes aggregate market data of supply and demand issues, should have indicated a reasonable potential of success. However, the emphasis on these factors would have misled the investors as to the level of business and market risk to which they were potentially exposed.

Further research identified the key activities in Austin's CBD to be government and financial establishments. Given that these activities were the major draws to the area, it was assumed that the associated uses would tend to link to those activities. Therefore, the market research effort needed to focus on tenant types in the area. The investigation identified lobbyists, lawyers, architects, accountants, and other professional and clerical services as the major users of space in Austin's CBD. Their activities were all concerned with marketing services to government and financial institutions. The developers' impression that oil clients would be in abundant supply in an overall Texas market was erroneous. Austin's economic base was government and university education, and this economic base did not support the developers' strategic and tactical plans.

A related key issue in the analysis of the CBD activities was that, at that time, only two enterprises in the community could be classified as corporate headquarters. Renters requiring large, contiguous space were limited. In fact, the average office size in the CBD was 4,000 square feet, and the largest office units were approximately 20,000 square feet—a third of the space needed by the developers' typical client. The larger CBD spaces were used by financial institutions, law firms, and accounting firms, which tended to own their own facilities. Often, they forced many of their outside consultants and other supportive services to rent space in their facilities. (This interrelationship of activities accelerated a downward spiral in office returns because of rapidly declining occupancy levels when the institutions went under.)

The developers accepted the advice that the market was not one with which they typically dealt. Given the smaller average size of the space rented (4,000 square feet versus the planned 60,000 square feet), a much more intensive marketing (and leasing) effort than had been used for their other facilities was judged to be required. Increased marketing and operating costs to the developer and a lower profit than previously projected were foreseen.

As this case shows, the productive attributes of a property determine its revenue and return. Location is a key element of the return, and economic location is heavily influenced by the primary activities in the area.

To truly evaluate an area, the key activities in the neighborhood must be identified; a functional study of the area, beginning with the general land uses, is needed. The study can be practically achieved by simple observation. A drive through the area and a schematic drawing of the immediate land uses can readily aid the decision maker. The drawing can be upgraded for sophisticated presentations and used over and over.

Rarely do rapid changes occur in an entire area over short periods of time. If changes are occurring rapidly within a short time period, identification of the changing uses is a key concern in the analysis.

Identification of these linkages and of the related uses that develop around them leads to a second concern: the association of land uses.

(d) ASSOCIATIONS

Association is concerned with the nature of the relationship among the various activities in the subject neighborhood. Activities may complement, serve, or compete with one another, or may be a total nuisance. The nature of their relationships is determined by the economic function of any particular use or set of uses.

Competitive automobile dealers who locate next to one another are an example of the interrelationship of functions. Shopping for a car, for most people, is not a matter of impulse. A car is a durable good that is purchased after one or several comparative shopping trips. Dealers find it mutually advantageous to be close to their competitors, even though they may be located on cheaper, out-of-the-way land. The significance of this example is that the nature of activities, and their associations, influences the use of land in any particular area.

Several categories of land use can be identified. The first general category is a dominant–subordinate use relationship; the chief activity of the subordinate enterprise *serves* the operation of the dominant activity. An example might be the development of a major printing facility in a community. The printer hires 1,000 employees at various ranks. In due course, the analyst can expect to observe ink suppliers appearing in the area, to service the large printing company. These subservient activities, in aggregate, may employ 100 additional people.

This same relationship can be seen where machine shops exist in close proximity to a manufacturing plant, or food jobbers are located in areas with low-cost access to fast-food restaurants and supermarkets, or lawyers are located near libraries, courthouses, or other facilities housing public records.

The dominant–subordinate relationship directly involves the subordinate land use activity in the dominant activity. Examples are: a distributor who furnishes supplies needed for a specific manufacturing process, or a professional or trades person who participates in a service (a lawyer in litigation at a courthouse).

The second general land use association is a dominant–ancillary linkage, in which the ancillary activity serves the clients or employees of the dominant use. Examples are candy, gift, or florist shops located on the first floor of an office building. The ancillary status is especially emphasized if the shop is oriented internally toward the building, with limited or no external access or exposure to the outside. For example, if a shop's major frontage is to the lobby, atrium, or foyer of an office structure, the shop is probably serving an ancillary function in relation to the use of the overall structure.

Another example of an ancillary use is the location of restaurants, bookstores, or computer shops in proximity to a university. The bookstores and computer shops may represent an overlap in the categories, because they provide direct inputs to the education of students (the product of the university). However, many of the ancillary products sold at these facilities are purchased for personal development, not directly for a degree program.

The third general category of land use/activity associations considers co-dominant uses and dominant–satellite uses. This category is often characterized by a shopping center or mall where the co-dominant uses are the large department stores, which are the major draws to the center. The co-dominant uses service the same customer demand. Therefore, this category could apply to the customers of the large department store and the center's adjacent ladies' shops, which are often selling similar, competitive, or comparable products.

The dominant–satellite relationships represent activities in which the satellite facilities capitalize on the dominant's draw. An example is a candy store in a shopping center or a restaurant in a hospital (sometimes the only 24-hour restaurant, in smaller communities).

The satellite function often takes on characteristics of a dominant–ancillary use, but the key is the service use capitalizing on the dominant's or co-dominant's draw.

Examples of co-dominant and dominant–satellite uses are not limited to shopping centers. They can be identified in a range of neighborhoods or trade areas. The earlier discussion of Austin's CBD illustrated that the base economic activities (co-dominant uses) were government and financial institutions. Government groupings (state, federal, and local) and agencies often serve the same clientele as do the competitive financial services (banks and savings and loans). Law firms, lobbyists, and other professional groups can be considered the satellite functions. The ancillary services in the CBD—shops, restaurants, lodgings, and recreation/entertainment facilities—are direct recipients of the base activity draws.

The quality and degree of land use associations afford great insights to the stability, strength, and development potential of a given property use or a neighborhood. Understanding the associations between land uses in an area over time enables a basis for investigating the direction of growth and future land use patterns.

(e) ACCESSIBILITY

The third aspect of location analysis is accessibility, which is concerned with the friction of movement of people or goods and services among the different activities. Friction is a resistance to movement, attributed to a lack of convenience, limited ease of access, volume of traffic or users, inability to choose direct paths, and similar factors; it is measured in terms of time, cost in dollars, and aggravation. Accessibility is akin to negative transportation cost: The more accessibility to major activities and complimentary use, the less the cost of accessing the property and the higher the potential site return.

Accessibility is a good that can be measured as the reciprocal of transportation cost.

Real transportation cost must consider all elements of the friction of travel. The lower the total transportation cost, the more accessible the site. The result is a consequential possibility of a higher income (rent) to the site or a higher market price. The importance of accessibility to a specific use, therefore, influences what one user will pay (over another buyer or user) for any specific site.

The relationship among activities, associations, and accessibilities allocates the land among different uses. An understanding of these relationships aids in the identification of the highest and best use or the probable use. The use then is the product for the market analysis.

(f) ACCESSIBILITY LEVELS

Consultants should be concerned with accessibility at two levels: the familiar site level that considers the ingress and egress to the property and the immediate area of the site, and the larger level that considers the flow of people between one area and another. Several concepts have been developed by urban land economists, geographers, and landscape architects to aid in this analysis.[10]

[10] See Andrews, *supra* note 2.

Macro Level

Macro-level accessibility is basically considered in the context of, or measured on, the opportunity trade-off of accessibility (via transportation cost) and the amenities and physical/economic location of the site (as represented by site rents and/or sale prices). Macro-level accessibility can be linked directly to the power of the draw of dominant land uses (or co-dominant uses).

In gravity models, this drawing power to an area is analogous to the relationship of distance and mass in physics. Often, the greater the number of competitors (dominant, co-dominant uses) in an area, the greater the total volume of possible consumers desiring access to that area.

This outcome, however, is contingent on specific land use types. For example, automobile dealerships are known to cluster near their competitors. This clustering process is termed economics of agglomeration. For automobile dealers, the economic advantage of clustering is that many dealers are offering only slightly differentiated product. The auto product is a shopping good that requires a comparative shopping trip, timely comparisons, and premeditated travel to the site of purchase. When a number of dealers are in proximity to one another, they function as a *group* dominant land use association and thus emit a gravitational pull. The gravitational pull, when combined with the limited travel and the accessibility of the alternative facilities after arriving in the "subject neighborhood," more than offsets any friction required to access the location.

Therefore, even in analyzing the macro-access level, it is necessary to get use-specific—to identify the relationships and linkages between land activities and to develop and understand the nature and operations of the activities.

On a macro level, the concern is with the competition of uses within the overall urban structure. The use competition is based on the capacity of a use to pay a competitive price for a desirable location. The location is often characterized by the uses for a given site (within the urban structure) and then by the transportation cost (the lack of accessibility) that must be incurred.

The economic trade-off between site rents and macro accessibility is the basis for explaining the economic structure of a city. This topic is addressed in § 3.7. At this point, it is important to recognize the importance of access to a given area on an aggregate level.

To investigate the relevance of accessibility to an area, analysts must describe or explain the character, direction, distance, and frequency of trips to and from a specific land use from related activities.

On a macro level, a neighborhood (trade area sector, and so on) can be studied in relation to the overall city. Reasons for the neighborhood focus are:

1. The neighborhood is a focal point for inward and outward trips relating to specific land uses (or an aggregation of land types).
2. The neighborhood holds a monopoly over certain pockets of movement and seems to account (within itself) for the majority of high-frequency short trips.

Therefore, if the travel within neighborhoods can define the micro-level accessibility (down to site ingress and egress), then travel between neighborhoods may form the basis of macro-level accessibility.

The capacity or potential of a neighborhood's draw and macro accessibility can be objectively delineated by the size and capacity of arterials, the nature of linkages, and the number and types of establishments within the subject neighborhood as compared to its competitors. The investigation of macro-accessibility analysis often entails the delineation of key roadways, public transportation, traffic counts, time–distance enumeration, and proximity to other linked activity centers (associated neighborhoods).

The macro-accessibility characteristics of a neighborhood often determine its ranking of desirability or status within the overall community. The ease or desirability of the access is an indicator of the area's potential for growth and the future direction of its growth.

A key concern associated with residential neighborhoods' macro accessibility is the *journey to work*. This neighborhood relationship to the overall urban structure is a key example of the scale of movement within a metroplex. The journey to work often involves neighborhood-to-neighborhood movement (or even sector-to-sector shifts). This large-scale movement of the draw of employment facilities relating to residential areas can be compared to the previous example of automobile dealers. The commercial equivalence of the journey to work is customers' trips across trade areas, which are chiefly generated by specialized goods or service offerings or by comparison shopping activities.

The observance of interneighborhood movement is helpful in identifying areas of potential development or growth. Geographers term these areas *zones of conflux*. They are land segments where the activities have a drawing power and the arterials and other infrastructures are developed such that vehicular traffic is forced into or attracted to the area. Examples of the combined infrastructural resources and economic activities are available in most cities. The delineation of these attributes in specific locales can be used to identify growth patterns (trends) and to assign location rankings. The process for the real estate decision maker is to identify the major economic activities within an area, their proximity or association with related activities, and their relation to major or popular roadways. The areas where the roadways intersect in volume of activities, or tend to converge in directional flow, can best be described as zones of conflux.

Micro Level

After the draw and accessibility to the area are considered, the prime objective of most real estate analysis is the micro-level accessibility concern. Micro-level accessibility is concerned with linkage relationships, movement between linked establishments, and issues of proximity. A linked relationship between establishments (or activities) is characterized by continuing or frequently recurring interaction. This interaction requires movement between loci (sites), and proximity may be a secondary component of the transportation of persons and goods.

Interrelationships requiring movement can have various orientations.[11] In general, the movements have an inward or outward orientation (to and from a land use or establishment). Further refinement distinguishes assembling movement, dispersive movement, and random movement. For example, the journey to work can be a dispersive movement from residential neighborhoods and an assembling movement for the labor market of employers. The dispersive movement is characterized by a spreading out from a central or focal point. On a micro level, this is dispersion or outward movement from a given site, subdivision, or neighborhood. On a macro level, it is the journey to work from the aggregated subdivisions and bedroom communities of the city.

The assembling movement is characterized by a convergence to a central or focal point. Examples of this type of movement are the journey to work at the central business district and the convergence of shoppers at a shopping center or mall.

The assembling movement is often indicated geographically by a configuration called a trapping point. The trapping point is a micro-level zone of conflux in which a site has gravitational pulls, infrastructural support, and a design configuration that attracts an influx of

[11] *Id.*, Part I.

people, goods, and activities to an area. Examples of trapping-point sites are Fountain Square in Cincinnati, Times Square in Manhattan, Fishermen's Wharf in San Francisco, and Fanevil Hall in Boston.

The random movement pattern is the movement of goods or persons among dispersed locations. A random movement (out from or converging toward) can occur at either end of a movement route.

Regardless of its pattern, movement is difficult to analyze without linking the movement to the activities of a specific use. However, the observance of existing activities and their movement patterns helps to identify the external and supportive network that surrounds a given site and that can determine and support the use (activities) and market for that site. All of those factors contribute broadly to a property's economic vitality. Therefore, the nature and orientation of the movement patterns must be considered, along with the frequency and volume of trips. For specific sites, uses, or activities, this measure can be obtained by survey. Examples are the number of trips to the supermarket per week and the typical dollars spent per trip. A secondary data source is traffic volume measurement.

The economic measures of access can be quantified in terms of dollar costs, time (and/or distance), frequency, and irritation. Each of these criteria varies in importance according to the mode of movement (or transportation) involved.

Dollar Costs

The dollar costs of movement are both fixed and variable. For public transportation, they are measured by taxes and/or user fees; the former are fixed, the latter vary with consumption of services. For private transportation, fixed costs can include the registration cost of licenses and title, insurance, and personal property tax. The variable costs include, among other expenses, fuel, lubricants, maintenance, fines, and parking expenses. All of the expenses of accessing an area or site can be considered as opportunity costs for occupying a given location. (Imagine capitalizing all costs of movement as a measure of the price paid to be located at a given site.)

Time

The issue of time as a measure of accessibility is key in urban areas; in rural areas, accessibility is often reflected as distance. Realistically, the time issue incorporates both distance and friction.

Measurement of time and friction often involves waiting costs, such as time spent in nonmovement, as additional costs of moving. These amounts may be quantified by opportunity costs or by productive income lost while in transit. Time costs also include time perceptions, often a function of the purpose of the trip, the urgency of the purpose, the route environment, or the conditions of traffic. For example, a shopping trip will tolerate a longer trip threshold than will a limited lunch break. This comparison involves both the purpose and the urgency of the trip, and the nature of either of these accessibility concerns can influence the use selection of specific locations. The location of a durable or shopping goods facility need not compete with the accessibility requirements of a convenience store, even though the more accessible appliance store or automobile dealer might have an edge over its competition. However, a convenience store, fast-food restaurant, or service station is highly certain of failure, if located on an inaccessible site.

The route environment, which is key to the time perception involved in site accessibility, is not only a matter of scenic views and amenities, although the trade-off of time versus scenery is familiar to anyone who has opted for a coastal highway versus an interstate. The route environment can be as simple or significant to site performance as the choice between shopping downtown or at regional malls. It is not unusual for shoppers to think a mall is more convenient than inner-city shopping, even though the mall parking involves a two-mile walk and the inner-city parking involves a walk around a block or from the second floor of an adjoining parking structure.

The perception of time also involves traffic conditions, which often overlap with irritation as a cost of access. Congested traffic extends the perception and reality of travel time. The condition of east–west traffic in relation to the north–south flow in midtown Manhattan is interesting. The north–south blocks are much shorter in physical distance than the east–west blocks; however, the east–west traffic appears much more dense, more slow-moving, and more time-consuming. It would be interesting to correlate the success–failure associations of various types of activities with whether they are situated on a north–south avenue or an east–west street in Manhattan.

An actual measure of time, geographically, within a city can be useful information. In larger cities, time/distance maps are often available from public sources. The city of Houston publishes such a map.

Illustrated in Figure 3.8 is a time study conducted in Austin, Texas, in 1985–1986. A time–distance study, as done by market research

Figure 3.8 Chart of Vehicular Travel Time and Distance for Austin, Texas

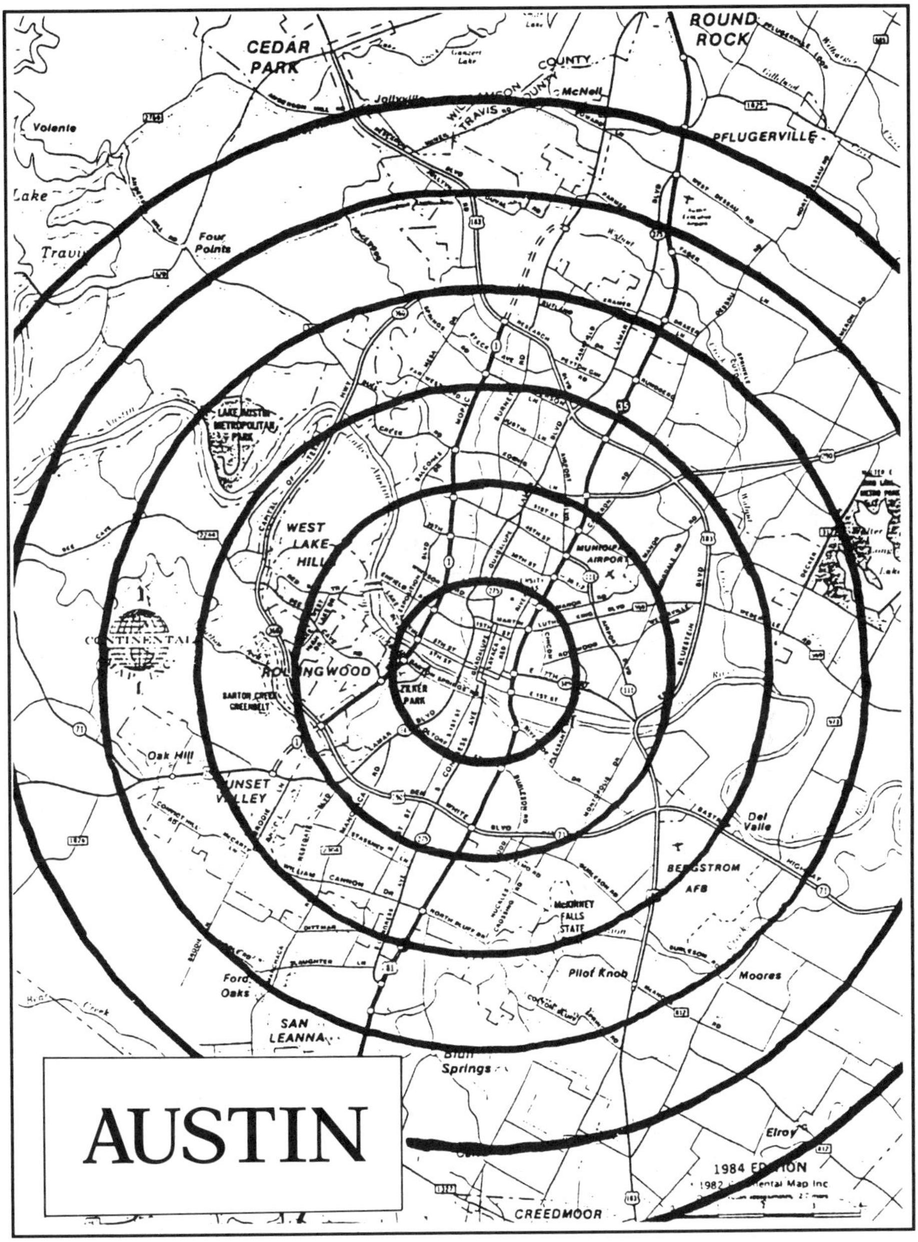

firms, usually involves a drive, with a stop watch, from a given site or area, such as the CBD. At certain time intervals, the driver's location is noted on a map. The equal time points on the map are then connected by lines (see Figure 3.8). For the best insight, the time markings should be done at consistent times during the workweek (both in rush hours and at off times), during the weekends, and on specific holidays.

The time–distance measures yield additional information that can help in selecting and comparing competitive sites and quantifying for economically different location adjustments.

One developer profitably combined all of the above time perception and trip frequency concerns in a resort/shopping development. Because the resort was oriented to family vacations, the development needed a mix of retail facilities that could be offered along with the housing/service facilities.

The developer's optimal strategy was to construct the shopping facilities at a distance just far enough from the resort that guests would opt to walk there rather than drive. This reduced the need for large parking facilities around the retail buildings and allowed more open space. Walking was also encouraged by the landscaping and design of walkways between the hotel and retail section.

Furthermore, assuming people would opt to walk because of the reasonable distance, the locations were far enough apart that visitors would not limit their shopping trip to less than an hour. Once at the shopping center, most families would spend half the day, including a mealtime. This linked the purpose and function of the trip to the economic success of the project by increasing the revenue of the retail tenants and increasing the enjoyment of the family vacationers, whose main function was to *kill time*. The developer had created a successful trapping point.

Frequency

The frequency of the trip is a key measure of economic accessibility. The frequency measure (and its significance) varies with the land use activities involved in the decision and the mode of movement. Trip frequency can be monthly, weekly, daily, hourly, or on a trips-per-day basis. The movement patterns on weekdays can vary, compared to the patterns over a weekend. Trip frequency can be affected by the sequence involved in accessing related activities and by the duration of movement and visitations.

Frequency of trips can be measured by the number of visits to a site per person or per family or household. The frequency can also be based on the waiting/opportunity cost involved in a trip.

Irritation

The final measure of accessibility is irritation. Because it is a psychological concept, irritation is not as easily quantified as the other measures. Irritation is a dynamic or behavioral concept; often, it is a response to the friction of movement. As such, it can be measured by ordinal ranking based on the judgment of people questioned in primary surveys linked to a specific site. Secondary data sources can be used to create ratios that may substitute as irritation measures, such as quantitative measures of congestion. Congestion, an economic misallocation of too many resources in the wrong place at the wrong time, is an indication of increased accessibility cost and negative location adjustments. A ratio measure as a proxy for congestion could be traffic volume at a given time, in relation to the distance that can be traveled in a given time. The measure of comparison would be the number of cars in the area per minute.

A definite issue of irritation is the availability of parking within proximity to a site. Availability could be measured by a ratio of traffic volume to parking stalls (or of parking area to total area). The indicator of irritation could be the potential unit of measure of the number of cars seeking a single parking stall.

Among other issues of irritation that overlap with the friction of movement issues is the inability to turn across traffic or to make right or left turns when needed, thus requiring circuity of travel, perhaps in the form of a large number of one-way streets.

Visibility

The visibility of a site can be linked to its accessibility, especially in the case of convenience goods or retail facilities and services that hope to attract mobile consumers. The operating success of fast-food restaurants, family restaurants, service stations, convenience stores, and other related activities is directly tied to a visible, accessible site. The extreme sensitivity of an enterprise's profit potential, based on whether the site is on the going-home or the going-to-work lane of traffic, or on the corner after a traffic light rather than the corner before it, has repeatedly been empirically shown.[12]

The direct effect in each of these situations is that accessibility is diminished. The lack of accessibility thus increases the cost of arriving at a given site. Accessibility, on both a macro and a micro level, is a key attribute of the property and influences its use, its marketability, and thus its value.

(g) ENVIRONMENT

The final element of situs analysis is the environment, or the total urban environment as it relates to a specific neighborhood. Like the neighborhood analysis, the analysis of the environment considers social, physical, economic, and institutional features. Even though these features are immobile, the environment is often described in terms of accessibility and activities—the surroundings through which goods and people must travel. The amenities or noneconomic attributes of an area are also classified as environmental components of a site's situs. The issue of situs environment is an eclectic area of discussion and investigation, and involves the external surroundings of a site that can characterize or define a neighborhood. As such, the environmental dimension of situs encompasses the spatial aspects of physical and legal productivity attributes but is external to the site (as opposed to specific site characteristics).

Environmental attributes are often characterized by nonmovement features and/or characteristics. Despite the feature of nonmovement, environmental attributes often overlap with accessibility in defining the gravitational draw of an area.

Environmental issues are often identified as areal amenities. However, investigation indicates that they are much broader and deeper spatial concerns encompassing issues of land use; physical, social, and cultural impacts on location; psychological responses to space and location; economics; and institutional and political topics and constraints.

The key to environmental (nonmovement externalities) analysis is that the array of topics listed above is linked to spatial impacts on realty and markets. Therefore, the economic environment is often the central concern of real estate decision makers. However, in a *broad* sense, the economic environment encompasses all of the other environmental

[12] Claus and Hardwick, *supra* note 7, at 143–144.

dimensions. In fact, all of the other environmental categories are interwoven to such an extent that any "true" breakdown, for discussion purposes, is artificial and is often the result of the various disciplines' studies of the different topical issues contained in real estate. Therefore, the following discussion offers a stepwise process to help real estate analysts and decision makers develop a way of addressing a qualitative dimension of realty. The breakdown used in the process includes the land use environment, the physical environment, the social and cultural environment, the psychological environment, the economic environment, and the institutional and political environment.

Land Use Environment

The land use pattern is based on a functional criterion. Related land uses are often clustered in any given area of a city. Therefore, the situs issues of use association discussed above can set the characteristics of the use and physical environment in a neighborhood. The land use associations of dominant–subordinate and ancillary–co-dominant can be further stratified as complementary, competitive, and infrastructural relationships.

The nature of the further stratified associations influences the land pattern qualities of the area and defines the potential for growth and stability over time. For example, the competitive uses can compete on an internal basis with other activities or facilities within the area. The internally competitive uses are often of a service nature to the local residents or customers within the primary trade area.

Externally competitive enterprises are exportive in the nature of their product or service and can be considered as draws to the neighborhood from consumers, suppliers, or others from outside of the immediate area. The end result is that the competitive association of the land use activities functions much like the economic base issues that are discussed later in this chapter. However, their effect on the immediate neighborhood does much to establish its overall character and environment. If the neighborhood or trade area can be characterized by a large number of externally oriented competitive land uses, the probability is high that the area will benefit or suffer from a large inward migration on a daily basis. If the neighborhood is best described as one of internally competitive land uses, external migration in the form of residents or customers will be limited or nonexistent. Therefore, the area may be desirable for land developments oriented toward privacy as a key property attribute. The availability of internally competitive land uses further suggests choice and convenience within proximity to existing land uses.

Internal competition of land uses within a neighborhood may be observed in the form of product or service competition. For example, an older neighborhood may offer supermarkets, convenience stores, meat markets, produce markets, and other specialty facilities; these alternatives for food purchases may not exist in many suburban areas. These diverse food facilities are substitutes or, in some cases, complementing sources for many consumers. The significance of this example is that land uses and the state of the competitive supply cannot be limited to only similar classes of uses or facilities. The level of competition must be delineated on a functional basis. Some of the current difficulties with oversupply in many areas might have been avoided with such a delineation.

Another dimension of the land use environment that is often neglected is the identification of adverse land uses and their impact on the neighborhood's situs quality. The presses of incompatible, nuisance, and even destructive land uses can color the perception of a neighborhood or location. The presence of nonconforming land uses has been a land use problem during the entire history of urban real estate. Examples are slaughterhouses, quarries, and other viable economic activities that may abut commercial or residential areas.

Environmental hazards are a growing concern of neighborhood conflicts and litigation. The presence of contaminated landfills, toxic waste dumps or spills, and manufacturing facilities that are contaminated because of previous economic procedures are now more than mere operational nuisances to surrounding land uses. The end results can be an accelerated life cycle for surrounding property uses and a rapid economic depreciation for specific facilities. All of these factors can have a major impact on the land use potential of an area.

Another land use concern often ignored for its influence on the spatial environment of an area is the infrastructural land use pattern. Infrastructural relationships are not limited to utilities or the route environment. Infrastructural land use patterns are concerned with the relationship between a neighborhood's land use activities and availability of utilities and the infrastructure, because that relationship influences neighborhood perceptions, access, and use clustering.

The propensity for clustering, as it relates to the infrastructure, is often tied to the utility system and must be addressed on the basis of whether the utility is a pure service operation, such as standard utilities' and fire and police departments' land use activities, or whether the service activity is tied to land use interdependencies, such as communications networks or production system linkages.

The land use environment is important to an understanding of location patterns, the quantity of land uses in particular areas, and the quality of the relationships among land uses. The quality of the relationships influences the duration of activities and use associations and the existing land use patterns. The quality level and duration of the relationships can impact the potential for an area's change and the spatial risk level of prices and returns. Information on the quantity of land uses and the amount of vacancies in an area is useful because location and market or investment analysis of the area (and of a given site) can be improved if the nature of the vacancies and their duration are understood. The issues can be linked to: the land use pattern and interrelationships and how the vacancies relate to overall project abandonment; the act of or potential for rehabilitation or remodeling in an area; and the overall relationship of vacancies, structural change, and area potential to structural use. Therefore, the land use environment is both the result of and a direct influence on the physical environment of a city and its subsections.

Physical Environment

As with the physical dimensions of an individual site, the physical environment of a neighborhood can be classified based on natural physical features and features created by human endeavor. Natural features consider the topography (traditionally identified in terms of grade and elevation), the fauna and topographical land cover, the atmosphere (or, specifically, the microclimate), the condition of soils (surface and subsurface), the bodies of water, and the surrounding natural phenomena.

Because all land uses adapt well to flat or gently rolling and well-drained land, extreme grades often become the concern of land use patterns, potential development, and the phenomena that often direct the nature of development and the behavioral patterns of a neighborhood. For instance, the entire community of El Paso, Texas, is influenced by and has evolved as a result of the economic significance of the physical proximity of the Rio Grande River and the Franklin Mountains. The extreme terrains of plush river valley, rugged mountains, and desert have definitely characterized the economic delineation of El Paso's neighborhoods.

Atmosphere and microclimate can be major determinants of a neighborhood's spatial development. The supra-surface dimension of real estate can influence structural development in respect to atmospheric conditions such as sun orientation and wind direction. An example of the atmosphere's impact on the built environment is witnessed in Boston, where additional maintenance is incurred because the wind coming off the Charles River causes windows to pop out of buildings.

In a more general sense, infrastructures such as street systems and sidewalks are developed in response to topography and wind direction. Also, as key components of the artificial physical environment, buildings are developed with an orientation to the street system.

The soil component of the natural environment is a common concern in terms of its capacity to support structures and to allow the installation of subsurface utilities (such as water, sewer, and gas lines). The soil's capacity to sustain vegetation is important as a competitive and esthetic condition of the environment. The extent to which a natural ground cover exists is quantified in dollars by the need for landscaping or the extent to which it is required in an area.

The summation of the natural physical environment must be linked to the artificial or built environment, because the natural terrain directs the design, cost, and physical development of improvements in an area. Often, there is a direct substitution between natural and built environmental factors. For example, if natural vegetation is lacking, a more extensive landscaping effort may be required to allow the subject area to compete with other areas.

Houston affords an example of the trade-off between the natural and the built environment. Physically, Houston is located on the theoretical "featureless plain" of urban economics and location theory. In reality, the plain is interspersed with waterways and plush vegetation. Therefore, to effectively create locational identity, the bulk of Houston's districts and projects (the Galleria area, the Greenspoint area, the Astrodome area, and the Rice University area) rely on unique physical design or features such as fountains, landscaping, or statues.

In many neighborhoods, the built environment is a major factor in reflecting the area's physical character. The environment can be described and qualitatively analyzed on the bases of the age of structures in an area, the density of building development and occupancy, the size of structures, the states of blight and maintenance, and the preference for or dominance of specific architectural designs and quality. The status of the built environment in a locale can further give insights to the strength of a developer's impact on an area, in conjunction or in conflict with local building controls.

The physical environment of an area influences and overlaps the land use pattern of the area and often forms the basis for the future development potential. This future potential and the existing structural pattern are often linked to the taste and preferences of the populace in the area. The taste and preferences, in turn, are tied to the social and cultural environment that is predominant within the spatial boundaries being investigated.

Social and Cultural Environment

The social and cultural environment of a spatial enclave is contingent on the network of residents, clients, or employees who live in or frequent the area on an on-going basis. The spatial patterns of the interacting groups are often observed in the ancillary land use associations characteristic of the neighborhood. For instance, a neighborhood bar situated across the street from a manufacturing or industrial plant can do much to establish a social dimension of a neighborhood and to expand the duration of activities in the area beyond a nine-to-five time frame. That dimension can be absent in a new industrial park.

The social and cultural dimension of the environment affords additional information on the land use potential of an area. This information is otherwise missing, if the data gathered are limited to the quantity of land uses in the area. Investigation of the social dimension allows insights to the efficiency of the land use associations. An efficient land use pattern is one that is characterized by a high degree of compatibility and inconsistency (not necessarily homogeneity) in activities in an area. The level of the compatibility and consistency is often depicted by the income levels, occupations, and life-styles of the occupants and clients of an area.

The essence of the social and cultural environment is the delineation and depiction of the life-styles of the occupants or clients within a neighborhood. A life-style is the total product resulting from the background and conditioning factors of the family and household that influence behavior patterns over the lifetime of an individual or group. Life-style involves an array of genetic influences, worldly circumstances, and growth—all conditioned by family mores, religion (or lack of it), formal education, special ethnic customs, and the behavior of the broader community.

All of the cultural components are strongly molded by the economic status of the household and the occupational condition, which establish personal and family status. Time and history give further conditioning. Despite this broad array of social concerns, real estate economics often synthesizes factors of sociocultural dimensions into measures of age, education, income, and occupation. The spatial dimension of life-style categories is represented by many market specialists' linking of life-styles to zip codes.[13]

The significance of this perspective is that the collective life-styles of an area direct the potential land use associations in terms of quantity, quality, and efficiency. An important dimension of the social and cultural environment is that it is in a constant state of change. However, because of the magnitude of the issues and the behavioral dimension of the attributes that are of concern, the pattern of changes is usually linear and easily forecast.[14]

The issues of the social environment that must be addressed, outside of the typical demographic variables used in market analysis, are tenure information as it relates to life-style, and the levels of communication among the neighborhood's residents, associations, and other political groups. Other concerns are the emphasis placed on historical tradition and custom; the fit of customers or clients to products, services, and existing or proposed activities in the area; and the significance of economic and political management within the neighborhood.

The social and cultural environment establishes the life-style framework that establishes much of the behavioral patterns characteristic of a neighborhood. These patterns are more thoroughly investigated in the context of the psychological environment of the situs concerns.

Psychological Environment

The consideration of the psychological environment is concerned with the spatial dimension of dynamic or marketability attributes and the behavioral perception of neighborhood intangibles. Where the social environment of an area is constructed on group value systems that are based on heritage and group experience and culture, the psychological dimension is often the individual's (and/or the household's) response to a group value system that contains psychological promptings that choose and then protect and promote urban neighborhood environs. Often, these promptings evolve into organized traditions.[15]

[13] Michael J. Weiss, *The Clustering of America* (New York: Tilden Press, 1988).

[14] Richard B. Andrews, *Situs Theory, Part III, Situs: Its Relation to Environment* (Madison: Center for Urban Land Economics Research, Graduate School of Business, University of Wisconsin, 1982): 33 (monograph).

[15] *Ibid.*, at 48.

For example, prestige is a common expression of an attitude that becomes a tradition. To understand the locational dimension of neighborhood prestige, prestige must be distinguished from status. Prestige is an ephemeral condition (in the long run) that describes the high esteem in which direct users and third parties hold a specific area, district, or neighborhood. Status is a more general condition that can prevail over a range of urban areas. Status areas are usually characterized by wealthy occupants or clients (as those who frequent Rodeo Drive in Los Angeles). Prestigious and status areas can be mutually exclusive. Prestigious areas need not be solely wealthy neighborhood, and high-status neighborhoods may not have prestige.

An example of a prestigious neighborhood not classified as a high-income area is Peachtree Hills, located in north-central Atlanta. Much of the original housing stock was developed in the late 1940s and early 1950s. The structures were small and deficient in functional design; in recent years, they often suffered from high levels of deferred maintenance. However, the area had been considered prestigious in the past, and, despite its decline to a low-income area and the condition of the structures at purchase, the perception of a prestigious neighborhood remained. The neighborhood then experienced a renewal of demand. The perception of prestige and the level of demand could be linked to the neighborhood's physical location in the north-central corridor of Atlanta. The area also benefited from its proximity to "the" Peachtree Street's economic and social connections and to an old-line prestigious and status neighborhood that includes the governor's mansion. The purchasers in this area tended to be young or middle-age couples with few or no children. The housing size was appropriate and much of the repair and remodeling was done on weekends by the purchasers themselves. This more urban area was chosen by many families over the plethora of status suburban neighborhoods being developed concurrently in the Atlanta area.

An individual's acceptance of an upwardly mobile meritocracy reflects a business-oriented value system of the overall community. This value system holds out the possibility of moving into traditionally desirable neighborhoods as a measure of social prestige.

Prestige areas are often characterized by "old money" (if wealth is a criterion). Other common delineating factors of a prestige area are that it includes many of the community's "best families"; it has distinctive architecture; and it has a perceived or actual historical tradition that defines the neighborhood and the demand for the area. An example that includes all of these factors and is developmentally similar to the Peachtree Hills area is the University Park section of Dallas. Like Peachtree Hills, it is comprised of older, 1950s-style, small houses that abut a major older (wealthy) status and prestigious neighborhood (Highland Park).

The University Park area has always been fairly prestigious. Currently, it is undergoing a renewal; the older housing is being purchased for remodeling, updating, and major enlargements, or solely for the site potential. In the latter cases, the original structures are being razed and replaced with new structures that often have zero-lot-line characteristics.

The locational perception of prestige or status neighborhoods is often linked to a rub-off effect. The potential for a rub-off effect exists where residential areas (such as Peachtree Hills and University Park) and retail facilities attempt to situate themselves as close as possible to the traditional or hierarchical prestige districts. This proximity urge or rub-off effect often results in a skewness in the land use pattern that can be used to infer or predict the directions and patterns of growth.

The concept of psychological environment is often identified as a factor in the choice of residential location. However, the issues of prestige and status are also relevant to the location of office and retail facilities. For example, professional and business operations often attempt to identify with specific office buildings and districts. The psychological environment of business activity is often defined by the street address. A location on Wall Street commands a premium for financial operations. Advertising is traditionally linked to Madison Avenue. The significance is that the locale must connect to the activity in which the neighborhood has a drawing and holding power, because of the perception of the area and its agglomerative effect on business potential.

Retail facilities can be drawn to the prestige of streets that accommodate high-class retail operations or enterprise zones that connote entertainment or unique experiences. The prestigious retail area discussed above, Rodeo Drive in Los Angeles, has a parallel in Fifth Avenue in New York City. Michigan Avenue represents a prestigious retail situs in Chicago. A major entertainment-oriented retail zone is the French Quarter in New Orleans; the prestige of this area is delineated by architectural style and history. Texas examples of entertainment areas are Sixth Street in Austin, the Riverwalk in San Antonio, and McKinney Street in Dallas.

Prestige in retail and commercial use areas is more fragile than in residential neighborhoods because of factors such as alternative site competition, the changing tastes of consumers and clients, changes in retailing methods, changes in perceptions of image and prestige, and the movement of anchor and draw uses.

Institutional activities such as hospitals, religious centers, and universities can generate prestigious subordinate and ancillary uses in their environs. But, because of their size and inward orientation, these uses do not seek or need prestigious environments. Many noted hospitals do not seek out convenient or prestigious situs. On a macro level, the Mayo Clinic's location in Rochester, Minnesota, is neither convenient nor prestigious. This same environmental pattern is evident on a micro level for the majority of city hospitals; their locational concern is an efficient location (the center of the metroplex), not psychological or social amenities.

Universities are frequently located in less desirable areas of a city, or in the bottom tiers of the hierarchy of cities, because they seek proximity to concentrations of population. However, as history shows, population can shift. At the time of a school's establishment, population patterns and the economic base of its locale may have been different.

Other attributes of psychological spatial perceptions are sentiment, inheritance, territoriality, and image making. An example of sentiment is the desire in small and rural communities to retain the old downtown area that has been superseded by new shopping centers. The displacement may have been earned by functional and external obsolescence, but the sentimental resistance is often sufficient to delay the neighborhood life-cycle and alter the pattern of decline into one of renewal. However, economic incentives are needed to enable survival.

Inheritance is often bound to sentiment. The psychological impact of inheritance prolongs the stages of a neighborhood's life cycle because of the vested interest of multiple generations living in the same area or in the same specific facilities. This impact on a neighborhood can be eroded by the increased mobility of society and the increasing tendency to follow economic cycles around the country.

The impact of territoriality and image making can be tied to the psychological perception or feeling that specific activities belong in a particular area. This perception and the activism that often results in formal or informal political action contribute to the homogeneity of land uses, income groups, and demographic patterns in specific areas and neighborhoods. The boundaries of a neighborhood are often established along distinctive lines that build over time and are composed of tradition, custom, life cycles, and sentiment.[16]

The psychological environment is important in developing the mental mapping of an area that often results in the patina of meaning that is given a neighborhood. The mapping and meaning are the basis for the holding power of the area and for the expectations of and for the area. These expectations are the key to spatial knowledge and often link to the potential and patterns of growth. The psychological expectations of individuals form the basis of subjective value decisions that can direct the external expectations of the market, which, in turn, establish the constraints of the economic environment of an area.

Economic Environment

The economic environment of an area is often denoted by the sales prices, the rental returns, the land use pattern, and the array of market participants in the neighborhood. The sales prices and rental returns are often stated in a range and tied to uses and distinct or unique property attributes. The market participants in the area are generally grouped into consumer, speculator, or investor classes. A descriptive analysis of each of the use categories and of the orientation of the market players often does much to establish the economic status of an area and its potential for and direction of growth.

Price can be viewed as an economic symbol of the area's expectations and its capacity to absorb and support alternative land uses. Price is an independent locational force. Because of this independence, the analysis of prices in relation to land uses and the economic environment can result in a causal dilemma: Does use determine price or does price determine use?

Price and use are highly interwoven; the principles of competition and substitution impact land use patterns in a neighborhood as well as on specific sites. On a micro level, the site's capacity to support a use indicates the return and the price paid (or, the value) for the site. This is the basis of and the approach to the principle of highest and best use. The use capacity of a site is determined on a locational basis by the surrounding economic environment and by the immediate activities in the area and their associations.

On a macro level, the competition for uses is reflected in the prices paid in an area. The immediate prices determine the use potential. The

[16] *Id.*, at 54.

end result is the economic topography of an area, depicted by price gradients and bid–rent curves. (The concept of land price gradients and bid–rent curves are addressed in § 3.7(f).) These concepts enable an analytical consideration of the competition of uses within the overall urban structure. The use competition further dictates the economic dimension of the area, because the immediate neighborhood functions like an organ within the overall organism. This relationship focuses on the concerns of micro- and macroaccessibility (discussed earlier) and emphasizes the relationship between the activities outside of the subject neighborhood and those within a delineated area. Given this relationship, economic occurrences and activities on the site and city levels can have profound effects on the price ranges in specific neighborhoods. In a price or rent context, the basis for comparison may be alternative neighborhoods rather than alternative tracts of land.[17]

The price and rental ranges identified in an area cannot be divorced from the market participants and their objectives. The concern of economics is choice. The economic context is often defined as choice under resource constraints with limited options. The limiting options in real estate are often proximity and location. All of the limiting options can be linked in general to the spatial context of real estate. Only so much space is available in a given area at a given time. If the users' needs in the area exceed the available inventory, then prices and/or rents are going to rise. If the available space greatly exceeds the amount of space required for users' requirements, then the prices and rent should decline. The issues of the changing directions must be further qualified by a time dimension. How long does it take the market participants (both buyer and seller groups) in an area to adjust?

Delineating the market participants on the demand side as consumers (or direct users), speculators, or investors enables increased analysis of an area. More description of the potential buyers helps to narrow the focus of the competitive objectives affecting the properties in an area. The nature of the buyers gives insights to the possible level of change and direction in an area. It may indicate the speed of the change and/or growth in an area and it allows an understanding of the prices paid in the neighborhood. In general, one might expect the final users to attempt to pay less than speculators. However, a financial analysis of a speculative purchase may show that the price

[17] Kenneth M. Lusht and Frederick Pugh, "Appraising Houses: A Research Note on the Effects of Changing the Search Area for Comparable Sales," *The Real Estate Appraiser and Analyst* (Winter 1981): 34–36.

paid by the speculators was influenced by advantageous financial terms and supported by tax law deductions that effectively lowered the actual cost.

Furthermore, the objectives of investors influence the expectations for properties in given locations. This effect can be illustrated in economic units such as sales prices, changes in prices, time adjustments, cap rates, discount rates, and changes in the rates of return in an area. Other factors reflecting change wrought by investors' actions are alternative levels of the income potential on given sites and other dynamic issues that can alter the patterns of growth and activities as well as the land use pattern in an area. Therefore, the economic artifacts of investments and transactions can indicate a fair level of activity in a neighborhood.

Another indicator of the economic environment in an area is the quantity of parking space in relation to specific land use patterns. For example, there is high correlation between the type of parking available in an area and the age and design of the buildings. Parking availability can also be linked to the architecture in an area.[18] The predominance of on-street parking in an area can be tied to older, high-density, developed structures. A legal requirement of off-street parking, or the presence of parking facilities on a site, can be linked to new buildings, in which specific floor-area-to-parking ratios were required.

An abundance of parking lots surrounding existing buildings can also be used as an economic indicator of a neighborhood in transition. Given the property tax structure in many areas, it is often economically rational to demolish existing structures and convert the land to parking space until construction is feasible or can be directly commenced.[19] Property taxes are considerably lower on parking lots than on buildings. The nature of interim land use activities can be used as an economic indicator of the future growth pattern of an area.

Financing terms and practices are key descriptors of an area's economic environment. The supply and availability of mortgage funds in an area portend the development and maintenance status of the neighborhood. The range of interest rates and terms available in a district can be used as both an indicator of the potential for growth and development and a measure of the risk level characterizing the neighborhood (as perceived by institutions). Several studies have been

[18] Andrews, *supra* note 14, at 94.

[19] David Segal, *Urban Economics* (Homewood, IL: Richard D. Irwin, Inc., 1977): 198–199.

conducted that indicate that debt costs vary in different cities and in neighborhoods within those cities.[20]

The sources of debt capital open to investors/users in given neighborhoods do much to characterize the risk levels of the area and its growth potential. The sources can be institutions such as banks, savings and loans, or insurance companies; participants in secondary mortgage markets such as the Federal National Mortgage Association ("Fannie Mae") and the Government National Mortgage Association ("Ginnie Mae"); or any of several Wall Street firms or individuals. The underwriting criteria of the institutions and secondary marketers are linked to the economic dimension of the neighborhood. Specific risk parameters must be considered. Individuals can vary in their underwriting standards; however, a high level of individual lenders in an area is often a clear indication of speculative markets or high risk perceptions.

In existing neighborhoods with older structures, the level of and activity in property improvement loans are clear indications of a renewal or a decline in the property life cycle. The use associated with the level of property improvement loans gives insights to the future economic patterns of a neighborhood. Existing structures can have various uses (which are often altered by the terms and conditions of mortgage financing and other loans).

The availability and volume of commercial credit in an area are attributes of the economic environment that cannot be ignored. Because land use patterns are tied to the activities in a neighborhood, commercial credit is a good indicator of financial support. The terms and availability of capital for the activities in the area measure the perceived strength and duration of the establishments' economies. The duration of the loans offers further insights to the risk potential of the economic environment.

Other indicators of an economic environment in transition are the levels of mortgage delinquency and foreclosure occurring in a neighborhood. The spatial concern of these economic issues must be segmented by the areas or loci of occurrence and the types of properties

[20] Limited work has been conducted on the spatial impacts of financing and its relationship to real estate markets. Two works that address this issue are: Ted. C. Jones, "Systematic Differences in Interest Rates for Conventional Fixed-Rate Residential Mortgage Loans Across Select U.S. Cities 1980–83," Ph.D. dissertation, Texas A&M University, available from University Microfilms, University of Michigan, Ann Arbor; and Alan R. Winger, "Regional Growth Disparities and the Mortgage Market," *Journal of Finance* (1969): 659–662.

involved. Besides the types and locations of the properties, the analysis must address the levels of debt on the property and the quality of the management involved. If a consistent pattern is noticed in the context of geographical location and property type, a projection of neighborhood trends is possible from the financial information.

In addition to the financial delinquencies, attention should be given to rental delinquencies and the availability of property insurance. Both of these criteria are useful as lead indicators of the economic environment of a property. Concerns must center around whether the delinquencies are locationally specific and whether they are tied to specific property types and/or management styles or groups.

The insurance availability in the area is linked to general and specific property issues. The insurance ranking, and hence its cost as a periodic expense impacting the income projections, often entails issues related to specific activities that may occur in spatial clusters. Therefore, analysts must be concerned with the levels of insurance in an area, the types of insurance available, the link of insurance coverage to levels of vacancy and use types, and institutional perceptions of risk levels in an area.

The economic environment is interwoven with the physical environment in the context of property maintenance. Maintenance also has a psychological link. The level of stewardship in an area is a direct indication of local-occupant versus absentee ownership. The legal tenancy in an area can offer insights to the current and future status of an area's economy and growth potential.[21] Maintenance involves the investment of additional capital and labor on a periodic schedule. These expenditures are not made if expectations of future returns are not possible. However, these returns can come in the form of monetary returns (rent, gains, and so on) or psychic returns (pride of ownership, standard of living, or a bequest to future generations). In either situation, the willingness to make further investment in existing structures illustrates a positive perception of the economic environment. Variations from the expectations of future economic potential, identified as rental or mortgage delinquencies, lack of maintenance, or income losses in an area, are all measures of economic or external obsolescence. The negative aspects of an economic environment are often incorporated into the valuation process as external obsolescence.

A major economic issue impacting an area's environment is technology. The status of an area is often linked to the adaptability of the area

[21] Ko Wang, Terry V. Grissom, and James Webb, "The Impact of Rental Properties on the Value of Single-Family Residences," *Journal of Urban Economics* (forthcoming).

and its structures to changing market (demand) standards based on perceived economic needs or comforts. As the needs of the activities occupying space change, the structural requirements demanded of given buildings and neighborhoods are altered. The valuation techniques used in appraisal address these economic environmental issues in the context of functional or internal obsolescence.

Technological developments have an economic impact on the physical structure and capacity of buildings and neighborhoods. This impact is reflected in the attraction of activities to certain areas of a city in part based on whether they are intensive or extensive users of space. Warehouse space is a classic example of how the intensive use of space can be altered by technology and rental and transportation costs. Historically, warehouses were located in the inner city. This location was linked to the technology of the time: transportation between cities was by water or rail and animal muscle provided the primary transportation within cities. The ports and the rails were often located at the city's central focus, because cities grew around these transportation activities. The warehouses were often high-rises; goods could be moved vertically or horizontally for equal costs. Therefore, warehouse space was intensively developed in inner-city areas.

With the technological development of diesel-engine trucks, the amount and cost of inter- and intracity transportation changed. Horizontal movement became less costly than vertical movement. As intercity travel between cities became tied to the highway system, it was advantageous to move the warehouses to cheaper land near the highways, on the fringes of the cities. The direct impact of technological changes in transportation was an alteration of the forms of buildings and cities. In this context, arguments can be made that northeastern cities are functionally obsolete and southwestern cities reflect current market trends. However, as experience shows, proximity to key activities can offset the deficiencies of physical form, and tradition and economic capital are important in location decisions. The compact nature of the traditionally structured cities offers communication advantages that are lacking in many of the younger cities. These communication advantages and the technological advances in communication facilities may hold the key structural impact of the future. Because technology can be a major molder of neighborhood environments, current patterns may be totally altered in the future.

The economic environment encompasses all of the other concerns regarding an area's physical, social, psychological, and institutional environment and its land use patterns. The information the economic environment offers decision makers is often in the form of economic artifacts distinguished as units of economic comparison. These economic units are descriptive and allow decisions based on returns, sales prices, or comparative cost. These units often enable a quantitative consideration of many subjective issues.

Institutional and Political Environment

The institutional and political environment of a neighborhood, like the economic environment, entails several of the other dimensions, especially the social and cultural and the psychological concerns of an area. The institutional concern in a spatial dimension often addresses issues of public laws, rules of behavior (both formal and informal), plans, and services. The social, economic, and psychological concerns discussed above covered many topics that can be considered institutional or political, but this environmental grouping is distinguished by the level or degree of organization involved in the various concerns impacting an area.

The level of organization is illustrated by the political organization and bureaucracy of the city; the neighborhood representational strengths, as witnessed by district or "at-large" elections; area contacts at city hall; formal or informal neighborhood associations; and the power of city planners. These various organizational levels can be observed in the availability of community services to specific neighborhoods as they compete with other areas of the city for services and limited benefits.

Neighborhoods can be defined by the scale and pricing of traditional services in an area. Because scale and cost can vary within a community, specific locations can be defined by institutional benefits and political clout. The availability of services can be linked to the cost of public services per area in the form of general tax bills, special assessments (which definitely take on a spatial dimension), and user fees (per area or property). In fact, the scale and quality of public services often can be related to specific locations and even to specific uses within specific locations. For example, to residential users, police protection may be more relevant than street maintenance, but the latter may be of prime importance to the commercial users in a neighborhood.

The institutional policies of a city may also discriminate against certain areas and give preference of other areas; older, less prestigious areas may not receive the same quality of service as newer areas that have more status. This may be linked, in part, to sources of property tax revenue. The institutional aspect of the assessment process has a major impact on a neighborhood.

Building codes and the implementation of housing are institutional factors that control the form and structure of neighborhoods and cities. The regulations prescribed by the codes, their enforcement, and the link of code compliance to services do much to augment the planning process in a city. The perceptions and philosophies of the strategic planners in a community contribute to the determination of the environment in which land use decisions and value estimates are made.

Strategic planning is not limited to the public sector. Private developers, financial institutions, and the processes that formulate land use policies all impact on the decision environment of neighborhoods and individual sites. Many municipal utility districts have been formed before individual property owners have had input to the inclusion or exclusion of their property from the system. The total environment of a neighborhood or site cannot be conducted without a high degree of political awareness.

The institutional and political environment of an area or neighborhood cannot usually be understood without linking it to the overall design and format of the urban structure. The site, like the biological cell, links to the neighborhood (its organ), and the neighborhood links to the urban complex (the organism).

(h) SUMMARY OF SITUS

Location is a complex subject that involves many dimensions. An understanding of location is essential to understanding the productivity of a given site (or even of a neighborhood). Unfortunately, the key components of a property's productivity are often limited to a subjective or qualitative discussion of the property and its surrounding environment. An investigation of the locational attributes of property can offer a process for addressing the gray areas of analysis that are often abused in the appraisals and market investigation of a property.

The process is based on the concept of situs, a theoretical premise that links the individual site to its environment. Situs divides the site into a land use function and a parcel of land. These two distinct dimensions of a property are related to the total urban environment in a specific time period. The analysis is then extended over time.

Based on this theoretical link between a site and the urban environment, the process of situs can be applied in a stepwise procedure by first delineating the area of concern and then identifying the activities in an area, the association among the activities, and the accessibility of the activities to one another and to the entire city. The relationship of these activities must then consider the impact of environmental concerns in the broad sense, addressing issues of land use, social and cultural concerns, psychological responses, economic concerns, and institutional and political impacts. Although the environmental concerns are often characterized by nonmovement, they are definitely dynamic forces directing the potential of a site and its neighborhood. However, to fully understand the context in which the situs analysis is defined, the location analysis must be expanded to the level of the city (the total urban environment). The urban structure and its related land use pattern and economic base are key to forecasting the potential of a specific parcel of land.

In making individual land use decisions, comparisons and contrasts of the impact of land use decisions and of property transactions in the aggregate are helpful. In general, individual decisions and urban form are influenced over time by market trends, institutional constraints, technology, and cultural preferences. These key issues in directing the pattern of aggregate urban growth were identified in the environmental component of situs.

§ 3.5 URBAN STRUCTURE: INTRODUCTION TO LEVEL THREE

Although real estate is physically fixed, it is economically flexible. This means that, even if a parcel of real estate is physically tied to a particular locus, the concept of location is an economic variable that can change over time. The essential point is that real estate is space being used in time segments to house an economic activity. As the surrounding neighborhood changes, the support system for the existing use can change. Change can affect the use of a property, the market for that property, and the transfer price that may be received for any given site. Therefore, the market for any given parcel of real estate cannot be analyzed without first analyzing the use. Consideration of the use will enable (1) a comparison between heterogeneous sites and (2) a measure of a degree of substitutability.

To understand real estate markets, then, the concept of spatially defined land use patterns and the use associations identified in situs analysis must be thoroughly understood. A link of the use, which defines the product, to the market structure must be identified. Because geographical or spatial dimension is a key element in real estate market structure, it is necessary to understand the urban structure of the city.

Urban structure is the social, physical, and economic aggregation of land uses in a community. An understanding of this aggregation of uses is needed because the existing activities in a community are the support system for the use on any given site. This support system of land uses directs the quantity, quality, and duration of returns and, hence, the value for a given site over time. These economic artifacts, as discussed in the preceding section, influence the demand for a given type of substitutable site and the availability of supply in a given city, area, or neighborhood.

Urban structure connotes an orderly arrangement of discrete and distinguishable economic functions as parts of a whole. The structure is an agglomeration of these parts that comprises all the essential functions—and their interrelations—by which a local population maintains itself.[22]

As the interrelationships get more complex, there is a tendency toward specialization of functions. Rational patterns of land uses evolve; where urban activities such as retailing, manufacturing, recreation, and other uses are concentrated, these patterns are composed of several functional areas.[23] The result in most cities is a delineation of major land use clusters.

As the city develops a network of functions, specialization of site function is concomitant with the evolution of the urban structure. The relationships between individual parcels of land can be viewed in the context of a "packet of functions."[24] Each site forms the base or locus of specific economic activities. A site can house a variety of activities that are influenced by surrounding land uses. The associated activities can be supportive, competitive, ancillary, or conflicting (see § 3.4(d)).

The associations contribute to a land use pattern (and resulting prices) that may not reflect the immediate and current space requirements of a community. The urban structure is the cumulative land needs of the community over a period of years. For example, in many

[22] Amos H. Hawley, *Human Ecology* (New York: Ronald Press Co., 1950): 206. This source and others cited to the end of this section represent the development of the conceptual basis of the space–time equation.

[23] Richard U. Ratcliff, *Urban Land Economics* (New York: McGraw-Hill, 1948): 368.

[24] Robert M. Haig, "Toward an Understanding of the Metropolis," *The Quarterly Journal of Economics* (February 1926): 414–420.

city areas, the skeletons of the street and utility systems are relics of the past.[25] Many buildings that are intermingled with current facilities may be representative of past generations. To understand the pattern of land prices, the factors influencing the urban structure and the structure's origin and changes over time must be identified.

§ 3.6 FORCES INFLUENCING URBAN STRUCTURE

The same basic structural tendencies appear in most cities, but topography, urban size, and other factors may cause them to vary. A city's initial situation is usually traceable to a primary activity or activities. For commercial, manufacturing, political, or social reasons, the activities may have been linked to those in other geographical areas. Often, the activities have evolved at points of transshipment or breaks in transportation modes (where one transportation mode terminates and another begins). Examples are water routes that terminate at superhighways or railroads.

Because an economic function brings people to an area, topographical features become the initial constraint or concern of the urban structure. The general attributes that encourage growth of cities are water sources and sharp variations in the levels of the surrounding terrain.

Cities originate at the most convenient point of contact with the outer world, and they grow along lines of least resistance or greatest attraction. The external convenience is best at the point of transshipment (the water's edge). The line of least resistance is often along a valley floor.

Many land economists perceive that the urban structure and the pattern of prices paid for land are based on ease of accessibility between predominant areas of activity. The price paid per square foot for a tract of land would then be inversely related to transportation cost or cost of access. The highest prices would be paid for the sites that offer the greatest number of people the highest quality of economic service. The service desired is convenience of location. The central business district, the center of the city, or areas of greatest functional activity are often the most convenient areas, and they serve the greatest number of people. The price paid for this convenience is also related to the available supply of land in any one area of a city. Land at the center of a

[25] Ratcliff, *supra* note 23, at 370–372.

city is limited; therefore, the price is driven up. The intensity of demand decreases at the periphery of the community because competing land sites increase as a squared function of the distance (D^2) from a given point (CBD). Often, the aggregation of activity at the edge of a city is illustrated by a price that represents the cost of platting and opening streets and/or discounting future expectations. The end result is that central-area increases in land prices may be attributable to the proximity of the CBD or of a maximum area of convenient economic activity.

Another general type of growth is axial growth along transportation routes. Accessibility makes this type of growth desirable. These alternative urban models will be discussed in a later section. At this point, it is key to understand that the urban structure influences individual land use decisions (and values) and that the basic economic functions of the city influence urban form.

As the pressure of demand pushes up the price of land in proximity to the most accessible point, topography as a constraint becomes less important and the amenities of terrain become attributes of attraction to specific functions. For example, high-income residential users may outbid lower-income groups for land on the high ground and near water sources (other than at initial transshipment points).

This general pattern of urban structure can be observed in many sites. The following factors also impact urban structure over time:[26]

- Government regulations and planning objectives
- Population changes
- Financing terms
- City size and age
- Tax rates
- Effective buying power (income levels)
- Available supply of land
- Transportation
- Expanded urban services
- Technology
- Employment centers
- Major groupings of economic activities.

[26] Paul F. Wendt, "Economic Growth and Urban Land Values," *Appraisal Journal* (July 1958): 427–443.

The impact of these factors can have different effects in different cities or in separate areas within a city. However, all the factors fall into the major categories of physical concerns shown in Figure 3.9: institutional constraints, market factors, economic base, technology, and cultural norms.

Figure 3.9 illustrates the *conceptual* relationship of the urban structure to (1) the forces that influence the form and structure of the city and (2) the urban land markets (and thus, by extension, a given site). The institutional constraints, market factors, economic base, technology, and cultural norms are considered in relation to *physical topography* because they influence the past, current, and future shape of the city; the physical attributes are the foundation supporting the various forces that shape both the city and the aggregate land price patterns.

Figure 3.9 Forces Influencing Urban Structure

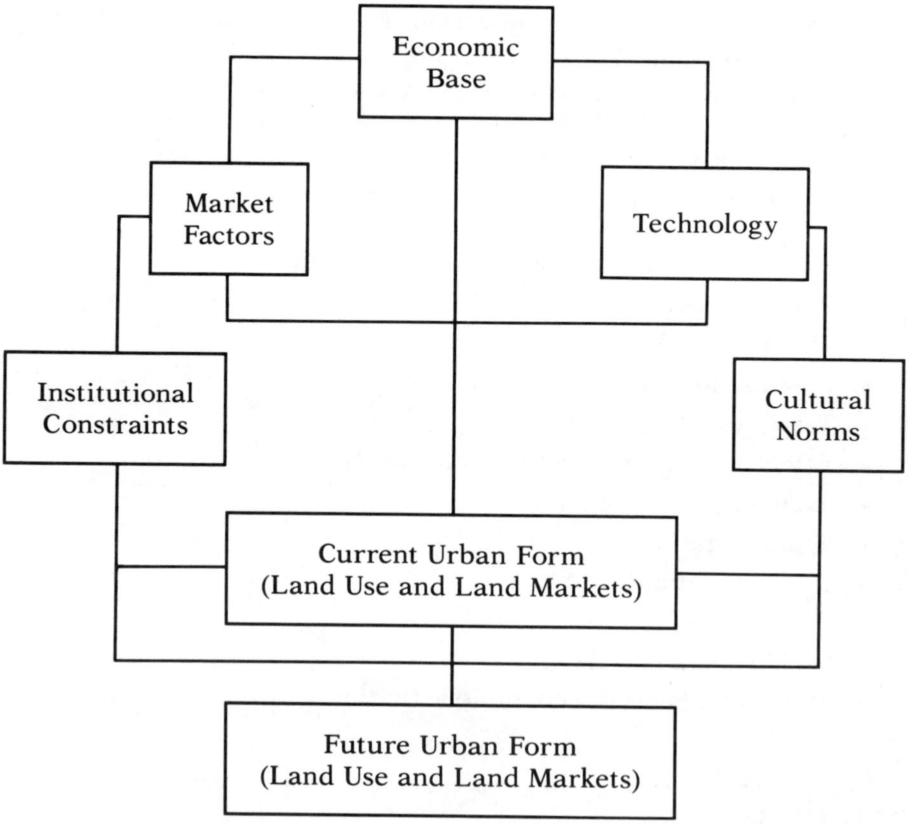

Therefore, the price pattern is linked to the physical terrain of a community. The forces considered are the broader expression of the environmental dimensions of situs.

The forces in operation on the physical terrain, as depicted in Figure 3.9, are individually significant. Institutional constraints range from the general to the specific. Examples of institutional constraints are found in property transactions, zoning, planning, and other governmental controls or regulations on individual land decisions. Institutional constraints also come in the form of the lending policies that are in effect at any one time, insurance requirements, and concerns for public safety.

Market factors are the elements of supply and demand, the potential for capture and absorption of land uses within given time frames, and a range of economic artifacts such as land prices, returns, rents or incomes, and costs to develop. These issues are discussed in § 3.8.

Another major force that affects the urban form is economic base. To fully understand a real estate market, the economic base of the community must be understood. Before the space for a certain type of use can be absorbed, there must be demand for the activities, goods, or services characterized by that use. A demand for a given use (and, hence, for space for that use) is evident when people are being employed in a given activity. Furthermore, that activity is conducted because the output of that activity—whether a product or a service—is being demanded by final consumers.

Technology relates to developments in products and methods of control and communication that enable (or even force) people to interact. Technological changes in modes of transportation and communication impact land values, because relative location can change. Technology can also determine whether existing real estate is esthetically or functionally desirable.

A community's norms reflect its perception of property rights. The community's desire to control and protect the environment can alter the land uses open to a parcel in any particular area of town. The level of this desire is often illustrated by the degree of political activism exhibited by neighborhood associations.

(a) THE ECONOMIC BASE MULTIPLIER

All of these concerns come together in the concept of the economic base multiplier. A general model of economic base analysis is illustrated in the following example of Glasgow, Kentucky.

The economic base of Glasgow is split 50–50 between agriculture and industry. The employment breakdown in the area is as follows:

Total employment (T)	= 13,650
Local employment (L)	= 6,780
Export or base employment (E)	= 6,870

The base employment is the economic reason the city exists: it produces a good or service to be consumed outside of the area. This production creates jobs and income within the local community, and the income enables a demand for goods and services locally. Therefore, as the base sector of the economy changes, there is a multiplier effect on the overall economy of the city. The relationship (k) of the total employment (T) to the base employment (E) is depicted as:

$$k = \frac{T}{E}$$

$$= \frac{13{,}650}{6{,}870}$$

$$= 1.9869$$

An alternate calculation is:

$$k = \frac{1}{1 - L/T}$$

$$= \frac{1}{1 - \dfrac{6{,}780}{13{,}650}}$$

$$= \frac{1}{1 - .496703}$$

$$= \frac{1}{.503299}$$

$$= 1.9869$$

The significance of the more complicated formula is that (L/T) is identified as the propensity to consume locally. The propensity to consume locally means that 49 to 50 percent of the employed income is directed toward jobs that are supplying local services. As discussed below, the local sector is significant to an economy because of an indirect income effect.

The direct impact is best illustrated by applying the multiplier to a new, autonomously generated industry that comes into Glasgow. Assume that the new plant employs 500 people. The following impact is projected:

$$\Delta T = \Delta E \frac{1}{1 - L/T}$$

$$= 500 \frac{1}{1 - \dfrac{6{,}780}{13{,}650}}$$

$$= 500\ (1.9869)$$

$$= 993.45, \text{ or (rounded) } 994 \text{ jobs created}$$

where:

ΔT = change in total employment
ΔE = employment change directly resulting from a new industry

The incoming plant would employ 500 people, but the potential overall growth in the community would be 994 jobs, because 494 jobs would service the needs of the city. The significance to real estate markets is in the direct effect of the incoming plant—industrial land is in demand—and in the indirect effect—supportive industrial, retail, and residential space is needed, and jobs are created in service functions that generate supplies for the new plant, provide its employees with food services, and satisfy their transportation needs, their residential needs, their banking and insurance requirements, and so on. These effects are quantified by the propensity to consume locally. A further effect is that the increased income of the area will generate other land use requirements. This effect is illustrated quantitatively by the employment-to-population ratio:

$$P_k = \frac{P}{T} = \frac{20{,}000}{13{,}650} = 1.465$$

$$\Delta P = T \times P_k = 994(1.465) = 1.456$$

This increase in population means more consumers.

The economic essence of the community (or neighborhood) directs the land use activities and land use patterns in an area. They, in turn, establish the geographical pattern of the real estate market and enable a projection of supply and demand for any given property use.[27]

§ 3.7 URBAN STRUCTURE MODELS

Several models have been developed over time, in an effort to understand the nature of city land use patterns and their growth paths. The first set of models can be collectively grouped as belonging to a social ecology school. The three general models in the set are descriptive in method and have titles such as the concentric zone model, the sector (wedge) model, and the radial corridor (axial) model. A fourth model, the multinuclei model, is a hybrid of two of the general models; as offered by the ecologist school, it connotes urban structure to many analysts. The models were developed from the 1920s to the 1940s and have received only moderate adjustments or extensions in the past 50 years.

Social ecologists see the urban topography as an ecological–social system of interrelated land uses. Although descriptive in form and static in origin, ecologist models can be used to predict where growth is likely to occur.

The direction and potential for growth or economic activity are key elements of market analysis. Furthermore, real estate market analysis must be considered in a spatial context. The urban structure models, because they are often presented in a physical and spatial design, are helpful in satisfying the segmentation requirements of market analysts. The models also form the basis for forecasts of how growth will affect the interaction of supply and demand in a spatial context.

Figures 3.10–3.13 illustrate the four ecologist models. In their static form, three of the models have a circular core, and one has an irregular center surrounded by disconnected points. The four models were developed by a sociologist, a land economist, a mortgage banker, and a pair of geographers. Because the models have their origins in different

[27] For a historical and case study approach that illustrates that the localized industries often evolve into base exporters, see Jane Jacobs, *Cities and the Wealth of Nations* (New York: Vintage Books, 1985).

disciplines, they tend to emphasize different issues of importance in spatial structure.

The following sections describe the various social ecology models.

(a) CONCENTRIC ZONE THEORY

In 1923, after studying several large urban areas, Ernest W. Burgess, a sociologist, concluded that a city expands radially from its center to form a series of concentric zones.[28] Figure 3.10 illustrates the concentric zone theory.

Zone 1 is the central business district, which contains a diversity of retail stores, offices, financial services, theaters, museums, and warehouses. This area is the urban central core, the heart of the major retail and service activities of the city.

Because growth of the city core encroaches on the surrounding occupied space, zone 2 tends to exhibit an unstable land use pattern. For this reason, zone 2 is a transitional zone; its characteristics are: light manufacturing, an outer belt of substandard dwelling units, and considerable crime and poverty.

Figure 3.10 Concentric Zone Theory Land Use Pattern

1 CBD
2 Zone of transition
3 Zone for workers' homes
4 Zone for middle and high-income units
5 Commuter zone

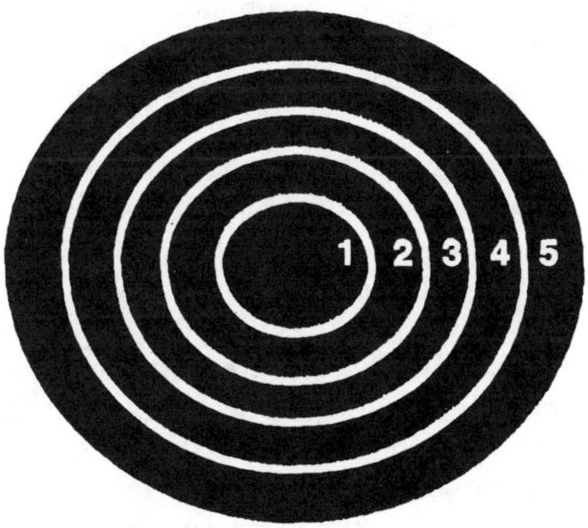

Adapted from T. V. Smith and L. D. White, eds., *Chicago: An Experiment in Social Science Research* (Chicago: University of Chicago Press, 1929).

[28] E. W. Burgess, "The Growth of the City," in *The City* (Chicago: University of Chicago Press, 1925).

Zone 3 is a relatively stable area because zone 2 absorbs most of the growth of the city core. Successful businesspeople tend to live in zone 3. Manufacturing displaced from the city core is located on the urban area's periphery, leaving zone 3 essentially untouched.

As industry expands, zone 3 begins to house mostly blue-collar workers who prefer to live close to work. As a result, the growing middle class moves out to zone 4, where lots and houses are larger than in zones 2 and 3. Zone 4 is often characterized as a zone of workingpeople's middle-grade homes or "better" residences.

Good transportation systems allow the more prosperous people to move into zone 5, an area surrounded by farms and recreational areas. Zone 5 is characterized as an area with non-urban-like uses of land. Because many of the people living in this area work in the city core, this region is identified as the commuters' zone.

Beyond the city's major functional areas lies the urban–rural fringe, a transitional zone between urban and rural uses that is functionally difficult to define and, in growing cities, is often characterized by an active level of speculative markets. The uncertainty of analysis and valuation in these areas is tied to the range of potential highest and best uses that can be projected for any given lot. The fringe ring is empirically shown to be more uncertain than the central core, based on the relative range of unit prices paid in the market.[29]

Burgess's theory, intended as a very general model, has been criticized as offering only limited descriptive and inferential power to the analysis of cities. Critics noted that Chicago was the reference point for the model and that, even in the 1920s, Chicago had a more defined CBD than was typical for American cities. Furthermore, the growth potential of the Chicago core was constrained by limited public transit (elevated trains and highways). (To this day, the central business district of Chicago is a commercial anachronism, compared to many cities where CBD growth has sprawled in many directions.)

Other criticisms were that the model does not consider topography (including drainage and slope) and the impact of the automobile on land use, and that Burgess emphasized residential activities more than commercial and manufacturing activities. However, because residential land use is the primary use in all cities, the relationships identified in the concentric zone theory offer some useful insights to the process and directions of growth in a city and to market delineation issues.

[29] Terry V. Grissom, "Land Price Patterns and the Urban Structure: Austin," Real Estate Center, Texas A&M University, Austin, Technical Report, December 1989.

The general model of Burgess's zonal relations offers an ordering of land use patterns. This ordering allows comparative studies among cities and analysis of the submarkets within cities, because the zones represent at least a central *tendency* for *all* cities.[30] With its emphasis on residential markets (beyond zones 1 and 2), the Burgess model stresses social status and income as key factors in land use development patterns. As a sociologist, Burgess also perceived the linkage among land use, social class, and family status. These are all concerns of real estate market analysis.

The forecasting elements or dynamics derived from the zonal model are based on the internal structural relationships between the zones. The essence of the zonal theory is the tendency of each inner zone to expand its territory outward by invading the next outer zone. Therefore, each outward move from a zone is influenced by the nature and conditions of the previous zone. The dynamics of growth in the orderly sequence of the zones is viewed as an "overflow effect," a decentralizing tendency in urban growth. As a central city with fixed boundaries continues to grow, vacant land is used up and growth may occur as higher density. With the decrease in available space (and an increase in prices), additional population spills over into the suburbs and outlying areas. The potential of the overflow effect is exponential. Before the growth rate reaches the central city boundaries, the suburban ring has a relatively slight development and density; it is often characterized by scattered suburbs and satellite cities. As the margin of development reaches the boundaries of the central city, the suburban population will rise at a faster pace than before. The suburban (or city fringe) growth then outstrips the central city growth.

One empirical method of measuring the overflow effect is to compare (regress) the density of population per square mile (or other spatial unit) to the percentage of population growth accounted for by the ring area (Census data are recommended).[31] The associations tend to show that the more densely developed the city, the greater the growth level (expressed as a percentage) of the suburbs. All new growth is in the suburbs, the original base is comparatively low, and the percentage change is greater than the change occurring in the large, densely settled city (which necessitates dividing by a large number). This high-density suburban growth is observed in the cities of the north and east

[30] Andrews, *supra* note 2, Part I, at 5.

[31] James Heilbrun, *Urban Economics and Public Policy* (New York: St. Martin's Press, 1974): 34–36.

(many of which follow the Burgess pattern) such as Boston, Philadelphia, and Chicago.

Many cities in the south and west reflect a low central city density and a low percentage change in the suburban fringe, even when they are high-growth cities, as Dallas and Houston were in the 1970s and early 1980s. The real estate development explanation behind these numbers is that, when low density exists in the city core, there is still potential for development there. When core development potential exists, the core and the suburbs are in competition for multiple land uses. For example, in older areas of Houston, new high-density housing is beginning to rival structures that are more distant from the CBD.

Further research[32] supports the overflow effect as it links to Burgess's zones by discussing the "methods" of the overflow movement. Commercial areas and some types of residential use (apartments) are described as having at least three distinct patterns or tendencies. One is that use areas "slide" along an axis outward from the core in one or more directions. The sliding can be the movement of the area away from its original nucleus or an extension outward from that point. The sliding pattern can be integrated with or distinct from the second method—"coalescence," the merging of one land grouping nucleus with a nucleus of the same use category, which originated in another location.

An example of the sliding phase as an independent movement is commercial growth along a major arterial. The coalescence force is observed in growth corridors where cities are pulled toward each other. Integration of the sliding and coalescence forces occurs in the growth of commercial activity along major arterials, in part, because of the attraction of intercity traffic flow.

The third category of movement is "jumping," the situation in which units of an area jump to disconnected points within the community. At these outward points, the mobile units, singly or with other units, create new nuclei. Jumping can also describe the movement of the entire original nucleus to an outward location.

A major contribution of the zonal theory is that it establishes limits to the urban area and its internal segments. The zones described above are determined by commutation limits. The trip length or the distance from one land use to another often sets the boundaries for the clustering of land use and social activities. The zonal model also affords a point of investigative initiation because the model is constructed on a

[32] Charles C. Colby, "Centrifugal and Centripetal Forces in Urban Geography," *Annals of the Association of American Geographers*, 23 (March 1933): 1–20.

single-center concept or mononuclear city format. The zones that experience the dynamics of the overflow effect hypothesize a development point from which the rest of the urban structure radiates.

The zone model offers real estate analysts a general pattern of land use ordering and a dynamic potential for identifying growth as an overflow from a single center of economic activity. It fails to consider the impact of topography, radial or axial growth, and nucleated neighborhood growth in all land use categories, but provides a general format in which to view these issues. (These issues are taken up further in the other models.)

The important point of Burgess's theory is that each inner zone tends to put pressure on the next outer zone for its residents and the land use they represent. Each ring builds on the previous ring.

(b) SECTOR (WEDGE) THEORY

In 1934, Homer Hoyt, MAI, a land economist, proposed the sector or wedge theory of land use patterns as being more accurate than the zonal theory in describing how an urban area takes form.[33] The study on which the sector theory is based was initially intended to be a case study of 64 cities for the U.S. Federal Housing Administration (FHA). The case analysis evolved into the sector theory of urban growth. The sector theory offers improvements over the generalizations of the zonal theory because it considers the importance of transport in the functioning of a city. Industrial land use also fits better into this scheme of urban development than it does into the zonal concept. The sector concept further expands on the dynamic potential of Burgess's model (as combined with the overflow effect) by considering the movement patterns of high-income residents and the concept of *filtering*. Filtering deals with the social/income mobility of people and its relation to the housing stock. In general, people are upwardly mobile; they ascend to higher-priced housing and status or prestige neighborhoods. On the other hand, the aging housing stock moves downward in a socioeconomic context. Older housing is purchased by the previous lower, but now upwardly mobile, income strata. Based on filtering, the sector theory indicates that urban growth is driven by high-income residential markets.

[33] Homer Hoyt, "Recent Distortions of the Classical Models of Urban Structure," *Land Economics*, 40:2 (May 1934): 199–211.

The sector (or wedge) theory also includes topographical impacts (from elevated ground, bodies of water, and terrain) on the direction of growth and development patterns of a city.

The sector model is monocentric, like the concentric zone model. (See Figure 3.11.) It accepts the origins of the city as being linked to economic activity and possible transshipment points. Hoyt identified (in general) the core activities of the city that generate land use conflicts. He then hypothesized that, once the contrasts in land use had arisen at the center, the differences were perpetuated as the city expanded.[34] Distinctive land use wedges were then likely to grow out from the center core, often oriented toward the major routes.

Figure 3.11 Sector (Wedge) Theory Land Use Pattern

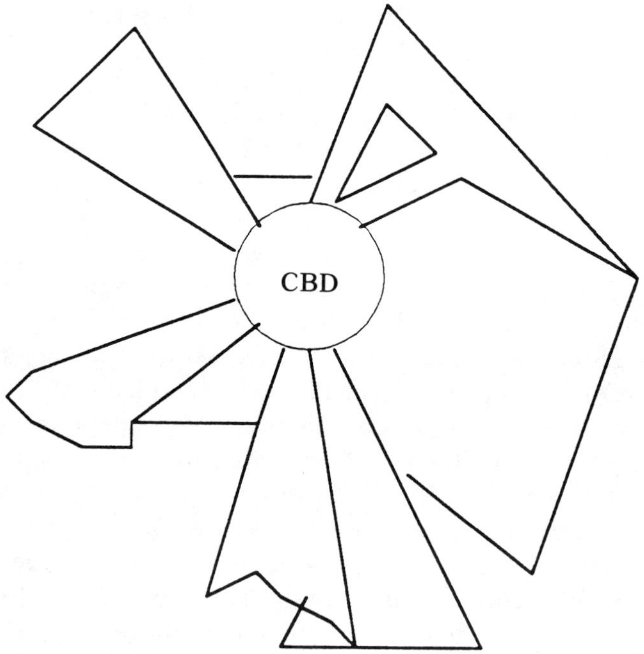

Adapted from Homer Hoyt, *The Structure and Growth of Residential Neighborhoods in American Cities* (Washington, DC: FHA; U.S. Government Printing Office, 1939).

[34] For further discussion, see James H. Johnson, *Urban Geography* (Oxford, England: Pergamon Press, Ltd., 1967).

Hoyt's theories of growth center on high-income or high-class housing: once a high-class housing district is established, the most expensive sites for new homes will lie at the outer edges of that district.

According to the sector theory, if a sector of an urban area develops first as a high-, medium, or low-rental residential area, it tends to retain that character for substantial distances as city growth causes the sector to expand outward. Each group of people tends to segregate, for working as well as for residence, on the bases of income and social position.

The tendency to assemble by income class is more a function of economics than of other factors. The poor and moderate-income residents of a city must comply with economic concerns guided by accessibility, amenities, and rent-paying abilities (or purchasing power). The wealthy can usually live where they choose and thus can make choices that may not comply with rational economic issues or economic premises. According to Hoyt, the high-income or influential residents of a city often lead the direction of urban growth. Thus, there are usually several sectors of populations within an urban area; as each group increases in population, it exerts pressure in one direction. Each group seeks the maximization of amenities and space. Socializing with others on a common educational, cultural, or social level is a secondary consideration relative to the income differentiation. Hoyt also observed that low-income families tend to locate in areas farthest from high-income areas, and they usually live on the least desirable land—alongside railroad, commercial, or industrial areas.

Bands of commercial retail businesses tend to string out along main thoroughfares, indicating the importance of access. Finally, as the urban area expands its perimeter, the city core is occupied by the poor or becomes unoccupied.

The net result over time is that a zone of high-class housing tends to be located on one side of the city rather than in a ring, as indicated by Burgess. The high-class housing tends to settle in the direction of the prevailing wind, upwind and upstream from the concentrations of industry.

The sector theory, in regard to high-class (income) residential locations, has the following general characteristics.

1. High-grade residential growth tends to proceed, from a given point of origin, along established lines of travel or toward other existing nuclei of building or trading centers. This latter concept is often referred to as scatterization. An example in a current context would be

the tendency of residential development to infill the sprawl that results when a mall develops in the urban–rural fringe, usually at a major intersection. The mall seeks the appropriate micro location, with expectations of residential growth in the area. However, as situs theory has shown, there is an interdependence in land uses such that the presence of the mall helps to attract the residential development. The concepts of scatterization and situs address one of the criticisms of the sector theory—that the model does not deal with the activity of the interstitial areas. These concepts consider the land lying between the transportation routes, the high-rent districts, and the commercial areas not covered in the basic theory.

2. The zone of high-rent (high-price) areas tends to progress toward high ground, which is desirable because it is free from the risk of flood, and to spread along lakes, bays, rivers, and ocean frontage, where such waterfronts are not used for industry.

3. High-rent residential districts tend to grow toward the section of the city that has free, open country beyond its edges and away from "dead end" sections that are limited by natural or artificial barriers to expansion.

4. The higher-priced residential neighborhoods tend to grow toward the homes of the leaders of the community.

5. Trends of movement of office buildings, banks, and stores pull the higher-priced residential neighborhoods in the same general direction (scatterization).

6. High-grade residential areas tend to develop along the fastest existing transportation lines.

7. The growth of high-rent neighborhoods continues in the same direction for long periods of time.

8. Deluxe, high-rent apartment areas tend to be established near the business center in old residential areas.

9. Real estate promoters may bend the direction of high-grade residential growth. Despite the general tendencies for residential growth to direct overall urban growth, given a desirable topography (hills and lakes) and some major arterials, developers, via advertising campaigns and marketing ploys, can alter the growth patterns of a city.

Hoyt noted that the age and condition of structures in residential areas are important factors in the determination of price and rent. The sector theory is the spatial embodiment of the housing policy that guided the FHA and hence contributed to the urban base in many communities. The essence of the policy, as noted earlier, is a concept called *filtering*: people are socially and economically mobile in an upward direction, toward more money and bigger and newer homes, and housing stock is mobile downwardly.

Filtering, in the context of the sector theory, would indicate that higher-income people move out from the central city into new houses built on the fringe of the city (suburbs). Their move opens up the existing housing, which was previously occupied by the high-income group, to the next lower socioeconomic tier. This sequence continues until the oldest or least desirable housing is occupied by the lowest income group. This concept of the mobility of people and the occupancy of existing housing stock was the guiding principle for government financing and financial reinsurance. The encouragement of capital funding, in this context, has contributed to the current urban form of many cities: a decaying central core or one that has heavy economic activity from nine to five and limited residential and economic activity afterward.

The filtering concept and its influence on capital investment became mixed with the impact of the automobile, which allowed urban decentralization first along major arterials and then in the interstitial areas. The mixture contributes to the general application of the sector model and the usefulness of its predictive potential in projecting directions of urban growth.

(c) MULTIPLE NUCLEI THEORY

In 1945, Chauncy Harris and Edward Ullman, both geographers, developed the multiple nuclei theory as a modification of the concentric zone and sector models.[35] The multiple nuclei theory holds that the spatial structure of an area does not necessarily develop from a single central core; instead, urban areas develop about several distinct nuclei. (See Figure 3.12.) The multiple nuclei concept shows a shift from the overflow premise of the growth to an emphasis on the automobile effect. In this theory, cities have a cellular structure, with distinctive types of land use grouping around the nuclei (or growth points) in given urban areas.

The grouping of the land use is tied to the needs of specialist activities. On a micro level, the nature of these associations of land use groups is addressed by the situs concept. The implications of using the

[35] Chauncey D. Harris and Edward L. Ullman, "The Nature of Cities," *Annals of the American Academy of Political and Social Science*, 242 (November 1945): 7–17.

situs concept on a macro level can be linked to four factors that influence in various ways the spatial distribution of activities within a city. First, certain activities require specialized facilities. These facilities can be grouped, based on the features of their sites, as either naturally endowed or produced by human endeavor (this links back to physical and legal productivity and the spatial dimension of these issues as situs environment). A macro-level example of the site endowments preferred by land uses requiring special facilities is the location of the CBD at the point of maximal accessibility within the overall community.

The second factor affecting urban structure is the premise that cohesion can generate profit. The expansion of situs association to a macro level is reflected in the issue of the economics of agglomeration. Profits can be made by grouping complementary or even competitive uses. The benefits of closely observing a major competitor cannot be overvalued.

The third factor is another macro-level extension of the associational dimension of situs. Associations can be detrimental as well as beneficial. Some land uses are best not placed in proximity to one another. As Hoyt pointed out, high-income residences are rarely near-neighbors to heavy industry.

Finally, as identified in the economic environmental dimension of situs, certain activities cannot afford the rents or prices of the most desirable sites (in the overall city). Therefore, the nature of the activities and their ability to pay for the economic commodity of location force them to group in areas of less costly land. Examples of the lower-end grouping because of economic competition for sites are cheaper housing and bulk storage facilities.

As shown in Figure 3.12, as the urban area grows, the number of nuclei increases. The multiple nuclei theory promulgates the economic fact that the internal geography of cities owes much to the unique characteristics of individual sites as they link to more general social and economic factors. Given these specialized requirements, the history of individual cities becomes important in understanding the existing and future land use patterns. The origin of a city and its economic base establish the general factors that encourage the sorting out of urban activities and the distinctive land use patterns that confirm and develop the preexisting pattern that forms the foundation of the future development pattern of a city. Therefore, the timing of the city's growth thrust (which may be cyclical) may influence the nature and pattern of the city over time.

The individual centers of development (nuclei) are connected to the central economic forces of the area by major transportation arteries

Figure 3.12 Multiple Nuclei Land Use Pattern

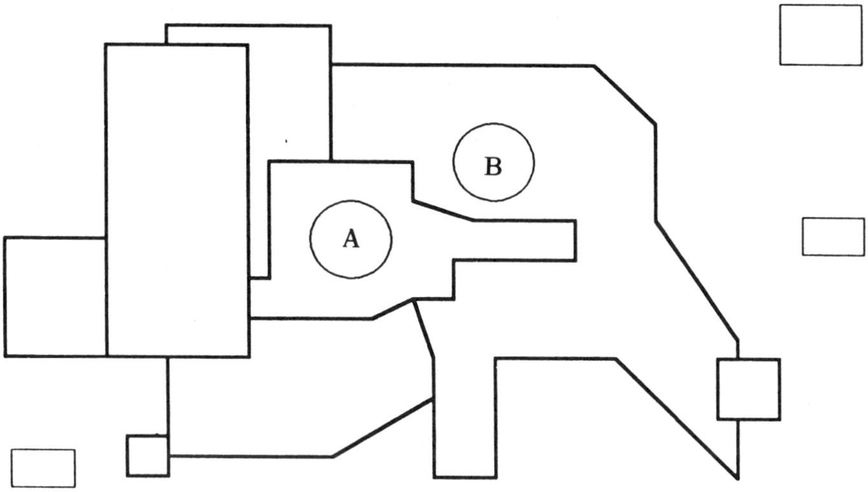

Adapted from Chauncey D. Harris and Edward L. Ullman, "The Nature of Cities," *Annals of the American Academy of Political and Social Science*, 242 (November 1945): 7–17.

that may cross areas of little or no development. Land located between the nuclei is usually raw land, held in expectation of a rise in value related to a change in its use. Areas A and B in Figure 3.12 are major economic nuclei of the city; they may consist of commerce, manufacturing, or a mix of other economic activities.

In summary, Harris and Ullman suggested that the development of urban spatial structure resulted from a combination of the following four factors:

1. Certain activities require specialized facilities; for example, financial institutions need easy access to law firms.
2. Certain land uses are priced out of locating in specific areas; for example, low-income families, unable to afford more desirable land, seldom locate next to the highest-priced housing.
3. Dissimilar activities are often detrimental to one another; for example, the odors from a petrochemical complex are incompatible with a high-class restaurant or the needs of commercial retailers for a clean environment.
4. Similar activities often group together because they benefit from proximity; for example, automobile dealers cluster to facilitate comparison shopping.

The multiple nuclei model is a general model in that it allows for unique urban situations and is an aggregation of the situs concept. The model is premised on basic economic issues that emphasize the competition of land uses for given sites or neighborhoods and attribute much of the current urban structure to the automobile effect. The automobile effect, a causal factor (along with the overflow effect) of decentralization, addresses the criticisms of the sector theory by considering the land use activities of interstitial areas. The "newer" cities of the west and south can be characterized by this effect, as can the suburban areas of the older cities of the north and midwest. The essence of the automobile effect as it relates to urban structure and especially to the multiple nuclei concept is that accessibility becomes a key component of understanding and forecasting land use patterns. (This issue is emphasized in the discussion of rent theory models in a later subsection.) The importance of transportation in land use is central to the axial theory of structure.

(d) RADIAL CORRIDOR (AXIAL) THEORY

The radial corridor or axial theory of urban structure is often viewed as a subset of either the zonal theory or the sector theory, even though it preceded both of those models.[36] Much of the arterial component of the sector theory is attributed to the influence of the radial corridor model. The radial corridor theory, attributed by many to Richard M. Hurd's 1903 classic book *The Principles of City Land Values,* is based on the observation that urban development often takes place along major transportation routes such as highways, railroads, and waterways. Figure 3.13 illustrates the radial corridor theory. Hurd, a mortgage banker, devised this concept to help his company make investment and mortgage underwriting decisions. Hurd took a historic approach; he studied American and foreign cities to identify the origins and patterns of development in cities, in order to more fully understand real estate decisions.

Hurd's practical approach to the problem resulted in the following observation about cities and land use patterns: Cities tend to be organic in composition and growth. Hurd stated that cities grow in conformity with biological laws and in harmony with the law of evolution; increasing differentiation is accompanied by increasing integration.

[36] Andrews, *supra* note 2, Part I, at 22.

Figure 3.13 Radial Corridor (Axial) Land Use Pattern

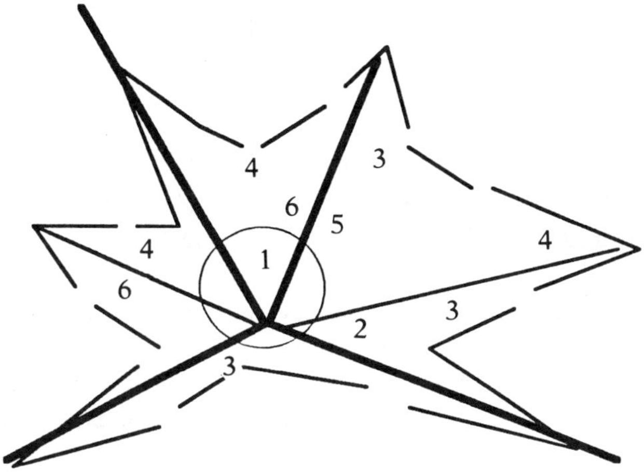

The organic view influences the perception of the origins of cities. According to Hurd, cities originate at their point of most convenient contact with the outside world (this supports the economic base concept and the transshipment-point premise). Therefore, all modern cities are created by the same factors (accessibility for economic functions or "activities"). Given this uniformity of creation, all cities grow in either a central (the overflow effect) or an axial pattern. (Hurd's theory preceded the automobile era; it therefore lacks the interstitial development explanation.)

Because growth is both central and axial, all growth in cities consists of movement away from the point of origin in all directions. This pattern of movement is due to aggregation at the edges and pressure from the center (market supply and demand). Because the city has an organic or cellular type of growth, the expansion is outward from "center points" (key activities). The points can be the center of the city or multiple subcenters.

In Figure 3.13, the central business district and the industrial area are shown as area 1. From that central core, retail and service-type businesses tend to locate along the transportation routes (e.g., area 2). Area 3 usually contains residential rental units that are inhabited by lower-income families because the area has lower rent levels and proximity to public transportation. The middle-class population is to be found in area 4. This area is far enough away from the busy commercial and industrial areas to be desirable, yet close enough to transportation corridors and public facilities such as hospitals and schools to be considered convenient. Beyond area 4 are located the higher-income residential areas and open spaces that provide seclusion.

Here again, urban growth causes each area to encroach on the adjacent area. Industrial parks and commercial facilities can be expected to spring up in areas 3, 4, and 5.

(e) SUMMARY OF SOCIAL ECOLOGY MODELS

The social ecology models, in general, indicate the relationship between socioeconomic factors and land use patterns. These models are basically expressed in physically descriptive modes, but they allow for the consideration of dynamic growth and causal explanations of the forms of land use patterns. The organic theme that runs through these models and their cellular context of growth (whether from one center or from multiple points of activity) are directly linked to the understanding and delineation of trade areas. The concept of bid-rent theory and the efficient location model offered by the trade-off between price or land rent and distance from the central business district cannot be separated from the socioeconomics of the ecology camp, nor can the distribution of demographic activities be separated from the general location of urban business activity and the hierarchy of land uses.

Given the link of social ecology to economic rationale, the academic need for the formulation of more analytical models is inseparable from the descriptive analysis of the social ecologist. The social ecology models also service the intuitive approaches required in many business decisions.

(f) RENT THEORY MODELS—GRADIENTS

A second school of thought on urban structure is that of rent theory. The rent theorist sees the city structure as a trade-off of site rents and transportation cost. Site rents are basically a location return over and above the return to the physical productivity of a parcel of land. Therefore, the return to a site is the result of a trade-off between the overall accessibility of a given site within the city and the competitive price that has to be paid to occupy a given locus in the urban terrain. By extracting the physical productivity of the site in the calculation of site rent, the measure of rent becomes the price of location. The rent theory school of urban structure views the overall city from the perspective of the economics of location. The central concern of the economics of location is to identify the allocation of income spent for location as an economic good in its own right. This perception of the city is illustrated by a model designed by William Alonso, a land economist. (See Figure 3.14.)

The Alonso model views location choices as being measured by the income or dollars allocated between the site rent and transportation cost, at varying distances from the CBD (see Figure 3.14). The vertical axis represents the income to be spent on location. The model suggests that, as one goes away from the center of the city (or the major focal point of any neighborhood), the site rents decline per unit of area (i.e., per square foot) and transportation costs increase. (See Figure 3.15.)

Alonso's model forms an analytical model of urban structure, by showing the location decision to be an economic choice. However, the basic Alonso model is limited to a demand perspective based on the trade-off between the choice of a given location within the overall city as measured from a central focal point and the cost of transport between the center and the location. The transportation cost can be viewed as negative accessibility.

In terms of real estate issues in the shaping of a city, the trade-off is between the site's relative position and the accessibility of the locus.

Figure 3.14 Alonso Model of Urban Structure

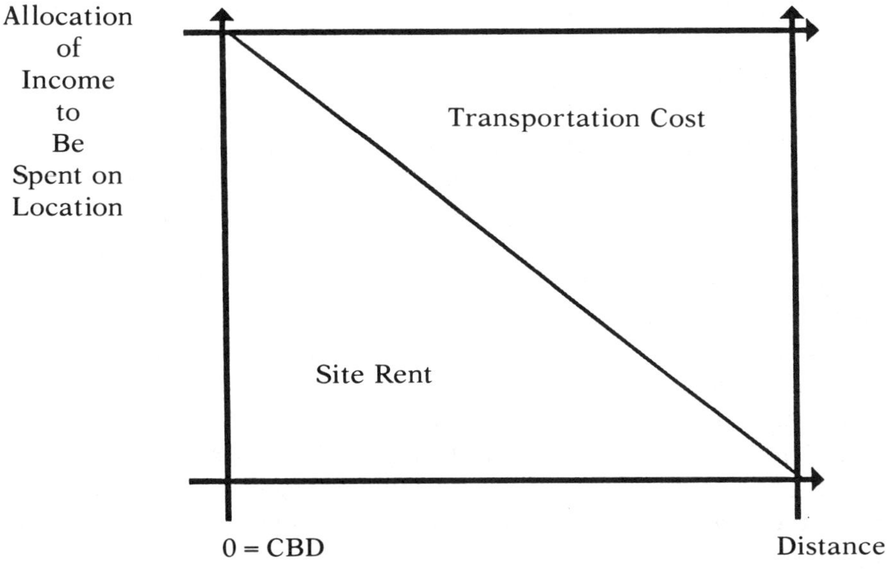

Figure 3.15 Land Use Competition Illustrated by Bid-Rents

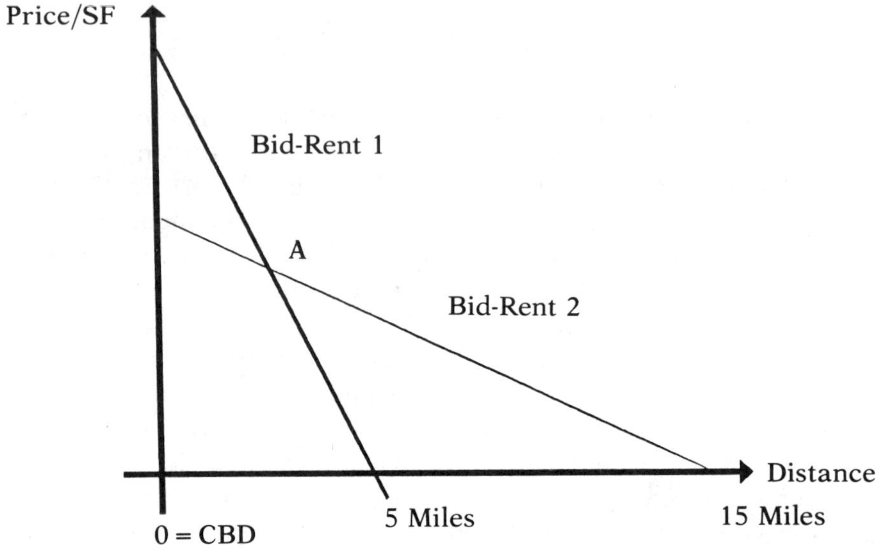

The economics of choice behind the Alonso model is important to real estate decisions because, on a competitive basis, the choice between location and accessibility within the overall city can help in the analysis of the competition of alternative land uses within a given area or general neighborhoods of the community.

The rate of trade-off between location and accessibility is the element of comparison. The trade-off is graphically represented by the slopes of the bid-rent curves for different land uses. The bid-rent curve concept represents the bid price for a use for a location within the overall city. The bid price for a use is relative to alternative or competitive uses. Figure 3.15 illustrates the bid-rent curves for two competitive uses within an urban structure. Bid-rent curve 1 represents the location/rent/transportation cost trade-off of office facilities. Bid-rent curve 2 depicts the schedule of a retail use's income as it would be allocated between location and transportation cost in the urban market.

The case depicted in Figure 3.15 shows that office use outbids retail use, out to point A. Within the urban structure, point A is approximately 3 miles outside the central business district. At 5 miles, office use bids zero for a location. From 3 miles to 5 miles, office use is outbid by other uses. At 5 miles, office facilities cannot make a rational or economic bid for location.

Bid-rent curve 2 shows retail use outbidding office space use from point A to the 5-mile marker. Therefore, in areas that are 3 to 5 miles outside the CBD, the land pattern should be *dominated* by retail uses. (In reality, other uses will be present within the zones. The concern of the model's theory is the dominance of use types.) As Figure 3.15 illustrates, of the two uses (office and retail), retail use dominates from 3 miles to 15 miles. At 15 miles, retail is outbid in the market. In this case, it can be surmised that agriculture outbids retail at the 15-mile distance from the CBD. Therefore, 15 miles can be considered the economic boundary of the urban land use (the economic city limits).

Figure 3.16 applies this concept of the economics of location as a process of analyzing urban structure to the general competition of commercial and residential land markets in Austin, Texas. The empirical test of the rent theorist's model, based on sales price per square foot per land use type, shows that the commercial market tends to dominate the residential market up to a distance of about 6 miles on the south side of Austin. It is essential to note that the residential market does exist within the dominant area of the commercial market; however, in the majority of site situations, commercial activities would tend to outbid residential uses for most sites. Any given site could alter the general pattern because of the attributes of the specific parcel.

Figure 3.16 Bid-Rent Curves, Austin, Texas

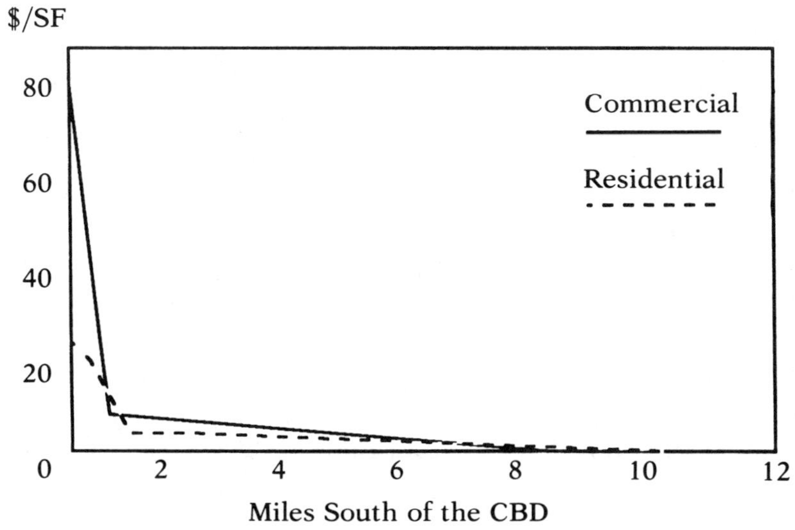

Another concern of the empirical comparison of the commercial and residential markets is that the trade-off of site rent (location) and accessibility to the CBD is not the strict linear relationship shown in the Alonso model. The trade-off depicted in the Alonso model is based on the demand perspective's allocating income between two distinct goods. The curvilinear nature of actual bid-rent curves (see Figure 3.17) depicts the market forces of (1) limited supply in proximity to the CBD and (2) demand allocation for the two goods. The impact of available supply on the form of bid-rent curves was addressed by Muth in his economic model of the city. Muth illustrated that the physical limits of supply in a mononuclear city result in asymptotic curves that decline rapidly from a high central city site rent to the lower rents per unit paid at the fringe of the city. This is partly attributed to the geometric potential increase in the competitive amounts of land available as distance from the city core is increased. No topographical or transportation problems are assumed in the city design.

The rent theory approach has also been applied to the density of population settlement within the geographical limits of the city. Most

Figure 3.17 Bid-Rent Curve Influenced by Limited Supply (Bid-Rent Curve = Aggregate Demand Curve for Location)

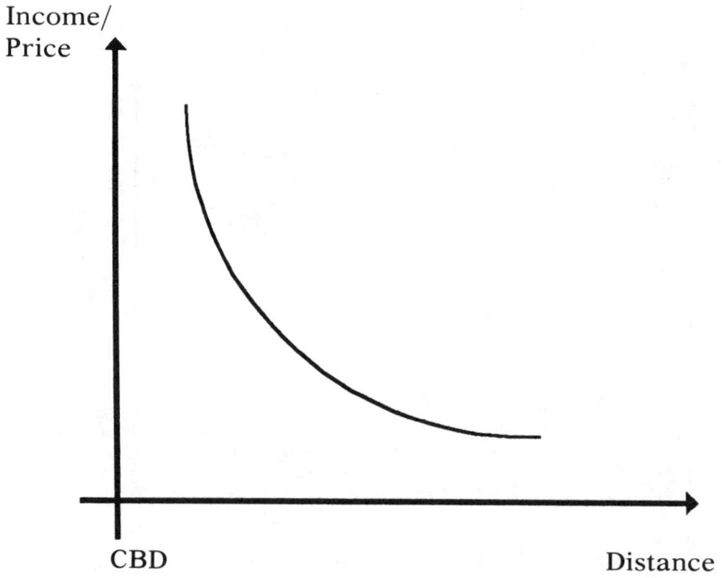

population gradient studies have shown the geometric pattern of the Muth bid-rent curves.

Although they make several assumptions that lose the descriptive insights and capacity for flexibility that characterize the social ecology models, the rent theory models enable an analytical framework that is missing in the ecologist models. They also contribute to market analysis because they are aggregate or macro-level applications of gravity models and central place theory, which are key to retail trade area delineation. Therefore, the rent theory format offers an alternative to the ecologist insight to the location decision process. Social ecologists view the overall environment; rent theorists extend the economics of the individual location choice to the underlying land use pattern of the overall city. The economics of location are key to the location decision of land uses and therefore to the process of market delineation.

§ 3.8 URBAN STRUCTURE AND REAL ESTATE MARKETS

These theories of urban structure are methods of understanding the impact of geography on real estate markets. Geographical impact enables the identification of substitutable tracts of land, land use support systems, and distinct market segments. Both approaches described above are useful for identifying land use clusters and directions of growth.

The urban structure of any city establishes the context of real estate market analysis. This context guides the conceptual structure of the market. Once the conceptual structure is understood, a process for analyzing markets can be established.

Both theories of urban structure described above can be linked to the delineation of retail market analysis. The conceptual linkage of multiple nuclei models and rent theory enables a delineation of the economic boundaries around specific nuclei. The economic boundary of the market, based on rent theory, is established where the combined cost of the site rent and the travel cost intersects with the combined cost from another site. The rent theorists' perception of the economic boundaries between two competitive facilities is depicted in Figure 3.18. The two sites, loci A and B, are depicted in both the multiple nuclei schematic and the rent theory graph. The site rent for locus A is the amount E. The site rent for locus B is C. The transportation costs for A and B are represented by the lines radiating out from the rent measures (E and C). The combined costs are the summation of the site rents and the delivery cost. The delivery cost is either the cost

Figure 3.18 Example of Multiple Nuclei Theory Linked to Rent Theory

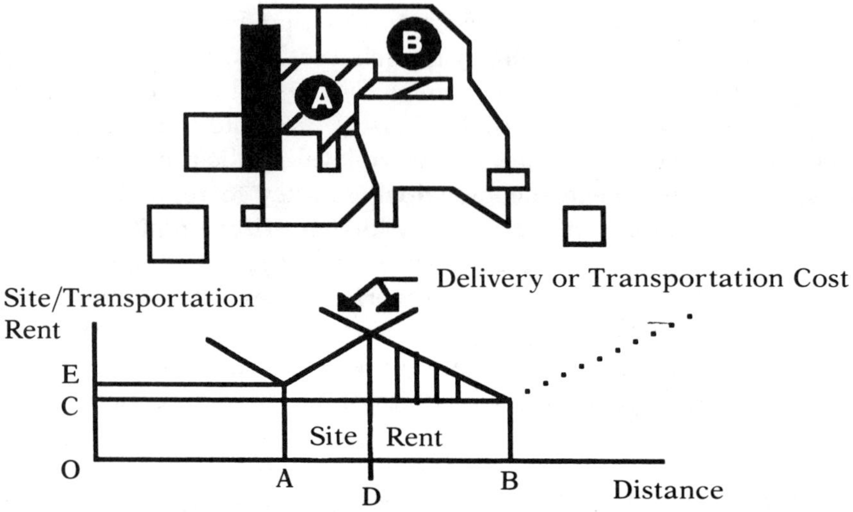

of delivering a good to a customer or the cost to the customer of acquiring a good. For example, the cost of a grocery item is not only the retail cost at the checkout counter but also the opportunity cost of time and travel to make the purchase. The point of cost intersection in Figure 3.18 is a point of indifference. If located at point D, a customer would have equal costs for acquiring goods from point A or point B.

The significance of Figure 3.18 is that it illustrates the relationship of rent theory to a location process that can help to explain or further document the socioeconomic and physical dimensions of the ecological models. These models can often be used for adjustments to the rent theory approach.

Figure 3.18 also illustrates the application of urban structure theory to market delineation—a connection that enables an understanding of economic location. The productivity of real estate is influenced by both economic and physical location, and economic location analysis is more than a simple identification of the physical position of one property in relation to another.[37] (The location analysis process was depicted in § 3.4 and linked there to the study of urban structure.)

Overall, both market analysis and location analysis begin with identifying the economic activities in the neighborhood or market area by

[37] Andrews, *supra* note 3, Chapter 2.

physical, geographical, political, and socioeconomic boundaries or giving them an economic time–distance delineation. The key activities or features to identify in a neighborhood are those that attract or motivate people. These economic magnets may be major employers, recreational activities, institutions, physical features such as rivers and roads, or services. In their ability to generate activities, they function like the major draws of a shopping center, attracting people from other neighborhoods into the subject area. Identification of these linkages and of the related uses that develop around them helps to define the associations between land uses. The processes of analyzing these locational activities were described in earlier sections on situs and urban structure theory. The key ingredients can now be addressed on both a micro and macro level.

The nature of the land use activity, the enterprise, and the location decision cannot be divorced in economic analysis. Activities may complement, serve, compete with, or be a total nuisance to one another. As the location process comes full cycle, the relationship among the concepts of structure, situs, and market analysis becomes obvious.

The linkage between the building blocks of location theory (situs and structure) and market analysis is based on real estate's being physically fixed in one location and yet subject to the ebb and flow of economic change in the surrounding environment. The environment—or, even more, the total urban environment as it relates to a specific neighborhood—is central to understanding value, returns, and risk of real estate. Like the neighborhood analysis, the analysis of the environment considers social, physical, economic, and institutional features. These features are immobile. Even so, the environment, the surroundings through which goods and people must travel, is often described in terms of accessibility and activities.

Understanding of the locational factors enables a thorough analysis of a specific parcel of real estate and allows the analyst to identify the relationship of the parcel to the total urban setting. The urban setting is the economic stadium in which the real estate game is played. By relating the urban setting to a specific site, aggregate urban data can be reduced to key points that influence the neighborhood and the subject parcel.

Finally, understanding the locational dimension of a site and its relation to the urban structure enables the development of real estate forecasting skills. The information afforded by each type of analysis can be pulled together for forecasting in the process of land use succession.

§ 3.9 LAND USE SUCCESSION

Urban structure theory establishes the spatial context in which real estate decisions must occur; succession theory investigates the effect of time on location decisions and the immediate market environment.

The process of land use succession is the concept behind neighborhood life cycles. Specifically, it identifies the highest and best use of land.

If locational analysis were to be viewed as an ecological chain that links one land use to surrounding activities, then succession would allow the identification of a break or a change in the ecological chain. By observing changes in the nature of activities and physical properties in the area, analysts can begin to foretell possible changes in a subject property. The areas surrounding universities provide a good example. Older, single-family homes are converted to boarding houses—a change in density, not a change in use or a major change in structure. As the demand for residential space near the universities increases, the old boarding houses are razed and new garden apartment buildings are constructed. They represent a change in structure but not in use. Over time, the apartment buildings suffer deterioration and obsolescence; they cannot compete readily with the newer facilities in the neighborhood. The next phase of the life cycle is to convert the existing structures into condominiums, continuing the residential use and superficially changing the physical structure. However, the conversion significantly changes the economic and legal structure. In total, the succession of uses experiences a break in the ecological chain. Initially, the activities and associations vary slightly; however, once the system is altered, the potential for change increases exponentially.

These trends can be identified in other scenarios. Residential facilities are frequently converted to office space—a change in use but not a major change in physical structure. The change may indicate the presence of market preferences that may support, in time, the construction of new office facilities in a previously residential neighborhood.

In this vein, various factors that may help the documentation of expected trends can be identified. These indicators may enable analysts to reduce the data found in a citywide forecast to useful information for the subject neighborhood and site. Andrews, in his classic work on urban land economics, identified several indicators of possible change (see Table 3.1).[38]

[38] Andrews, *id.*, Chapter 5.

Table 3.1 Potential Land Use Change Indicators

1. Investment return	6. Use controls
2. Market competition	7. Situs quality
3. Vacancies	8. Property turnover
4. Physical	9. Family cycle
5. Structure density	10. Structure value

Source: Richard B. Andrews, *Urban Land Economics and Public Policy* (New York: Free Press, 1971).

Despite the variety of indicators of succession, the economic issues causing and resulting from land use changes are of two general types: functional weakness in the existing properties, and external competitive pressures that force a change in the existing situs pattern.

Firm productivity analysis results from the ability to identify patterns and the various degrees of changes in the patterns. If productivity analysis is done well, the complications of the market analysis are often reduced. The space–time nature of a real estate product forms the basis of the unit of comparison and the revenue unit. These two concepts are key measurements in market analysis.

Market analysis is concerned with supply and demand for specific or alternative uses. By linking the succession potential of change to the spatial dimensions of situs and structure, the key elements of the urban real estate product can be linked to the supply and demand issues underlying market analysis. The productivity attributes of a parcel—its physical, legal, and locational attributes—must be matched to the desires and wants of potential buyers. The principle of substitution, defined by the delineation of the competitive supply of properties, is the heart of market analysis and the basis for a property's valuation or investment analysis. Therefore, the analysis of a property's productivity attributes (the fundamentals of real estate or any product) is essential to estimating value, analyzing investment returns, and ultimately arriving at appropriate real estate decisions.

§ 3.10 RELATIONSHIP BETWEEN PRODUCTIVITY AND REAL ESTATE MARKET STRUCTURE

Market analysis is primarily concerned with the analysis of supply and demand for a product. First, however, the product must be understood. Because real estate is physically fixed, it must be recognized in market analysis within a spatial or geographical context and characterized as a heterogeneous product. The basis for its heterogeneity is that each parcel is unique because of its location and its physical characteristics, both of which illustrate the spatial context. However, this basis can be misleading, if limited to the geographical context. The economic essence of real estate is that it is space to be used by an economic activity over time. The economic activity, in turn, relates to other activities at various locations.

The recognition of real estate as a space–time product in a spatial–locational context enables two important aspects in the analysis of supply and demand. One aspect is that, even if real estate is perceived to be heterogeneous and unique, there is still a relatively flexible degree of substitution between different sites, which allows them to be compared. A site with certain physical attributes—for example, a rolling terrain located near an intersection, with exposure to an interstate highway and rail access—can be a viable alternative to a nearby site that has level topography, rail access, frontage on a major highway, and good exposure, but indirect access to the interstate.

The second aspect is that real estate, though physically fixed, is economically flexible. A parcel of real estate may be physically lined to a particular locus, but the concept of location is an economic variable that can change over time. Real estate is space being used in time segments to house economic activities. As the surrounding neighborhood changes, the support system for the existing use can change, and that change can affect the use of the property, the market for the property, and the transfer price that may be received. Therefore, the market for any given parcel of real estate cannot be analyzed without first analyzing the use. If the standard for value estimation is the market value concept, then the standard for use must be the highest and best use concept. The analysis of the use will then enable a comparison between heterogeneous sites and a measure of the degree of substitutability.

To understand real estate markets, then, the concept of highest and best use must be thoroughly understood. How is use, which defines the product, linked to the market structure? As described previously, a key element in real estate market structure is the geographical or spatial dimension; the existing activities in a community are the support system for the use on the site being appraised. This support system of land uses directs the quantity, quality, and duration of returns and the value for a given site over time. From these are derived the demand for a given type of substitutable site and the availability of supply in a given city, area, or neighborhood.

An understanding of the economic base of the community is essential for any appraisal. Before the space for a certain type of use can be absorbed, there must be demand for the activities, goods, or services characterized by that use. Evidence for a demand for a given use (and hence, space for that use) is illustrated by employment of people in that activity. The activity, whether a product or a service, is conducted because of a demand for it among final consumers.

The economic essence of the community (or neighborhood) directs the land use activities and land use patterns in an area. These establish the geographical pattern of the real estate market and enable a projection of supply and demand for any given property use.

§ 3.11 CHARACTERISTICS OF REAL ESTATE MARKETS

The geographical characteristics of real estate markets may require alteration of the basic assumptions of an efficient market that are often used in analyzing financial markets.[39] The productivity attributes of real estate can even lead to this question: Are the assumptions of an open or purely competitive market, which underlies the traditional appraisal process, appropriate?[40]

The efficient market is a concept based on assumptions about the behavior of buyers and sellers and the characteristics of products. Acceptance of the heterogeneity of the real estate product, based on its physical, legal, and locational attributes, can result in a broad range of reactions toward the economic behavior of different parties in the spatial confines of realty markets. The decision criteria and the motivations on the part of end users, investors, and speculators can result in a very diverse market pattern in a given neighborhood or even for a specific parcel. The result is that real estate markets can illustrate a lack of the characteristics often associated with a high degree of efficiency. The following description of the attributes of an efficient market and those associated with real estate demonstrates this point.

The goods or services in an efficient market are essentially homogeneous items that can be readily substituted for one another. The goods are assumed to be fungible; that is, they can be readily substituted or easily mixed and separated.

[39] American Institute of Real Estate Appraisers, *The Appraisal of Real Estate*, 10th Edition (Chicago: AIREA, 1988).

[40] Byrl Boyce and William Kinnard, *Appraising Real Property* (Lexington, MA: D. C. Heath and Co., 1984).

Except in the abstract sense, real estate is not fungible. The heterogeneity of real estate is considered unique. Each parcel of real estate is one of a kind, and its location is fixed. No two parcels of real estate are physically identical; certain parcels may be economically similar and substitutable, but they differ at least geographically. This emphasizes the importance of productivity analysis in delineating the market for real estate.

In an efficient market, a large number of buyers and sellers create a competitive, free market, and none of these participants has a large enough share of the market to have a direct and measurable influence on price. This is not often the case in markets that are spatially delineated.

In real estate, usually only a few buyers and sellers are acting at one time, in one price range, and at one location for any type of property. This suggests that, because of the geographical nature of real estate, an oligopolistic structure exists in real estate markets and price setters are active in those markets. The high relative value of real estate requires strong or debt-supported purchasing power. Real estate markets are highly sensitive to changes in wage levels, the stability of income, and the number of individuals employed. Construction costs, housing costs, and rent levels are affected by the ability of market participants to pay.

Insights to the oligopolistic nature of real estate can help analysts to recognize the key players in any given market. Because there are usually only a few players, an understanding of their decision process is important. The nature of oligopoly is that, because there are only a few suppliers in any given market, the actions of each supplier (seller, developer, subdivider, and so on) can affect the market and impact on the actions and decisions of every other player. The behavior of each seller, buyer, or investor is important.

This interrelationship is contrary to pure competition, in which no one player can influence the direction of the market. By contrast, in real estate, one major developer can alter not only a given neighborhood but an entire city's form. To best understand the process of estimating value and returns, appraisers must understand the objectives, goals, and mind-set of the individuals who comprise a local market. This understanding is achieved in real estate by linking the urban structure to the market form and to the decision criteria of the key players in a local or given market.

Buyers and sellers in an efficient market are knowledgeable and fully informed about market conditions, the behavior of others, past market activity, product quality, and product substitutability; buyers and sellers in real estate often are not. A premium is often paid for real estate information in the form of appraisal and market analysis services. Information on bids, offers, and sales, which is readily available in efficient and competitive markets, is often nonexistent in real estate markets.

Buyers and sellers in real estate markets are not always well-informed about the product. Because most people do not buy and sell real estate frequently, they are not familiar with the procedures and do not know how to judge a property. Information on bids, offers, and sales, related to a particular property or similar properties, is not readily available to buyers or sellers. Therefore, it is important to not only identify the relevant information required in real estate but also to determine how the information is analyzed and processed by the influential players in the specific market under study. Real estate market analysis is concerned with determining the decision criteria and objectives of the markets' movers and shakers.

The analysis process is helped by the spatial dimension and its link to productivity analysis. The spatial dimension on both a micro and a macro level affects market structure. The spatial distribution of suppliers and sellers and the existing and potential demand are sensitive components of the market structure. The result is often unequal bargaining powers that determine how property is used and valued. Spatial constraints that limit the number of suppliers of real estate services alter the competitive characteristics of the market and direct how the negotiating, marketing, and pricing of realty facilities are determined.

In real estate markets, demand can be volatile. Population may suddenly shift into or out of a locality. A sudden influx of population results in high prices, because months or years may be needed to construct buildings or develop an area. A sudden outward migration caused by economic conditions could result in an oversupply relative to previous periods and, therefore, in lower prices. The general summation of these market qualities is that real estate markets are risky, if not uncertain, and require decision and analysis models that incorporate these issues. The timing issue reflected in absorption analysis and the spatial dimension of competition delineated by capture potential are key elements that help to integrate the real estate market concerns with the oligopolistic form, uncertainty, and spatial market forces.

The end result of this integration may be a hierarchy of valuation techniques rather than the traditional equivalence of the three approaches. To fit the format of the spatial oligopoly, the process might emphasize the application of the income analysis, sales comparison techniques that emphasize a market inference approach, and, finally, cost analysis, but only in an investment context so that it reflects the effect of competition.

The income approach, specifically the discounted cash flow and yield capitalization models, allows explicit consideration of expectations and decision criteria on a year-by-year basis over an intermediate-length time frame. The sales comparison approach is limited to the short term, when attempting to emphasize expectations. The cost approach approximates value theoretically only in the long run and almost exclusively for new buildings. It allows limited analysis of market or investor expectations. The significance of these issues will become evident in the application of market analysis to different property types and, specifically, as market analysis is linked to the appraisal process.

Valuation cannot be appropriately conducted or documented without sufficient market analysis and an understanding of market structure. Market structure is contingent on the productivity of the asset and the spatial dimension of real estate. Location is an essential concern of asset productivity and a spatial market structure. Therefore, real estate valuation, investment, market and risk analysis, and development cannot be conducted without a thorough understanding of location on both a macro and micro level.

§ 3.12 CONCLUSION

Location, an important fundamental in establishing the economic worth of real estate, can be considered on three levels: (1) the specific site and its internal design, (2) the situs relating a specific parcel and its land use to the immediate neighborhood and to the total urban environment, and (3) the urban structure, which considers the site and the neighborhood in relation to the aggregated market and anatomy of the city (or metroplex).

The three levels displace the old adage of location, location, and location as being the three most important factors in the value of real estate. However, when considered as three levels in a continuum from the microscopic view of the site to the macro-level concerns of the city, the locational or spatial dimension establishes the basis for understanding of a distinct capital asset and the market structure or environment in which it functions. In terms of a process, the location analysis links to the market structure, which then sets the context for decision making and the selection of appropriate decision tools.

Four

Alternative Cash Flow Returns and Related Real Estate Mathematics

§ 4.1 INTRODUCTION

The process proposed in this chapter illustrates the real estate mathematics that equates the productive physical space that is possible on a given site to the projection of a proforma cash flow. A solvency model is given, for allocation of the alternative cash flow returns from operation among the property, the financial structure, and the tax benefits.

Anticipated benefits are a major reason for the ownership of real estate. Therefore, the principle of anticipation is central to the value of realty.

Solvency, the comparison of money coming in to money going out, is the basis or chief measure of the principle of anticipation. The measurement of solvency reduces the analysis of real estate to its basic elements: the conversion of the space–time relationship (space to house an economic activity over time) to one of money–time. The essence of financial analysis is that money is being converted or compared over time.

The mathematics of finance is concerned with the cost of time choices; it measures pleasure in dollars and uses immediate gratification as the basis of comparison. A dollar received today gives the recipient a dollar to spend today on goods that can be traded for the dollar. Waiting a day costs the recipient the pleasure that the dollar can bring if it is received today. The key to the principle of anticipation is that *sooner* is *better* than later.

If the present is the best time to receive pleasure or money, then deferring the receipt of a benefit has a cost, in the form of lost opportunities. In financial terms, one opportunity would be to invest a dollar at the going interest rate today. However, because the dollar is not received today, it cannot be invested today. For each day the dollar is not received, the owner has lost interest for a day.

For example, if interest is 10 percent a day (that is, the return is 10 cents on a dollar), a dollar received and invested today will result in $1.10 by the end of tomorrow. However, if the person who owes the dollar does not pay it back until tomorrow, the opportunity to make the 10 cents is lost because the dollar was not available for investment. Because of this 10-cent loss, a dollar to be received tomorrow at a 10 percent interest rate is worth about 90 cents today. (Again, the basis is immediate gratification.)

The receipt of pleasures, benefits, or dollars today rather than tomorrow is the basis of the concept of compound interest. The mechanics of the procedure is to add the interest rate to the original amount and then multiply the procedure by the number of time periods. For example, if the interest rate is 10 percent per year and a dollar is invested today, the value of the investment three years from now would be calculated as:

$$\$(1 + .10)(1.10)(1.10) = \$1.331$$

A shorthand way of writing the procedure is $(1.10)^3$; a general way of symbolizing it is $(1 + i)^n$, where i = the interest rate and n = the time period.

To reverse the procedure and discount future dollars (to get an estimate of pleasure today), the mechanics of the financial model is the reciprocal of the compound interest process. The general discounting formula is $1/(1 + i)^n$. For the example of 10 percent over three years:

$$1/(1 + .10)^3 = 1/1.331 = .7513$$

The process implies that the value of a dollar to be received three years from today, discounted at 10 percent, is approximately 75 cents.

The usefulness of this mechanical process is that it can apply to any dollar measure, as shown for the following random amounts:

Dollar Amount	×	Factor: 10 Percent, Three Years	=	Value Today
$ 1.00	×	$\frac{1}{(1.10)^3} = .7513$	=	$.7513 ~ $.75
551.52	×	.7513	=	414.37
1,000.00	×	.7513	=	751.31
10,000.00	×	.7513	=	7,513.15

The above excursion into the mathematics of finance sets up the mechanical component of the money–time issue of real estate. The mathematics of finance brings closure to the issues of solvency and value relationships. The anticipated benefits or money received over time can be collapsed or discounted to a *value today.* The reduction of the cash flow over time to a single number, a value today, helps the decision maker's choice process.

The key to successfully understanding real estate lies in linking the space–time component of real estate to the money–time mechanics. As experience has shown, few investors have done this well.

§ 4.2 SPACE–TIME, MONEY–TIME EQUATION

The essence of real estate (especially in urban areas) is the space that can be used over time. The quantity and quality of the space are defined by the physical dimensions of a property.

An example is shown in Figure 4.1. A lot measuring 150 feet by 100 feet is situated at the intersection of two major streets. The lot abuts a residential neighborhood. The zoning classification supports the development of a moderate-to-high office facility and requires a 5-foot setback on the side of the property that abuts the residential land. A 10-foot building line, required at the rear of the property, prevents building on the 10-foot strip that ends at the rear property line. However, this 10-foot strip can be used for parking, unlike the 5-foot strip

Figure 4.1 Site Plot Plan, Commercial Use Adjacent to Residential Use

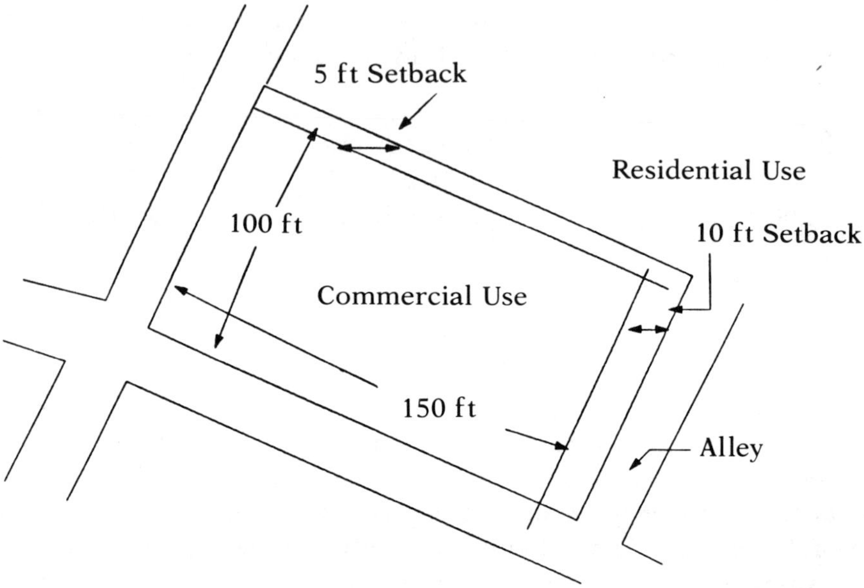

Lot	(150 ft. × 100 ft.)	= 15,000 sq. ft.
Setbacks; or areas lost to use	(150 ft. × 5 ft.)	= 750 sq. ft. on residential side lost to use
	(*95 ft. × 10 ft.)	= †950 sq. ft. at rear with restricted use

*Allowing for setback on residential side (100 ft. – 5 ft. setback = 95 ft.).
†This area can be paved and used for parking.

abutting the residential property, under the zoning specifications. The zoning restrictions allow the following land to be usable:

Land area (150 ft. × 100 ft.)	= 15,000 sq. ft.
Less set back (150 ft. × 5 ft.)	= 750
Land available for use (building and parking)	14,250 sq. ft.

The development regulations in this area and zoning class require that 300 square feet of parking be allotted for each 300 square feet of net leasable building area that is planned. The planned building efficiency based on the market trend is 85 percent.

Given the above legal constraints on the site, as specified in this case by the city's Land Development Department, there is a potential for determining a land use design equation, which yields a land allocation unit called a land unit equivalent (LUE).

General standards of building/parking ratios for the nation can be found in Urban Land Institute publications. In many areas, the parking ratio can be linked to gross building areas; restaurants' basis is often the number of seats in the restaurant. To understand the impact of specific physical and legal constraints on a property's cash flow, this information should be gathered from public and regulatory agencies in the jurisdiction where the property is located.

In this case, the city requires one parking area of 300 square feet for each 300 square feet of net leasable building footage constructed on the site. Because the example is based on a net leasable area requirement, the concept of the building efficiency ratio is introduced. The building efficiency ratio is the amount of the leasable or usable space in a building, in relation to the total building area. This ratio can be established initially by legal requirement or by market standards. The actual building efficiency in this case is the result of the final design. The 85 percent ratio was estimated from a comparison with similar facilities in the area. Three comparable office structures had the following net-to-gross area relationships:

	Comparable Facilities		
	1	2	3
Net leasable area (NLA)	17,275	13,050	11,146
Gross building area (GBA)	21,513	15,000	13,051
Building efficiency ratio (Er)	.803	.87	.854

The indicated range is 80.3 percent to 87 percent building efficiency for similar structures. Facility 3 is most similar to the subject property in style, design, and size. Based on this comparative analysis, the building efficiency ratio applied to the subject's design is *approximately* 85 percent.

The legal, physical, and market constraints on the proposed project result in the following information regarding the project's land allocation unit:

1. Regulations—For each 300 square feet of net leasable area (NLA) planned for the facility, 300 square feet of parking must

be allowed on the ground. The 300 square feet in the parking unit include not only the parking stalls, each measuring, say, 15 feet by 10 feet, but also allow for ingress and egress space, turning capacity, and door swing.

2. Market constraints—A building efficiency ratio (Er) of 85 percent is used to convert the net area to a gross area dimension to be allocated on the ground surface. This allocation is termed the building foot print (f.p.).

With 300 square feet of net leasable area (NLA) required for one parking unit (Pu), net area is converted to gross area by dividing the NLA by the building efficiency ratio (Er), to yield the gross building unit foot print ($GBA_{f.p.}$). The formula is:

$$\frac{NLA}{Er} = GBA_{f.p.}$$

Each $GBA_{f.p.}$ requires one parking unit (Pu), including parking stalls and access area. Using the information given on the subject property, that each 300 square feet of net leasable building area requires one 300-square-foot parking unit:

$$\frac{300}{.85} = 352.94 \text{ sq. ft.}$$

Adding the basic building foot print (352.94 square feet) to the parking unit (300 square feet) yields a base land unit of 652.94 square feet. This would be the end of the spatial calculation, if the subject structure were a one-story facility. However, the subject building is a three-story office building. Under the regulations, 300 square feet of parking (one Pu) must be allocated in the same ratio for the two stories above the ground level.

To comply with the regulations, the next step of the procedure is to convert the vertical requirements of the regulatory impact to the horizontal surface of the lot. The following addition to the base foot print equation is then introduced:

$$\text{Total parking requirements} = \text{Parking unit} \times \text{Number of stories}$$
$$TPU = Pu(S)$$

For the three-story office building in the example, where each parking unit must be 300 square feet:

$$900 = 300(3)$$

The total land allocation unit equation is then:

$$\begin{aligned} &\text{Building foot print} + \text{Surface parking} = \text{Total land per land allocation unit} \\ &352.94 \text{ sq. ft.} \quad + \quad 900 \text{ sq. ft.} \quad = 1{,}252.94 \text{ sq. ft.} \end{aligned}$$

Consideration of the number of stories affected by the parking unit regulations results in the basic land area per land allocation unit (LUE):

$$\begin{aligned} \text{Land area per LUE} &= GBA_{f.p.} + Pu(S) \\ &= 352.94 \text{ sq. ft.} + 300(3) \text{ sq. ft.} \\ &= 1252.94 \text{ sq. ft.} \end{aligned}$$

The land allocation unit used to allocate the usable site (total land area less unusable setbacks) between the land and building is:

$$\begin{aligned} LUE &= \frac{\text{Usable land area}}{\text{Land area per land allocation unit}} \\ &= \frac{14{,}250 \text{ sq. ft.}}{1{,}252.94 \text{ sq. ft.}} = 11.373 \text{ sq. ft.} \end{aligned}$$

See Appendix 4A for the overall LUE model stated in an algebraic format.

The land allocation unit is used to construct the allocation of the usable site between the total gross building area (as a foot print on the ground level) and the total parking area required by regulation and subject to the physical constraint of the site. (The foot print is the gross building area per floor.)

The format of the overall land and building area is:

$$A - Sb = GBA_{f.p.} \times LUE + Pu(S) \times LUE$$

where:

$A - Sb$ = usable area of site after setback is deducted ($A = 150 \times 100$ ft.; $Sb = 150 \times 5$ ft.)

Using the example:

$$A - Sb = (352.94 \times 11.373) + (300(3) \times 11.373)$$
$$= 14{,}250 \text{ sq. ft.}$$

An alternative format for land use allocation can be presented as follows:

	Total $GBA_{f.p.}$	Net Area per Foot Print ($GBA_{f.p.} \times Er$)
Building area per floor (352.94 sq. ft. × 11.373)	= 4,013.98 sq. ft.*	3,411.00 sq. ft.†
Parking area (900 sq. ft. × 11.373)	= 10,235.7 sq. ft.	
Total restricted site or usable site area	= 14,250.0 sq. ft. (rounded)	

* For computational use, revenue and expenses based on these physical dimensions are rounded to the nearest dollar.

† The net building area per floor is stated for convenience and is the basis of future revenue projection. It is calculated by ($GBA_{f.p.} \times LUE \times Er$) or 4,013.98 × .85 = 3,411.00.

The gross area of the structure establishes the basis for its cost. The net area identifies the space that can be leased out. The net leasable area establishes the maximum revenue potential of the subject site. The gross building area establishes the cost to construct the facilities.

The proposed building with finish-out is estimated to cost $50 per square foot of total area to construct. This dictates the following (simplified) cost measure.

The per-square-foot ground area or foot print is multiplied by the number of stories to arrive at the gross building area. The formula is:

$$B = GBA_{f.p.} \times S$$
$$= 4{,}013.98 \text{ sq. ft.} \times 3$$
$$= 12{,}041.94 \text{ sq. ft. (or 12,041 rounded)}$$

where B = total gross building area. B is the basis for the building cost of construction or development.

The formula for the total NLA is:

NLA = B × Er
= 12,041 sq. ft. × .85
= 10,233 sq. ft. (approximately, based on 3,411 sq. ft. per floor as rounded previously)

(a) ESTIMATED IMPROVEMENT CONSTRUCTION COSTS

	Area	×	Cost/sq. ft.	=	Total cost
Building:	4,013.98 sq. ft. per floor × 3 floors	×	$50/sq. ft.	=	$602,097
Parking:	10,235.7 sq. ft.	×	$3/sq. ft.	=	30,707
Landscaping				=	10,000
Total improvement cost					$642,804
Land value:	15,000 sq. ft.	×	$10/sq. ft.		150,000
					$792,804

The net area forms the basis for the net leasable area. In this example, no common-area fees are charged. A straight rental rate is charged, with the owner to pay expenses (as discussed in the next subsection).

(b) ANALYSIS INCOME

Assume that market research indicates that the subject property, by type and location, can expect a normal rental of $10.67 per square foot per year (net leasable area in 3 years). This assumes that year 3 is the stabilized income phase. As a new building, the subject's rents are lower initially than in year 3, with correspondingly greater vacancy levels. Therefore, potential gross income (PGI) per year (initially) is:

Area	×	Rent	=	PGI
3,411.0 sq. ft. per floor × 3 floors	×	$10.67/sq. ft.	=	$109,186

The PGI of $109,186 is based on a totally rented area of 3,411.0 square feet per floor for three stories (10,233 square feet total). Assume that market analysis has indicated a typical vacancy rate of 6 percent for similar office buildings in the subject neighborhood. (The vacancy rate should be representative of actual market conditions, including the impact of other potentially competing buildings currently under construction.) Therefore, the effective gross income (EGI) is 94 percent of the PGI. The EGI at this point is the amount that the property might be expected to earn in a stabilized situation.

Typical operating expenses, both fixed and variable, are running about $2.67 per square foot; the fixed expenses are about $1.07 per square foot and the variable expenses are approximately $1.60 per square foot (15.975 percent of the PGI). Total operating expenses are 25 percent of the potential gross income. A 1-year operating statement (year 3, in this example) for a stabilized year is indicated as:

PGI	$109,186	
Less: Vacancy rate (6%) equivalent	6,551	
EGI	$102,635	
Less: Operating expenses		
Fixed	$ 10,918	(1.06694 per sq. ft.)
Variable	16,378	(15.9575 percent of PGI)
Net operating income (NOI)	$ 75,339	

The analysis of expenses is more complicated than is illustrated in this example. The fixed costs must consider expenses such as insurance, property tax, and management.[1] The costs of these and other items must be paid, regardless of the level of occupancy in the building. Variable expenses will fluctuate or vary with the level of occupancy. For example, costs of electricity, heating and cooling, security, and other factors will change with the building occupancy. In some situations, the variable costs may run opposite to the occupancy level. Security could cost more in an unoccupied or low-occupancy building than in one that is fully rented.

Because this is a proposed project, the above is not the first-year cash flow statement; stabilized income will not occur until a later time

[1] Real estate is management-intensive; management can determine the success or failure of a project. For more insights into the relationship of management to the solvency and value of real estate, see "Asset Management in a Down Market: A Suggested Valuation–Underwriting Process," Real Estate Center, Texas A&M University, College Station, TX, Publ. 679, 1988.

period. In this case, the stabilized phase should begin in year 3. (See § 4.3 for the first-year income.)

The three spatial dimensions of real estate (length, width, and height) establish the cost of development and the revenue potential of a particular property. The space afforded by development is used over time. Therefore, income analysis must be expanded to consider a fourth dimension, time.

The time element of real estate emphasizes the concept that realty is created to house alternative (or various) economic activities for a given economic period. To appropriately represent the impact of time on real estate, decision makers must make forecasted or projected proforma income statements and then discount their projections to a common time period.

A projection requires a number of assumptions. In practice, the first assumption concerns various growth or decline rates (or more appropriately, rates of change) as they affect the potential gross income, the fixed and variable operating expenses, and the changes in vacancy.

Rates of change are the focus because rents and expenses can drop as well as increase. In the past, many growth projections were linked to the rate of inflation and/or the consumer price index (CPI). Several factors must be considered, especially in areas and times of active inflationary pressures. Investors must be aware that rents can decline in inflationary periods, if demand for space declines or the inventory of space increases.

Other sources of information on growth/change rates used in discounted cash flows are: the experiences of the subject property and the patterns and trends in comparable properties. The economic principle of substitution is in effect for rental markets as well as fee simple estates. The principle of substitution assumes that, given rational economic behavior, no one will pay more than the price demanded (or received) on other similar properties.

Therefore, the rental potential of a property is highly influenced by market alternatives. A given property may do better than the market trend, if it possesses distinct attributes or amenities that offer it a monopoly position in the competitive arena. On the other hand, the property may suffer competitively, realizing lower potential rental returns, because of undesirable attributes.

The significance of investigating the competitive rental position of a property reinforces the need to understand the spatial dimensions of real estate and to conduct a fundamental analysis of the physical, legal, and locational attributes of a specific property. Given the heterogeneous nature of real estate, productivity analysis cannot be ignored; it enables good judgment and the assumptions and estimations used in the projection of expenses and incomes over time.

Continuing the earlier example based on the spatial dimensions, the income statement can be projected over time. Additional data required are the rates of change in expenses, in revenues, and in the expected selling price or market value. The rates used in the example are based on the market trends in the subject area and on the CPI.

§ 4.3 DISCOUNTED CASH FLOW AT NET OPERATING INCOME LEVEL

Income is projected to grow at approximately 3 percent per year. The rate of growth, based on a slow to stabilizing market, is assumed to barely approximate the anticipated level of inflation.

It should be pointed out that year 3 is the stabilized income phase, as illustrated earlier. As a new structure, the subject building's rents are lower initially than they will be (probably) in year 3, and the vacancy rate is higher. Because a preleasing effort was made by the owners during the preconstruction and construction phases, the property is assumed to have a 65 percent occupancy in the first year. An 80 percent occupancy is projected for year 2, based on market analysis. The annual rental rate is projected to increase at approximately 3 percent, yielding rental rates for years 1 through 5 of $10.00, $10.35, $10.67, $11.00, and $11.33 per rentable square foot, respectively. Fixed expenses are projected to grow at 5 percent after the third year, based on actual property proforma, market trends, and the CPI. As Table 4.1 illustrates that the productivity of the property can be determined by linking its spatial capacity to the use of the property over time. Although the potential gross income (PGI), based on physical space, varies from $102,330 to $115,940, market constraints and economic forces can limit the property's *effective gross income* (EGI). The EGI rises from a low of $66,515 in year 1 to $108,983 in year 5. The impact of competitive properties and economic forces introduces uncertainty into the cash flow analysis. The potential range is $13,610 ($115,940 – $102,330). The effective income range is much greater—$42,468 ($108,983 – $66,515). The market issues that can generate these differences cannot be dismissed from the analysis of a specific property, despite the convenience of

Table 4.1 Example of Discounted Cash Flow

	Years				
	1	2	3	4	5
Vacancy (%)	35%	20%	6%	6%	6%
Rental (per sq. ft.)	$10.00	$10.35	$10.67	$11.00	$11.33
PGI	$102,330	$105,912	$109,186	$112,563	$115,940
Vacancy ($)	35,816	21,182	6,551	6,754	6,956
EGI	66,515	84,729	102,635	105,809	108,983
Operating expenses					
Fixed*	10,918	10,918	10,918	11,464	12,037
Variable†	10,614	13,521	16,378	16,885	17,391
Total expenses	21,532	24,439	27,296	28,349	29,428
NOI (EGI less Total expenses)	$ 44,983	$ 60,290	$ 75,339	$ 77,460	$ 79,555

* Assumed to be static for the first 3 years and increasing by 5 percent per year thereafter.
† Based on a static 15.9575 percent of EGI.

canned cash flow programs. The EGI must be recognized as representing the comparative market position of a property. The comparative analysis of the PGI and EGI identifies the impact and levels of market and business risk characterizing a property.

As expenses are deducted from the EGI, the productivity of the real estate is quantified. The NOI represents the productive capacity of the property. All cash outflows required in the day-to-day operation of the property are deducted at this point of analysis. The residual is the *cash* return to the property. Discounted cash flow analysis is a cash accounting procedure; it is not the accrual income analysis used in traditional appraisal, which may allow for amortized or stabilized reserves for replacement. In cash flow analysis, as the expenses are incurred, they are deducted from the effective revenues of the property.

The NOI as the cash return to the property is a measure of the property's productivity. If analysis of the *overall* property is the objective or need of the analyst or decision maker, then the NOI is the level of discounted cash flow to seek out. In the example, the NOI increases from $44,983 in year 1 to $79,555 in year 5. The range of variance is $34,572. The NOI variation is less than that of the EGI, but greater than that of the PGI.

If the decision requires a financial capital analysis or an evaluation of the income tax impact, then the discounted cash flow must be extended.

§ 4.4 FINANCIAL POSITIONS IN CASH FLOWS

The NOI, as a measure of the productivity of real estate, is the basis from which the investment interests are compensated. If the deal is an all-equity investment, then the NOI is a measure of the equity cash flow return. If debt capital is borrowed to finance the deal, then the return to the equity is reduced by the amount of the periodic debt service.

The periodic debt service is generally calculated in two ways: (1) by use of the mortgage constant and the loan amount, and (2) by applying the debt coverage ratio to the net operating income. Both of these techniques consider the lenders' desired return and elements of risk management.

The techniques and concepts involved are illustrated in the following section.

§ 4.5 LOAN-TO-VALUE APPROACH TO DEBT SERVICE

Continuing the earlier example, the subject property's overall cost of construction and land was $792,804. The lender, predisposed to loan on this property, wants to limit the possibility of default by requiring the borrower to put a 25 percent down payment (equity) into the deal. This means the lender will loan 75 percent of the project's cost. This loan-to-value ratio of 75 percent is a risk management technique on the part of the lender. The loan-to-value ratio is a policy decision that sets the loan amount as a percentage of the value (or cost). The policy is established to prevent 100 percent financing and to require the borrower to have assets exposed to loss, to reduce the likelihood of default.

Seventy-five percent of the cost ($792,804) is a loan of $594,603. The loan value (V_M) is then multiplied by the mortgage constant (R_M) to arrive at the debt service on the property.

The mortgage constant is a capitalization rate for the mortgage value. The rate is determined by the effective interest rate, the loan payment frequency, and the amortization term of the loan. All of the terms are subject to the policy decisions of the lender and the constraints of the financial market.

Assume, in this case, the interest rate is 10 percent, payable monthly, with an amortization period (period over which to pay back) of 30 years. Based on this information, the mortgage constant is .105309 (an annualized monthly rate of 0.008776 times 12 months). The mortgage constant can be found in precalculated tables or derived by use of the financial keys on most business calculators. The mortgage value (V_M) times the mortgage constant (R_M) equals the debt service (DS):

$$V_M \times R_M = DS$$

$$\$594{,}603 \times .105309 = \$62{,}617$$

The calculated debt service based on the loan-to-value ratio is then deducted from the NOI in the cash flow format.

§ 4.6 DEBT COVERAGE RATIO APPROACH TO DEBT SERVICE

An alternative calculation for the debt service is to divide the lender's required debt coverage ratio (DCR) into the NOI. The current DCR, in this example, is 1.20. This ratio signifies that the lender desires a 20 percent cash flow buffer between the income and the debt service; the technique allows an equity "cushion," to protect the debt service position. The debt coverage ratio is often applied to a stabilized income measure. As stated previously, the stabilized income level is projected to occur in year 3. The DCR of 1.20 and year 3's stabilized income indicate the following debt service payment:

$$\frac{NOI}{DCR} = \frac{\$75{,}339}{1.20} = \$62{,}782$$

In this case, the two forecasts of DS (by the loan-to-value ratio and DCR methods) are close in amount (\$62,782 – \$62,617 = \$165). Either method can be used. For ease in calculating the mortgage balance, the principal at resale, and the interest payments, the loan-to-value method is used in the following example, to determine the before-tax cash flow (BTCF):

	Years				
	1	2	3	4	5
NOI	\$ 44,983	\$60,290	\$75,339	\$77,640	\$79,555
DS	62,617	62,617	62,617	62,617	62,617
BTCF	\$(17,634)	\$ (2,327)	\$12,722	\$14,843	\$16,938

As the cash flow analysis indicates, the project is insolvent in the first two years of operation. The income from the property cannot cover the operating expenses and debt service. The return to the equity or the before-tax cash flow (BTCF) does not turn positive until year 3.

The BTCF example also illustrates why the term mortgage constant is used for the mortgage cap rate. The total debt service is a constant annual payment of $62,617 (monthly payments of $5,218.07). This payment can be allocated between interest and principal as follows (all payments are rounded or truncated to fit a whole dollar payment schedule):

	Years				
	1	2	3	4	5
Principal	$ 3,305	$ 3,651	$ 4,034	$ 4,456	$ 4,923
Interest	59,312	58,966	58,583	58,161	57,694
Debt service	$62,617	$62,617	$62,617	$62,617	$62,617

Given the use of the standard amortizing loan, the periodic debt payment is allocated between principal and interest. Initially, the predominant payment is for interest and only a small amount of principal is paid off. In the first year, the principal repayment is $3,305. The next calculation is based on the loan's being reduced by the amount of the annual principal payment. The interest in the second year is then calculated based on the outstanding balance (in this example, the payments are monthly, so the effective rate for the year is greater than 10 percent).

The overall pattern in the debt service payment, given standard amortization, is that the principal payments increase over time and the interest payments (given a declining loan balance) decline. Despite the changing relationship between the principal and interest payments, the overall debt service payment remains constant.

The economic significance of the interest-to-principal ratio is realized in the taxable income calculations.

§ 4.7 TAX ANALYSIS IN CASH FLOWS

Cash flow analysis in the after-tax situation is based on several issues that are the result of legal or legislative initiatives, not straight economic concerns.

To estimate the taxes due or the tax shelter potential on a particular project, the taxable income must first be estimated. The taxable income is developed by deducting the interest paid on the project and the book depreciation.

Tax depreciation is a legal/economic concept; it does not represent an actual loss in the value of a property. Book depreciation is a legal concept that allows the periodic recapture of a long-term durable asset. The social purpose of allowing recapture via depreciation is to encourage people to invest in capital assets that may not generate an immediate return.

Long-term capital formation is thus accounted for (or rewarded) by allowing the periodic recapture or sheltering of income from taxation, by allowing a depreciation deduction from the income of the property.

The NOI is the productivity measure of the property. The productivity is reduced for tax purposes by a depreciation allowance, representing periodic recapture or a subsidy for long-term capital investment. The productivity is also reduced by any financial obligations, such as the interest expense on the property. Principal payments are not deducted, because borrowing is not taxable.

The depreciation allowance, under the 1990 tax law's phase-ins, continues the 1986 legislation. The allowance is limited to straight-line depreciation over a mandated economic life. For income residential property, the term is 27.5 years. For nonresidential property, the term is 31.5 years.

The subject of the example (the three-story office building) requires a 31.5-year term. The federal government publishes schedules that detail the allowable depreciation deductions, based on the month when the asset is placed in service.

The depreciable amount over the 31.5-year period is $642,804 (land not included). Assuming that the property is placed in service in January, the allowable depreciation is 3.042 percent for year 1; for years 2 through 5, it is 3.175 percent of $642,804. The year 1 amount would vary according to the month when the property is placed in service.

	Years				
	1	2	3	4	5
NOI	$ 44,983	$ 60,290	$ 75,339	$ 77,460	$ 79,555
Less:					
Interest	(59,312)	(58,966)	(58,583)	(58,161)	(57,694)
Less:					
Depreciation	(21,984)	(20,409)	(20,409)	(20,409)	(20,409)
Taxable income	$(36,313)	($19,085)	($ 3,653)	$(110)	$ 1,452

As the above calculations indicate, the property has negative taxable income projected for the first four years of operation. Although the property can cover its debts and operating obligations after year 2, the depreciation deduction allows for the potential of *tax shelter* through the fourth year.

The taxes are calculated by applying the marginal tax rates (the effective tax rate of the investor, to the estimated taxable income per period to the taxable income. Assume in this case that the investor is in a 33 percent tax bracket. This is the effective rate for an individual in the 1986 law's 28 percent bracket, after the disallowance of interest on personal debt.

In the fifth year, the taxable income is $1,452. Therefore, the income tax is $479.16 (479 rounded).

The taxable income is negative in the first four years, reflecting a deficit of $36,313 in the first year and a decline to $1,110.00 in the fourth year. A negative taxable income is the basis for the potential of tax shelter being generated by this project. The possible tax savings on other income (TSOOI) is estimated by applying the marginal tax rate to the taxable income loss. The tax rate used is 33 percent.

	Years				
	1	2	3	4	5
Taxes or (tax saving) on other income (TSOOI)	$(11,983)*	$(6,298)	$(1,205)	$(366)	$479

*33 × −36,313.

It is important for investors/analysts to note how rapidly the tax shelter potential declines. As the income increases over time, the interest shelter declines. If there is a legislative return to accelerated depreciation, this source of tax savings will also reflect a declining base.

The after-tax cash flow (ATCF) is calculated as follows:

	Years				
	1	2	3	4	5
NOI	$ 44,983	$ 60,290	$ 75,339	$ 77,460	$ 79,555
DS	(62,617)	(62,617)	(62,617)	(62,617)	(62,617)
BTCF	(17,634)	(2,327)	12,722	14,843	16,938
Less: TSOOI	(11,983)	(6,298)	(1,205)	(366)	479
ATCF	$(5,651)	$ 3,971)	$ 13,927	$ 15,209	$ 16,459

The cash flow analysis to this point has illustrated that the ATCF is negative only in the first year. *With the application of the TSOOI as a form of cash return,* the example illustrates positive cash flow to the project from the second through the fifth year. In fact, from the third year on, the income (ATCF) appears more stable than in the before-tax situation.

Understanding the mechanics of cash flows helps the decision maker to understand the value of tax savings on other income. The key to the value of ATCF, however, lies with the tax laws themselves. Currently, incomes are classified as passive, active, or portfolio incomes. As the laws currently stand, real estate income in most investor–limited partnership scenarios is classified as passive income. Therefore, the shelter potential of real estate can be used only to offset other passive income returns. If the investor does not have other sources of passive income, then the TSOOI has no immediate value. The tax savings items can be deferred (carried forward) to offset future passive income.

If an investor makes less than $100,000, a portion of active income (similar to salary or wages) or portfolio income (dividends or interest) up to $25,000 can be offset for tax purposes. This deduction for up to $25,000 is lost if the investor's income is over $150,000 per year.

The relevance of this general discussion of the tax law is that the potential cash generated by TSOOI is a creation of the law and varies for individual situations. Therefore, the value potential of tax shelters can vary because of applicability and timing (deferred interest), despite the mechanics of the cash flow.

In general, the current tax laws benefit investors that have existing, solvent real estate deals. Therefore, the importance of understanding solvency and leverage on a before-tax basis is greater than ever. An understanding of TSOOI also illustrates the importance of an individual project to a portfolio of properties and/or investments.

§ 4.8 OVERALL CASH FLOW PROJECTION

The discussion to this point has segmented the periodic income of the cash flow into the following general components or alternative forms of cash return:

- The productivity or positive cash flow generated by the overall property;

- The residual return or positive cash flow to the equity position;
- The TSOOI, as a cash return to the property;
- The link of real estate to a portfolio design.

Aggregating the separate returns enables the presentation of a before- and after-tax cash flow proforma. The overall cash flow (considered both before and after taxes) provides an analytical tool for evaluating the performance of a real estate project.

§ 4.9 AFTER-TAX CASH FLOW

As shown in Table 4.2, the cash flow down to the NOI level represents the productivity of the real estate project. It is similar to the NOI of a company or enterprise; it reflects the cash returns to the business from the operation of the project, because it is influenced by management skills and market competition. This level of analysis in real estate

Table 4.2 Traditional After-Tax Cash Flow Model

	Years				
	1	2	3	4	5
PGI	$102,330	$105,912	$109,186	$112,563	$115,940
Vacancy ($)	35,816	21,182	6,551	6,754	6,956
EGI	66,515	84,729	102,635	105,809	108,983
Operating expenses					
Fixed	10,918	10,918	10,918	11,464	12,037
Variable	10,614	13,521	16,378	16,885	17,391
Total expenses	21,532	24,439	27,296	28,349	29,428
NOI	44,983	60,290	75,339	77,460	79,555
Depreciation	21,984	20,409	20,409	20,409	20,409
Interest	59,312	58,966	58,583	58,161	57,694
Taxable income	(36,313)	(19,085)	(3,653)	(1,110)	(1,452)
Plus: Depreciation	21,984	20,409	20,409	20,409	20,409
Less: Principal repayment	(3,305)	(3,651)	(4,034)	(4,456)	(4,923)
BTCF	(17,634)	(2,327)	12,722	14,843	16,938
Less: Taxes	0	0	0	0	479
Plus: TSOOI	11,983	6,298	1,205	366	0
ATCF	(5,651)	3,971	13,927	15,209	16,459

would be the concern of appraisers, lenders, property taxing authorities, and equity investors, such as pension funds.

The next level of concern would be the BTCF, which represents the flow of funds to the equity position, after consideration of the debt encumbering the property. This level of income analysis is the concern of investors that use debt financing and of lenders. The lenders would be concerned because, if properly understood, this level of the cash returns enables insights to the potential for default. This level of income would also be a concern for appraisers, if the market standard for properties is debt financing.

The next level of the cash flow is twofold: taxable income and the derivation of income taxes or TSOOI are calculated. The taxable income level of the cash flow is of interest to the Internal Revenue Service (IRS) because this level establishes the potential for TSOOI as a form of cash return to taxable investors. Cash flow is of interest to the IRS and to individual, corporate, and some institutional investors. It is also a concern for investors that have a property-specific interest and those that are interested in real estate in the context of a portfolio.

In summary, cash flow analysis can be done on various levels for various purposes. The four levels for conducting the analysis are:

- Overall property level, using NOI
- Debt-equity level, using BTCF
- Before-tax basis, with debt financing, using BTCF, or without debt financing, using NOI
- After-tax basis, using ATCF.

The traditional cash flow analysis can also be expanded to consider the solvency potential and risk of a property.

§ 4.10 ALTERNATIVE CASH FLOW PERSPECTIVE: SOLVENCY MODEL

The ATCF is composed of two return components: the potential cash (after taxes) and debt spin-off from the operation of the property, and the tax savings generated by the subject property, which can be used in sheltering other income (TSOOI). However, TSOOI is only a source of cash return if passive income from other sources is available. Therefore, a cash flow method that separates the after-tax cash return to the property from the tax shelter would aid investment decision-making abilities. Such a model would emphasize the solvency potential of the property.[2]

The solvency issue may be dealt with by covering insolvent periods with a working capital loan (WCL, or alternatively, periodic infusion of additional equity).[3] A WCL is the amount of short-term capital borrowed in order to maintain solvency. The WCL consideration is inserted into the discounted cash flow between the tax deduction and the TSOOI.

The mechanics of the solvency model are illustrated in the cash flow example (Table 4.2) and the WCL analysis (Table 4.3). As Table 4.2 shows, the property operation is insolvent by $17,634 at the end of year 1. To maintain operations into the second year, a $17,634 loan is borrowed at 14 percent. The WCL interest rate can change periodically; it is short-term. However, for ease of demonstration, the interest charge is held constant. This outstanding debt, created by the project's insolvency and beginning at the end of year 1, is carried against the property's potential income until the end of year 2. At that time, the short-term loan must be paid off with interest ($20,103). However, in this example, the cash from operations (CFO) is negative again. The negative CFO at the end of year 2 is $2,327. Another WCL of $2,327 plus the outstanding WCL from year 1 must be borrowed ($17,634 of principal plus $2,469 of interest = $20,103). The calculation of the growing and then declining WCL (plus interest), and thus the state of the property's solvency, is illustrated in Table 4.4.

The primary function of the WCL analysis is to indicate the periodic solvency/insolvency potential of the property over time, as measured by the spendable cash after taxes (SCAT). Because the cash flow is usually a proforma statement, the WCL (plus interest) is an extension of the traditional cash flow model. *The extension enables decision makers to formulate strategies that are important in planning sources of additional capital, as solvency needs arise.*[4]

The solvency model in Table 4.3 indicates the impact of negative cash flow and the implied opportunity cost via the operation of the

[2] Terry V. Grissom and James L. Kuhle, "An Alternative Cash Flow Method for Real Estate Analysis," *The Real Estate Appraiser and Analyst,* 49:4 (Winter 1983): 52–58.

[3] *Ibid.,* at 57.

[4] Stephen D. Messner and M. Chapman Findlay III, "Real Estate Investment Analysis: IRR Versus FMRR," *The Real Estate Appraiser* (July–August 1975): 10–12.

Table 4.3 Solvency Cash Flow Model

	Years				
	1	2	3	4	5
PGI	$102,330	$105,912	$109,186	$112,563	$115,940
Vacancy ($)	35,816	21,182	6,551	6,754	6,956
EGI	66,515	84,729	102,635	105,809	108,983
Operating expenses					
Fixed	10,918	10,918	10,918	11,464	12,037
Variable	10,614	13,521	16,378	16,885	17,391
Total expenses	21,532	24,439	27,296	28,349	29,428
NOI	44,983	60,290	75,339	77,460	79,555
Depreciation	21,984	20,409	20,409	20,409	20,409
Interest	59,312	58,966	58,583	58,161	57,694
Taxable income	(36,313)	(19,085)	(3,653)	(1,110)	1,452
Plus: Depreciation	21,984	20,409	20,409	20,409	20,409
Less: Principal repayment	(3,305)	(3,651)	(4,034)	(4,456)	(4,923)
BTCF	(17,634)	(2,327)	12,722	14,843	16,938
Less: Taxes	0	0	0	0	479
Cash from operations	(17,634)	(2,327)	12,722	14,843	16,459
WCL	17,634	22,430	12,848	0	0
SCAT	0	0	0	196	16,459
Plus: TSOOI	11,983	6,298	1,205	366	0
SCAT + TSOOI	$ 11,983	$ 6,298	$ 1,205	$ 562	$ 16,459

property. A comparison of Tables 4.2 and 4.3 illustrates that the property is not only insolvent for years 1 and 2 as previously indicated; the early insolvency of the property can strain the cash returns of the property through year 4.

The solvency model, in comparison to the traditional cash flow, also shows that the TSOOI is not the major return for the first two years, as implied in Table 4.2, but it is the sole return through the third year and comprises 65 percent ($366/$562) of the return in the fourth year.

The additional benefits of solvency analysis are: it identifies additional opportunity cost in the control of real estate (interest on the WCL) and the sensitivity of real estate returns to the tax laws, and it illustrates the need to find deep pockets in real estate. Solvency analysis shows that, prior to an investment, buyers should be lining up other investments that are liquid or solvent. Real estate investment should

Table 4.4 Working Capital Loan with Interest: A Measure of Insolvency

	End of Years				
	1	2	3	4	5
	$(17,634)				
1. $(17,634)(1.14)		$(20,103)			
		(2,327)			
		$(22,430)			
2. $(22,430)(1.14)			$(25,570)		
			12,722		
			$(12,848)		
3. $(12,848)(1.14)				$(14,647)	
				14,843	
			SCAT	$196	

increasingly be viewed from a portfolio perspective, even if the investor has limited options.

§ 4.11 CASH AT SALE

The investigation to this point has addressed only the periodic returns from income flows. Real property is also characterized by a loss or gain when sold. To achieve the resale estimate at the end of the holding term (in this case, 5 years), the resale price must be projected. This projection can be accomplished by two techniques. One technique is to project the future sales price, based on an accumulated growth rate (or decline) applied to the original purchase price of the property. For example, the original purchase price (based on cost of construction, in this case) is $792,804. If the market illustrates a price increase of 2 percent per year, the projected resale price is $875,320 ($= 792{,}804 \times (1.02)^5$) at the end of the fifth year.

A second method commonly used to estimate the resale value in discounted cash flow is the capitalization of the sixth year's net operating income. The sixth-year cash flow is calculated as:

PGI	$119,418
Less: Vacancy ($)	7,165
EGI	112,253
Less: Operating expenses	30,552
NOI	$ 81,701

The sixth-year NOI of $81,701 is then capitalized into a value estimate for resale. Because the income is forecast to grow at a moderate rate of 3 percent per year, reflecting a slow but growing economy, the terminal cap rate is expected to drop, but only slightly. The growth expectations are offset by the moderate degree of physical deterioration in the property. The stabilized cap rate (year 3) is 9.5 percent. The cap rate applied in year 6 is 9.4 percent.[5] Therefore, the resale value, based on a capitalization approach, is:

$$\$81{,}701/.094 = \$869{,}160$$

§ 4.12 RESALE CALCULATIONS

Using a reconciliation of the two resale (terminal value) estimating techniques ($875,000 versus $869,160), a future salesprice of $872,500 is indicated for the property. The cash received by the owner at the time of sale must reflect deductions for sales expenses, the outstanding mortgage debt, and the taxes at sale.

The taxes at sale are a side issue that influences cash flow analysis. Although there is not a rate difference between capital gains and ordinary income as of the 1986 tax law, the concepts still apply to different forms of return. Effective in 1991 the maximum rate on capital gains will be 28 percent. However, the effective rate will exceed 28 percent for taxpayers affected by exemptions and itemized deduction phaseouts. This point was addressed in the marginal tax rate discussion. Therefore rate used here is 33%. This would result if say $3,300 more

[5] An aside on the terminal cap rate issue. The traditional rule of thumb implies that the terminal rate is 1–2.5 percent higher than the going-in cap rate. The only reason for such an opinion is that real estate is subject to physical deterioration. In an income perspective, the emphasis must be on the economic changes or expectations related to the property. The decision rules for terminal cap rate selection must then be linked to whether the property value is expected to decline, appreciate, or remain constant. The direction of value change leads to the following set of decision rules:

	Going-In Rate	=	Going-Out Rate
Value declines	R_o	$<$	R_n
Value constant	R_o	$=$	R_n
Value appreciates	R_o	$>$	R_n

taxes after deduction were due on $10,000 more income. The tax components are indicated in Figure 4.2

$$\$3{,}300 \div \$10{,}000 = .33$$

The owner has depreciated the property over the 5-year holding period. The total depreciation is $103,620. The original cost less the accumulated depreciation indicates a basis of $689,184 in the property. The portions subject to income tax at resale are labeled A and B in Figure 4.2. Assume that total selling expenses paid by the seller amount to 6 percent of the sales price. (Typical expenses would likely be in the 6 to 8 percent range; the more optimistic 6 percent is selected for this example.) The monetary difference is the variance between the resale price less the sales expenses ($872,500 – 52,350), or $820,150, and the adjusted tax basis of $689,184. The difference, $130,966, is subject to a tax rate of 33 percent.

Therefore, the taxes at sale are:

$$\$130{,}966 \times .33 = \$43{,}219 \text{ (rounded)}$$

Along with the taxes at time of sale, the terminal sales price will be reduced by the outstanding mortgage balance and sales expenses. If

Figure 4.2 Tax Components at Resale

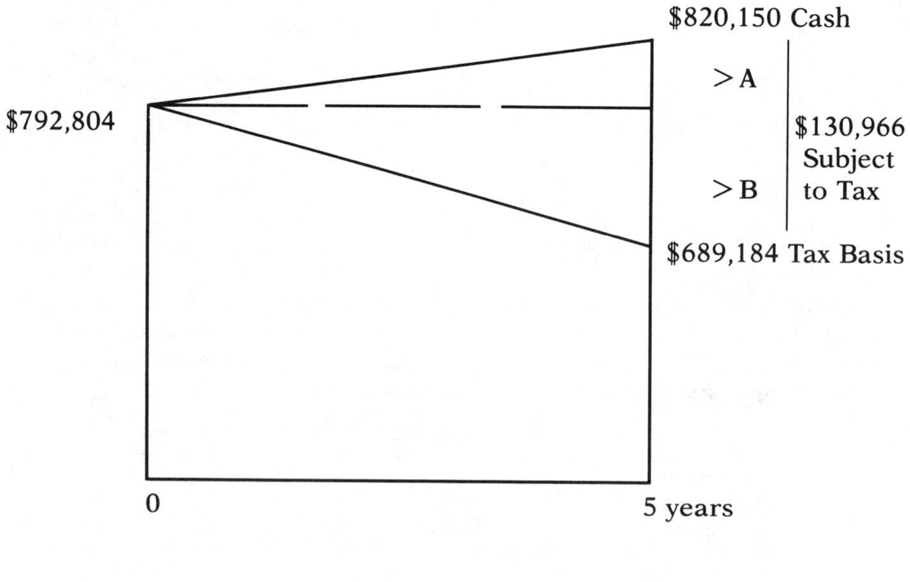

Table 4.5 Net Proceeds from Sale of Property

Total sales price	$872,500
Less: Selling expenses (6 percent)	52,350
Available cash at sale	820,150
Less:	
Mortgage balance	574,234
Taxes	43,219
Working capital loan	0
Cash proceeds from sale of property	$202,697

the solvency model is used and the project does not reach a positive cash flow from operations, then the WCL balance would be deducted from the sales price. An example of the cash proceeds at time of sale is given in Table 4.5.

The implication of the information in Table 4.5 is that $202,697 in cash will be generated at the sale of the property (if all assumptions of growth are realized), over and above the mortgage and income tax. The cash received at the end of the fifth year would then be the $202,697 at sale plus the $16,459 of spendable cash generated by the property's operation.

§ 4.13 PRESENT VALUE

Although cash flow is a direct measure of a property's solvency, it is also a basis for estimating value. The principle of anticipation states that value is the present worth of future anticipated benefits. The benefits are the cash flows controlled by property ownership.

The objective of valuation via cash flow analysis is the discounting process, discussed earlier, that equates periodic flows at different times to a common time period. A useful time perspective is the present. Both the traditional cash flow model and the solvency model can be adjusted at a desirable discount rate and collapsed to a single value estimate. The solvency analysis via a cash flow thus becomes a discounted cash flow (DCF) analysis.

The desirable discount rate used in both examples is 13 percent. This rate, like the earlier rates used here, is derived from the market for similar properties, which reflects a range of 12–15 percent. The property returns are further supported by financial markets that indicate a

10–11 percent interest rate and a 2–5 percent risk loading for the attributes, illiquidity, and nature of the real property. The cash flow from the traditional model is:

	Years					
	1	2	3	4	5	Resale
ATCF	(5,651)	$3,971	$13,927	$15,209	$16,459	$202,697
P.V. factor (13%)	.88496	.78315	.69305	.61332	.54276	.54276
Present value of periodic flows	$(5,273)	$3,110	$ 9,652	$ 9,328	$ 8,933	$110,016
P.V. of equity	$ 136,038					

Total property value based on traditional cash flow analysis:

Equity value	$136,038
Original mortgage	594,603
Total value	$730,641

The cash flow from the solvency model (discounted at 13 percent) is:

	Years					
	1	2	3	4	5	Resale
SCAT + TSOOI	$ 11,983	$ 6,298	1,205	$562	$16,459	$202,697
Present value of periodic flows	10,604	4,932	835	345	8,933	110,016
P.V. of equity	$135,666					

Total property value based on solvency cash flow analysis:

Equity value	$135,666
Original mortgage	594,603
Total value	$730,269

A comparison of the solvency model to the traditional cash flow model indicates that a slightly lower present value is calculated as a result of the potential insolvency of the property and the dependence in the early years on the tax shelter alone. Insights to the insolvency of the property help identify why the overall property's present value is below the cost of construction. The present value analysis indicates a tight value range of (rounded) $730,250 to $730,650. The cost estimate is $792,804 (including $150,000 in the land).

The cash flow analysis indicates the potential for market, business, and financial risk in a property. In the subject example, the cash flow analysis, in which value is less than cost, suggests that the project design and financing might need to be rethought and renegotiated before this deal is undertaken. A drop in the discount rate (to 12 percent) does not improve the present value-to-cost relationship. The feasibility of this development or investment is highly suspect, yet the example was a very common scenario over the past decade.

§ 4.14 SUMMARY OF CASH FLOW ANALYSIS

Cash flow analysis is concerned with the cash returns to a project over time. Cash returns can come in alternative forms; the forms vary with the sources and basis of the cash flow.

The return linked to the productivity of the real estate is the NOI. It is the income available after allowances for vacancy and operating expenses are covered. The NOI is linked to the operation of the enterprise and is subject to elements of business and market risk.

The second return often considered in a cash flow format is the before-tax cash flow or the cash flow to the equity position. The equity cash flow is a residual return after the consideration of debt financing. The BTCF is the measure of return to an equity capital investment and often becomes the first element of a solvency measure.

The taxable income as a cash flow measure is an intermediary step in the development of the after-tax cash flow. The ATCF is the key cash flow return in many canned analysis programs. The ATCF is the cash flow return after debt and taxes. The after-tax considerations are prime measures of solvency in many real estate projects.

Two major decision criteria are served by cash flow analysis. The first is solvency analysis. Solvency is concerned with the ability of a project's operations to meet and cover the project's operating and debt responsibilities. Failure to meet these responsibilities often results in loss of control or of ownership of the project. As a solvency measure, cash flow is a strategic tool that helps the decision maker to identify and control the source of wealth and value generated by a given asset.

The second decision criterion derived from cash flow analysis is a value estimate—or, more precisely, a present value estimate. Value is denoted as the present worth of future anticipated benefits. The benefits of concern are the cash flows, in the form of income and gain, from the ownership or control of a property.

Cash flow analysis is a mechanical process. Many people limit their knowledge and use of the technique to the mechanical level. The technique is expandable into a tool of strategy and decision making.

APPENDIX

General Land Allocation Unit Model:

$$\text{LUE} = \frac{\text{A} - \text{Sb}}{\dfrac{\text{NLA}}{\text{Er}} + \text{Pu(S)} + \text{O}}$$

where:

A = total site area or size
Sb = area of setback, via regulation
NLA = net leasable area
Er = building efficiency ratio
Pu = parking units (in area)
S = number of building stories
O = open space requirements after stated as square footage per some unit of decision (square foot, number of units, or cubic measures); in this case, no open space requirements are in effect

$$\text{LUE} = \frac{15{,}000 \text{ sq. ft.} - 750 \text{ sq. ft.}}{\dfrac{300 \text{ sq. ft.}}{.85} + 300(3) + \text{O}}$$

$$\text{LUE} = 11.373 \text{ sq. ft.}$$

Five

Income Analysis: Alternatives to Discounted Cash Flow Analysis

§ 5.1 INTRODUCTION

This chapter identifies the general structure of income models that are viable alternatives to the discounted cash flow. An overview of the general attributes of the models considers their implicit assumptions and delineates the information and variables that must be explicitly investigated, analyzed, and gathered to employ a specific model.

The models can be grouped into ratio models, yield capitalization models, and discounted cash flow (DCF) models. The yield capitalization and DCF models are subdivisions of a more general class termed yield models. The alternative forms of the DCF were described in the previous chapter.

Discounted cash flow (DCF) analysis is the model predominantly used by a variety of professionals for considering the income/benefit flows from real estate and linking them to the value of a given property.

Figure 5.1 Income Analysis Models: Explicit Identification of Assumptions Affecting Value

	Ratio Models			
	Before Tax			
1 Gross Income Multiplier	2 Overall Capitalization	3 Equity Residual Model	4 Underwriter's Model	5 Band of Investment
Gross Income	Gross Income −Vacancy	Gross Income −Vacancy	Gross Income −Vacancy	Gross Income −Vacancy
×	Effective Gross Income − Expenses	Effective Gross Income − Expenses	Effective Gross Income − Expenses	Effective Gross Income − Expenses
	Net Operating Income	Net Operating Income	Net Operating Income	Net Operating Income
(Gim)	$\div R_o$	Debt Service (DS) Cash Throw Off (CTO)	(NOI)($\div$ DCR) = Debt Service	$\div R_o$
		$+R_E$	NOI − DS = CTO $\div R_E$ DS $\div R_M$	Where $R_o = (MR_M) + (1 - M)R_E$
		V_E + V_M (Original Mortgage)	V_E $+V_M$	
V_o	V_o	V_o	V_o	V_o

Source: Real Estate Center at Texas A&M University

Figure 5.1 (*Continued*)

Yield Models				
Before Tax			After Tax	
6 Akerson	7 Ellwood Model	8 Fishers After Tax Ellwood	9 Discounted Cash Flow	10 Alternative Discount Flow
Gross Income −Vacancy	Gross Income −Vacancy	Gross Income −Vacancy	Gross Income −Vacancy	Gross Income −Vacancy
Effective Gross Income − Expenses	Effective Gross Income − Expenses	Effective Gross Income − Expenses	Effective Gross Income − Expenses	Effective Gross Income − Expenses
Net Operating Income	Net Operating Income	Net Operating Income	Net Operating Income	Net Operating Income
$\div R_o$	$\div R_o$	$\div R_o$	−Depreciation −Interest	−Depreciation −Interest
			Taxable Income +Depreciation −Principal	Taxable Income +Depreciation −Principal
Where $R_o =$ (MR_M) $+$ $(1 - M)Y_E$ $-MP1/s_n Y_E$ $-\Delta_o 1/s_n Y_E$	Where $R_o =$ $Y_E - MC$ $-$ $\Delta_o 1/s_n Y_E$	Where $R_o =$ $Y_E - MC$ $-$ $\Delta_o 1/s_n Y_E$ $-MR - Bdt$	Cash Throw Off	Cash Throw Off
			−Taxes	−Taxes
			Cash from Operations	Cash from Operations
			Tax Savings on Other Income	Working Loan
			After-Tax Cash × Discount Factor	Spendable Cash After Taxes
				+Tax Savings on Other Income
				× Discount Factor
V_o	V_o	V_o	V_o	V_o

As shown in Chapter 4, DCF enables a decision maker to segment the cash generated by the productivity of the property from the benefits that are directed to (or received from) the financial components and the taxing authority. The details of the cash flow segmentation are illustrated in the last (right-hand) column in Figure 5.1.

The essence of the DCF is to depict how the flows of benefits from control of the property are identified over time. This depiction then helps the decision maker to address problems directly, by using a solvency standard, or indirectly, by using the discounting process to convert the cash flows to a present value.

Although the DCF is the most commonly recognized form of income analysis being used in business, banking, and real estate (by accountants, bankers, appraisers, and financiers), alternative income methods have evolved over time. Many of the alternative models to the discounted cash flow were developed before the DCF model came into general practice; the universal appeal of DCF can be tied directly to the availability of the personal computer. Prior to the advantages of the computer, many of the techniques presented in Figure 5.1 were conceived as shortcuts to the generation of a discounted cash flow by hand.

§ 5.2 ALTERNATIVE INCOME MODELS

The array of income models illustrated in Figure 5.1 evolved over time. The bulk of them preceded the employment of the tool of the DCF model (if not its concept). Because many of the income models presented are simple, they can be considered as more directly linking income to value than does the DCF. However, they often are not as realistic as the DCF, in reflecting the issues of concern. These models, as traditionally employed, are limited to the estimation of value as their sole decision criterion; they do not present the actual pattern of solvency experienced by a given property. As future research on risk analysis is conducted, a broader application of these traditional models is expected.

The gross income multiplier (GIM) model, illustrated in the first column of Figure 5.1, is one of the simplest and most direct income–value models. It is direct because it identifies a multiplier or ratio relationship between the gross income of a property and its value. The formula is:

Gross income × Gross income multiplier = Value

or, in short form:

GI × GIM = Value

This formula is far less complicated than the DCF model. In the models presented in Figure 5.1, the number of steps in the models expands, as read from left to right; more and more information is required to develop each new model. In each model, more of the issues and determinants of value must be made explicit.

The GIM model involves only three steps to arrive at an estimate of value. The decision maker/analyst must (1) appropriately determine the gross income of a property, (2) select an income multiplier, and (3) calculate the property value via multiplication. The GIM model is one of the most implicit and heroic models that can be used. When a decision maker employs the GIM model, he or she is assuming away much of the world. For example, the research effort in this model is concerned with the level of the gross income. In the GIM model, gross income and market rentals must be thoroughly investigated and documented by analyzing the income pattern of the property over time. With the DCF program, the historic patterns might reveal an irregular income return, varying with market conditions. However, the GIM model is seeking only one income measure, a stabilized annual income, which is constructed to represent the typical return of the property over time. A demonstration of the stabilization process would be:

	Years				
	1	2	3	4	5
GI	$15,000	$14,000	$16,000	$15,000	$14,500

The typical or average income can be selected as $15,000. The decision is ultimately judgmental, but should be based on observation and rational analysis of comparable properties as they are examined and contrasted with the subject property.

The average income ($15,000) is then converted to a value by a multiplier. The selection of the multiplier could be based on an investment policy stating that the investor will pay five times the gross income, or on the methodology of the professional appraiser, which requires a documented multiplier developed from comparable sales.

The technique of developing GIMs from the market requires confirming a number of sales and obtaining the annual gross income and the sales price of the property. For example, five similar sales in the area of a potential investment may reflect the following information (multipliers are rounded to nearest 100):

	Sales				
	1	2	3	4	5
Sales price (SP)	\$100,000	\$110,000	\$125,000	\$80,000	\$95,000
Gross income (GI)	\$ 15,000	\$ 16,000	\$ 15,000	\$10,000	\$13,500
GIM = SP/GI	6.67	6.87	7.81	8	7.04

The consideration of similar sales in the area indicates a range in GIMs from 6.67 to 8. This is a spread in multipliers of 1.33 points (8 – 6.67). Given a \$10,000 income, a difference between the extremes of the estimated range is a value variance of \$13,300. This potential variation is based on the multiplier range (\$10,000 × 1.33 = \$13,300). Therefore, interpretation of the market data above can result in a possible valuation error.

A decision rule must be employed to use any model. In this case, the market data indicate that there is not a precise range of ratios being paid for specific income streams, but there is a fairly consistent pattern. The key to employing the GIM model (and all the other models depicted), when used in a market (and market value) context, is to choose the multiplier generated by the transaction of the property most similar to the subject. This similarity is often based on like characteristics shared by the sale and subject properties.

In the example above, assume the most similar property is sale 1; a GI of \$15,000 times a GIM of 7 (rounded) equals a value of \$105,000. The analysis would be helped by insights to the characteristics and motivations of the parties involved in the transaction.

Although the GIM model involves only three steps, it is conceptually complex and requires many assumptions. A key set of assumptions is that all similar properties have the same vacancy level and the same operating expenses and that the buyers have the same financing resources, opportunities, and tax incentives. These are heroic assumptions, yet they are implicit within the model.

In Figure 5.1, as the reader moves from the GIM model in column 1 to the alternative cash flow model in column 10, the models require a more explicit documentation of the input and a heightened level of knowledge about the property (and the market). The explicit documentation of the variables employed in each model can help in the insights needed to evaluate any project or investment.

For example, a model not illustrated in Figure 5.1 is the effective gross income (EGI) model, a multiplier model based on the effective gross income of a property. The formulas are:

Gross income − Vacancy = Effective gross income (EGI)

EGI × EGIM (an effective gross income multiplier) = Value. Conceptually, the value should be the same as that generated by the GIM model. In reality, it will probably vary because of the imprecision in the market data and the subjective interpretation of the market by various individuals.

The EGIM model requires not only a documentation of the gross income and the range of multipliers, as in the GIM model, but also an investigation of vacancy levels. The vacancy levels can be based on the historic level for the subject, the current and historic level of the competitive market, or a combination of both the market and the subject. For example, assume the market's and the subject property's vacancy level is 6 percent. Based on a $15,000 gross income, the effective gross income is:

GI	$15,000	
Less: Vacancy	900	($15,000 × .06 = $900)
EGI	$14,100	

EGI × EGIM = Value
$14,400 × 7.45 = $105,000 (r)

(EGIM is based on a market search of comparables, as in the GIM.) The concern here is not only with the mechanics of the GIM and EGIM models, but with the reality that each income model requires an additional or different set of information. Therefore, as the models depicted in Figure 5.1 are read from left to right, the additional attributes of each model require a more explicit and detailed investigation of the data that are characteristic of the model, the property, and the market.

§ 5.3 CAPITALIZATION

All the models depicted in columns 2 through 8 in Figure 5.1 are traditional capitalization models. Figure 5.1 divides the capitalization models into two general model groups: ratio models (direct capitalization) and yield models. Both groups are concerned with the capitalization process, the conversion of an income into a value estimate. The income used in the capitalization models (both ratio and yield) is a stabilized annual income. This is the same concept as is used in the multiplier models; however, here a net operating income is stabilized, not a gross income. A stabilized net operating income (NOI) is not an actual cash flow return, but an income measure created by considering typical deductions and expenses incurred (or expected to be incurred) over time. The stabilized income processed is based on accrual accounting procedures, not cash accounting as in discounted cash flow models. The stabilized income is the typical return expected to accrue to the property, over time, after the deduction for various cash outflows and expenses. Unique to income analysis in appraisal capitalization is the deduction of reserves for replacement, to arrive at an estimate of the NOI. Reserves for replacement consider the periodic amortized payment for a short-lived capital item, such as a replacement in 5 years of the roof on a building that has a remaining economic life of 25 years. The roof has an economic life of 5 years before it must be replaced again. Under cash accounting, the roof construction would be deducted from the cash flow in the year when the expense is incurred. With the stabilized income, a periodic deduction is taken over the economic life of the roof. For example, if the roof cost $10,000 to repair, a $10,000 deduction would be subtracted on the cash flow statement in 5 years. Under the stabilized method, the $10,000 is amortized on a straight-line basis over the economic life of the roof, say five years. Therefore $10,000/5 = $2,000 deducted per year from the similarly stabilized income estimate.

After the income estimate is stabilized, it is capitalized by the alternative methods presented in columns 2 through 8 in Figure 5.1.

The *ratio* capitalization models presented in Figure 5.1 are the overall capitalization rate model, the equity residual model, the underwriter's model, and the band of investment model. The *yield* capitalization models presented are the Akerson model, the Ellwood model, and Fisher's after-tax Ellwood model.

(a) RATIO MODELS

Ratio models are concerned with the direct capitalization of an income to a value. The rates used in these models are a direct ratio of a single-period income to a specified value amount. Another term for ratio capitalization is direct capitalization. The key to a general characteristic in ratio capitalization is that the rates derived, representing a single-period ratio, directly reflect an explicit relationship between the income and the appropriate value.

The simplest ratio or direct capitalization model, and a prime example of ratio capitalization, is the overall cap rate model. The rate is calculated as the index of NOI to the sales price or overall value:

$$\frac{NOI}{V_o} = R_o$$

where:

NOI = net operating income
V_o = actual sales price of a sale, or an estimated value
R_o = overall cap rate

The application of the model reverses the development of the cap rate (R_o). The format of $NOI/V_o = R_o$ is used to abstract a rate from comparable transactions. The market-derived cap rate (R_o) from comparable sales (as illustrated for the gross income multiplier) is then applied to a property that is being valued. For example, five sales of offices are investigated to determine their transaction prices and NOIs. The investigation indicates the following five cap rates: 9.5, 8.5, 10.5, 10.0, and 11.0 percent respectively. After these rates are calculated, the properties are compared, based on their physical characteristics (age, size, design, and so on), income and risk potentials, location, and any other relevant factors, to arrive at the sales indicator that is most similar to the subject property. This comparative process is the basis for selecting the rate that is appropriate for the subject property. In this case, assume that the appropriate cap rate is 10.5 percent.

The overall capitalization model requires that a stabilized NOI be first derived and then converted into a value estimate by dividing the income by the market-derived overall cap rate. The model's format is illustrated as:

PGI	\$15,000	(stabilized as derived in GIM model)
Less: Vacancy (6%)	900	(6 % × \$15,000 = \$900)
EGI	14,100	
Less: Operating expenses	3,000	(Operating expenses are stabilized estimates based on a market standard; in this case, the market indicated fixed and variable expenses (including reserves for replacement) to be 20% of PGI (.20 × \$15,000 = \$3,000)
NOI	\$11,000	(stabilized estimate)

Capitalization Model

$$V_o = \frac{NOI}{R_o}$$

$$= \frac{\$11,100}{.105}$$

$$= \$105,714 \text{ (rounded to } \$106,000)$$

where:

V_o = overall value estimate
R_o = overall cap rate (as derived from market sales)
NOI = net operating income

Conceptually, the overall capitalization rate model should not result in a value significantly different from that of the GIM model. However, the potential for value differences is indicated by the increased consideration that must be given to deductions and other factors that are explicitly addressed in each model. The GIM assumes that vacancy and expenses, as well as financing and tax implications, are similar among all comparable properties. The overall cap rate model explicitly documents the deductions from income based on vacancy levels typical in the market (or for a specific property that is similar to the subject property). A thorough investigation of the expenses, both fixed and variable, is conducted to arrive at the NOI in the overall capitalization model. In this example, the increased data and explicit documentation of variables indicate a $1,000 ($106,000 – $105,000) value difference.

Like the GIM model, the overall capitalization model assumes that the financing and income tax are similar for the comparable properties (and buyers). Therefore, many of the variations in cap rates and values used and resulting from the valuation process can be attributed to the implicit assumptions of the models. Like the GIM, direct capitalization is a simple procedure but a complex concept.

(b) MORTGAGE-EQUITY ANALYSIS

The ratio models depicted in columns 3 through 5 and the yield models in columns 6 through 8 of Figure 5.1 all explicitly address the issues of the financial impact on value.

The mortgage-equity models in columns 3 through 5 are ratio (direct) capitalization models. A discounted cash flow analysis can divide the income stream after the NOI into a debt component (the debt service cash flow) and the equity component (the cash flow to equity). Similarly, the capitalization models divide the overall cap rate (R_o) into a debt rate (R_M) and an equity rate (R_E). The combination of the debt and equity rates is dependent on the structures of the capitalization method employed. For example, in column 3 of Figure 5.1, the equity residual model's treatment of the debt and equity components is initially different from that of the band of investment model, in column 5. However, an in-depth comparison shows that both result from a weighted rate approach.

(c) EQUITY RESIDUAL MODEL

To a degree, the equity residual model is a hybrid cash flow/capitalization approach. It uses the stabilized income (NOI) concept but divides the property's NOI into debt service income and equity income.

The income stream, segmented into debt and equity components, is then capitalized into debt value and equity value components. The conversion of the income components into value components is accomplished by using a mortgage cap rate (the mortgage constant, R_M) and an equity cap rate (R_E).

The format follows the overall capitalization process, but instead of the NOI being divided by the overall cap rate (R_o), the debt service is divided by the mortgage constant (R_M) and the cash throw-off (CTO; also identified as cash flow to equity, or cash on cash flow) is divided by the equity dividend rate (R_E, also referred to as equity cash flow cap rate).

To develop the mortgage constant and equity dividend rates, the mortgage and equity markets must be investigated and the terms typical and applicable to properties like the subject property must be identified.

Assume that, at the time this analysis is occurring, the current mortgage terms available for commercial properties similar to the subject property are: a 75 percent loan-to-value mortgage at 12 percent interest for 30 years, payable monthly. The annualized mortgage constant is .123434. (The constant is carried out to six places as a matter of convention; see standard financial tables, or develop the rate using the financial keys on a calculator, as explained in Appendix.)

Market research has indicated that an acceptable equity dividend rate is 5 percent. This is the cash on cash rate of return sought by typical investors for properties comparable to the subject property.

Another aspect of the equity residual technique that is similar to the discounted cash flow model is that the debt service must be known (or, at least, the overall value and/or mortgage amount must be known, in order to calculate the DS) along with the mortgage constant. The fact that the NOI and DS can be determined or known has given the model its name—equity residual model. The equity cash flow is the resulting return, after debt is deducted from the property's overall productivity.

Based on the financial/investment data required for the equity dividend model, the following format is offered as the equity residual model (same as the overall capitalization model; see Figure 1.5, columns 2 and 3):

PGI	$15,000
Less: Vacancy (6%)	900
EGI	14,100
Less: Operating expenses	3,000
NOI	11,100
Less: DS	9,813*
CTO	$ 1,287

*Mortgage value amount (V_M) ($79,500, or .75 × $106,000), based on overall cap rate model; $79,500 × .123434 = $9,813 (approximations).

$$V_M = \frac{DS}{R_M}$$

$$= \frac{\$9{,}813}{.123434} = \$\ 79{,}499.98$$

$$V_E = \frac{1{,}287}{.05} = \underline{\ \ 25{,}740}$$

$$\$105{,}239.98 \text{ (rounded to } \$105{,}000)$$

$$= \frac{CTO}{R_E}$$

The equity residual model considers the allocation of a property's productivity (NOI) between debt and equity positions. The model requires the explicit identification of the financial and equity terms typical of the market. Specific financial terms can be applied within the model's criteria matrix.

The equity residual model illustrates that the debt claim on income flows supersedes the equity claims.

The equity residual model, as compared to the overall cap rate and the GIM models, makes the capital structure explicit. As this example illustrates, it conceptually should fall within a reasonable range of the value estimates of the GIM and overall cap rate models. In practice, this will not necessarily occur, because of the broad array of forces influencing the capital markets and real estate markets. However, if the constraints of the market are appropriately investigated and delineated in reference to a given property, the variation should be minor. If significant differences occur, the variation between the models may be an indication of changing market conditions. A comparison of the model's assumptions may help identify the changing forces.

§ 5.4 UNDERWRITER'S MODEL

The underwriter's model is a capitalization technique that incorporates the issue of financial solvency. This incorporation employs the lenders' risk management tool, the debt coverage ratio (DCR). The DCR is similar to the loan-to-value ratio (M) in that it mechanically enforces a buffer of equity protection in the cash/income flows.

The loan-to-value ratio requires that the borrowers have some money (of their own) in an investment; the ratio ensures a partial loan, supposedly preventing a 100 percent financing.

The DCR also ensures a buffer of income flowing to the equity position, which mechanically prevents all of the property's NOI (productivity) from being directed to debt service.

The DCR is calculated as:

$$\text{DCR} = \frac{\text{NOI}}{\text{DS}}$$

where:

NOI = net operating income of property
DS = debt service as determined by underwriting guidelines

Therefore, with a continuation of the previous example:

$$\text{DCR} = \frac{\text{NOI}}{\text{DS}} = \frac{\$11{,}100}{\$9{,}813} = 1.131153 \text{ (rounded to 1.13)}$$

This result implies that the lender is requiring a 13 percent buffer of income between the property's net operating income and the amount of periodic debt carried by the borrower.

For capitalization purposes, the DCR concept can be turned around and used as a technique to determine the amount of debt that can be safely carried by the income potential of a given property. The context of reversing the model is that value (and hence the loan amount and debt service) is unknown, but the lender has specific underwriting standards that must be fulfilled. In this case, the requirement is a DCR of 1.13.

Given this underwriting requirement regarding the property's income potential, and the information on debt and equity capital requirements as explicitly incorporated in the equity residual model, the underwriting model will take the following form (as per previous models):

PGI	$15,000
Less: Vacancy (6%)	900
EGI	$14,100
Less: Operating expenses	3,000
NOI	$11,100

$$DS = \frac{NOI}{DCR}$$

$$= \frac{\$11{,}100}{1.13} \qquad = \underline{\$\ 9{,}823}$$

$$CTO = NOI - DS$$

$$= \$11{,}100 - \$9{,}823 \qquad = \$\ 1{,}277$$

$$DS + CTO = NOI \qquad = \$11{,}100 \text{ (check)}$$

$$V_M = \frac{DS}{R_M} = \frac{\$9{,}823}{.123434} = \$79{,}580.99$$

$$V_E = \frac{CTO}{R_E} = \frac{1{,}277}{.05} = \frac{\$25{,}540.00}{\$105{,}120.99} \text{ (rounded to \$105,000)}$$

If the information used in the models is consistently employed, the same (or a similar) value conclusion is derived. In this case, the productivity for the property and the financial and equity terms are consistent with prior models. The DCR is based on the financial terms established by the loan-to-value format; this is not always the case. However, a consistent relationship between the DCR and M criteria used to evaluate and manage risk should be consistently employed by lenders.

§ 5.5 BAND OF INVESTMENT MODEL

The final ratio model illustrated in Figure 5.1 (column 5) is the band of investment (BOI) model—the most employed direct capitalization model observed in a sampling of mortgage-equity techniques.[1]

The BOI model is a strict capitalization model; it does not employ cash flow attributes, like the equity residual model, or solvency concerns, like the underwriter's model. All the mortgage-equity concerns are developed within the rate structure. The orientation has evolved because the appraisal assignment is to estimate value. Only the productivity of the property has been estimated at the beginning of an appraisal analysis; value is not known, nor is the mortgage amount, nor

[1] Kenneth M. Lusht, "Appraising Income Property: Empirical Evidence on the Relationships Between Appraisal Theory and Appraiser Behavior," College of Business Administration, The Pennsylvania State University, Working Paper, February 1979.

the debt service. Announcement of this information typically concludes an appraisal assignment.[2]

However, initial and asset capital terms of lending institutions and equity markets—loan-to-value ratio, typical financing rates, term periods, and payment frequency—can be identified. This financial information, along with the equity dividend, is sufficient to develop a traditional BOI model, as follows:

PGI	\$15,000
Less: Vacancy (6%)	900
EGI	14,100
Less: Operating expenses (20% PGI)	3,000
NOI	\$11,100

$$V_o = \frac{NOI}{R_o}$$

$$R_o = (M \times R_M) + (1 - M) \times R_E$$

where:

M = loan-to-value ratio of 75 percent
R_M = mortgage constant of .123434 based on 12 percent interest, monthly, for 30 years
$(1 - M)$ = equity of 25 percent = (1 − .75)
R_E = equity dividend rate of 5 percent (derived from equity markets)

Therefore:

$$.75 \times .123434 = .092575$$
$$.25 \times .05 = .0125$$
$$R_o = .105075 \text{ (rounded to 10.5 percent)}$$
$$V_o = \frac{\$11,100}{.105} = \$105,714 \text{ (rounded to \$106,000)}$$

[2] For the definition of an appraisal assignment, see the Uniform Standards and Practices of the Appraisal Foundation, available from the Appraisal Institute, 430 North Michigan Ave., Chicago, IL 60611-4088.

Again, with the consistent employment of the data explicitly incorporated into the market, a tight value range is depicted. The BOI model is most consistent with the overall cap rate model; both are strict capitalization models, having similar constraints. To incorporate attributes of cash flow calculations, the underwriter's model and equity residual techniques require additional knowns.

The BOI is depicted as the last ratio model in Figure 5.1 because it is the conceptual building block for the yield capitalization models depicted in columns 6, 7, and 8.

§ 5.6 YIELD CAPITALIZATION MODELS

Before the yield capitalization models can be appropriately discussed, it is necessary to reconcile some of the variables of direct capitalization and to summarize the symbols employed in contemporary appraisal. This summary allows a presentation of the relationship between ratio capitalization and yield models. The primary objective of yield capitalization is to collapse the attributes of the cash flow model to the traditional direct capitalization model.

This is desirable for two major reasons:

1. To equate investment requirements and criteria to the limited data available in a highly inefficient market;
2. To enable a documentation of rational behavior patterns behind vague market artifacts (units of comparison, effectively created by analysis, perhaps after the fact).

The syntheses of ratio capitalization variables and yield issues are depicted in Table 5.1, which shows the relationship among specific values, incomes, cap rates, and yields.

The general capitalization model of $V = I/R$ can be applied for each component or standard—the overall property (o), the mortgage component (M), or the equity position (E). Therefore, $V_M = DS/R_M$ or $R_E = CTO/V_E$, the rationale for capitalization's being perceived as a ratio or direct income-to-value conversion process.

Yield capitalization requires that additional information be incorporated and made explicit in the development of a model. All of the ratio models are characterized as capitalizing a stabilized income stream into

Table 5.1 Symbols for Variables and Concepts

Component Concepts	Values	Incomes	Ratio Rates	Yields
Overall property	V_o	NOI	R_o	Y_o
Mortgage	V_M	DS	R_M	Y_M
Equity	V_E	CTO	R_E	Y_E

where:

V = value measure; subscripts identify whether the value is an overall property value (o), a mortgage value (M), or an equity value (E)
R = rates of capitalization for overall property (o), mortgage constant (M), and equity (E = equity dividend)
Y = yields to overall property (o), mortgage (M – the interest rate), and equity (E – the equity yield rate before taxes)

perpetuity (an infinite time period)—an interesting characterization, given that only a one-period (annual) income is capitalized. This implicit time dimension is the reason for the stabilized income concept's importance in direct capitalization. The stabilization process allows for an up-front consideration of possible income and value changes, over time.

The time dimension, an addition to ratio capitalization, is made explicit in the yield models. Yield analysis is conducted in the context of a holding period, investment horizon, or advantageous taxing period. The holding period in yield capitalization is equivalent to the time frame used in the DCF model. As capitalization, it links cash flow concerns to value theory. Given that value is the present worth of future anticipated benefits, ratio capitalization forecasts the benefits indefinitely, and yield capitalization identifies a holding period of, say, 5 years, is yield analysis not reflecting a major investment value component?

The missing value component is the capitalized value of the income flows between the end of the fifth year and the end of time (infinity). Although an extreme concept in a theoretical sense, it collapses to a very practical application. Given that value is the present worth of future benefits, then the capitalized or discounted value of the income from the end of the fifth year to infinity is the future sales price (resale value) at the end of the fifth year.

A yield is the rate that is earned based on a comparison of current value (the purchase price) to the benefits received from ownership over a given time period. These benefits can be received as incomes or as future sales prices. The yield can be used as the rate that equates the purchase price (or a current value) to the cash flows (income, recapture of original capital, and capital gains) over time. In this scenario, the yield mechanically equates to an internal rate of return.

As a rate for relating a cash flow (incomes or future sales prices) over time to a current value, the yield equates the yield concept to the present value technique. This present value process is the crux of yield capitalization.

The formula for a yield (using the standard appraisal symbols) for the overall property is:

$$Y_o = \sqrt[n]{\frac{\Sigma NOI + V_{o_n}}{V_o}} - 1 = \text{overall property yield}$$

where:

n = holding period term
Σ = summation of NOIs over holding period
V_o = purchase price or current overall value estimate
V_{o_n} = future overall value at end of holding period

The basis of the yield capitalization concept and how it relates to direct (ratio) capitalization can be observed if the yield formula is considered over a one-year period, as follows:

$$Y_o = \frac{NOI_1 + V_{o_1}}{V_o}$$

where:

NOI_1 = NOI for one year
V_{o_1} = resale (future sale) at end of first year

With some rearrangement:

$$Y_o = \frac{NOI_1}{V_o} + \frac{V_{o_1}}{V_o}$$

where, with extension or substitution:

$NOI_1/V_o = R_o$ or cap rate

V_{o_1}/V_o = ratio of future value to present value; if 1 is subtracted, this will be illustrated as the appreciation growth over the year: $V_{o_1}/V_o - 1$

Therefore:

$$Y_o = \frac{NOI_1}{V_o} + \left(\frac{V_{o_1}}{V_o} - 1\right) \quad (1)$$

or, equivalently, if stated as a percentage change:

$$\frac{V_{o_1}}{V_o} - 1 = \frac{V_{o_1} - V_o}{V_o} = \Delta_o$$

where Δ_o is the percentage change in the overall value over the year.

Therefore:

$$Y_o = \frac{NOI_1}{V_o} + \frac{V_{o_1} - V_o}{V_o} \quad (2)$$

With substitution, the yield calculation is shown to be:

$$Y_o = R_o + \Delta_o \quad (3)$$

Using the prior formulas with the property information employed in the previous direct capitalization models gives these results:

NOI = \$11,000

V_o = \$106,000 (based on previous value estimation or purchase price)

V_{o_1} = \$111,300 (given future value or resale price; for the example, it can be considered an actual occurrence)

For equation (1):

$$Y_o = \frac{NOI_1}{V_o} + \left(\frac{V_{o_1}}{V_o} - 1\right)$$

$$= \frac{\$11,100}{\$106,000} + \left(\frac{\$111,300}{\$106,000} - 1\right)$$

$$= .1047 + (.05)$$

$$= .1547 \text{ (rounded to 15.5\%)}$$

For equation (2):

$$Y_o = \frac{NOI_1}{V_o} + \left(\frac{V_{o_1} - V_o}{V_o}\right)$$

$$= \frac{\$11,100}{\$106,000} + \left(\frac{\$111,300 - \$106,000}{\$106,000}\right)$$

$$= .1047 + .05$$

$$= .1547 \text{ (rounded to 15.5\%)}$$

For equation (3) (R_o = cap rate as derived from the market):

$$Y_o = R_o + \Delta_o$$

$$= .105 + .05$$

$$= 15.5\%$$

Therefore, in a simplified context, the yield is equal to the cap rate plus the expectation of value change over time, stated as a percentage.

The rearrangement of equation (3) enables the use of yield analysis in a capitalization context:

$$R_o = Y_o - \Delta_o \qquad (4)$$

If the overall yield or cost of capital is known (as in many discounted cash flow analyses) and the expected or actual gain or loss in value over a holding period is available (as per DCF models), then a cap rate can be mechanically derived.

In this case:

$$R_o = Y_o - \Delta_o$$
$$= .155 - .05$$
$$= .105$$

$$V_o = \frac{NOI}{R_o} = \frac{NOI}{Y_o - \Delta_o} = \frac{\$11,100}{.105} = \$105,714 \text{ (rounded to \$106,000)}$$

Equation (4) in a generalized form is called the universal cap rate. It is the basis of all yield capitalization models. The universal cap rate premise underlies the mortgage equity models displayed in Figure 5.1, columns 6, 7, and 8.

§ 5.7 AKERSON'S MODEL OF MORTGAGE-EQUITY ANALYSIS

The Akerson model is an interesting yield capitalization technique because it relates the ratio procedure of the band of investment (BOI) to the universal cap rate model (yield capitalization). Because the Akerson model makes this connection between traditional capitalization and the cash flow models, it relates the familiar to the unfamiliar; by building on the familiar, it offers a yield capitalization technique that is generally preferred by students of appraisal.

Akerson initially presented his model as "Ellwood Without Algebra."[3] However, as will be seen, all capitalization is a matter of deterministic algebraic equations, beginning with the traditional BOI. Component X is the mortgage position in the property; component Y is the equity. However, the mortgage component has already been presented as a loan-to-value ratio, symbolized by M, and the equity position of the overall value is denoted by (1 – M). Each of these capital positions is multiplied by its perspective capitalization rates. The traditional BOI model is then:

$$(M \times R_M) + \{(1 - M) \times R_E\} = R_o$$

[3] Charles Akerson, "Ellwood Without Algebra," *The Appraisal Journal*, 39:4 (July 1970): 325–335.

Akerson extended the basic ratio model to yield capitalization by substituting the equity yield rate (Y_E) for the equity dividend rate (R_E).[4] Therefore, the first phase of the Akerson model is:

$$M \times R_M + (1 - M) \times Y_E = R_o$$

(R_o here is only an approximation of the overall cap rate. This factor must be further delineated. See Figure 5.1, column 6.)

Two concerns result from this substitution:

1. The mortgage rate is combined with an equity yield;
2. A percentage of the principal is paid off during the holding period.

When a mortgage ratio rate (R_M), the mortgage constant, is combined with an equity yield, Y_E, a component of the mortgage shifted to the equity must be explicitly considered. Yields and cap rates are not the same (R is not equal to Y). In essence, for Y to equal R, the following relationship must occur:

$$R = Y - \Delta_a$$

For the equity yield rate (Y_E) to equal the equity dividend rate (R_E), a change in the equity value (Δ_E) over the holding period must be estimated and deducted on an annual basis (a = annualizer). The equation for the equity position considered within the rate structure is:

$$R_E = Y_E - \Delta_{E_a}$$

The situation is complicated by beginning with the band of investment, as per Akerson, because the model's initial phase begins with a mortgage *ratio* rate (R_M) and an equity *yield* rate (Y_E). Therefore, it

[4] The difference in the Akerson yield format (as a mortgage-equity model) and the traditional band of investment, which is the conceptual origin of the Akerson model, is the use of an equity yield rate (Y_E) rather than an equity dividend rate (R_E). The difference between the yield and ratio rates is the consideration of the expected change in value over a given holding period. The formula reflecting the relationship in the equity position is:

$$R_E = Y_E - \Delta_{E_a}$$

is not adequate to simply address the change in equity *value* ($(V_{E_n} - V_E)/V_E$, as per the earlier yield discussion). Akerson had to also address the value change in the relationship between the mortgage and the equity position; this position is generally called the equity build-up.

Equity build-up occurs with the repayment of principal on a loan from the property's income stream over the term of the holding period. The rate and the amount of repayment are determined by the combined consideration of the terms reflected in the mortgage constant and the length of the holding period.

In the earlier example, the mortgage constant is .123434, based on a 30-year mortgage at 12 percent interest, payable monthly. The rate is illustrating that both principal and interest are paid over time ($R_M = P_r + I$, where P_r is the percentage of principal paid over the year and I is the rate of interest; therefore, $.123434 = .0003434 + .12$). The rate is based on the 30-year mortgage term in this example.

The second concern in yield capitalization is the amount of principal paid off over the investment holding period. In a cash flow analysis, this amount could be determined by summing the principal payments for the investment holding period (5 years, in the example). The problem is that the yield capitalization technique is probably being used, because sufficient information does not exist to generate a DCF model (that is, V_o is unknown).

To address the percentage of principal paid off during the holding period, Akerson borrowed Ellwood's equation for calculating the percentage of equity build-up (within the rate structure):

$$P = \frac{R_M - I}{R_{M_p} - I}$$

where:

P = percentage of principal paid off over the holding period

R_{M_p} = a contrived mortgage constant that considers (hypothetically) that the mortgage amortization term is the holding period (in this example, 5 years), not the contracted mortgage amortization term (in the example, 30 years).

The contrived R_{M_p} is .266933 (see the Appendix for calculator key strokes). Therefore:

$$P = \frac{R_M - I}{R_{M_p} - I}$$

$$= \frac{.123434 - .12}{.266933 - .12}$$

$$= \frac{.003434}{.146933}$$

$$= .023371$$

The percentage of the mortgage paid off over the holding period (of 5 years) is 2.3371 percent. As the equity yield and mortgage constant are weighted by the loan-to-value ratio (M) and equity portion (1 – M) respectively, so too must the equity build-up position be weighted by its contribution to the overall property. The 2.3371 percent change in the mortgage–equity relationship is being shifted from the mortgage component (M). In terms of its weighted position to the overall property, the equity build-up component (change in the debt-to-equity position) is effectively concerned with the debt position of M.

Also, the 2.3371 percent change is for the entire term of the holding period (5 years). Because the model is attempting to convert a yield concept (over time) to a one-period ratio model, the change must be annualized. This is achieved in Akerson's model by a sinking fund factor at the equity yield rate.[5] The equity yield rate is employed because the value interest is being shifted from the debt side to the equity side, and the appropriate opportunity cost is the equity return.

Summarizing the concerns of the equity build-up concept, Akerson offered the second step of his model with the following equation:

$$Ebu = M \times P \times 1/s_{\overline{n|}}$$

where:

Ebu = equity build-up
M = loan-to-value ratio
P = percentage of principal paid off during holding period
$1/s_{\overline{n|}}$ = sinking fund factor at equity yield rate, used to annualize P

[5] The sinking fund factor conceptually is the amount to be set aside each period to accumulate to a specific amount in the future at a given reinvestment rate. The sinking fund factor (mathematically and conceptually) is the reciprocal of the future worth of 1 per period. It is approximately the same as $1/n$, where n = the economic term with a reinvestment assumption.

The combined steps of the Akerson model to this point are:

$$\begin{array}{llcl} & M & \times R_M & = MR_M \\ + & (1-M) & \times Y_E & = (1-M)Y_E \\ - & M \times P & \times \dfrac{1}{s_{\overline{n|}}} & = MP\dfrac{1}{s_{\overline{n|}}} \\ \hline & & & Y_o \end{array}$$

The Akerson model is interesting at this point, because it represents the property's overall cost of capital. Y_o is the overall yield to the property. If both debt and equity capital are used, then the overall yield is the combined rate that considers the weighted effect of the capital components and their effective terms.

In this case, the combination of a mortgage at 12 percent interest for 30 years (payable monthly), with equity dollars seeking a 15.5 percent yield over a five-year holding period, results in the following overall cost of capital:

$$\begin{array}{llll} M \times R_M = MR_M & & .75 \times .123434 & = .092575 \\ +(1-M) \times Y_E = (1-M)Y_E & + & .25 \times .155 & = .038750 \\ -M \times P \times \dfrac{1}{s_{\overline{n|}}} = MP\dfrac{1}{s_{\overline{n|}}} & - & .75 \times .023371 \times .146855 & = .002574 \\ \hline Y_o & & & .128751 \end{array}$$

The overall cost of capital for the example case lies between the .123434 mortgage constant rate (and above the 12 percent mortgage interest rate, Y_M) and the yield rate (Y_E) at 15.5 percent.

The overall discount rate (Y_o) is often called the basic rate, symbolized by r in Ellwood modeling.

By emphasizing the development of the overall yield rate in the Akerson model, the level of analysis can be switched to the overall property rather than to either the mortgage or the equity component. Earlier, it was shown that, to equate Y_E to R_E, the change in the equity value would need to be calculated. This, however, is difficult to isolate, given the inefficiencies in the real estate market and the lack of data about specific properties. It is also difficult as a matter of logic; the property has not been sold twice over the holding period, so V_{En} and V_E are hard values to estimate.

However, by converting to the overall property level, the concern is focused on the change between the current (V_o) and future (V_{o_n})

overall values of the property, which may be estimated based on market activities. Δ_o, the overall property change as a percentage

$$\left(\frac{V_{o_n} - V_o}{V_o}\right),$$

can be approximated, based on the time adjustment abstracted from a comparison of similar properties in the local market. Δ_o is the same as the property appreciation or growth rate used in the DCF models.

The yield analysis example that follows uses a 5 percent per year increase, or a cumulative appreciation of 25 percent (5 percent × 5 years), in the subject property over the holding period. However, this 25 percent, as for the equity build-up via amortization, must be annualized in order to collapse the yield multiple period concerns to a ratio model. The annualizer for the expected overall value change in the Akerson model is a sinking fund factor, at the equity yield rate. (See the last phase of the Akerson model in Figure 5.1, column 6.)

The entire Akerson model is thus shown as:

$M \times R_M$		$.75 \times .123434$	$= .092375$
$+(1 - M) \times Y_E$	$+$	$.25 \times .155$	$= .038750$
$- M \times P \times \frac{1}{s_{\overline{n}\rceil}}$	$-$	$.75 \times .023371 \times .146855$	$= .002574$
$- \Delta_o \times \frac{1}{s_{\overline{n}\rceil}}$	$-$	$.25 \times .146855$	$= .092038$
R_o			$.092032$ (rounded to 9.2 percent)

The yield capitalization rate is different from the ratio rates, which were fairly consistent in the concluded estimates of the prior ratio models. In this example, the yield cap rate is about 1.3 percent lower than the ratio cap rate of 10.5 percent (10.5 − 9.2 = 1.3 percent). This variation can be attributed to the change in opportunity cost used to discount the value over a holding period, and the consideration of equity build-up as a form of explicit return. The overall value change and build-up are implicitly considered in the ratio models; however, the explicit consideration of the aspects of the yield model can result in a different rate calculation (hence the moderate change in the rate).

Incorporating the explicit additional concerns of yield capitalization, the Akerson model collapses to the traditional overall cap rate model of:

$$V_o = \frac{NOI}{R_o} = \frac{\$11,100}{.092} = \$120,652 \text{ (rounded to } \$121,000)$$

Why would value increase by \$15,000 to \$16,000 (\$121,000 – \$106,000 or \$121,000 – \$105,000) with the consideration of 5 percent per year appreciation for 5 years and of equity accumulation via mortgage amortization? This issue gives an insight to financial risk exposure that must be addressed through the leverage concept.[6]

The explicit consideration of income, value, and capital changes over time can have a significant impact on value. Small changes in cap rates (given fixed or stabilized income measures) can have magnified effects on value estimates. The explicit consideration of real estate economic and financial variables can improve the analytical capacity of decision makers. The insights offered by the Akerson model are offered in the other yield models.

§ 5.8 ELLWOOD'S MODEL

The Ellwood model, in column 7 of Figure 5.1, is the conceptual basis for all the yield capitalization models. Akerson's model was derived to link Ellwood's innovations to the traditional BOI models. As Gibbons[7] shows, the Ellwood model underlies the general premises of what was later called the "universal cap rate model." The universal cap rate model is constructed as:

$$R = Y - \Delta_a$$

The model begins with a yield and deducts the changing value component of a return, to collapse to a capitalization ratio.

The Ellwood model begins with the *equity yield rate* and deducts the equity build-up component and the overall property value change, to derive the overall cap rate to a property. This overall process is similar to the Akerson model, but the origin (or basis) of the model is the equity position, not the debt and equity bands of the investment. This model's origin must be emphasized, to explain the procedural differences between Ellwood and Akerson. The reasons for the difference in origin will be explained later.

[6] The risk exposure of leverage is taken up in Chapter 7.

[7] James Gibbons, "Equity Yield," *The Appraisal Journal*, 48:4 (October 1980): 49–56; Appraisal Institute, *Appraising in a Changing Economy* (Chicago: AI, 1982): 132–157.

Because the Ellwood model begins with the equity yield rate to derive the overall cap rate, it has been argued that the model takes on an investment orientation rather than a market value perspective. However, whether a model is an investment application or a market value application depends in great part on the information used in the model. If the equity yield rate is supported by a comparison with other properties, then the yield rate used can be equated to a market yield, as in the examples used to show the market derivation of the GIM and R_o.

The Akerson and Ellwood models are mechanically and conceptually the same model. The difference in the basis or origin of the model is attributed to analytical tradition and the needs of various decision makers.

Because the Ellwood model is a technique that begins with a yield construct and collapses to an overall rate, the universal cap rate can be used to simplify the Ellwood model.

The universal cap rate illustrates the relationship between the overall cap rate (R_o) and the overall yield rate (Y_o). Therefore:

$$R_o = Y_o - \Delta_{o_a}$$

The Ellwood equation is:

$$R_o = Y_E - MC - \Delta_{o_a}$$

Therefore, if the capital structure is already blended to arrive at the overall cost of capital:

$$R_o = Y_o - \Delta_{o_a} = Y_E - MC - \Delta_{o_a}$$

A comparison of the two equations shows that both are calculating an overall cap rate (R_o), and both employ the overall change in property value, which is annualized (Δ_{oa}, allowing for either appreciation (a gain in value) or depreciation (a loss in value)). The difference in the models lies in the symbols Y_o and $Y_E - MC$. For the Ellwood and universal cap rate models to equate, Y_o must equate to $Y_E - MC$.

In the discussion of the Akerson model, Y_o was pointed out to be the overall cost of capital to a leveraged property. Therefore, Y_o is a weighted combination of the debt and equity components in the yield analysis.

In Ellwood's model, MC represents the amortization or equity build-up over the holding period, as it affects the overall property. This amortization of the debt is deducted as a form of return from the equity yield rate, in the process of equating the yield rate to the overall cap rate.

The Ellwood model explicitly states that the equity return rate is comprised of the income (stabilized measure) received by the property plus the return of the capital via the amortization of debt over the holding period and the capital gain (or loss) received at the resale of the property. The income component as a rate is symbolized by R_o, the amortization return is symbolized by MC, and the gain at sale is Δ_{o_a}. MC and Δ_{o_a} are deducted to arrive at the R_o component. The practicality of this model is that NOI via the appraisal process can reasonably be developed by market data. The debt information is available from lending institutions and the equity yield information can be derived from investor surveys or abstracted from market data.

The key to understanding the Ellwood model lies in the component MC. M is the loan-to-value ratio established in the BOI model; C is a concept Ellwood termed the mortgage coefficient. This coefficient, which quantifies the equity build-up to a property in the rate structure, has the following components:

$$C = Y_E + P(1/s_{\overline{n}|} - R_M)$$

None of the symbols is new:

Y_E = equity yield rate (see Akerson and BOI models)
P = percentage of mortgage paid off over holding period (see Akerson model)
$1/s_{\overline{n}|}$ = sinking fund factor at equity yield rate (see Akerson model)
R_M = mortgage constant (see Akerson and BOI models)

Intuitively, the mortgage coefficient is seen as quantitatively adjusting the equity yield rate for the equity build-up derived from mortgage amortization over the holding period. This dynamic adjustment allows for the change in the debt and equity position over the holding period (that is, the change in the loan-to-value ratio). The percentage of the mortgage paid off over the holding period is added to the equity yield rate (Y_E).

As in Akerson's model, the percentage over the entire holding period is annualized (by the sinking fund factor at Y_E), in order to get a yield estimate (for a period of years) to collapse to a ratio rate (for only one *stabilized* year). The reinvestment via the equity yield rate reflects the shifting of the principal from the debt position to the equity position.

The increased yield rate ($Y_E + P(1/s_{\overline{n|}})$) is then reduced by the mortgage constant to derive the differential between the equity and the debt positions ($Y_E + P(1/s_{\overline{n|}} - R_M)$). The differential can almost be perceived as a periodic cash flow difference that represents the difference between the gains received by the equity holder and the cost of ownership attributed to the debt obligation (that is, the capitalization of the leverage advantage, if there is one).[8]

The mortgage coefficient ($C = Y_E + P(1/s_{\overline{n|}} - R_M)$) is then weighted by the loan-to-value ratio, because all of the gain to the equity position from amortization has occurred in the mortgage component of the property. Therefore, the combined effect of the equity yield and the mortgage amortization should quantitatively equal the overall yield or weighted cost of capital to the property. This result is illustrated with the following check, using numbers from the ongoing example (see § 5.7):

$$
\begin{aligned}
Y_o &= Y_E - MC\ (C = Y_E + P(1/s_{\overline{n|}} - R_M)) \\
&= Y_E - M(Y_E + P(1/s_{\overline{n|}} - R_M)) \\
&= .155 - .75(.155 + .023371(.146855) - .123434) \\
&= .155 - .75(.155 + .003432 - .123434) \\
&= .155 - .75(.034998) \\
&= .155 - .026249 \\
&= .128751 \text{ (see Akerson model)}
\end{aligned}
$$

Ellwood called the Y_o component, reflecting the combination of debt and equity capital within the property context, the basic rate and he used the symbol r. In retrospect, Ellwood's $r = Y_o$, and the Ellwood model is a special case of the universal cap rate:

$$R_o = Y_o - \Delta_{o_a}\ (a = 1/s_{\overline{n|}} \text{ at } Y_E)$$

Given input from the example case:

$$
\begin{aligned}
R_o &= .128751 - (.25 \times .146855) \\
&= .128751 - .036714 \\
&= .092037 \text{ (rounded to 9.2 percent; see Akerson solution)}
\end{aligned}
$$

[8] See Chapter 7 on risk analysis (and leverage).

For a value, Ellwood shows:

$$V_o = \frac{NOI}{R_o} = \frac{\$11{,}100}{.092} = \$120{,}652 \text{ (rounded to \$121,000; see Akerson solution)}$$

A full statement of the Ellwood model is:

$$\begin{aligned} R_o &= Y_E - MC - \Delta_{o_a} = Y_E - M(Y_E + P(1/s_{\overline{n}|} - R_M)) - \Delta_{o_a} \\ &= .155 - .75(.155 - .023371(.146855) - .123434) - .25(.146855) \\ &= .092037 \end{aligned}$$

The above example illustrates that the Ellwood and Akerson models result in the same value answer, despite their different origins. Conceptually, they are the same model. This is illustrated in the Akerson general-derivation beginning:

$$\begin{array}{lll} & M & \times R_M \\ + & (1 - M) & \times Y_E \\ - & M \times P & \times \dfrac{1}{s_{\overline{n}|}} \\ - & \Delta_{o_a} & \underline{} \\ & & R_o \end{array}$$

With an initial rearrangement of the format:

$$\begin{aligned} R_o &= (M \times R_M) + (1 - M)Y_E - (M \times P(1/s_{\overline{n}|})) - \Delta_{o_a} \\ &= (M \times R_M) + Y_E - MY_E - MP(1/s_{\overline{n}|}) - \Delta_{o_a} \\ &= Y_E - MY_E - MP(1/s_{\overline{n}|}) + (M \times R_M) - \Delta_{o_a} \\ &= Y_E - M(Y_E + P(1/s_{\overline{n}|}) - R_M) - \Delta_{o_a} \end{aligned}$$

and, since $C = (Y_E + P(1/s_{\overline{n}|}) - R_M$, then:

$$R_o = Y_E - MC - \Delta_{o_a}$$

Therefore, the Akerson model, as an extended or yield BOI model, collapses to the Ellwood model.

The preceding exercise is not an idle academic activity. It illustrates not only the relationship between the Akerson and Ellwood models, but the relationships between mortgage-equity yield models and mortgage-equity ratio models. This link can then be expanded to demonstrate a conceptual relationship between direct or ratio capitalization and discounted cash flow models. The extent of the relationships must be demonstrated by the capacity of the model to make relevant decisions, and the proof must lie in the uniformity of the data employed in the various models.

The relationship between yield capitalization analysis and discount cash flow analysis, which is often presented in an after-tax analysis, is illustrated by Fisher's Ellwood after-tax extensions (Figure 5.1, column 8).

§ 5.9 FISHER'S AFTER-TAX ELLWOOD MODEL

Fisher's after-tax Ellwood model is an extension of Ellwood's basic yield model that allows for the value contribution of the tax shelter potential that can accrue to real estate.[9] In the classical yield models, the tax shelter components of value are considered within the rate structure, not within the income flow. As in the other yield models, the tax shelter components are deducted from the before-tax equity yield as the explicit multiperiod concerns of yield analysis are collapsed to a single-term ratio model.

The Fisher model extends the traditional Ellwood model with a combination of factors, to allow for the cash flow returns derived from the reduced taxable income to real estate projects, resulting from an interest deduction and the depreciation allowance (as a taxable deduction). The Fisher model takes the following form:

$$R_o = Y_E - MC - \Delta_{o_a} - MF_t - B_{dt}$$

[9] A previous after-tax yield capitalization model was developed by Charles H. Gushee; see *Financial Capitalization Rate Tables* (Chicago: AIREA, and Boston: Financial Publishing Co., 1974). A comparison of the Fisher and Gushee models is necessary to understand the calculations yield.

where:

R_o = after-tax cap rate (per Fisher's model, it may be more appropriate to identify the cap rate as R_t)
Y_E = before-tax equity yield rate
M = loan-to-value ratio
C = Ellwood mortgage coefficient, $C = Y_E + P(1/s_{\overline{n}|}) - R_M$
Δ_{o_a} = overall property change for the holding period, annualized; the annualizer (a) is a sinking fund factor at the before-tax equity yield rate ($a = (1/s_{\overline{n}|})Y_E$)
F = composite factor that allows for the geometric decrease of the interest deduction over the holding period (see page 000)
t = marginal tax rates
B = balance of property value that is depreciable
d = annual depreciation rate; depreciation component stated as a percentage

To apply the after-tax rate analysis, additional information must be made explicit. This information would be required to conduct an after-tax cash flow analysis.

First, the financial data must consider the interest components of the debt service for 5 years. For a cash flow analysis, this would require knowing the amount of the loan (or having prior knowledge of the value—which is the objective of the appraisal, and is therefore supposedly not known at the time of the appraisal). As in the example for

Table 5.2 Interest Components of Debt Service (DCF)

	Years				
	1	2	3	4	5
V_M	\$79,500	\$79,227	\$78,921	\$78,578	\$78,194
	× .12	× .12	× .12	× .12	× .12
Interest	9,540	9,507	9,470	9,429	9,383
DS	9,813	9,813	9,813	9,813	9,813
Less: Interest	9,540	9,507	9,470	9,429	9,383
Principal	273	306	343	384	−430
V_M	79,500	79,227	78,921	78,578	78,194
Less: Principal	273	306	343	384	430
	\$79,227	\$78,921	\$78,578	\$78,194	\$77,764

the equity residual model, a mortgage is around \$79,500. The interest rate is 12 percent and the amortization terms are monthly payments for 30 years. A discounted cash flow would require the calculations shown in Table 5.2 (interest calculations are rounded to the nearest dollar). The \$77,764 at the end of the fifth year is the balance of the mortgage. Over the holding period, \$1,736 of principal has been paid off (and shifted to the equity position). The equity build-up, in effect, places additional equity in the project. The total interest paid over this period is \$47,329. At a 33 percent tax rate ($t = .33$), approximately \$15,618.57 (\$47,329 × .33) is a tax deduction. This interest allowance can be used as a shelter against other passive income received by entities controlling the example property.

The Fisher model considers this interest deduction at an effective rate of .35 to .4 percent per year over the holding period in the F factor. The F factor allows for the periodic decline in the interest write-off over the holding period. Insertion of the financial information into the F factor formula generates the following financial situation for the example:

F = tax saving effect due to interest write-off

$$F = \frac{1}{a_{nY_t}}\left[\frac{a_{12nY_t/12}}{a_{12MY_M/12}} - \frac{1}{s_{12MY_M/12}}\left(\frac{1 - v^{12n}_{Y_t/12}(1+Y_{M/12})^{12n}}{Y_{t/12} - Y_{M/12}}\right)\right]$$

where:

- a = present worth of 1 per period (monthly) at either Y_M (interest rate) or Y_t (after-tax equity yield)
- s = future worth of 1 per period (month)
- v = present worth of 1 at the Y_t rate
- $v^{12n}_{Y_t}$ = present worth of 1 due in n periods [the holding or projection period (times 12 = monthly discounting)] at the after-tax equity yield
- n = holding or projection period
- M = years of mortgage life (times 12 = monthly)
- $a_{nY_t/12}$ = present worth of 1 for n periods (holding/investment term) at the after-tax equity yield (divided by 12 = monthly effective yield)

The decomposition of the rate structure, to estimate the present worth of interest on a direct reduction loan, is difficult. Therefore, Gushee's methodology is used rather than Fisher's. Gushee's procedure is set up to deduct the present worth of the principal repayment from the value (present worth) of the whole loan, to arrive at the present value of the interest. The present value of the whole loan is

$$\frac{1}{a_{12M\,Y_M/12}}$$

(symbol for installment to amortize, with reinvestment at the interest rate (Y_M)). This amount is multiplied by $a_{12n\,Y_t/12}$, which is an annuity at the after-tax yield tax (Fisher's modification of Gushee's tables).

The present worth of the principal repayments is the amount

$$\frac{1}{s_{12M\,Y_M/12}}$$

that is, the first principal payment (a sinking fund factor for the mortgage term at the monthly interest rate). This is multiplied by the present worth of 1 per period (ordinary annuity $1 - v_{Y_t/12}^{12n}$ for the holding period at Y_t), growing at a ratio of the compound interest rate monthly for the holding period $1 + Y_{M/12}^{12n}$. This present value of the growth annuity is divided by the difference in the after-tax yield (monthly) and the effective interest rate.

The difference between the present worth of the whole loan and the principal payments is the present value of the interest. This is multiplied by the factor to amortize the value for the holding period at the after-tax equity yield rate. The weighted effect of all these components comprises Fisher's F factor.

The numerical example of the F factor components is as follows. The problem is for a holding period of 5 years ($n = 5$) calculated monthly ($\therefore\ 12n = 12 \times 5 = 60$ periods). The mortgage term is 30 years (monthly considerations result in $12 \times 30 = 360$ periods).

After-tax equity yield is 18 percent ($Y_t = 18$ percent monthly $= \sqrt[12]{1.18} = .01388$.

$$F = \frac{1}{a_{\overline{5}|.18}}\left[\frac{a_{\overline{60}|1.388}}{a_{\overline{36}|01}} - \frac{1}{s_{\overline{36}|01}}\left(\frac{1 - v_{1.388}^{60}\,(1 + Y_{M/12})^{60}}{8/12 - 12/12}\right)\right]$$

$$= .319778\left[\frac{40.538376}{97.218331} - \left(.000286\right)\left(\frac{(1 - .437109)(1 + .01)^{60}}{.01388 - .01}\right)\right]$$

$$= .319778\left[.416983 - (.000286)\left(\frac{(.562891)(1.816697)}{.00388}\right)\right]$$

$$= .319778[.416983 - (.000286)(263.557274)]$$

$$= .319778[.416983 - .075377]$$

$$= .109238$$

where:

$Y_t/12$ = 1.388 percent (per month) for $Y_t = 18$ percent
M = 360 months (30 years)
$Y_M/12$ = 1 percent (per month)

The F factor must be weighted by the loan-to-value ratio, to appropriately attribute the value impact of this tax feature to the debt component of the property.

This weighted factor (MF) is then multiplied by the tax rate (t = .33), to approximate the tax flow impact as a rate equivalent explicitly considered in the cap rate (as a deduction from the yield rate). The combined equation for the financial deduction is MF_t or (.75 × .109238 × .33 = .027036).

A similar procedure is applied to estimate the tax flow component as a rate factor for the depreciation component of the after-tax valuation. This component analysis has been simplified by the current tax laws, which allow only straight-line depreciation.

Fisher's depreciation components are B, d, and t. B is the percentage of the property that is depreciable. In the case example, this is the 80 percent of the property value that represents the improvements (20 percent of the value is land). In reality, this ratio can only be established by having a land value appraisal performed (especially if the property is improved). In this case, B = .80; d is the effective rate adjustment, considering the impact of depreciation. Because the property is commercial, the depreciable economic life allowed by statute is 27.5 years. The d factor is a ratio of the periodic depreciation allowance of 1/27.5 = .036364 to an annuity factor at the after-tax yield rate.

The annuity factor is for the holding period of 5 years ($n = 5$) at the after-tax yield rate of 18 percent. The formula for the straight-line depreciation impact is:

$$d = \frac{x}{a_{nY_t}}$$

$$= \frac{.036364}{3.127171} = .011628$$

where:

x = periodic depreciation allowance of $\frac{1}{T} = \frac{1}{27.5}$

T = 27.5 years, or tax depreciation term allowed

n = 5-year holding period

Y_t = 18 percent

The tax rate is 33 percent ($t = .33$). The combined equation for the depreciation is B_{dt} or ($.80 \times .011628 \times .33 = 0.003070$).

The tax at sale must also be considered in the Ellwood equation. Neither Fisher nor Gushee addresses this issue. The tax at sale is \$13,834, when calculated as a cash flow (see page 000). In the rate structure, the tax at sale component in a valuation is composed of the summation of the periodic depreciation deductions for the holding period, discounted as a lump sum (the concern is the present worth of 1 per period), times the tax rate. This is the amount of tax that must be paid, based on the deferment resulting from the periodic depreciation deduction from the cash flow. The tax at sale as a rate is:

$$\text{Tax at sale rate} = xn\text{vt}$$

where:

x = the periodic depreciation deduction of .036364 (1/27.5)
n = the holding period term (5 years)
v = present worth of 1, received at the end of 5 years (a discount factor)
t = tax rate

The tax at sale deduction is added into the capitalization formula because it is an expense at sale. The impact in this case example is:

$$\begin{aligned}\text{Tax at sale rate} &= xn\text{vt}\\ &= (.036364 \times 5 \times .437109 \times .33)\\ &= .026227\end{aligned}$$

The Ellwood model numerical example is expanded to the Fisher model with the inclusion of the tax at sale. The format is:

$$R_t = Y_E - M(Y_E + P(1/s_{\overline{n|}}) - R_M) - \Delta_{o_a} - MF_t - B_{dt} + xn\text{vt}$$

$$= .155 - .75(.155 + .023371(.146855) - .123434) - .25(.146855) - .75(.109238)(.33) - .80(.011628)(.33) + (.036364 \times 5 \times .437109 \times .33)$$

$$= .092032 - .027036 - .00307 + .026227$$

$$= .088153$$

The traditional capitalization formula is employed using the modified Fisher after-tax cap rate:

$$V_t = \frac{NOI}{R_t} = \frac{\$11{,}000}{.088153} = \$125{,}917 \text{ (rounded to } \$126{,}000)$$

Note that this value is explicitly calculated after taxes. Conceptually, the tax benefits are implicitly considered in all of the previous capitalization models. In fact, the variation in market cap rates (R_o) could be attributed to varying expectations of property growth (or gain) and the individual tax situations of the market participants (as well as the differences in after-tax equity-yield expectations). This possibility exists because the R_o is the ratio of the productivity of the realty asset, which can be constrained via productivity factors (physical, legal, and location attributes), competition within a tight range, and the transaction price, which can vary with financing and taxing situations, as the mortgage-equity analysis illustrates.

§ 5.10 DISCOUNTED CASH FLOW (DCF) MODEL

The objective of this chapter is to illustrate alternatives to the DCF model. Figure 5.2 compares a traditional DCF model with the capitalization models previously discussed.

To achieve the chapter's objective, even more information must be made explicit. Up to this point, the property's productivity has been consistent because all of the capitalization models use the accrual accounting concept of a stabilized income. A cash accounting concept can deal with a variable income.[10] In the example case, the income and expenses are projected to increase at a constant (compounding rate) of 3 percent per year. This is an explicit variable that should be considered along with the financial, tax, and property change variables. For consistency, the income and expenses could be held constant over time (0 percent growth), but a concern of this analysis is to show the impact on value conclusions of explicitly considered variables.

Table 5.3, a cash flow projection over a 5-year holding period, acknowledges all of the variables explicitly and implicitly considered in the previous models (Figure 5.1, columns 1 through 8).

[10] Capitalization models can deal with consistent income patterns and changes (see the J and K factor concepts in Chapter 7).

Table 5.3 Cash Flow Projection (All figures rounded to nearest dollar)

	Years				
	1	2	3	4	5
GI	$14,139	$14,563	$15,000	$15,450	$15,914
Vacancy (6%)	848	874	900	927	955
EGI	13,291	13,689	14,100	14,523	14,959
Operating expenses (20% PGI)	2,828	2,913	3,000	3,090	3,183
NOI	10,463	10,776	11,100	11,433	11,776
Less: Interest	(9,540)	(9,507)	(9,470)	(9,429)	(9,383)
Depreciation	(3,084)	(3,084)	(3,084)	(3,084)	(3,084)
Taxable income	(2,161)	(1,815)	(1,454)	(1,080)	(691)
Plus: Depreciation[1]	3,084	3,084	3,084	3,084	3,084
Less: Principal	(273)	(306)	(343)	(384)	(430)
CTO or BTCF[2]	650	963	1,287[3]	1,620	1,963
Less: Taxes or Plus: Tax savings[4]	713	599	480	356	228
ATCF[5]	1,363	1,562	1,767	1,976	2,191
PV factor at 18%[6]	.8475	.7182	.6086	.5158	.4371
PV	$1,155	$1,122	$1,075	$1,019	958

[1] Depreciation requires a knowledge of cost or value; in this case, the capitalized value of $106,000 is used. Eighty percent (.80) of the value is depreciable (see the Fisher model). Therefore, the depreciation base is $84,800, which is then multiplied by the annual percentage of .036364 (1/27.5 years). The result will vary from the IRS tax schedule. The annual estimate for the depreciation deduction is $3,084 (r).

[2] BTCF = before-tax cash flow.

[3] See CTO/BTCF calculation in equity residual model.

[4] This project generates tax savings or, more appropriately, tax savings on other income, for each year in the holding period. The tax savings are calculated by multiplying the *negative* taxable income by the tax rate of 33 percent. The first year calculation is: (2161) × .33 = $713.

[5] ATCF = after-tax cash flow.

[6] The present value factor is an after-tax discount at 18 percent. This is 2.5 percent more than the before-tax yield of 15.5 percent. The 2.5 percent difference is not a standard, but the after-tax yield should tend to be higher, as long as tax benefits contribute to value.

The periodic cash flow from operations must be added to the cash received upon sale, at the end of the holding period. This cash calculation is:

Future sales price based on 25% appreciation and before sales commission	$140,957
Less: 6% sales commission	8,457
Net sales price	$132,500
Less: Mortgage balance	77,764
Taxes at sale*	13,834
Cash at sale	$ 40,902†

* The taxes at sale are on the difference between the net gain ($132,500) and the depreciated basis ($106,000 − $15,420 = $90,580). Therefore, $132,500 − $90,580 = $41,920 × .33 = $13,834. ($15,420 = depreciation of $3,084 per year × 5 years.)

† The present value of the cash at sale is $40,902 discounted at 18% for 5 years (the factor is .4371).

The present value of the cash at sale is added to the present value (PV) of the 5-year cash flow of $5,329 ($1,155 + $1,122 + $1,075 + $1,019 + $958) and the original mortgage value (V_M) of $79,500, to arrive at the present value (V_o) of the property by the discounted cash flow model. Therefore:

PV income	$ 5,329
Cash at sale	17,878
V_M	79,500
V_o	$102,707 (rounded to $103,000)

§ 5.11 SUMMARY AND CONCLUSIONS

Nine models as alternatives to the discounted cash flow have been presented in this analysis. The models include two gross income multiplier models, four direct (ratio) capitalization models, and three yield capitalization models. All but the EGIM model are depicted in Figure 5.1.

These nine models have been compared to a traditional discounted cash flow (DCF) model. The comparison is to show, in part, that as the models depicted in Figure 5.1 progress from left to right, more and more information is made explicit. This progression requires an increase in the number of assumptions needed for each calculation, but a decrease in the amount of variables (and/or information) that are assumed away.

The projection and comparison of the models also show that, even though the models implicitly consider variables that are explicit in models placed farther to the right in Figure 5.1, the explicit consideration of a variable may potentially impact value conclusions.

In the numerical example carried through the investigation, the impact of explicitly considering financing terms had little or no effect on the value conclusion in the multiplier and ratio models. In fact, the value estimates in the examples were consistently in the $105,000 to $106,000 range.

With the inclusion of the time dimension in the yield models, which allow for a dynamic consideration of the amortization effects of financing and the consideration of expectations of growth (or occurrences of decline), a significant change in the value conclusions is observed.

The example shows that the yield models are not only similar, but are identical with a value estimate of $121,000. This is approximately $15,000 (or 14.2 percent) more than the ratio and multiplier models indicated. However, this $15,000 is *approximately* the present value of a 25 percent increase in value ($132,500) over a 5-year period and a 2.3 percent shift ($1,829) of mortgage debt to equity collateral, resulting from mortgage amortization.

Therefore, the yield models not only make more variables explicit, they consider additional factors that may contribute to value. If expectations of property appreciation were held constant, the yield models would indicate a value within $2,000 of the ratio-multiplier models. The $2,000 is attributed to equity build-up due to amortization over the holding period. This could be greater if the leverage were more positive.

The Fisher yield model has very similar conclusions and indicates a value within $5,000 of the other yield models. Again, this value variance is more than the explicit consideration of variables; it results when additional components of value are identified and capitalized. The models depicted in columns 8 and 9 of Figure 5.1 introduce the benefits of tax shelter to value estimation. The DCF also allows for an increase in the income stream each year, and has a value within $2,000–$3,000 of the ratio models.

These variables, to a limited extent (as long as they follow a consistent pattern), can mathematically be considered in the yield models through such techniques as the J and K factors to be explained later.

The Fisher model did not allow for the varying income pattern that is part of the DCF model, but this is partially offset by its lack of consideration of taxes at time of sale (capital gains taxes). Inclusion of this factor increases the after-tax rate in proximity to the 9 percent level. A major contributor to a difference in the yield models and the DCF after taxes is that many of the components are discounted at the before-tax yield rate (Y_E), but all components in the DCF are discounted at the after-tax yield rate.

If the income growth is held constant and there is no potential for tax benefits, the DCF and Fisher models should equate to the Akerson and Ellwood models. Therefore, another key concern of this analysis has been to show that there is a relationship among all of the income models that have evolved over time.

The key differences in the models are their basis of origin (the income level capitalized and the variables assumed to be implicit to the models), the emphasis placed on specific variables, and the situation in which the models can properly be employed. The issues of emphasis on different information and appropriateness of a model at different times address the utility of the models. Because it is an imperfect world of limited information, a specific model may be the only tool available to help a decision maker at a given place, situation, or time. However, as this analysis shows, all of the models are generally related.

APPENDIX

Calculator Keys

To calculate the mortgage constant for the holding period (R_{M_p}):

5 g n
12 g i
1 (chs) PV
PMT = .022244
.022244 × 12 = .266933

To calculate a sinking fund factor (at 15.5 percent):

(f) (Reg) or (f) (Fin)
5 n

15.5 i
1 (chs) FV
PMT = .146855

Figure 5.2 Income Analysis Models: Hypothesized Value Estimates

	Ratio Models					
	1 GIM	1a EGIM	2 Overall Cap*	3 Equity Residual	4 Underwriter's Model	5 Band-of-Investment Model*
Explicit variables	None	Vacancy Estimate	Vacancy All operating expenses (OE)	Vacancy OE Debt service (DS) Mortgage constant (R_M) Equity dividend date (R_E)	Vacancy OE DS Debt coverage ratio (DCF) R_M R_E	Vacancy OE Loan-to-value Ratio (M) R_M R_E
Value estimate per example	$105,000	$105,000	$106,000	$105,000	$105,000	$106,000*

*Note the similarity in the value estimates of the strict rate models, where all issues are addressed in the rate development (columns 2 and 5) and the similarity in the conclusions of the model, requiring information in the forms of income, rates, and multiplier ratios (columns 1, 1a, 3, and 4). The difference in yield rates as discounting factors is a major reason for value differences.

Yield Models				
6	7	8	9	10
Akerson	Ellwood	Fisher's Ellwood After-Tax	DCF	Alternative DCF
Vacancy	Vacancy	Vacancy	Vacancy	Same
OE	OE	OE	OE	
M	M	M	M	
R_M	R_M	R_M	R_M	
Y_E	Y_E	Y_E	Y_E	
Percentage of mortgage paid off (P)	P	P	P	
Overall property value change (D_o)	D_o	D_o	D_o	
Reinvestment assumptions at Y_E	Reinvestment assumptions at Y_E	Reinvestment assumptions at Y_E and Y_t	Reinvestment assumptions at Y_t	Plus insolvency after taxes
		Tax rate (t)	t	
		Depreciation schedule (d)	d	
$121,000	$121,000	$126,000	$103,000	

Calculator key strokes:

Mortgage Constant Input	(HP example) Financial Keys
30	g n
12	g i
1	(chs) PV
(PMT) = .010286	(effective monthly rate)
$R_M = .010286 \times 12$ (months) = .123434	

If financial calculator does not have g function of HP, then keys are:

Input	Financial Keys
$30 \times 12 = 360$	n
$12 \div 12 = 1$	i
1	PV
PMT = .010286	

Six

Direct Capitalization

§ 6.1 INTRODUCTION

Direct or ratio capitalization is the process of converting a single-period income into a value by use of a capitalization rate. Traditionally, direct capitalization has been employed as a valuation tool. This chapter exhibits the development of direct capitalization theory and techniques, and sets the foundation for using direct capitalization as a tool of solvency and rate analysis—a task approached in later chapters. The income capitalized should be a stabilized income measure, if the objective is a market value estimate. Often, a first-year income, which may not be a typical operating income, is used. The overall cap rate may also be used to reflect the ratio between any periodic income measure and a periodic value measure. This single-term ratio can be used for a temporal measure of how a property meets the productivity-to-asset-worth expectations. As a periodic measure of productivity to asset worth, the pattern of change in periodic cap rates is a useful barometer, when used in conjunction with a discounted flow projection (see Chapter 7).

§ 6.2 OVERALL CAP RATE

The direct cap rate calculation can be used as a comparison of current property productivity and expectations of asset worth because it is a ratio of net operating income to asset value (or current price):

$$R_o = \frac{NOI}{V_o}$$

where:

R_o = overall cap rate
NOI = net operating income—the income derived after deducting a vacancy allowance and all operating expenses, fixed and variable, from the effective gross income

NOI is a measure of productivity because it represents the potential revenue received by the real property after deductions for maintenance, operations, and other services needed to sustain the activity or enterprise housed by the real estate. After the deductions, the residual income is the price paid for the use of the real estate space over time.

The sales price (V_o) or current value estimate is a current capital amount that represents the present worth of future expected benefits. Therefore, the cap rate implicitly considers:

1. Return of the initial capital investment;
2. Return on the overall investment;
3. Allowance for expectations of appreciation or value decline;
4. Allowance for changes in financial structure over time, if financing is used.

§ 6.3 ORIGINS OF DIRECT CAPITALIZATION

The origins of the income approach, historically presented as a discounting (annuity) or capitalization process, can be linked to two major issues. One issue was the need for economists to make aggregate economic (capital) allocation decisions. This influence is seen in the efforts of mathematicians and economists as far back as 1662, when Sir William Petty summed the annual rents of estates into land value, and 1668, the year of John Newton's tables of compound interest. The evolution of modifications on this basic theme has continued into the twentieth century.[1]

[1] James H. Burton, *Evolution of the Income Approach* (Chicago: AIREA, 1982).

The second issue was the economic depression of the 1930s. The lack of market activity and valid arm's-length transactions forced an emphasis on the purchase of property for its revenue potential. Lenders and regulators then, as now, were forced to become asset managers. The premises for the income emphasis of real estate, expressed in the works of Babcock and Mertzke in the late 1920s and early 1930s, were heavily influenced by Fisher's body of work, which spanned the years 1906 to 1930.[2] Fisher's definition of value as the present worth of future income is now universally accepted. After completing a vigorous theoretical analysis of three approximations of the rate of interest, Fisher deduced that the rate was theoretically determined by investment opportunity, time preference, and the market. Fisher illustrated that the discounting process (reciprocal of a given compound interest rate) collapses to the overall direct capitalization rate, as follows:

$$V = \frac{NOI}{y} = \left(\frac{1}{(1+y)} + \frac{1}{(1+y)^2} + \; . \; . \; . \; + \frac{1}{(1+y)^\infty}\right) NOI = \left(\frac{\frac{1}{1+y}}{1 - \frac{1}{1+y}}\right) NOI$$

where:

V = value on amount function
y = discount rate (the effective interest rate or change per period)

Fisher was the first economic writer to emphasize the direct capitalization technique.[3]

The relationship of the cap rate to the interest rate (and the compounding/discounting methods) supports the contention that the cap rate implicitly contains consideration of opportunity costs, time

[2] The literature influencing the income analysis perspective of real estate is observed in the classic works of Frederick M. Babcock, *The Valuation of Real Estate* (New York: McGraw-Hill, 1932); Arthur J. Mertzke, *Real Estate Appraising* (Chicago: National Association of Real Estate Boards, 1927); Irving Fisher, *The Nature of Capital and Income* (New York: The Macmillan Co., 1906), and *The Theory of Interest* (New York: Kelley and Willman, 1930).

[3] Fisher, *supra* note 2, at 52. The symbols and factors have been converted to real estate jargon.

preferences, and market influences. Fisher made an interesting conceptual link that is useful in decision making: the individual's investment/ consumption rate of time-preference at the margin of choice tends to harmonize with the market rate of return. Human impatience to spend and enjoy income is translated and crystallized into a market rate.

Some issues that are important for understanding direct capitalization in the context of computers (and, consequently, multiple-year cash flow analysis) emerge from this historical background:

1. Direct capitalization was designed to enable capital allocations in an era of limited data, less advanced technology, and outmoded constraints.
2. The cap rate implicitly contains the elements of a measure of total investment return.

This second issue lays the foundation for the remainder of this chapter and is the basis of Chapter 7's discussion of yield capitalization.

The investigation of direct capitalization given here is structured to examine the link of the cap rate to the market and its capacity to aid in comparing investments or selected properties. The market relationship allows the abstraction of risk levels, recapture allowances (physical and investment), financial components, and expectations of change. Each of these direct capitalization issues is considered in turn.

Because the direct capitalization concept was developed as a tool of convenience, the simple technique for deriving a ratio of income to price inherently contains complex issues (investment preferences, expectations, opportunity cost, and measures of productivity). These issues are conceptually tied to the market and potentially contain information that can be abstracted for comparison and analysis.

The technique of dividing income (as a perpetual measure) by a rate, to derive value, establishes several issues (yield capitalization, discounted cash flow, and other techniques that address income and resale measures) that cause direct capitalization to deviate from standard investment analysis. The direct capitalization methods propose that all value is based on a stabilized income measure. Therefore, the potential gains to be received from the future resale (or terminal) value must be considered in the rate structure (or the income estimate). The time horizon of a typical investment term is not reflected in the perpetuity model; if considered relevant, it must be considered in the rate structure. Issues of risk, the recapture of initially invested capital, financial structure, and physical components are also contained in the rate structure.

§ 6.4 OVERALL CAP RATE: THE MARKET SALES ABSTRACTION TECHNIQUE

The overall capitalization rate can be derived by abstraction from comparable property transactions (the market derivation) or as a result of a built-up rate (see § 6.5).

The preferred method of developing a capitalization rate for a market value estimate is to derive it from market sales transactions. In many cases, the capitalization rate can be considered a market artifact, because it is a contrived measure of market performance that can be used as a benchmark for comparing the subject property with other properties.

The objective of the market abstraction technique is to select an appropriate set of comparable sales, to be used as the indicators of an estimated cap rate for a subject property that has not recently been sold. Properties with similar risk levels and exposures, and comparable revenue patterns and returns, would meet the standards of investment comparison. The physical, legal, and locational attributes of the property can also be matched. Examples of the physical attributes are building size, construction materials, location, and other property/market attributes.

Five sales are identified in the following example of the comparable sales selection process:

	Sales				
	1	2	3	4	5
NOI	$ 10,000	$ 12,000	$ 20,000	$ 15,000	$ 18,000
Sales price	100,000	140,000	180,000	150,000	200,000
Cap rate (R_o)	.1000	.0857	.1111	.1000	.0900

The range of cap rates is approximately 8.5 to 11 percent. The subject property's stabilized income estimate is $10,000. Based on the range of cap rates, the possible value range for the subject is $90,000 (based on the 11.11 percent rate) to $117,647 (based on the 8.5 percent rate).

A significant insight at this point is that the lower rate indicates a higher value is paid for a given income stream. This will be more clearly explained in the discussion on yield capitalization, in Chapter 7. It is sufficient to note at this point that a high cap rate may not be desirable as a high investment yield (it may connote the opposite). A high cap rate may indicate that the deal was premised on the strength of the current income and is not dependent on expectations of great gains upon resale. The key is to identify the appropriate relationship between the stabilized income estimate and the value (sales price–asset worth).

In the example above, sales 1 and 4 are similar to the subject, in terms of income patterns, risk levels, location, and physical condition. Based on these factors, a 10 percent cap rate is considered appropriate to the subject property. The value of the subject property, using the sales comparison, is:

$$V_o = \frac{NOI}{R_o} = \frac{\$10,000}{.10} = \$100,000$$

The market sales abstraction technique is mechanically a simple process in which emphasis is placed on the collection and analysis of data. However, despite the technique's being mechanically simple, it is conceptually complex. The overall rate, in equating the productivity of the property to the asset's worth (the present value of future benefits) via the NOI, implicitly considers future value changes (expectations of gains or loss), returns on and of investment, and any amortization during the holding period, if debt capital is considered. It can even be argued that tax shelter benefits are incorporated in the rates, because the value (purchase price) would be based on all benefits of ownership and the NOI is before tax and financing.

The concerns of risk and return implicitly incorporated in the overall tax rate as indicated by market abstraction can be made partially explicit in the built-up technique of overall rate development.

§ 6.5 BUILT-UP RATES

The issues implicit in the overall cap rate allow a breakdown of the rate into its component parts. On the other hand, the concept of the direct capitalization rate's allowing for a return on and of the investment and the consideration of risk allow the cap rate to be built-up.

The components of the built-up rate are dependent on the periodic status of financial and real estate markets.

The primary issues to be considered involve a return on and of the investment. The components of return on investment are: a risk-free rate that identifies the time preference of investors, an inflation consideration, a financial administrative cost allowance (stated as a percentage), the base or minimum opportunity cost, and a risk premium that is appropriate to the nature and characteristics of the property type. (The risk premium should contain an allowance for nonliquidity, given real estate alternatives.)

The nature of direct capitalization requires a return of the investment, because all value in direct capitalization is contingent on the NOI level (V = I/R). No consideration is given for a recapture of capital via a resale of the property (return via gain or loss at resale). The potential for final value change is addressed by a loading (deduction) within the cap rate. This loading traditionally was approached as a recapture rate, to allow for the physical/economic depreciation of the property.

The concern with or perception of the physical and conceptual differences between real capital and land is essential to understanding the recapture loading and the return of the investment within the rate structure.

The origins of the split rate can be linked to Adam Smith's theory of distribution, which suggested four factors of production: labor, capital, land, and coordination (entrepreneurship). Each factor of production was to receive a return. Specifically, capital would receive interest (if financial capital) or other forms of income (if real capital), and land would receive a residual return called rent. The real capital had finite economic life and would thus depreciate (physical deterioration is emphasized, but there are also elements of functional obsolescence—a deficiency in design or capacity, in terms of market references). These expectations that a property's value would decline over time required a periodic deduction from the income stream, resulting in a lower value (overall). Three techniques of recapture have evolved: the straight-line, Inwood, and Hoskold methods.

(a) STRAIGHT-LINE RECAPTURE METHOD

Several alternatives were developed over time, to allow for the periodic recapture of capital. In each case, the recapture rate was added to the overall return on the investment.

The simplest technique is recapture on a straight-line basis. The straight-line recapture identified the expected term or economic life of the depreciable property and developed an annual recapture rate by taking the reciprocal of the term. For example, the property of concern has a projected economic life of 40 years. This implies a periodic recapture rate of 2.5 percent (1/40). The recapture rate is added to the return rate (summation of time value component management and risk premium) to derive the overall built-up rate. Assuming it is 9 percent, the cap rate is:

Return on investment	.09
Recapture	.025
Overall cap rate (R_o)	.115

(b) INWOOD RECAPTURE METHOD (ANNUITY RECAPTURE)

An even older capitalization/economic issue than the difference between permanent land and wasting real assets is the debate concerning the appropriate reinvestment approach in the recapture rate. Should the recapture be conducted by using a reinvestment rate in a sinking fund equation or an annuity equation? The sinking fund and annuity equations are examined in more detail in Chapter 7.

In 1811, William Inwood wrote a book of annuity tables derived from the work of Francis Bailey and John Smart.[4] The tables are based on the assumption that an investor must invest the difference between his or her annual income and the interest on that income, at a rate of interest that is equal to the rate of return, in order to replace the original investment. Over time, this has been known as the Inwood premise.

The Inwood premise requires the economic term of recapture and the rate of return. The built-up overall cap rate is the summation of the rate of return and a recapture rate at the rate of return.

Return on investment	.09
Sinking fund factor at the annuity rate (9% over 40 years) (recapture)	.00296
Overall cap rate	.09296

[4] Burton, *supra* note 1, at 31.

(c) HOSKOLD RECAPTURE METHOD (SINKING FUND RECAPTURE)

In 1877, Henry Hoskold developed a method of capitalization that added a return on investment (interest) rate to a sinking fund factor, at a lower rate of interest (often a "safe rate") than the speculative rate at the return on investment level.

Hoskold's premise was that the reinvestment rate would ordinarily be lower than the required return on capital. Hoskold's immediate concern was dealing with the reserves in a quarry. The recapture at a "safe rate" was considered important because quarries and related mineral deposits are depleting assets. Therefore, opportunity costs are limited and the loss is a certainty, not a risk or unknown occurrence.

Based on the model's origins in the context of depleting assets, the Hoskold premise has been assumed to have limited applicability. Hoskold's approach was attacked because the interest rate plus a sinking fund is mechanically and mathematically the same as a straight annuity factor. However, the contribution of the Hoskold premise in a modern context is that a split rate, which allows for an alternative reinvestment rate, may be relevant and realistic in several situations.

The split rate is appropriate in any situation where investors' resources and opportunities for alternatives are limited. The limitations are set by the marginal opportunity cost or marginal returns open to an investor who has limited resources and options. The reinvestment return may be constrained by limited options in a given short-term market controlled by limited information and constrained knowledge. A longer-term market often has longer periods, allowing more information flow and multiple options. The split rate of the Hoskold premise underlies the modified interval rate of return concept. The Inwood premise underlies the internal rate of return.

The Hoskold premise requires knowledge of the economic terms, the return on investment, and a reinvestment at the marginal opportunity cost. The Hoskold example is:

Return on investment	.09
Sinking fund at marginal or safe rate (6% over 40 years)	.006462
Overall cap rates	.096462

§ 6.6 SUMMATION OF RECAPTURE METHODS

The various methods of recapture—straight-line, Inwood, and Hoskold—are informative because of their mechanics and the reinvestment assumption. The effects of the mechanics illustrate that the reinvestment rate assumption affects the cap rate. The higher the reinvestment rate, the lower the cap rate. The straight-line method assumes no recapture and has the highest cap rate. For a given income (say, $1,000), a low value (relative to Inwood and Hoskold) is estimated; that is, $1,000/.115 = $8,695.65, versus $1,000/.09296 = $10,757.31 and $1,000/.096462 = $10,366.77 via the Inwood and Hoskold methods:

	Straight-Line	Inwood	Hoskold
Reinvestment rate	0	.09	.06
R_o	.115	.09296	.096462
Value	$8,695.65	$10,757.31	$10,366.77

The variation in rates and values illustrates the significance of investment (or reinvestment) assumptions on value. The high reinvestment rates (and hence, the lower cap rates and higher value) are realized because improved reinvestment opportunities reflect additional returns expected to be offset to the real estate (original investment). By analogy, the Inwood and Hoskold premises extend real estate valuation/analysis to a portfolio context. As noted in Chapter 1, the reinvestment assumptions are the foundation of the alternative models for internal rates of return (IRR, MIRR, and so on). The built-up/split rate models also are related to the physical residual models, through the issue of recapture of wasting assets.

§ 6.7 PHYSICAL RESIDUAL TECHNIQUES

The physical residual techniques have their origins in the land and real capital dichotomy of classical economists. Based on this conceptual dichotomy and the simplicity of application (in an environment of limited technical support: no calculators or computers), the residual techniques were widely used by practicing appraisers for three decades (the late 1920s to the 1960s).

Three residual techniques evolved over time—the land residual, the building residual, and the property residual.

The debate over their applicability has ebbed and flowed over the decades, with recent literature and practice favoring the emphasis of financial implications. The debate has further centered on a preference for one model over another; a set of criteria for delineating when each approach is most appropriate has therefore developed.

The residual techniques are split rates that follow the built-up procedure of blending a return (rate) on and of the investment for depreciable assets and a singular return on the permanent land asset. The blended rate is summed to represent an overall cap rate.

The property residual rate separates the income stream from the property (or reversion/resale) value over time and in the current term. The income and property reversion are usually discounted as annuities. The income component is often treated as a (level) annuity and value component distinct from the resale of the property. Hence, the property's future resale value (discounted) is treated as a residual value component. Although, using the Inwood premise, the property residual views the components as annuity, the land and building residuals were initially devised on a straight-line basis, as would be applied to an annuity process. Extensions of the physical residuals have used the Inwood premise. The use of the Hoskold premise has also been employed over the ensuing years.

The traditional physical residuals incorporate the philosophy of treating permanent land differently from wasting (depreciable) real assets. Because improvements were perceived as wasting assets, a recapture allowance was built into the building cap rate. This was then added to the return on the investment, as in the basic built-up rate.

The land component of the residual model was considered a permanent asset. As a gift from God, it did not deteriorate physically (nor, by extension in this model, economically). Therefore, the land income was capitalized at a rate illustrating only a return on the investment. There was no need to periodically recapture the land value because, as a nonwasting asset, the land value was permanent and could be resold at the original land price—a view that seems to neutralize the reality of land speculation and the need for appraisal analysis!

(a) LAND RESIDUAL METHOD

The land residual technique mechanically splits the income flow between the building and land components of a property. The building income is considered as the basis of the improvement (building) value (initially), and the remaining income (difference between the overall NOI and building revenue) is attributed as a residual return to the land.

In the following examples, the NOI is \$20,000, the documented current building cost is \$100,000, and the return on the investment is 9 percent. The economic life of the depreciable physical components is 40 years. Based on the economic life, the straight-line recapture is .025 (= 1/40 yrs.).

Straight-Line Recapture

V_B = building value
I_B = building income
R_B = building cap rate
V_L = land value
I_L = land income
R_L = land cap rate

NOI	\$ 20,000
Income imputed to building ($V_B \times R_B = I_B$):	
\$100,000 × .115 (.09 + .025)	− 11,500
Income imputed to land	\$ 8,500
Land value estimate: ($I_L/R_L = V_L$) \$8,500/.09	\$ 94,444
Plus: Building value (based on cost)	100,000
Overall property value	\$194,444 (rounded to \$195,000)

Annuity Recapture

NOI	\$ 20,000
Income imputed to building ($V_B \times R_B = I_B$):	
\$100,000 × .09296	− \$ 9,296*
Income imputed to land	\$ 10,704
Land value estimate ($I_L/R_L = V_L$): \$10,704/.09	\$118,933
Plus: Building value	100,000
Overall property value	\$218,933 (rounded to \$219,000)

*The Inwood premise at 9 percent annuity return plus a sinking fund factor based on a 9 percent return over 40 years.

The land residual technique is most appropriately used (1) for newly improved lots, when the building components are proper improvements (buildings developed at their highest and best use), and (2) when there are limited or no land sales available in a neighborhood. This would suggest that the land residual technique is an appropriate technique to use in built-up areas and as a test for highest and best use.

(b) BUILDING RESIDUAL METHOD

Like the land residual model, the building residual technique divides the property's NOI into land and building components. A split-rate (built-up) approach is used, with R_L reflecting only a return on the nonwasting land asset and R_B comprised of a return on and of the wasting physical improvements. The building residual emphasizes a prior calculation of the land income based on a land value documented by current land transactions (comparable sales in the subject property's area). The land income is deducted from the property's NOI, to arrive at the building income. This residual income is then divided by the R_B to arrive at the contributory value of the buildings (and hence, summed to estimate the overall property). The following example uses the same information contained in the land residual technique problem. However, in this example, the building value (cost) is not known and the land value is $95,000, based on the analysis of three comparable sales in the immediate neighborhood.

Straight-Line Recapture

NOI	\$ 20,000
Income imputed to land ($V_L \times R_L = I_L$):	
\$95,000 × .09	8,550
Income imputed to building	\$ 11,450
Building value estimate ($I_B/R_B = V_B$):	
\$11,450/.115	\$ 99,565
Plus: Land value (based on comparable sales)	95,000
Overall property value	\$194,565 (rounded to \$195,000)

Annuity Recapture

NOI	\$ 20,000
Income imputed to land ($V_L \times R_L = I_L$):	
\$95,000 × .09	8,550
Income imputed to building	\$ 11,450
Building value estimate ($I_B/R_B = V_B$):	
\$11,450/.09296	\$123,171
Plus: Land value	95,000
Overall property value	\$218,171 (rounded to \$218,000)

The building residual technique is appropriate in areas of middle life (or older) buildings (reflecting the condition of the subject property). The subject building's cost status at this time would be economic history and would be subject to measure (valuation) error, especially in the depreciation estimation. This approach is also appropriate in areas where land sales are active and current, limited new facilities are currently developed, and expanded facilities are expected in the near term. In this method, the existing facility must be at its highest and best use.

(c) COMPARISON OF STRAIGHT-LINE AND ANNUITY RECAPTURE IN LAND AND BUILDING RESIDUALS CONTEXT

As depicted in Table 6.1, alternative values are developed by the different residual techniques and the recapture methods used.

When the assumptions of return and recapture are consistent in the land and building residual techniques, the value conclusions are consistent (if not equivalent). The failure to recognize the importance of this consistency resulted in a concern, prior to the 1960s, regarding the manipulation of these techniques to arrive at either a higher or lower value (depending on the client's or appraiser's desire). An appraiser/investor might employ the land or the building residual, depending on the desire for a high or low value. However, as the previous examples have shown, the ability to alter the value conclusion is not inherent in the mechanics of the model, but in the assumptions emphasized by the model user. The key difference in these examples lies in the reinvestment assumptions of the recapture model and the consistency of an opportunity cost.

Table 6.1 Residual and Recapture Alternatives

	Land Residual	Building Residual
Straight-line recapture	$195,000	$195,000
Annuity	$219,000	$218,000

The implications of the assumptions are depicted in Table 6.1. The $23,000–$24,000 ($218,000 or $219,000 – $195,000) difference between the land and building residual techniques, using straight-line or annuity (reinvestment) recapture, can be attributed to the assumption of reinvestment used in the models. The annuity method's assumption of capital reinvestment of depreciating assets takes on the aspect of a portfolio of realty and financial capital management. The combined portfolio attributes create the value difference.

The annuity concept as used in the physical residuals (with immediate reinvestment of wasting capital) is incorporated in the property residual technique.

§ 6.8 PROPERTY RESIDUAL TECHNIQUE

The property residual technique reflects the issues that are the foundation of yield capitalization (discussed in the next chapter). This residual

Figure 6.1 Value Components, Property Residual Model

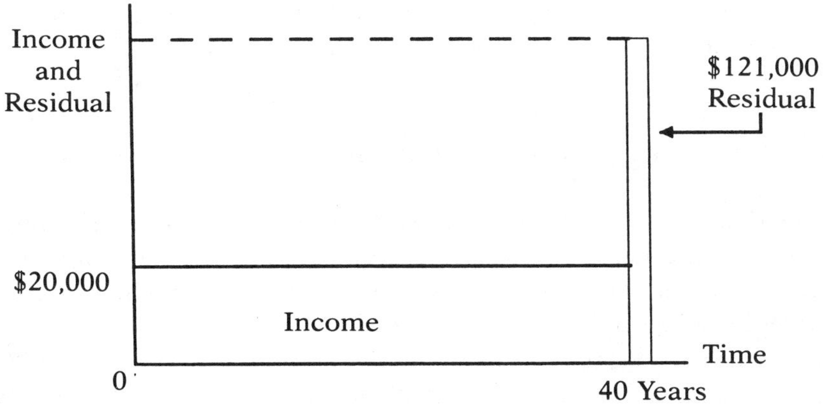

technique separates the property's value into two return components: the value derived from the income over the economic (or physical) life of the property, and the current value of the residual or future sales price (terminal value) of the property. The future resale value can be viewed as the residual component.

Using the information in the prior land and building residuals, the property residual model considers a $20,000 NOI for 40 years and then the future resale price at the end of the term. Both value components are discounted at the 9 percent annuity rate (and hence, 9 percent annuity factors) for the appropriate terms.

The components are illustrated in Figure 6.1. The present value of the income component is calculated as follows:

$20,000 × 10.75736*	$215,147
$121,000† × .031838**	3,852
	$218,999 (rounded to $219,000)

* Present worth of one per period annuity factors for 40 years at 9 percent.

† Future resale value based on a current value of $218,000 – $219,000, as determined by previous residual annuity models.

** Present worth of one for 40 years at 9 percent.

The above present worth factors will be discussed in Chapter 7.

As this technique illustrates, the property (or, effectively, its future resale value) is the residual value component. The estimation of the resale value is subject to broad variation and estimation. Any deviation from the $121,000 used in the example would result in a different value conclusion. The $121,000 is approximately a 1.1 percent decline per year off the current value (based on the other residual techniques). The usefulness of the property residual model may be as a process to check or test future resale value forecasts.

§ 6.9 PHYSICAL RESIDUALS AS A BLENDED RATE

The physical residual technique illustrates the important point that income and value can be allocated among the different components of property. At this point in the analysis, the allocation can be considered between building and land components.

As illustrated in the previous land/building residual, the NOI of $20,000 can be broken up, with approximately $8,500 attributed to the land and $11,500 to the building. In this example, approximately 42.5

percent of the *income* is derived from the land and 57.5 percent from the building.

The *value* is allocated between the components at 48.71 percent for the land and 51.29 percent for the building. The variation between the income and value percentages is attributed to built-up rate differences between the permanent land and wasting building components and the assumptions addressing their treatment. The informational contribution gleaned from the models is that, if income can be divided between the land and building components, and if value can be separated between land and building, then the ratio rate of income to value can also be allocated among the physical components. Using the NOI as a known ($20,000) and the value as the basis of the rate components, a banded rate approach can be developed.

If the basic value model is:

$$V_o = I_o/R_o$$

and:

$$V_o = V_B + V_L$$

where:

V_o = overall value
V_B = building value
V_L = land value

and:

$$I_o = I_B + I_L$$

where:

I_o = overall income (NOI)
I_B = building income
I_L = land income

then:

$$R_o = \frac{I_B}{V_B} + \frac{I_L}{V_L} = R_B + R_L$$

where:

$$\frac{I_B}{V_B} = R_B$$

$$\frac{I_L}{V_L} = R_L$$

However, for appropriate summation to arrive at the overall rate, the land and building rates must be weighed by the percentage value component of the land and building to the overall value. This weighting allows for the recapture differences.

The effective model is:

$$R_o = \left(\frac{V_B}{V_o}\right)R_B + \left(\frac{V_L}{V_o}\right)R_L$$

$$= \frac{\$100{,}000}{\$195{,}000}(.115) + \frac{\$95{,}000}{\$195{,}000}(.09)$$

$$= (.512821)(.115) + (.487179)(.09)$$

$$= .058974 + .043846$$

$$= .102821$$

Incorporating the weighted rate into the basic valuation model results in a value of:

$$V_o = \frac{NOI}{R_o}$$

$$= \frac{\$20{,}000}{.102821}$$

$$= \$194{,}513 \text{ (rounded to } \$195{,}000)$$

The illustration of the banded rate and the link to residual income, with a potential allocation between physical components, establishes the basis for mortgage-equity analysis within the direct capitalization models.

§ 6.10 MORTGAGE-EQUITY ANALYSIS

As early as the 1920s, appraisers and economists began to criticize the physical residual techniques and to emphasize the impact of financing on the valuation process. The relevance of financial implications became dominant in the 1960s, with the expanded analysis afforded by yield capitalization. However, the mortgage-equity analysis during the 1940s and 1950s was still constrained by the tautology of direct capitalization analysis—that valuation is totally dependent on the income measure. Any departure from this simplified model required (1) extensive assumptions that had to be explicitly documented and (2) an improvement in the technology of analysis. Until these advances were available or required, the state of mortgage-equity analysis was developed along the lines of the split rate capitalization used in the physical residual techniques.

The mortgage-equity models of direct capitalization are based on the assumption that overall value can be divided between an equity component and a mortgage component. This is depicted as:

$$V_o = V_M + V_E$$

where:

V_o = overall value
V_M = mortgage value
V_E = equity value

As in the physical models, the financial models are based on the assumption that, if value can be allocated to debt and equity components, then the income can be separated between the NOI that covers debt (debt service payments) and the remaining or residual income that accrues to the equity position. This relationship is illustrated as follows:

$$NOI = I_o = I_M + I_E$$

where:

NOI = net operating income
I_o = overall income
I_M = mortgage income
I_E = equity income

A key component of mortgage-equity analysis is that, based on both economic logic and contractual reality, the equity income is a residual return. By contract, it is normal for the lender to require that the mortgage payments have first claim on any income produced by a property. This contractual requirement is based on the economic logic of positive leverage, in which the debt funds have a lower cost of capital because of a lower risk. The risk is lower, in part, because the lender—specifically, the debt capital—has a prior claim to income returns generated by an investment. The financial claim is usually preceded only by the government's tax claims and any skilled labor or mechanic's liens incurred in the development of a parcel of property.

As in the physical residuals, if the income, like the value, can be allocated between debt and equity, then the rate (stated as a simple ratio) that equates value and income can also be separated into debt and equity ratios. Therefore:

$$\frac{I}{V_o} = R_o$$

$$\frac{I_M}{V_M} = R_M$$

$$\frac{I_E}{V_E} = R_E$$

where:

R_o = overall cap rate
R_M = mortgage cap rate
R_E = equity cap rate

Over time, the various rates and incomes have been institutionalized and given specific (or even alternative) names. The mortgage cap rate (R_M) is generally called the mortgage constant. The mortgage income has been termed debt service.

The equity position has been less formalized; the component names often vary with regions of the country or within varying industry segments. The equity income has been called the cash flow, the equity cash flow, the equity dividend, the cash on cash return (or flow), cash throw-off, and net income (NI = NOI − DS; not to be confused with net operating income, NOI, the overall income I_o to the property).

The equity cap rate has been referred to as the cash on cash rate of return, the cash flow rate, the equity dividend rate, the cash throw-off rate, and the equity cash flow rate (among other names).

Table 6.2 Alternative Financial Positions of Value, Income, and Rates

	Value	Income	Rates
Overall	V_o	Net operating income (NOI)	R_o
Mortgage	V_M	Debt service (DS)	R_M
Equity	V_E	Equity cash flow (CF)	R_E

The significance for direct mortgage-equity capitalization is that several values, incomes, and rate positions must be identified and understood, to develop financial capitalization analysis. These same concepts are significant in yield capitalization. The symbols and concepts are depicted in Table 6.2.

§ 6.11 EQUITY RESIDUAL TECHNIQUE

The information depicted in Table 6.2 can be incorporated into the equity residual capitalization technique. The equity residual model is a good introduction to direct mortgage-equity analysis because it is mechanically similar to the physical residual techniques, it follows the format of the familiar discounted cash flow model, and it emphasizes the legal and economic concepts of equity as the residual return in real estate (or any investment).

The equity residual model requires a knowledge of the property's NOI (in this case, $20,000). NOI is derived after deductions for vacancy and for fixed and variable operating expenses. Other inputs for the equity residual technique are the debt service of the property, the mortgage constant, and the equity cash flow rate. In this example, a property has a mortgage at 9 percent interest for 20 years, with monthly payments. The acceptable equity dividend rate is 6 percent. To use the equity residual technique, either the mortgage value (amount) or the debt service amount must be known, along with the mortgage constant. In this case, both are given. (Numbers are truncated or rounded to the nearest dollar for ease of display.) The amounts are:

$$
\begin{aligned}
NOI &= \$20{,}000 \\
DS &= \$16{,}883 \\
R_M &= .107967 \\
R_E &= .06
\end{aligned}
$$

Therefore, the mortgage value is:

$$V_M = \frac{DS}{R_M} = \frac{\$16,883}{.107967} = \$156,371$$

The equity residual technique format is:

NOI	\$20,000
Less: DS	16,883
CF	\$ 3,117

$$V_E = \frac{CF}{R_E} = \frac{\$3,117}{.06} = \$51,950$$

$$V_o = V_M + V_E$$
$$= \$156,371 + \$51,950 = \$208,321 \text{ (rounded to \$208,500)}$$

The effective overall cap rate in the equity residual analysis is:

$$R_o = \frac{NOI}{\sim V_o} = \frac{\$20,000}{\$208,500} = .0959 \text{ (rounded to .096)}$$

This can be compared to the overall weighted physical residual rate of 10.28 percent. The value difference indicates possible potential in the employment of positive leverage.

The equity residual technique illustrates the essence of mortgage-equity analysis. The income, value, and rates are split among the financial components of the realty asset. The equity residual technique is similar to the income analysis procedures used in discounted cash flow analysis, except that it is a one-period accrual model using a stabilized income procedure (see Chapters 2 and 6).

Despite the equity residual technique's simplicity, it was not the first direct mortgage-equity technique. The first mortgage-equity technique was the band of investment model, using the interest rate.

§ 6.12 BAND OF INVESTMENT WITH THE INTEREST RATE

The band of investment technique is a weighted, split rate approach to developing a direct capitalization rate. The *bands* considered in the technique allow for the debt component (or financial band) and the equity component (band). The mechanics of the technique follow the banded rate model used in the physical residual discussion: weights are derived from the land and building percentages of the overall property. In mortgage-equity analysis, the weights are the loan-to-value (M) ratio for the debt component and the residual percentage (1 – M) for the equity component.[5]

The first band of investment model was presented by Thurston Ross, a professor at the University of Southern California, in 1937.[6] Ross's model used the interest rate (Y_M), a yield concept, to derive the weighted rate for the debt band. The equity band used the return on equity rate. The equity rate was not clearly explained in Ross's article but has been demonstrated, over time, as the equity cash flow rate (R_E).

If the model combines a yield rate on the mortgage (Y_M) with a ratio rate on the equity (R_E), the model has several basic structural flaws. The primary flaw is discussed in Chapter 7, and the secondary flaw is addressed in the next section. The overall process of the basic band of investment model (with an interest rate) is illustrated as:

$$\begin{array}{lll} M & \times Y_M = .75 \times .09 = & .0675 \\ (1 - M) & \times R_E = .25 \times .06 = & \underline{.0150} \\ & \sim R_o & .0825 \end{array}$$

where:

M = loan-to-value ratio of 75 percent
$1 - M$ = equity-to-value ratio of 25 percent
$\sim R_o$ = approximation of the cap rate

The interest rate (Y_M) of 9 percent and the equity dividend rate (R_E) of 6 percent are used in the previous equity residual technique.

The symbol $\sim$ is used with the overall cap rate symbol of R_o because, at best, it is an approximation. The fallacy of using the interest rate with the equity dividend rate is illustrated by the value conclusion of Ross's model as compared with that of the equity residual model. The equity residual value was $208,500, based on the property's $20,000 NOI. Ross's band-of-investment model indicates the following value, using a $20,000 NOI:

[5] For insights into the basic mortgage equity equation, see Charles Akerson, *Income Capitalization: Technique and Theory* (Chicago: AIREA, 1986).

[6] Thurston H. Ross, "Rate of Capitalization," *The Appraisal Journal* (July 1937): 217.

$$V_o = \frac{NOI}{\sim R_o} = \frac{\$20{,}000}{.0825} = \$242{,}424 \text{ (rounded to \$242,500)}$$

The difference between the equity residual model and Ross's model is \$33,924 (\$242,500 − \$208,500). This value difference is explained by the structural (and conceptual) flaw of combining a yield with a ratio rate. The initial problem is the failure of the yield rate, as presented, to allow for capital recapture for the debt or overall property (from the income stream), as is inherently considered in the direct capitalization model. The recapture allowance deficiency was corrected by Edwin Kazdin in 1944,[7] with the use of the mortgage constant.

§ 6.13 BAND OF INVESTMENT USING A MORTGAGE CONSTANT

Kazdin's modification to the band of investment model correctly incorporated a recapture allowance into the weighted return model for a *direct* capitalization process. Direct capitalization must consider a periodic recapture of the original investment within the rate structure; it does not allow for a future resale allowance of the property. Kazdin's use of the mortgage constant allowed for the periodic recapture process of direct capitalization within the band of investment technique. Kazdin's modification is illustrated as:

$$\begin{array}{lll} M \times R_M & = .75 \times .107967 & = .0810 \\ (1 - M) \times R_E & = .25 \times .06 & = \underline{.015} \\ R_o & & = .0960 \end{array}$$

The value per modified band of investment is:

$$V_o = \frac{NOI}{R_o} = \frac{\$20{,}000}{.0960} = \$208{,}333 \text{ (rounded to \$208,500)}$$

The modified model is equivalent to the equity residual model and is consistent with the basic premise of the direct capitalization tautology (that is, that value is based on a stabilized income measure with an allowance for periodic recapture of the original investment). As such, if

[7] Edwin Kazdin, "Capitalization Under Present Market Conditions," *The Appraisal Journal* (October 1944): 310, 311.

value and income can be allocated between debt and equity components, so can the rate structure that equals the two features.

Ross's use of a yield rate (mortgage interest rate) in the band of investment would only be appropriate if combined with an equity yield rate. The format would be:

$$\begin{array}{lll} M & \times Y_M = .75 \times .09 = & .0675 \\ (1 - M) & \times Y_E = .25 \times .15 = & \underline{.0375} \\ & Y_o & = .105 \end{array}$$

(The equity yield rate used, 15 percent, exceeds the previous equity dividend rate of 6 percent.)

The end result would be an approximation of an overall yield rate (Y_o) of 10.5 percent. This is *not* a cap rate; it is an approximated discount rate or overall cost of capital rate that must be applied to a series of cash flows, one of which could be a future resale price. The weighted yield rate is not appropriately applied to a single stabilized income measure, because it does not consider issues of return on and of an investment as a capitalization process. However, the (weighted yield rate) discussion example sets up the potential relationship between cap rates and yield rates, which is considered in Chapter 7.

§ 6.14 DIRECT CAPITALIZATION APPLICATIONS IN A CHANGING ECONOMY

Direct capitalization is a *deterministic* model based on a tautology, which means that each imputed variable, and hence the value conclusion, is a certainty. The model does not account for variability in the relationships or for the possibility of alternative outcomes (especially since the traditional model is stated as a tautology: that value is defined to be a function of income, because valuation is totally dependent on the income measure.

This defined relationship has been qualified, over time, by identifying the components of value, income, and rates to be composites of varying physical and financial returns. Historically, the physical residual, mortgage-equity, and built-up or summation approaches were developed to construct rates when direct observations were not available from market transactions. This technique was relevant in the past (as it is currently) because data were (and are) often limited in the real estate market, creating the need for the built-up techniques. The significance of this need (resulting from data poverty) is observed in the fact that the weighted rate approach of the band of investment was developed before the equity residual technique. The simplicity and logic of the equity residual technique are applicable only if the debt service and/or mortgage value (or overall value) are known (this same information is required to apply the discounted cash flow model). However, in the appraisal process, the overall value is unknown and the mortgage amount—and hence, the debt service—is often contingent on the quantity of the overall value.

The band of investment establishes an algebraic relationship between known standard lending terms, such as the current interest rate, and time terms, which are the basis of the mortgage constant, and combines this relationship with the loan-to-value ratio. The debt bands of the overall rate are simply information on the institutional policies of banks toward risk (loan-to-value ratio) and returns (interest rates and recapture allowances).

Once the lenders' institutional requirements are gathered (or known), the residual equity band is explicitly considered in the cap rate structure and the only market or property information required is the income level.

Therefore, the built-up processes of direct capitalization were born out of necessity in an environment of limited information and a need for analysis and observation of heterogeneous observations and samples. These procedures are weak and easily criticized in the context of today's technology and evolving data bases (that is, until necessity again requires their employment).

The employment of direct capitalization in computerized discounted cash flows requires a realization that the direct cap rate is a market artifact that enables the comparison or analogy of the prices paid for given income streams of fairly similar properties. The overall cap rates derived by comparing the ratio of a stabilized income to the transaction price of other investment alternatives ($R_o = NOI/V_o$) enable benchmarks of analysis to constrain and reinforce cash flow projections and allow further insightful analysis of income properties. The capitalization ratio is a unit of comparison.

Therefore, the emphasis of direct capitalization should be on deriving overall cap rates from the market (and hence, approximations of market returns). Once these objective measures are derived, theory and practice allow the income, value, and rate measures to be separated into physical, financial, or risk components. This decomposition can be useful in further analyzing the actions of investors, overall markets, and market participants. The segmentation of overall cap rates into physical, risk, or financial components is not different from the segmentation of stock or investment returns and loadings into classes of market premiums, illiquidity, and other factors that may help explain the actions of market participants or competitors. The segmentation of the components enables insights and information to help the decision process. The key for application in current and future markets is not to limit direct capitalization to building up rates in periods or areas of limited data. Instead, information should be abstracted from the overall market (or property) derived rates that enable an explicit determination of the information inherently present in the artifact rate that depicts market motivations.

Direct capitalization cannot be limited to value estimation as its sole decision function. An emphasis on solvency measures and rate analysis (considering both return and risk issues) in the context of real estate decisions can be developed, with the employment of direct capitalization techniques. However, to fully employ these skills and link them to the technology available (now and in the future), the concept and practice of yield capitalization must be investigated.

Seven

Yield Capitalization

§ 7.1 INTRODUCTION

Yield capitalization was originally developed as a valuation decision tool in implementing the theory and mechanics of annuity capitalization. Annuity capitalization (and yield capitalization) is concerned with the conversion, over a finite term, of a series of income flows into a value estimate. The objectives of this chapter are to identify the development of the theory and techniques used in yield capitalization and to expand their use in helping to address decisions based on solvency and rate analysis (as well as value).

Chapter 6 indicated that many of the more complicated and comprehensive models used in yield capitalization were developed before the currently applied models, which are simpler, more straightforward, and more easily explained.

§ 7.2 RELATIONSHIP BETWEEN YIELD RATES AND CAP RATES

James Gibbons, in developing a method for abstracting prospective yield rates from stock market data, published the first example of the "universal cap rate," the technique that illustrates the relationship between yields and capitalization rates.[1] The key element illustrated by Gibbons was the change in value over a given holding period. Gibbons's

[1] James Gibbons, "Influence of Inflation on Real Estate Valuation and Investment Analysis," *The Appraisal Journal,* 48:4 (October 1980): 485–502; also published as "Equity Yield," in *Appraising in a Changing Economy: Collected Writings of James E. Gibbons* (Chicago: AIREA, 1982): 132–160.

model was based on Ellwood's 1959 mortgage-equity capitalization model (to be discussed later), but enabled an analysis of income investments, regardless of the investment vehicle or the nature of the debt structure. Gibbons's model also considered Gibbons's requirement that realized yield take account of both terminal values and annual net incomes, converting both issues to a rate structure. The consideration of both the income flow over time and the gain (or loss) at resale (or as an expectation of gain or loss in the future) in a rate context is the basis of yield capitalization.

The link of yield capitalization to the financial model of overall return and its evolution to the universal cap rate is developed as follows. The total return to an investment, the decision criterion often sought in the analysis of investments, is a combination of the income component and the appreciation return. In securities analysis, the total return (for one period) is identified as the dividend and appreciation, stated as a combined rate:

$$r = \frac{D_t + (p_{t+1} - p_t)}{p_t}$$

where:

r = overall yield for the period
D_t = dividend for time t
p_t = purchase price in time t
p_{t+1} = future sales price in time t + 1

The same concept can be considered in real estate for the overall property or any of its component parts. The concept, using real estate symbols, is:

$$Y_o = \frac{NOI_1 + (V_1 - V_o)}{V_o}$$

$$= \frac{NOI_1}{V_o} + \frac{(V_1 - V_o)}{V_o}$$

where:

Y_o = yield to the overall property, based on the effective cost of capital (this depends on the combination of debt and equity funds)
NOI_1 = net operating income in year 1

The above formula shows a one-period investment model. The yield concept introduces time into investment analysis. The total yield is concerned with the sum of the income for each year of the holding period plus the gain at a future resale. As with the ratio rates and the appreciation rates, the total return can be allocated between the capital components of the property. This will be developed later.

(a) CAP RATES AS A MEASURE OF TOTAL RETURN

If the cap rate is understood to be a surrogate for total return, then the cap rate can be used as a measure of total return when more thorough or available data are lacking. The concept of yield capitalization introduces the factor of time into the capitalization process. The traditional cap rate capitalizes the stabilized income into perpetuity. This function is based on the premise that value is the present worth of future anticipated benefits. Therefore, if current value is the capitalized value of all income flows into infinity, then the property is the summation of the income stream for the holding period plus the capitalized value of the property from the end of the holding period into infinity.

In terms of yields, the overall yield to a property is the cap rate plus the appreciation rate. This concept is illustrated by the formula for the ratio and appreciation rates, to be discussed in more detail later:

$$Y_o = \frac{NOI_1 + (V_1 - V_o)}{V_o}$$

This equation can be broken down as follows:

$$Y_o = \frac{NOI_1}{V_o} + \frac{(V_1 - V_o)}{V_o}$$

The symbols R_o and Δ_o can be substituted in the formula for the yield:

$$Y_o = R_o + \Delta_o$$

This formula illustrates a one-period analysis; it can be expanded to multiple periods by adjusting Δ_o with an annualizer. The formula can also be transposed so that:

$$R_o = Y_o - \Delta_o$$

Therefore, if cap rates can be derived from the market, then either the cost of capital or the expected change in property values can be derived, given that sufficient information can be obtained to support one of the other factors in the equation. (If one of the other issues can be supported by research or knowledge, the third factor can be derived.) Based on the yield capitalization concept, cap rates are an approximation of total returns that can be gathered from most real estate markets.

The availability of cap rates allows a measure of total return that permits comparison of real estate investments with other investments of all types. However, the comparison of rates alone is not sufficient to make investment decisions. Risk is also a primary concern.

§ 7.3 IMPACTS OF INCOME AND FUTURE VALUE PATTERNS AND CHANGES ON PRESENT VALUE

(a) INCOME AND GROWTH PATTERNS

Because yield analysis and value estimation are concerned with income and resale returns received over specific time periods, the income and growth patterns experienced or typically expected for a property or specific property types are important. Variations in income and growth patterns can have a major influence on value return and solvency estimation. The alternative income patterns are illustrated in Figure 7.1.

Figure 7.1 Alternative Income Patterns

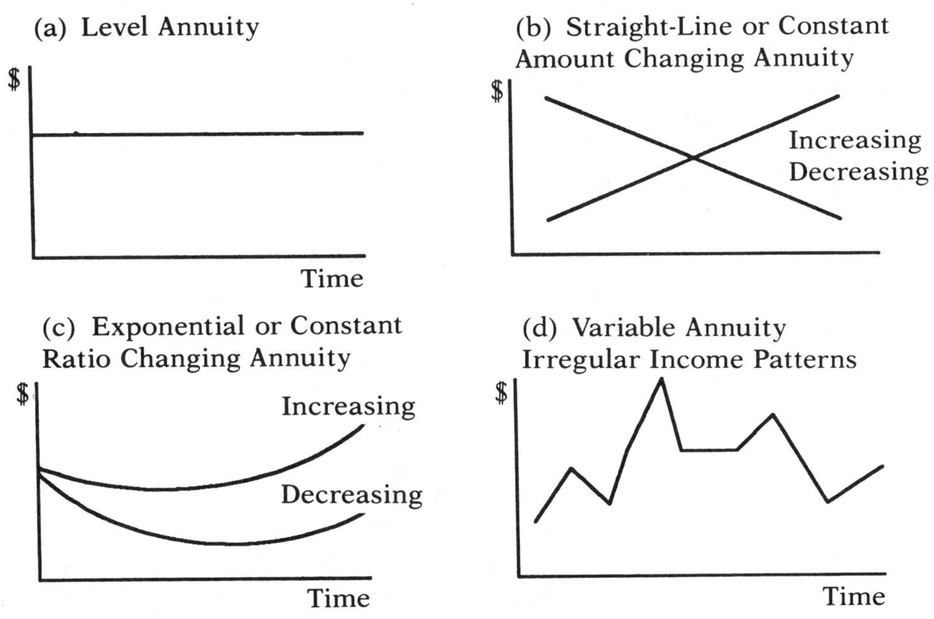

The immediate impact of the income pattern can be observed in properties that are limited to income as their basis of value. Examples are company-owned property and family estate ground leases that will be held into perpetuity or for a given period of ownership. The basis of yield capitalization for an income stream over a specified time period has its roots in annuity capitalization.

(b) FLOW OF BENEFITS—A GIVEN TIME PERIOD

Annuity capitalization is concerned with the flow of benefits over a given time period. These benefits can come in the form of income or cash gains at resale. Annuity capitalization differs from direct capitalization in that a stabilized income is not (necessarily) used. Annuity capitalization can be applied to alternative income patterns as well as to gains at resale. Given this flexibility, an input of annuity capitalization is a specified time period other than perpetuity. Therefore, investment holding periods and mortgage amortization periods can be considered in the capitalization process (the conversion of periodic benefits into a current value).

Annuity capitalization, in effect, is discounting, but not always in the context of the familiar DCF model. The DCF, which often deals with an irregular income pattern, is a subset of or an equivalent model to annuity capitalization, and annuity capitalization can address the variety of income patterns depicted in Figure 7.1. The concept of an annuity has expanded over time from a clear to a very muddled term. Initially, an annuity was a level, or constant, annual payment. The concept was expanded via descriptive adjectives to consider increasing or decreasing annuities and variable or irregular annuities. An annuity need not describe annual payments; it can refer to monthly, quarterly, or irregular payment schedules. Currently, the only consistent description of an annuity is that it is a periodic payment over time, with some regularity expected in the frequency of the payment schedule. With this variation in mind, it is possible to expand annuity capitalization to address the variety of income streams observed in various properties.

§ 7.4 VARIETY OF INCOME PATTERNS

(a) IRREGULAR INCOME PATTERNS

The traditional discounted cash flow model often deals with an irregular income stream, as depicted in Figure 7.1(d). In this irregular income case, each annuity is treated as a separate and distinct capital flow, isolated or described by the year in which it is incurred. Annuity capitalization employs the mathematics of finance as they apply to the concept of compound interest. Irregular or variable annuities (the typical DCF) use the discounting model of the present worth of 1 per period. This model, the reciprocal of the compound interest formula, is 1 divided by 1, plus the interest rate raised to the specific year that the cash flow is received. This factor is called the present worth of 1 factor; its format is:

$$V_n = \frac{1}{(1 + i)^n}$$

where:

V_n = present worth of 1 factor, for a given period or term
i = interest or discount rate
n = investment or holding period

Because the concern is yield capitalization, the traditional symbol (i) is replaced with y, to denote a yield. Therefore:

$$V_n = \frac{1}{(1 + y)^n}$$

This is the factor used for each year. As explained earlier, annuity capitalization is concerned with income received over a period of years. The present value is determined by discounting each separate year by the appropriate (discount or opportunity) cost–yield rate, and then summing the value for each year (after discounting). This procedure is necessary because the time differential has been adjusted and each year is now at current terms. The overall formula for an irregular income flow for n years is:

$$V_o = \frac{NOI_1}{(1 + y)^1} + \frac{NOI_2}{(1 + y)^2} + \quad . \; . \; . \quad + \frac{NOI_n}{(1 + y)^n}$$

A shorthand notation for this summation is:

$$V_o = \sum_{i=1}^{n} \frac{NOI_i}{(1 + y)^i}$$

Therefore, at a 12 percent discount rate (y = .12) for 3 years (n = 3), with variable incomes of \$10,000, \$7,000, and \$11,000, the value is:

$$V_o = \frac{\$10{,}000}{(1 + .12)^1} + \frac{\$7{,}000}{(1 + .12)^2} + \frac{\$11{,}000}{(1 + .12)^3}$$

$$= \$8{,}928.57 + \$5{,}580.35 + \$7{,}829.58$$

$$= \$22{,}338.51$$

The discount factors for years 1, 2, and 3 respectively are: .892857 + .79719 + .71178.

The above formula addresses only income flows, because the current concern is capitalizing different income patterns into a value estimate. Gains at sale will be considered in § 7.5.

The present concern is that the income stream varies each year: each income flow must be treated separately, that is, each year must be discounted individually. However, if a constant level income is received, the process of analysis can be shortened by the use of the present worth of 1 per period factor.

(b) LEVEL INCOME PATTERNS

If the investment is recognized to have a level income, then the model can adopt the Inwood factor as a shortcut in capitalization. The Inwood factor is a fixed multiplier (which varies with the term and discount rate). The shorthand value notation is:

$$V_o = \sum_{i=1}^{n} \overline{NOI}_i \left(\frac{1}{(1 + y)^i}\right)$$

where:

$\overline{NOI}_i$ = a level income flow (in this case, \$10,000 per year for 3 years)

As the notation indicates, the Inwood factor (and discounting premise) is concerned only with the summation of the discount factor for the holding period term. The previous variable or irregular income analysis reflected annual discount factors of .892857 + .79719 + .71178 for years 1, 2, and 3; the Inwood factor, or present worth of 1 per period, is 2.4018. Using this factor, the value of the 3-year, \$10,000 annuity is \$10,000 × 2.4018 = \$24,018.

This result can be tested against treating the level annuity as three distinct or separate $10,000 returns, as in the variable income model. The answer is the same, $24,018. The difference between the variable annuity and the level annuity is attributed to the income pattern and the timing of the income flows. The first year, in both scenarios, is $10,000 (discounted at 12 percent for one year). The second year's difference of $3,000 ($10,000 – $7,000) reflects the value of the level annuity (in this case); however, this major decline in the second year has a greater impact than the $11,000 annuity (over the $10,000) in the level investment, in the third year. Analysts and decision makers must always be concerned with the income flow and the timing of the returns. With the application of annuity capitalization, traditional capitalization has turned from a process of division, in which an income is divided by a rate (I/R = V) to arrive at a value, to a process of multiplication. The multiplier is the discount factor (F). The discount factor (F) times the level income (I × F = V) equals the value estimate. In fact, to some extent, the discount annuity factor is the reciprocal of the cap rate. This is illustrated in the formula for the Inwood factor:

$$a_{\overline{n}|y} = \frac{1 - \dfrac{1}{(1+y)^n}}{y}$$

Using the 3-year term and the 12 percent discount rate from the previous example, it can be demonstrated that the discounted value of $1 of income for 3 years is $2.40 (plus). This is developed using the formula:

$$a_{\overline{n}|y} = \frac{1 - \dfrac{1}{(1+.12)^3}}{.12}$$

$$= \frac{\dfrac{1-1}{1.404928}}{.12}$$

$$= \frac{1 - .7117802}{.12}$$

$$= \frac{.2882197}{.12}$$

= $2.4018 (rounded to $2.40)

This is the annuity factor developed by the previous summation of the discount factors for each year. This entire process can be related back to Fisher's formula for the overall cap rate, in Chapter 6.

(c) CHANGING INCOME PATTERNS

Direct capitalization illustrated that changing variables can be applied within the cap rate structure. This same flexibility is possible within the annuity factors. In fact, the annuity factor can be adjusted for the value impact of a straight-line increase (or decrease) in an income flow (or projection).

A straight-line income increase is a growth of income by a constant amount. Therefore, for the $10,000 annuity indicated above, an income growth of 2 percent would be $200 per year for three years, in a straight-line income growth pattern:

Straight-Line (Constant Amount) Changing Income

		Years		
Base	Change	1	2	3
$10,000	2% ($200 per year)	$10,000	$10,200	$10,400

This constant amount of growth can be considered within the discount factor, using the following formula:

$$V_A = (d + hn)\, a_{\overline{n}|} - \frac{h(n - a_{\overline{n}|})}{y}$$

where:

V_A = present worth measure (either overall value or factor)
d = starting or base income (1, in factor calculation)
h = annual increase or decrease after year 1; if positive, h connotes an increase; if negative, −h depicts a decrease
n = number of years
$a_{\overline{n}|y}$ = annuity for n years at y rate (actuary symbol)
y = yield rate (used as discount rate)

The following example uses the 3-year projection of growth at a constant of $200 per $10,000, or 2 percent. The level annuity factor is at 12 percent for three years:

$$V_A = (1 + .02(3))2.4018 - \frac{.02(3 - 2.4018)}{.12}$$

$$= (1.06)2.4018 - \frac{.02(.5982)}{.12}$$

$$= 2.545908 - .0997$$

$$= 2.446208$$

The V_A factor (in this example) of 2.446208 is then multiplied by the \$10,000 starting (base) income, to arrive at the present value of the straight-line increasing income stream. The value is:

$$V_o = I \times V_A$$
$$= \$10,000 \times 2.446208$$
$$= \$24,462.08$$

This process could be shortened by using d = \$10,000 as the base income. The key issue in discounting factors is: what is true for \$1 is true for \$10,000 (see Chapter 5). If \$10,000 is used, however, the input for h would be \$200 rather than 2 percent.

The consideration of the impact of the straight-line increasing income on value, as illustrated by adjusting the annuity factor, is supported by discounting the 3-year income stream at the 12 percent discount rate (via the DCF procedure):

	Years				
	1		2		3
Income	\$10,000		\$10,200		\$10,400
F	× .892857		× .79719		× .71178
V_o	= \$ 8,928.57	+	\$8131.33	+	\$7,402.51
	= \$24,462.42 (differs from previous V_A measure because of rounding)				

The factor and value for the straight-line increasing income are moderately higher than for the level annuity capitalization. A comparison of the capitalized values directly reflects the impact of the income pattern on value (however moderate the impact).

Exponential Curve (Constant Ratio) Changing Income

As with the straight-line changing annuity, a compounding (or exponential) income growth pattern can be analyzed within the format of annuity capitalization. The compounding income stream is capitalized using the following present worth equation:

$$V_c = \frac{1 - \frac{(1 + c)^n}{(1 + y)^n}}{y - c}$$

where:

c = compound growth rate
Y = yield/discount rate
n = term

Using the information from the previous example, the first-year income is \$10,000, the discount rate is 12 percent, and the growth rate is at 2 percent compounding:

$$V_c = \frac{1 - \frac{(1 + .02)^3}{(1 + .12)^3}}{.12 - .02}$$

$$= \frac{1 - \frac{(1.061208)}{(1.40492)}}{.10}$$

$$= \frac{1 - .755346893}{.10}$$

$$= 2.446531$$

The original income of \$10,000 × 2.445631 equals a value of \$24,465, a slightly greater value than the straight-line income for the 3-year period. However, it is clear that the income pattern can alter the value estimation. In fact, as the income term expands, the present value difference increases. This relationship is illustrated in Figure 7.2.

The comparison of level, straight-line increasing, and exponentially increasing incomes, as illustrated in Figure 7.2, shows that these differences increase over time. In the example depicted, the initial years indicate similar measures of income. This pattern is supported by the numerical examples discussed earlier. Therefore, the straight-line or exponential growth patterns are minor until the magnitude of the

Figure 7.2 Relationship of Various Income Patterns over Time

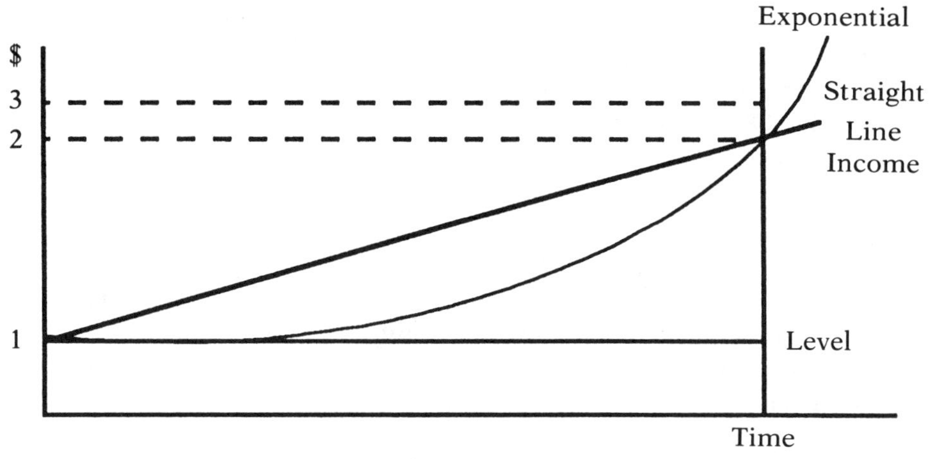

income level is applied. However, the longer the term of the lease (or income stream), the greater the income differences, especially as compared to the level annuity. The income difference over time is modified by the application of the discount factor. The end conclusion is that income patterns do alter the value estimate of a property. Furthermore, the annuity capitalization concept is simply a shorthand application of the discounted income approach. Annuity capitalization mechanics are equivalent to the DCF for variable irregular annuities but offer shortcuts for distinctive income patterns, such as level annuities (and, by extension, graduated payments, which are a series of segmented level annuities), income changing on a straight-line basis, and income changing exponentially.

§ 7.5 TOTAL RETURN AND YIELD CAPITALIZATION

The previous discussion on annuity capitalization emphasized the significance of the income pattern and of the discount factor technique that was appropriate to convert a distinctive pattern into a value estimate. This same relationship of growth pattern to capitalization technique is possible when the terminal value (or future resale price) is considered. The resale price can reflect both a return of and on the investment, if a gain at sale is realized. The return on is appreciation in value/price over time.

If the property sells for less than the original purchase price (or indicates a loss in equity), then a value decline or depreciation is incurred and the property gives no return on the investment and only a partial return of the original investment at resale.

Either a gain or a loss (realization or expectation) has an impact on current value. This impact can be observed in the context of the traditional cash flow model (for irregular incomes), as illustrated by:

$$V_o = \sum_{i=1}^{n} \frac{NOI_i}{(1+y)^i} + \frac{V_n}{(1+y)^n}$$

where:

n = finite period (say, 5 years), not infinity
V_n = future value, resale value, or, specifically, a value in time period n

The time period is less than the infinite term used in the annuity capitalization format, and the discounted value of the future is considered as a benefit or form of return to the overall property. The DCF and annuity capitalization process resemble the property residual technique discussed in Chapter 6.

This yield/annuity capitalization model reflects a measure of total return. Total return considers the income return over the investment holding period and the gain (loss) at resale. As illustrated earlier, these elements are reflected in the overall yield model of total return (for one period):

$$Y_o = \frac{NOI_n + (V_n - V_o)}{V_o}$$

where:

$V_n = V_1$ = value at the end of one period
n = 1

The total yield is then allocated between the appreciation rates and the income ratio rates. (These are more fully discussed in the subsections that follow.) The income ratio rate at this point is the cap rate. The appreciation rate in this example is a positive rate of change at resale (again). The overall discount rate is:

$$Y_o = \frac{NOI}{V_o} + \frac{V_n - V_o}{V_o}$$

In standard appraisal symbols, the equation is:

$$R_o = \frac{NOI}{V_o} \text{ and } \Delta_o = \frac{V_n - V_o}{V_o}$$

Therefore:

$$Y_o = R_o + \Delta_o$$

The synthesis and symbol substitution illustrate a relationship among DCF analysis, annuity capitalization, and the cap rate. The context of analyzing yield issues within the cap rate format is termed yield capitalization. Yield capitalization can be a shorthand approach to the complexities of DCF by collapsing the cash flow analysis to the direct capitalization model. That is:

$$\frac{NOI}{Y_o - \Delta_{o_a}} = \frac{NOI}{R_o}$$

To illustrate the cash flow–capitalization relationships, it is useful to show the application of yield capitalization to the array of income patterns discussed earlier. Because total return is the emphasis of yield capitalization, the models are now expanded to reveal the impact of asset growth patterns (or decline) on value estimates as well.

To add this latter dimension (value change) to the basic capitalization model, it is necessary to convert the holding period change component of return (Δ_o or $V_n - V_o/V_o$) to an annual increment. This is achieved with use of an annual modifier. The accepted symbol for the annualizer is (a). Therefore, the yield capitalization factor takes into consideration the overall cost of capital (Y_o) and the impact of the investor's expectations or realizations (Δ_o) as an annualized factor.

The modified formula, which is now a present worth technique that collapses expectations (realizations) over time to a current value measure, is:

$$R_o = Y_o - \Delta_{o_a}$$

This formula has been called the "universal cap rate model." It is a general-purpose formula in which the annualizer (a) varies with the patterns of the income and asset growth trends. The formula's general application is illustrated in the following scenarios.

(a) LEVEL INCOME, NO CHANGE IN VALUE

When income and value are not expected to change, the capitalization is in perpetuity, as in the annuity capitalization example discussed earlier. In this case, Δ_{o_a} equals zero, so $R_o = Y_o - \Delta_{o_a}$ collapses to $R_o = Y_o$. Therefore, without an expectation of change in value, the cap rate becomes the overall yield rate (or the weighted cost of capital, as will be demonstrated later). The model applicable in this scenario is:

$$R_o = \frac{\text{NOI}}{Y_o - \Delta_{o_a}}$$

$$= \frac{\text{NOI}}{Y_o} = \frac{\text{NOI}}{R_o}$$

$$= \frac{\$10{,}000}{.12} = \$83{,}333 \text{ (rounded to } \$83{,}500)$$

(b) LEVEL INCOME, CHANGE IN VALUE

In this scenario, the effect is a combination of a level annuity income with a built-up value. As demonstrated in the annuity capitalization analysis, a level annuity is capitalized with the Inwood premise, which was shown to be the summation of the discount factor (present worth of 1). Implicit in the Inwood premise is the assumption that reinvestment is at a given yield rate (the overall yield at this point, for example, Y_o).

The objective in the yield capitalization analysis is to break out the reinvestment component of the Inwood premise and use it as the periodic annualizer (a) of the expected appreciation (or depreciation) over the holding period. The reinvestment component can be isolated by taking the reciprocal of the Inwood formula:

$$a_{\overline{n|}i} = \frac{1 - \dfrac{1}{(1+y)^n}}{y}$$

resulting in:

$$\frac{1}{a_{\overline{n|}y}} = \frac{i}{1 - \dfrac{1}{(1+y)^n}}$$

which is the partial payment factor or the amount to amortize a loan. The partial payment factor is the mortgage constant, and the mortgage constant is a cap rate that considers a return on and of the principal invested by the lender. The return of the principal component is a sinking fund factor. This can be tested by calculating a sinking fund factor or looking one up in financial tables, and adding the *effective* interest rate to the sinking fund. The answer will correspond to the mortgage constant at the contract rate.

To be mathematically consistent with a level annuity, the value change must accrue in the pattern of an accumulating sinking fund. Therefore, the appropriate annualizer in the application of yield capitalization is a sinking fund factor ($SFF = 1/s_{\overline{n}|}$) at the Y_o rate. In the prior examples, the subject property generated a $10,000 income for 3 years, with expectations of a 12 percent yield. If the property is expected to appreciate by 6 percent over the holding period, its current value (or an appropriate purchase price) would be:

$$V_o = \frac{NOI}{Y_o - \Delta_{o(1/s_{\overline{n}|})}}$$

$$= \frac{\$10{,}000}{.12 - (.06)(.296349)} \quad \text{where } \left(SFF = \frac{1}{s_{\overline{n}|y}}, \text{ where } n = 3 \text{ and } y = 12 \text{ percent}\right)$$

$$= \frac{\$10{,}000}{.12 - .01778094}$$

$$= \frac{\$10{,}000}{.10221906}$$

$$= \$97{,}829$$

The present value of the contribution of the expectation of 6 percent appreciation over 3 years is:

Level income:	
With change	$97,829
With no change	83,333
	$14,496

The above comparison illustrates the impact of expectation to value, to overall real estate analysis, and to decision makers. Although the risk of realizing the expectations is important and must be considered, the overall expectations are a driving force in the market. Yield capitalization enables analysis of the impact of expectations on real estate activities; although a technical process, it enables an analysis of investors' and market participants' behavior. However, to appropriately apply yield analysis to specific properties (or property types), the model must match the assumptions of the income and growth (loss) patterns. When dealing with level income flows and changing values, a sinking fund factor is the most appropriate annualizer.

(c) STRAIGHT-LINE, CONSTANT-DOLLAR CHANGES

When income and value are expected to change (increase or decrease) by fixed amounts (often based on a first year's or a specifically designated year's income) according to a straight-line pattern, the present value can be estimated by a straight-line (recapture) annualizer.

Given the property above, the 6 percent growth would be annualized on a straight-line format of (1/3 years = 33 percent per year). The result of .333 × .06, or .01998 percent per year, rounds to 2 percent. Within the context of the universal cap rate, the procedure would be:

$$\frac{\text{NOI}}{\text{Y}_\text{o} - \Delta_{\text{o}(1/n)}} = \frac{\$10{,}000}{.12 - .06(1/3)} = \frac{\$10{,}000}{.10} = \$100{,}000$$

where:

$$\frac{1}{n} = \frac{1}{3} \text{ or } .333$$

In this case, the straight-line recapture or annualizer rate is greater than the sinking fund factor (.333 > .296349). This mechanically results in a larger deduction from the yield rate, and thus in a smaller cap rate and a higher value.

The higher deduction under the straight-line method occurs because the sinking fund factor in the level annuity model allows for reinvestment at the desired yield rate. In part, the deduction results from two economic premises reflected in the mechanics of the model: (1) the SFF requires that less of the appreciation be recaptured each period from the income stream, because of the reinvestment strategy; (2) the straight-line model assumes that both the *income* and *value* are increasing at the constant amount of 2 percent of the base income. The final value, therefore, represents both the income and the asset value growth that is expected over the 3-year holding period. The difference

($2,171) in the values of $100,000 and $97,829 can be attributed to a difference in the growth patterns of the appreciation in both models and the increasing straight-line income growth in the second model versus the level annuity of the first model.

(d) EXPONENTIAL GROWTH OR CONSTANT RATIO GROWTH

In this scenario, income and value are expected to change at a constant ratio. This pattern, which follows the exponential curve of compound interest, is the growth pattern often projected in canned DCF projections. To apply this model, the annualizer would be the *n*th root of the growth factor plus the original investment.

Consistency with the previous examples would involve taking the third root (3) of 1.06, or the 6 percent growth over the 3-year period, plus the original dollar of investment (the growth is occurring like compound interest). Therefore, the annual growth is:

$$c = \sqrt[n]{\frac{FV}{PV}} - 1 = \sqrt[3]{\frac{1.06}{1}} - 1$$

$$= \sqrt[3]{1.06} - 1$$

$$= 1.0196 - 1$$

$$= .0196 \text{ or } 1.96\%$$

where:

c = compound rate
FV = future value
PV = present value
n = three years

This process is a little more complicated than the others, but can be easily incorporated into the general formula by treating the annualized rate itself as the required input. The modified formula is therefore:

$$\frac{NOI}{Y_o - c} = \frac{\$10{,}000}{.12 - .0196} = \frac{\$10{,}000}{.1004} = \$99{,}601$$

Often, the application of this model is easier than that of the other scenarios, because the input can be reduced initially to the annual growth rate. For example, rather than stating that the property will appreciate by 6 percent over 3 years, it might be more typical to say that property value or income is growing at 1.96 percent per year (more probably 2, 3 or 4 percent per year, depending on the market). Because the use of the annual growth rate is typical in most DCF models, the problem would probably be viewed as: What is the present value of a property that is to be held 3 years, has an initial income of $10,000, and has both the income and value growing at 1.96% per year?

(e) COMPARISON OF INCOME AND GROWTH PATTERNS

The overall returns, like the various income patterns, are based on income and appreciation patterns that can be compared by depicting their growth assumptions over time. The alternative scenarios are illustrated in Figure 7.3. The implications are that all three scenarios can be projected to grow from $1.00 to $1.50 in 20 years (or to 6 percent in 3 years). At issue is the process by which the accumulation of growth occurs in the model. For example, the straight-line pattern increases at a constant amount and is the most aggressive growth pattern in the beginning and middle periods. The compound rate is the second most aggressive (or fastest) growth pattern in the beginning and middle years, but in later years it begins to exceed the straight-line pattern, arriving at the same concluding value ($1.50, in this case).

The accumulated sinking fund pattern, which is the slowest growth rate in the initial and middle years, becomes the most aggressive of the

Figure 7.3 Relationship of Various Income and Value Growth Patterns over Time

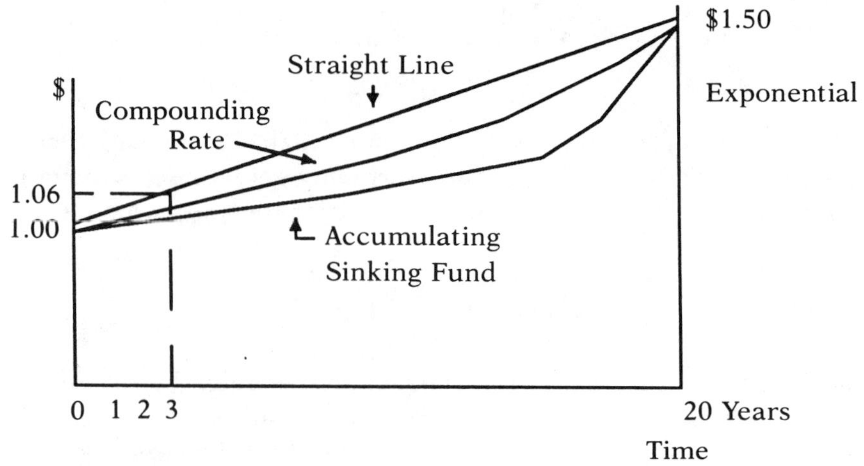

three scenarios. This technique lags the other two methods initially, but arrives at the terminal value measure with the others.

The relative position of the premises is the same, regardless of the time period used. For example, given a 3-year term, all three models would arrive at the 1.06 amount. The time period alters the periodic input, not the final accumulation, which is based on the anticipated forecast.

§ 7.6 PHYSICAL RESIDUALS AND YIELD CAPITALIZATION

As developed in direct capitalization, incomes, values, and rates can be allocated between the land and the improvement components of a property. Yield capitalization has shown that value based on the concept of the present worth of future anticipated benefits can be allocated between income returns and expectations (or realizations) of gain or loss at resale.

Techniques have evolved that combine these two concepts, allowing decision makers to address more complex real estate situations, such as analysis of the value of a property that may have a depreciating building (in terms of a real economic loss rather than book depreciation) and appreciating land values. The combination of the physical residual techniques and yield capitalization can be a useful tool for valuing properties located in transitional neighborhoods.

For example, assume a decision maker must analyze a property in an area that is evolving from a residential area to a professional office area. The large, existing residences were built initially in the 1920s; they are on the fringe of the CBD. The residences, even as office conversions, are perceived as declining in contributory value, while the land in the area, perceived as sites of future office structures, is increasing in value. What is an appropriate valuation technique? At the point in time when a (purchase/sell) decision must be made, no land sales will have occurred in the area. The purchasers may have stated their intention to remove the converted residences and construct moderate-rise office facilities. However, none of the property has been razed for 4 years, and none is expected to be razed in the next 3 years. What is the estimated property value?

The current rental income (office use–residential structure) is $10,000 per year. Several properties similar to the subject property have been purchased and improved as office facilities. The purchase price range is $90,000 to $120,000. The improvement and conversion costs have ranged from \$20,000 to \$50,000. The property most similar to the subject was purchased for \$120,000 and had a \$20,000 renovation cost. Of the \$120,000, \$80,000 of it was attributed to the improvements. Given the transition occurring in the neighborhood, the improvements are expected to decline by 50 percent in the next 5 years. The land is expected to appreciate by 50 percent over the same period. Investors are seeking 10 percent overall return (a standard based on available information on financial structures and terms in the area, as will be explained later).

Based on the above information, a physical residual yield capitalization model is applied using two options: (1) a sinking fund recapture, and (2) a straight-line recapture. The residual yield format for improvement income is:

$$V_B \times (Y_o + \Delta_{B_a}) = I_B$$

Then:

$$NOI = I_o$$

$$I_o - I_B = I_L$$

$$\frac{I_L}{R_L} = \frac{I_L}{Y_o - \Delta_{L_a}} = V_L$$

such that:

$$V_B + V_L = V_o$$

$$R_B = Y_o + \Delta_{B_a}$$

where:

V_B = improvement value
Y_o = overall yield
Δ_B = change in building value over projection period
I_L = income imputed to land
NOI = net operating income
I_o = NOI or overall net operating income
I_B = income imputed to improvements (building)
R_L = land cap rate
Δ_L = change in land value over projection period
V_L = land value
V_o = overall property value
R_B = building cap rate

For option 1, the sinking fund recapture (annualizer), the rate is 12 percent for 5 years:

NOI	$25,000
Income inputed to improvements:	
$80,000 (purchase) + $20,000 (renovation) =	
$100,000 × (.12 – (–.50)(.1574097) =	
$100,000 × (.1987048)	19,870
Income imputed to land	$ 5,130

$$V_L = \frac{\$5,130}{.12 - .50(.1574097)} = \$124,227 \text{ (rounded to } \$124,000)$$

The current land value, based on the expectations of the area's transition, is $124,000. The improvement value is $80,000 (contributory value of purchase price) and requires a $20,000 capital investment to make it a competitive interim (or short-term) use. The income allocation is somewhat distorted because a high rate (SFF) is required to recapture the investment in the improvements, given their short projected (or planned) economic life. The economics of the area's transitional status is supported by the excess of the capitalized land value over the improvement's contributory value ($V_L > V_B$ or $124,000 > $80,000).

The combination of overall economic (market) analysis, physical residual theory, and yield capitalization gives insights for decision making. The capitalization model as used here can be viewed as an acid test that may require a more fully detailed cash flow projection that compares various development alternatives, strategies, or timing. The key is that various property components can be identified.

In this example, a land residual technique was used. A building residual is just as plausible. The appropriate model is determined by the problem situation.

For option 2, the straight-line recapture (annualizer), the holding period is 5 years:

NOI	$25,000
Income imputed to improvements:	
$80,000 + $20,000 =	
$100,000 × (.12 – (–50)(1/5))	22,000
I_L	$ 3,000

$$V_L = \frac{\$3,000}{.12 - (.50)(.20)} = \$150,000$$

The straight-line approach indicates a higher land value than did the sinking fund method, because the periodic recapture is greater under the straight-line mechanics than under the sinking fund method. An implication is that the appreciation of a nonwasting asset is deferred at a greater periodic allowance. The cumulative effect is that more heavily weighted deduction of the deferred appreciation results in a higher value estimate.

The mechanics of this technique also fits the format of a building residual model. Furthermore, the combination of varying property/value components in a yield context opens up the possibility of expanding yield capitalization to mortgage-equity analysis.

§ 7.7 MORTGAGE-EQUITY AND YIELD CAPITALIZATION

As illustrated in Chapter 6, the income, value, and rates in real estate investment analysis can be allocated between debt and equity positions. This allocation of the financial structures can also be achieved within the context of yield capitalization. The components of yield capitalization are the yield rates, the ratio rates, and the appreciation/depreciation rates.

Mortgage-equity, in the context of yield capitalization, is concerned with the changes in debt and equity positions over a stated holding period. The mortgage and equity ratios change because of the mortgage's amortization features.

The concerns of mortgage-equity yield capitalization are illustrated in Figure 7.4. The impact of traditional mortgage amortization over the 5-year holding period is an increase in the terminal equity position. As the mortgage is paid, the principal component of the periodic debt service is shifted from the debt portion of the balance sheet to the equity portion. The mortgage component depicted in Figure 7.4 is originally $75,000. This is a loan-to-value ratio of 75 percent. The amortization period is for 30 years, payable monthly. The interest rate is 10 percent. With the monthly debt service payment of $658.17, approximately $625 is paid as interest and $33 as principal. The $33 of principal is shifted from the mortgage component of the property to the equity position. This reduces the mortgage balance to $74,967 after the first month. The interest payment in the second month is $624.73. This allows a second-month principal deduction of $33.44. The pattern of increasing principal and decreasing interest payments continues (out of the constant debt service payment of $658.17) over the holding

Figure 7.4 Changes in Mortgage-Equity Positions over a 5-Year Holding Period with Terminal Sale (with Appreciation)

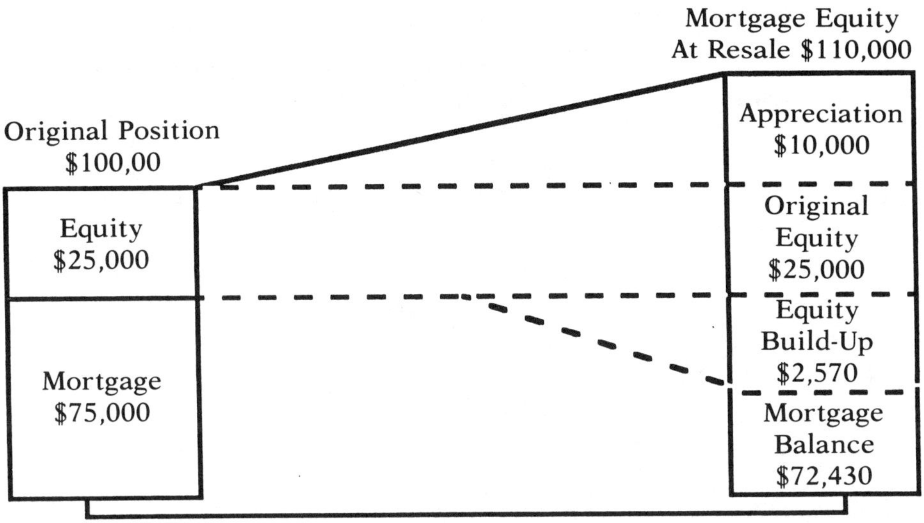

period. At the end of the 5-year holding period, $2,570 of mortgage has been paid off. (See Figure 7.4.) The mortgage balance at the time of sale is $72,430; the terminal equity is $37,570. The $37,570 in equity represents a return of the original $25,000 investment and a return on the investment of $12,570 (the equity build-up component can be viewed as additional equity investment over the holding period, although it is a cash return to the seller at the time of the transaction). Therefore, the overall yield, based only on the gain at sale, is:

$$Y_o = \sqrt[5]{\frac{FV}{PV}} - 1$$

$$= \sqrt[5]{\frac{37{,}570}{25{,}000}} - 1$$

$$= 1.08487 - 1$$

$$= 8.49\%$$

This yield measure reflects only the cash (or capital gain) at time of resale; it does not consider the income generated over the 5-year holding period. This income must be considered, in order to derive the two major components of an overall yield measure. The yield measure can take the value components depicted in Figure 7.4 and express them in the context of rates. This conversion is necessary, in part, because the overall value is the quest in valuation, and the mortgage amount cannot be established without having an opinion of the overall value beforehand. Therefore, the various components of yield measurement must be investigated.

§ 7.8 COMPONENTS OF RATE OF RETURN MEASURES

There are several methods for the measurement and identification of returns in real estate or other investments. Generically, the techniques can be categorized as ratio rates, appreciation rates, and yield rates or total return rates.

(a) RATIO RATES

The ratio rates (also called dividend rates) are derived from dividing the reported or estimated income by a value or purchase price. In addition to the term ratio to represent a general category of rates, several other names are used in describing this measure or level of return: the overall capitalization rate, the equity dividend, the equity cap rate, or the cash on cash rate of return. Examples of various rates, as they relate to capital components of property, are illustrated in Table 7.1.

Cash throw-off represents the same income return as the before-tax cash flow or the equity dividend.

(b) APPRECIATION

Investment value is concerned with the present worth of future expected benefits. The benefits in real estate can be considered in two general forms: (1) the cash flow and its pattern over time, and (2) the cash received from appreciation at the future resale price. Property purchased for investment is not limited to income properties; other properties can be acquired solely for capital gain. This latter form of return may be the only type of compensation received from the investment in single-family residential real estate and raw land (though, with only a few exceptions, these are not the property types purchased by many institutions).

Table 7.1 Ratio Rates

Rate	Component of Value	Formula	Rate Symbol
Overall capitalization rate	Total property value	$\frac{NOI}{V_o}$	R_o
Mortgage constant	Original loan amount	$\frac{DS}{V_M}$	R_M
Equity dividend rate	Original equity amount	$\frac{CTO}{V_E}$	R_E

where:

NOI = net operating income
V_o = overall property value or purchase price
R_o = overall rate of capitalization
DS = debt service
V_M = original mortgage value
R_M = constant rate of mortgage
CTO = cash throw-off
R_E = rate of equity dividend

The appreciation return for non-income-producing investment property must still consider the potential of cash flows. These cash flows are negative—property tax payments and debt service payments (if the property is encumbered with a loan). Given these concerns, an investment decision standard for a non-income-producing property must be based on a comparison between the expected appreciation rate and the holding or waiting costs. The holding costs are composed of the opportunity cost of capital (the existing interest rate on the debt or returns that would be obtainable if investing in other investments of similar risk) and the property tax rate. The opportunity cost must include a factor for inflation. With the total holding cost identified, the investment decision criterion for non-income-producing property is based on a comparison of the appreciation rate to the holding cost stated as a rate. A decision proxy can be the point at which the appreciation rate is equal to or exceeds the opportunity cost of capital plus the tax rate.

The major concern with investment in real estate is that the purchaser is tied to a long position (gain can only occur if the future price is greater than the original price). Usually, this only happens in a growth market or if the property has a unique or monopoly position.

Table 7.2 Appreciation Rates

Rate	Component of Value	Formula	Rate Symbol
Overall appreciation rate	Total property value	$\frac{V_1 - V_o}{V_o}$	Δ_o
Equity build-up rate	Decline in debt amount	$\frac{V_M - B}{V_M}$	P
Equity apreciation rate	Change in equity amount	$\frac{V_{E1} - V_E}{V_E}$	Δ_E

where:

V_1 = future resale price
Δ_o = overall appreciation rate
B = mortgage balance at time of resale
P = percentage of mortgage paid off over holding period
V_{E1} = future equity value at time of resale
Δ_E = equity appreciation rate

Appropriate leveraging can offset part of this exposure, when the equity build-up or pay-down (amortization) of the mortgage exceeds the decline in property value. Based on this insight, Table 7.2 considers appreciation rates for the various components of the property, building on the description of the ratio rates in Table 7.1.

The percentage of the mortgage paid off during the holding period is the value shifted from the debt portion to the equity portion of the balance sheet ($P_E\Delta_M$). The percentage paid off is a percentage change in the mortgage value. This is a build-up in the equity value at the time of sale. If the market falls and this component exceeds a decline in the overall or equity value, the investor may still receive a return on or an increasing yield to the investment.

The concept or calculation of P is a rate representing the percentage of the mortgage paid over the holding period. This percentage is the gain in the equity because of the mortgage amortization. Using the information for the subject property of Figure 7.4, the amount of P is the ratio of the principal paid off ($2,570) to the original mortgage amount ($75,000). The ratio indicates that 3.4256 percent of the mortgage has been paid off over the holding period.

An alternative method often required for valuation (because the mortgage and principal payments are unknown until the value is estimated) is derived by using the mortgage constant ratios:

$$P = \frac{R_M - I}{R_{M_p} - I}$$

where:

R_M = mortgage constant for amortization period
R_{M_p} = mortgage constant for holding period
I = nominal interest

Using the mortgage terms for the property in Figure 7.4 (30 years' amortization, 10 percent interest, payable monthly over a 5-year holding period):

$$P = \frac{.105308 - .10}{.254964 - .10} = \frac{.00530}{.15496}$$

$$= .034256$$

Consideration of the ratio rates, the appreciation/depreciation concerns of the property, and the amortization process enables the development of mortgage-equity yield analysis.

§ 7.9 BASIS: BAND OF INVESTMENT

As in direct capitalization, the band of investment (BOI) technique is a reasonable basis for developing mortgage-equity yield analysis. The BOI in yield analysis differs from direct capitalization BOI in that the equity yield rate (Y_E) is used in the weighted equity rate, rather than the equity dividend rate (R_E). This, however, creates an inconsistency in the developed cap rate. The combination of the mortgage constant (R_M) with the equity yield rate (Y_E) is improper. As in the direct capitalization procedure, ratio rates can be combined (R_M and R_E) or yield rates can be combined (Y_E and Y_M, the interest rate). The consistency of combined ratio rates and combined yield rates is required because of the difference between dividend or income return rates and total yield rates. The latter consist of income and property value changes, as discussed in § 7.7.

Therefore, the yield model based on Y_E must be altered for the equity build-up component and the property value change (appreciation or depreciation) at the end of the holding period. The format established by Akerson[2] was discussed in detail in § 5.7, where the equivalents were given as:

$$\begin{array}{lll} M & \times & R_M \\ +(1-M) & \times & Y_E \\ -\ M \times P & \times & \underline{SFF} \\ & & Y_o \\ & & \underline{-\Delta_o}(SFF) \\ & & R_o \end{array}$$

where:

- M = loan to value ratio
- R_M = mortgage constant
- 1 − M = equity-to-value ratio
- Y_E = equity yield
- P = percentage of mortgage paid off during holding period
- SFF = sinking fund factor at the equity yield rate; used as periodic recapture rate or annualizer for the equity build-up and overall property value change; $1/s_{\overline{n}|}$ is equivalent symbol
- Y_o = overall weighted cost of capital
- Δ_o = overall property value change—appreciation or depreciation
- R_o = overall cap rate

The Akerson format can be applied to the case depicted in Figure 7.4. However, more information is now required. Besides the financial information on the mortgage (30 years, 10 percent interest, monthly payments, and a five-year holding period), an equity yield rate must be established, a sinking fund based on equity yield rate and holding

[2] Charles B. Akerson, "Ellwood Without Algebra," *The Appraisal Journal*, 39:4 (July 1970): 325–335.

period must be calculated, and the expected change in value must be projected. In this case:

$$
\begin{aligned}
M &= .75 \\
R_M &= .105308 \\
Y_E &= 15\% \\
P &= .034256 \text{ (based on previous calculation for Figure 7.4)} \\
SFF &= .148316\text{; 5-year sinking fund factor at 15\%} \\
\Delta_o &= 10\% \text{ over 5 years}
\end{aligned}
$$

$$
\begin{array}{lll}
M \times R_M & = .75 \times .105308 & = .078981 \\
+(1 - M) \times Y_E & = .25 \times .15 & = +.037500 \\
- M \times P \times SFF & = -.75 \times .034256 \times .148316 & = -.003810 \\
\hline
Y_o = & & = .112671 \\
-\Delta_o(SFF) = & .10 \times .148316 & = -.014831 \\
\hline
R_o = & & = .097838
\end{array}
$$

The cap rate (R_o), developed by considering the impact of amortization and appreciation at the end of the holding period, is applied in the traditional direct capitalization model. In this case, the property was generating a stabilized NOI of $10,000 per year. Therefore, the estimated value of the property is:

$$V_o = \frac{NOI}{R_o} = \frac{\$10{,}000}{.097838} = \$102{,}209 \text{ (rounded to \$102,000)}$$

The $102,000 value is significantly close to the $100,000 used in the predetermined value to document Figure 7.4. A partial explanation of the $2,000 of added value is that the equity build-up and expectations of 10 percent appreciation in 5 years have been (discounted) capitalized into the current value estimate.

The Akerson format, based on the BOI technique, is a restatement of Ellwood's[3] original mortgage-equity yield model, which was stated in the universal cap rate (yield context) later developed by Gibbons. The Ellwood model is:

$$Ro = Y_E - M(Y_E + P \times SFF - R_M) - \Delta_o(SFF)$$

[3] L. W. Ellwood, *Ellwood Tables for Real Estate Appraising and Financing*, 4th Edition (Cambridge, MA: Ballinger Publishing Co., 1977).

Continuing the previous case:

$$
\begin{aligned}
R_o &= .15 - .75(.15 + .034256 \times .148316 - .105308) - .10 \times .148316 \\
&= .15 - .75(.0497727) - .0148316 \\
&= .15 - .0373295 - .0148316 \\
&= .097838
\end{aligned}
$$

The cap rate calculated by the Ellwood model is equivalent to the rate calculated by the Akerson model. This is important because the Ellwood model begins with the equity yield, which is the concern of many investment or lending groups. Ellwood's model was developed to help corporate real estate decisions.

The Akerson model is based on the weighted cost of capital (Y_o) that results from considering the debt and equity bands of investment. The Akerson model has its roots in traditional appraisal analysis.

The significance of comparing the two models is that, despite their orientation and origins, they are equivalent models, as illustrated in the following equations:

$$
\begin{aligned}
R_o &= Y_E - M(Y_E + P \times SFF - R_M) - \Delta_o SFF \\
&= Y_E - MY_E - MPSFF + MR_M - \Delta_o SFF \qquad (1) \\
&= (1 - m)Y_E + MRM - MPSFF - \Delta_o SFF
\end{aligned}
$$

Reorganized, equation (1) can be illustrated as:

$$
\begin{array}{lr}
M & \times R_M \\
+(1 - M) & \times Y_E \\
- M \times P & \times \underline{SFF} \\
 & Y_o \\
 & \underline{-\Delta_o(SFF)} \\
 & R_o
\end{array}
$$

Both the Akerson and Ellwood models are alternatives to the discounted cash flow (DCF) model. As yield models, they consider the impact on present value of changing values over time, the amortization of debt, and the significance of a stabilized income. Fisher[4] and Gushee[5]

[4] Jeffery Fisher, "Ellwood After Tax—New Dimensions," *The Appraisal Journal*, 45:3 (July 1977): 325–330.

[5] Charles H. Gushee, *Financial Capitalization Rate Tables* (Chicago: AIREA, and Boston: Financial Publishing Co., 1974).

have even demonstrated that Ellwood and mortgage-equity yield capitalization can be calculated after federal income tax. Canaday and Colwell[6] have shown that mortgage-equity yield capitalization is equivalent to a cash flow model with specific stabilized or smoothing assumptions.

Although presented here as an alternative or shortcut to discounted cash flow, appraisers must often use this method because information to generate a traditional cash flow is incomplete. The DCF, in terms of debt service, rate calculation, and growth projections, often requires an initial value estimate. This beginning point in many DCFs is the objective of the appraisal process. Therefore, appraisers are often forced to analyze within the context of the rate structure.

A major concern with the mortgage-equity yield rates is the emphasis on a stabilized income projection. This concern has been addressed with the application of the J and K factors.

§ 7.10 J AND K FACTORS

The J and K factors are modifiers employed in the cap rate formula to adjust for the value impact of a changing income stream and forecasted value.

(a) J FACTOR

The J factor was devised by Ellwood to allow for the impact of a changing income (increasing or decreasing) on the fixed value estimate. The J factor functions like an accumulating sinking fund. The accumulating sinking fund is based on estimating the base amount to be added to the income stream each year and then letting the income addition (the sinking fund amount) grow in the pattern of a future worth of 1 per period factor (compound interest) on an added dividend per period. For example, if the income is projected to increase by 5 percent per year, then, over the 5-year holding period, the income has increased by 27.6 percent $= (1.05)^5$, if the project assumes discounting and compounding as do most DCF programs. This increase must be considered,

[6] Roger Canaday and Peter Colwell, "A Unified Field Theory of the Income Approach to Appraisal—Parts 1, 2, 3," *The Real Estate Appraiser and Analyst,* 47:1,2,3 (First Quarter, Summer, Fall 1981): 5–10; 29–43; 25–37.

Table 7.3 J-Factor or Accumulated Sinking Fund Income Pattern

Year	1 Base Income	2 SSF Amount		3 Compounding Factor for $1 per Period		4 Income Adjustment	5 Projected Income
						(2 × 3)	(1 + 4)
0	$10,000	0	×	1	=	0	$ 10,000
1	10,000	$409	×	1	=	$ 409	10,409
2	10,000	409	×	2.15	=	879	10,879
3	10,000	409	×	3.47	=	1,419	11,419
4	10,000	409	×	4.99	=	2,041	12,041
5	10,000	409	×	6.74	=	2,757	12,757
						$7,505	$ 67,505
				Plus resale at end of year 5:			110,000

The present worth of column 5 plus $110,000 discounted of 15% per year (47,556) equals $115,061 (rounded to $115,000).

along with the forecast that the property's resale value will increase by 10 percent (to $110,000 in 5 years).

Using the J factor, the sinking fund base is taken from the difference between the first year's income and the income at the end of the holding period, as:

$10,000 × 1.27628 = $12,762.80

$12,762.80 − 10,000 = $2,762.80

$2,762.80 × .148316 = $409.76 (.148316 = SFF for 5 years at 15%)

As shown in Table 7.3, the income increases as an accumulating sinking fund. This method was adopted by Ellwood to remain consistent with the procedure used in the property appreciation and equity build-up components of the Ellwood/Akerson model. The sinking fund concept is based on the traditional amortization schedule.

This method was devised before the advent of the micro-chip calculator/computer. To make the analysis more feasible, Ellwood devised a set of J factor tables, based on varying series of yield rates and terms. They are calculated with the following formula:

$$J = \frac{1}{s_{\overline{n}|}} \times \left(\frac{n}{1 - \frac{1}{(1 + y)^n}} - \frac{1}{Y} \right)$$

where:

n = the holding period
Y = the yield
$\frac{1}{s_{\overline{n}|}}$ = sinking fund factor at Y

Therefore, the J factor at 15 percent for five years is:

$$J = .148316 \times \left(\frac{5}{1 - \frac{1}{(1 + .15)^5}} - \frac{1}{.15} \right)$$

$$= .148316\left(\frac{5}{(1 - .497)} - 6.6667\right)$$

$$= .148316(9.9438 - 6.6667)$$

$$= .148316(3.2768)$$

$$= .4861$$

The J factor is then applied to the projected change in the income over the holding period plus 1, and divided into the Ellwood equation to arrive at an overall cap rate that is adjusted for changing income stream:

$$R_{o_J} = \frac{R_o}{1 + \Delta J} = \frac{Y_E - M(Y_E + P \times \frac{1}{s_{\overline{n}|}} - R_M) - \Delta_o s_{\overline{n}|}}{1 + \Delta,J}$$

$$= \frac{.097838}{1 + .2762(.4861)}$$

$$= \frac{.097838}{1.1342}$$

$$= .08625$$

(.097838 is as calculated with the Akerson or Ellwood models.)

The cap rate, adjusted for the increasing income, is lower than the cap rate for the stabilized income. This results in a higher value, when divided into the stabilized income (or initial year's income) as in the traditional capitalization model:

$$V_O = \frac{NOI}{R_{O_J}} = \frac{\$10{,}000}{.08625}$$

$$= \$115{,}942 \text{ (rounded to } \$116{,}000)$$

The impact of the increasing income on the present value is $14,000 ($116,000 – $102,000) more than the original Ellwood/Akerson calculation.

Because value is the present worth of future expectations, the expectation of income growth (or decline) will impact the present value estimation.

(b) K FACTOR

The K factor is similar to the J factor in that it allows for the impact of a changing (increasing or decreasing) income stream on present value. It varies from the J factor in that it allows for a compounding annual income change and does not require the sinking fund assumption. The K factor has been applied to the stabilized income and, like the J factor, it can be used within the rate structure.

As applied to the income, the annual increases (in this example, 5 percent per year), the yield rate (15 percent), and the holding period (5 years) are considered. The K factor, based on the above parameters, is 1.0902. This is multiplied by the $10,000 of NOI and then capitalized at the original Ellwood/Akerson rate of 9.7838 percent:

$$\$10{,}000 \times 1.0902 = \$10{,}902$$

$$\frac{\$10{,}902}{.097838} = \$111{,}429 \text{ (rounded to } \$111{,}500)$$

As with the J factor, the K factor reflects the impact of the compounding income on value. Therefore, the K factor value is above the traditional Ellwood value ($111,500 – $102,000); the K factor value, however, is less than the J factor value ($116,000 – $111,500), because the J factor accumulates the growth in the earlier years and the K factor increases more rapidly in the later years. The growth patterns for the J and K factors are illustrated in Figure 7.5.

Figure 7.5 J Versus K Growth Patterns

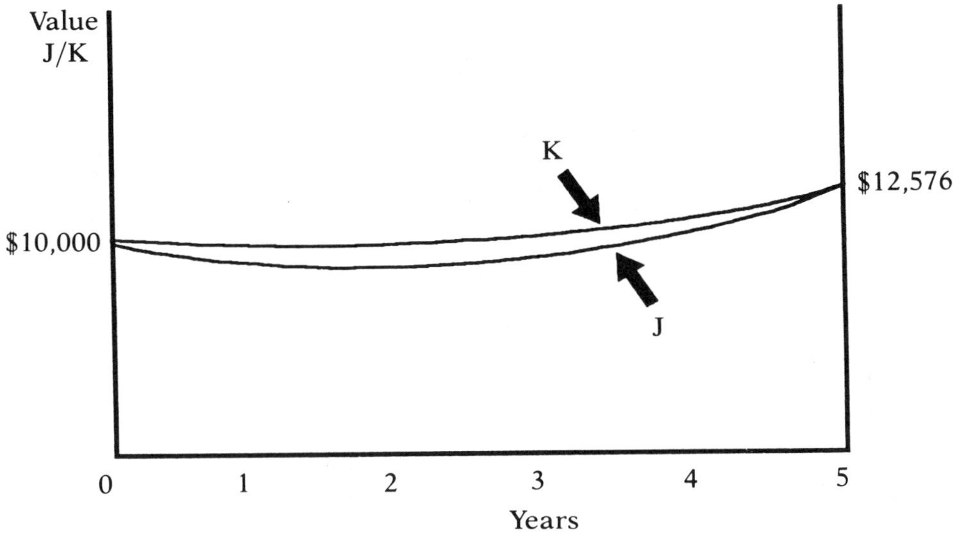

The formula for the K factor, as applied to the income, is:

$$K = \frac{1 - \dfrac{(1+d)^n}{(1+y)^n}}{(Y\text{-}d)a_{\overline{n|}y}}$$

where:

d = income change per year (5%)
y = yield rate
$a_{\overline{n|}y}$ = present worth of $1 per period (annuity) factor based on the 15% yield rate

The $a_{\overline{n|}y}$ rate is:

$$\left(\frac{1 - \dfrac{1}{(1+y)^n}}{y}\right)$$

Therefore,

$$a_{\overline{n|}y} = 3.352155.$$

Thus:

$$K = \frac{1 - \frac{(1+.05)^5}{(1+.15)^5}}{(.15-.05)3.352155}$$

$$= \frac{1 - \frac{(1.27628)}{2.01135}}{(.10)3.352155}$$

$$= \frac{1 - .634538}{.335216}$$

$$= 1.09023$$

Above, the K factor modified the income stream (NOI). It can also be used like the J factor, to modify the Ellwood/Akerson cap rate:

$$R_{OK} = \frac{R_o}{K} = \frac{Y_E - M(Y_E + P \times \frac{1}{s_{\overline{n}|y}} - R_M) - \Delta_o \frac{1}{s_{\overline{n}|y}}}{K}$$

$$(K = 1.0902)$$

$$= \frac{.097838}{1.0902}$$

$$= .089743$$

$$V_o = \frac{\overline{NOI}}{R_{OK}} = \frac{\$10{,}000}{.089743} = \$111{,}429 \text{ (rounded to \$111,500)}$$

Effectively, $K \simeq 1 + \Delta_I J$ = \$111,500 versus \$116,000.

In summary, the J and K factors are approximations of one another and enable the consideration of specific patterns of income growth and future property appreciation on present value. With the addition of the factors to the capitalization process, the variability of the DCF model is possible within rate analysis.

§ 7.11 RISK ANALYSIS

Yield capitalization offers a major contribution to the analysis of investment risk over time. A transposition of the formula $R_o = Y_E - M(Y_E +$

$P \times \frac{1}{s_{\overline{n}|y}} - R_M) - \Delta_o \frac{1}{s_{\overline{n}|y}}$ allows the abstraction of the expected change in property value based on the market relationship among income, value, and financing. Taking $R_o = Y_E - M(Y_E + P \times \frac{1}{s_{\overline{n}|y}} - R_M) - \Delta_o \frac{1}{s_{\overline{n}|y}}$, then the formula is $R_o = Y_o - \Delta_o SFF$. This equation can be transposed to $\Delta_o = R_o - Y_o/s_{\overline{n}|y}$. Therefore, if financing and income are known, the expected changes driving a specific transaction can be derived from the market. This is significant in forecasting.

Another use of the abstraction of the expectation of change is in the analysis of syndications or various real estate security investments, where numerous service (fee) loads are taken up front and a return (guaranteed, secured, or risky) is to be taken from the proceeds of sale at the end of the stated holding period.

For example, a 6 percent return per year is projected over a 3-year period in a prospectus. The unit is sold in \$10,000 shares. Therefore, the return in 3 years should be \$10,000 × 1.191 = \$11,910.16. This is a return of 19.1 percent, which is marginally above the current rate.

However, the syndicate selling the shares takes a commission up front. This commission is not only the selling fee; it also includes an acquisition fee of 6 percent and a 2.5 percent management fee (on the deal). The end result is that 14.5 percent is deducted for real estate services. Operating expenses, legal fees, financing costs, and property and loan management fees are also deducted, until only 66 percent of each dollar is invested in real estate. Therefore, the perceived 19.1 percent return on each dollar invested (\$10,000 in all, growing to \$11,910) must be generated by the \$0.66 per dollar (or \$6,600).[7] This is an 80-plus percent increase in value over a 3-year period. (See Figure 7.6.) The actual return would have to be 21.7 percent. The test for the decision maker is whether this return complies with the market trends.

§ 7.12 SUMMARY

Yield capitalization is the missing link between discounted cash flow and direct capitalization models. Yield capitalization, like DCF, considers the impact of changing debt and equity relations on value and the

[7] Terry V. Grissom, "Real Estate Syndications," *The Appraisal Journal*, 54:3 (July 1986): 376–398.

Figure 7.6 Return Potential Based on Expectations in a Syndication Investment

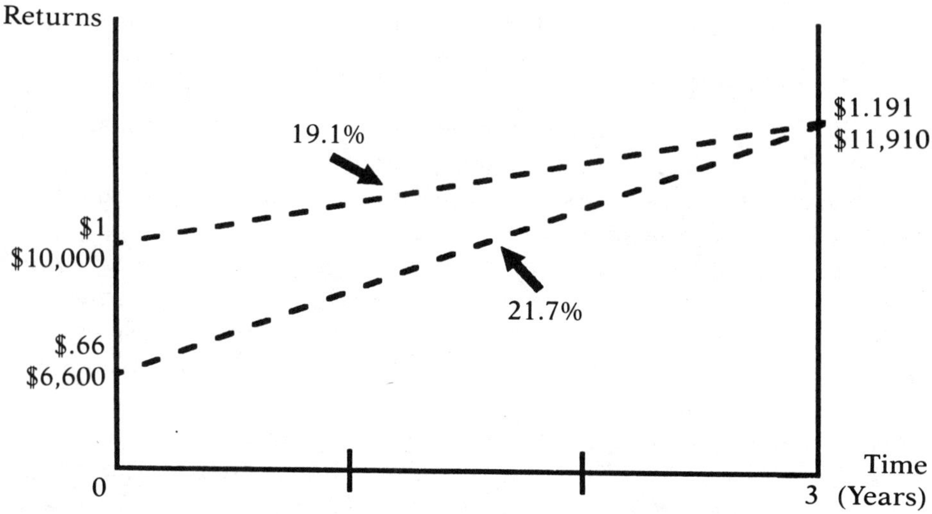

changes in property value over projected holding periods. It also enables a measure of total return from market transactions.

In this age of computers, DCF is more easily accomplished than yield capitalization, in cases where numerous inputs are readily available. However, many of the market/financial parameters in real estate are missing and unavailable. The yield capitalization enables an approximation of the DCF.

As the link between direct capitalization and DCF, yield capitalization affords many insights. Overall cap rates derived from the market can be used to forecast or investigate buyer/investor expectations at the time of purchase. As illustrated in the risk analysis, yield capitalization that focuses on the expected changes in property value furnishes additional information required by investors.

Eight

Real Estate Market Analysis and the Decision Process

§ 8.1 INTRODUCTION

There has been an incomplete integration of documented market information into the traditional appraisal process. Depictions of the appraisal process in most books illustrate a lack, or at least an incomplete representation, of market information and its relevance to appraisal analysis.[1] An objective of this book is to address this deficiency and directly integrate market analysis into the decision process.

§ 8.2 APPRAISAL THEORY AND MARKET ANALYSIS

Understanding the relationship of market analysis to appraisal theory will help decision makers and users of appraisals to understand the

[1] A review of several appraisal books and articles shows no or little delineation of market analysis in the alternative appraisal processes presented. Implicit considerations of market concerns are identified in the data collection steps. However, data collection alone does not imply analysis. Exceptions that did identify market issues were Fred Case, "The Theory of Valuation," in *Recent Perspectives in Urban Land Economics*, Michael Goldberg (Ed.) (Vancouver, BC: The University of British Columbia Press, 1974) and James A. Graaskamp, *The Appraisal of 25 N. Pinckney, A Demonstration Case for Contemporary Appraisal Methods* (Madison, WI: Landmark Research, Inc., 1977).

purpose and use of market research as it relates to valuation and overall decision making. Economics is a matter of choices. These choices are made with the constraint of limited resources and in the context of a competitive environment. The issue of limited resources is delineated with an analysis of the productive attributes of a property within the context of competitive supply and limited demand. The exposure of the limited productive resources to competitive supply and demand is the basis of value in real estate. The constraints of supply and demand also establish the context in which a property is valued.

Appraisal is concerned with the estimation of value, and value estimation is approached on three distinct levels. These levels are concerned with issues of value theory, valuation theory, and appraisal theory.[2] The first two levels are traditionally defined in economic analysis. Economics has identified value theory as the issues concerned with the basis of worth in an asset. Valuation theory is the techniques or processes by which value is measured, estimated, or forecast. Appraisal theory is defined as the logic process by which valuation theory is linked to value theory, as it is applied to a specific land use or parcel.[3]

Appraisal theory has evolved with the maturing of the appraisal profession and has developed an increasing relevance with the instigation of regulatory concerns such as memoranda R-41b and c of the Federal Home Loan Bank Board, the Comptroller of the Currency mandates, and the (CEBA) and Federal Deposit Insurance Corporation (FDIC) regulations. Despite the growing importance of appraisal theory that stresses the relationship of value factors to valuation techniques, little effort has been placed on developing and understanding value and appraisal theory. Most appraisal literature deals with the issues of valuation techniques[4]—the concerns of estimating or measuring the quantity of value.[5]

[2] Terry V. Grissom, "Value Definition: Its Place in the Appraisal Process," *The Appraisal Journal,* 53:2 (April 1985): 217–225.

[3] *Ibid.*, at p. 218.

[4] An investigation of the topics identified in *Bibliography of Appraisal Literature (1981–1986)*, published by the Appraisal Institute's Research Department, indicates that only approximately 27 articles out of about 2,000 (1.3 percent) concern value theory and only 5 (.25 percent) address appraisal theory issues.

[5] *The Appraisal of Real Estate,* 9th ed. (Chicago: AIREA, 1987), has an introductory chapter and three other chapters that may be considered to deal with value theory (chs. 1, 2, 3, and 6). Three chapters consider appraisal theory (chs. 4, 23, and 24; Chapter 4 is on the valuation process). All the remaining chapters consider data collection, property description or analysis, and valuation techniques.

The integration of what has been separately termed market analysis is most appropriate in the value section of the appraisal process. Overall, this integration is a necessary step in linking a property's productive attributes to the value or income the property generates, and is a key component in the real estate decision process proposed in this book. The potential of this integration is observed in the basic components of value theory. As identified by the Appraisal Institute's Body of Knowledge Committee, the components of value are utility, scarcity, desire, and exchange. Utility is a functional use of the land, not the psychological measure made by marginalist economists. The alternative use analysis of a property is both the function of the market analysis process and the highest and best use section of an appraisal. The market analysis component of the appraisal investigates the support for a use, a range of uses, or the use possibilities of a particular site. It furthermore identifies and documents appropriate market support for existing or probable uses.

The documentation of the appropriate market support and financial feasibility of a probable use is the functional purpose of a market analysis.[6] This purpose is reflected in two of the components of value theory, utility and scarcity. Scarcity in value theory means that value arises as the result of a limited supply of a commodity, asset, or resource (all of these are used to describe real estate, depending on the property type or problem situation). As will be observed in the analysis of competitive supply and market absorption, a large quantity of properties on the market, in relation to the amount of demand at any one time, generally tends to reduce the probable selling price of a typical property. A limited amount of alternative facilities can cause prices to rise in the short run, for various property types.

The quantity of the competitive properties available in relation to demand potential has an impact on the absorption or marketing period of a given property or property type. The value of a property is then adjusted by the impact of opportunity cost, holding cost, waiting cost, or ripening cost, as discussed in Chapter 4. All of these costs or issues concern the time value of money and hence the present value of a property.

The issues of the amount of competition impacting value at a point in time, or influencing value as a matter of time, illustrate that market analysis is appropriate whether the basis of value is the premise of value in exchange (emphasizing the principle of substitution) or present value based on the present worth of future anticipated benefits (emphasizing

[6] John B. Bailey, Peter F. Spies, and Marilyn Kramer Weitzman, "Market Study + Financial Analysis = Feasibility Report," *The Appraisal Journal*, 45:4 (October 1977): 550–577.

the principle of anticipation). The nature of the appropriate value premise in a report is identified in the purpose of the appraisal. The consideration of the appropriate value principle (substitution/anticipation) aids the gathering of the necessary data, the emphasis of the discussion and documentation of the market analysis, and the selection of the appropriate valuation techniques to use or emphasize in the reconciliation. The linkage among value theory, valuation techniques, and the documentation of the value estimate is the concern of appraisal theory, with market analysis being the cohesive factor.

Desire and exchange are the value issues representing demand. Value theory and market analysis are concerned with measures of effective demand. Effective demand represents the ability of people who desire a good or commodity to act on their desire in an economic context. Demand analysis leads to the segmentation of markets, and the ability to segment markets aids the consultant in property use analysis and valuation. The demand for uses delineates the appropriate comparable properties, the financial and value ranges for various property types, and the timing issues identified in the concern of scarce supply.

The relation of supply and demand at any one time is the key issue in estimating a value. In a growth market, the supply of any kind of real estate is (relatively) limited. The supply is inelastic. The implication of these features is that the level of demand has the most immediate impact on value or probable selling price. In an overbuilt market, the quantity of existing and proposed supply has an immediate impact on the valuation concerns. The ability to estimate a value in any environment or market structure (except a stable market) is totally dependent on market analysis for the thorough understanding that is needed. The interaction of supply and demand is basic to the estimation of value. Value theory, as defined, emphasizes the issues of market analysis and highest and best use. The comparison of a specific property to the market is an essential component of appraisal analysis. Therefore, appropriate analysis and documentation of market activity are keys to the valuation process.

§ 8.3 PLACEMENT OF MARKET ANALYSIS IN THE REAL ESTATE PROCESS

Based on the relationship of market research to value theory and valuation, the appropriate place for market analysis in the real estate process is as documentation of the key factors of value theory. Market analysis should enable an analyst to empirically and logically document the elements of uses, the extent of effective competitive demand, and the scarcity of competitive supply that exist for a particular property type at a specific time or in a given market environment over time.

If it is accepted that market analysis is the process for documenting the value issues of appraisals, and that a major component of that documentation is to identify whether support exists for present or alternative uses of a site, then market analysis is an extension of highest and best use analysis in many assignments.

Figure 8.1 is the traditional appraisal process, with the extension of the highest and best use section, which is described in detail in Figure 8.2.[7] Highest and best use must consider a general problem of value theory: the determination of use. In the appraisal process, use determination involves the concept of highest and best use—the probable use that produces the highest present value at the date of the appraisal. A direct relationship between use (a value theory factor) and valuation is identified in the appraisal. The basis of the most profitable use (highest value) is linked to the attributes of the site. As seen in Figure 8.2, the productivity of the site's attributes is considered in the preliminary analysis of the alternate uses possible on a given site. These attributes can be generally grouped into physical, legal, and locational attributes. These attributes determine the productivity of the property and are the basis for identifying the market appeal and thus the marketability of a site. The issues of a property's productivity analysis help the appraiser in identifying the market appeal of a given tract and enable the linking of the property to the market and the market to the methods for estimating value. The productivity market analysis of a property links the attributes to the market's behavioral response to the property's attributes. With the aid of general economic information and an ability to match the attributes of comparable sales with the subject property and with other comparable properties, an economic value or return can be estimated for the varying levels of market appeal.

Real estate is physically fixed but economically flexible. Because the attributes of a property can support various uses, the highest and best use analysis is a comparative process that must consider the appropriate support of two market levels. The first level is the competition between uses for a given site. Success in the competition usually goes to the use that generates the highest return and thus the highest present

[7] Stephen F. Fanning and Jody Winslow, "Guidelines for Defining the Scope of Market Analysis in Appraisal Assignments," *The Appraisal Journal*, 56:4 (October 1988): 466–476.

Figure 8.1 The Valuation Process

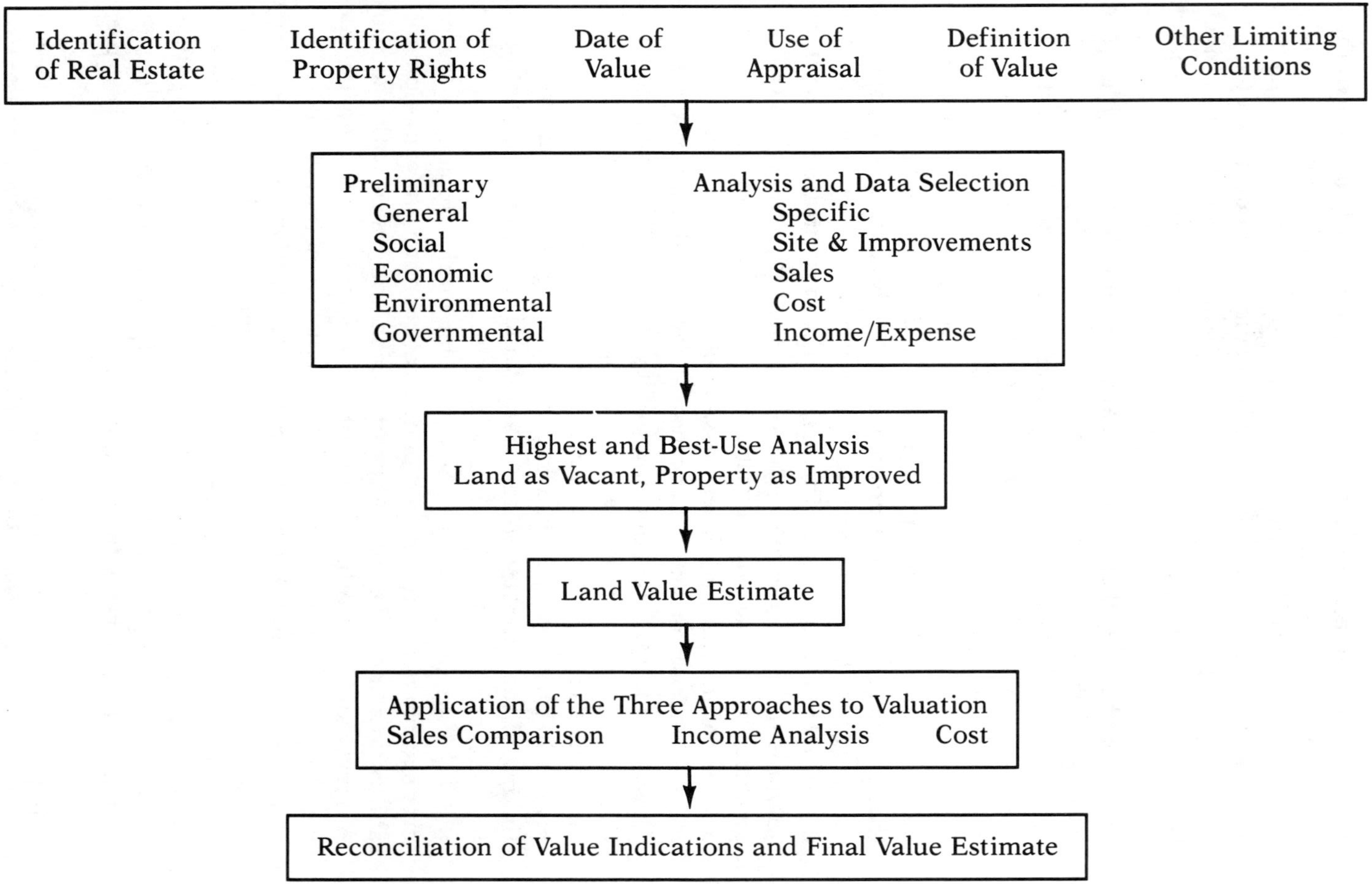

Figure 8.2 Highest and Best-Use Analysis Process

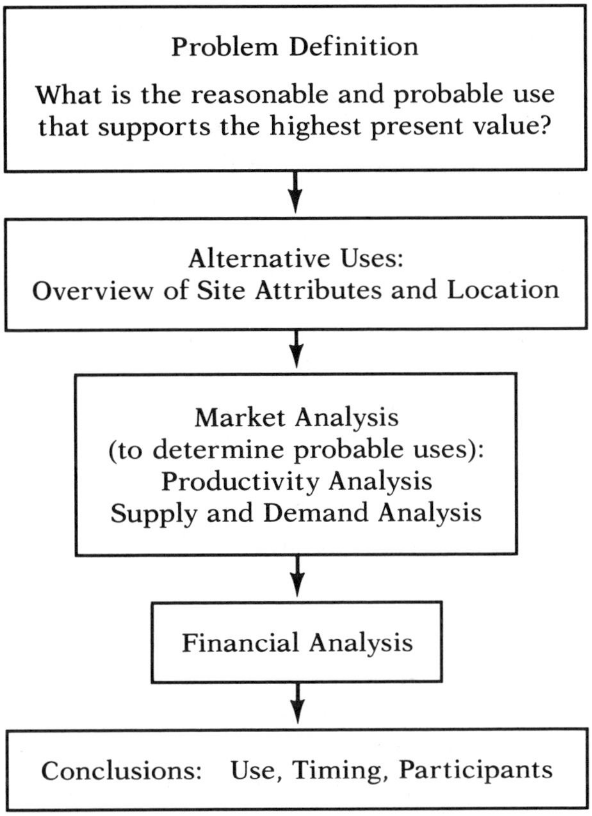

value, compared to other uses. The second level is the competition between users. Once the uses have competed, there is a market allocation among alternative users.

As an example, residential and commercial uses are in competition for a given site. The commercial uses, based on physical and locational attributes, outbid the residential uses. The commercial alternatives are office, office-warehouse, general retail, and local retail. The allocation among the competing uses is influenced by the level of competitive supply and effective demand. Immediate supply alone can eliminate the office and office-warehouse possibilities in this area. The productivity attributes may determine whether the subject site has a comparative advantage (or even a monopoly potential), such that, regardless of the quantity of the supply, it may be a successful property as an office or office-warehouse. In this case, the potential does not exist.

Supply and demand analysis in the immediate neighborhood and trade area may support a retail use. The property attributes are appropriate for either general or local retail. The second level of analysis aids this further segmentation of uses, by identifying the market support of competitive users of space and products in the subject's trade area.

With the synthesis of the above issues, the appraiser is able to specify the appropriate land use for the site, the existing market conditions, and the probable market participants for a given site. The objectives of market analysis, integrated into the highest and best use analysis, are depicted in the last block of Figure 8.2.

Consideration of an appropriate place to link valuation or decision models and the market research process results in the identification of common elements in objectives and formats. Both valuation (in the strict sense) and market analysis are concerned with the research process. An investigation of the general research process can help gain further insights to the place of market research and analysis in appraisal theory. The common elements of market research and analysis, appraisal theory, and investment analysis are the foundation for an overall real estate decision process.

§ 8.4 RESEARCH PROCESSES

A common link between appraisal and market analysis is that they are both research processes initiated to help make decisions on real estate problems. Therefore, to understand the relationship of market analysis and appraisal, an investigation of the general research process is appropriate.

The overall research process is concerned with an organized approach to problem solving. Most research concerns begin with the identification of the problem to be investigated by the research effort. The best known research process is that of scientific method, but it is not the only organized approach to problem solving nor the only research process that merits a general discussion. Other research formats are institutional studies, structuralism, humanistic studies, behavioral analysis, and others.[8]

The scientific method's format offers an appropriate investigative approach for dealing with economic situations and enables empirical

[8] R. J. Johnston, *Philosophy and Human Geography: An Introduction to Contemporary Approaches* (London: Edward Arnold Publishers, 1983).

documentation in the context of value estimation. An analogy involving appraisal analysis, market analysis, and scientific method is presented to show the overall integration of the market research process and appraisal/investment analysis.

Scientific methodology begins with an identification of a problem. The appropriate delineation of the problem can often be 90 percent of the solution. The appraisal process also begins with the identification of a problem, but the range of the situations is more limited. The problem situation in the appraisal is stated in the function of the report. The function is concerned with the decision that needs supportive information, documentation, and analysis.[9] The general classifications of appraisal problems are:

- Transactions—acquisition or disposition of a property;
- Extension of credit—estimation of collateral value;
- Indemnification—compensation for loss;
- Taxation;
- Development or redevelopment of real estate;
- Alternative use considerations;[10]
- Real estate portfolio analysis and management.

As Figure 8.1 illustrates, the problem statement in the appraisal process also begins with an identification of the property. The property description is concerned with a street address, a physical description, and a legal description.

The market analysis process has a broader range of problem situations than does the appraisal process. The variation in the problems to be solved is a key difference in the two processes. The area of overlap between the appraisal process and the market analysis process is the employment assignment (or engagement of employment), which is property-specific.

The second step in research methodology is the statement of a hypothesis or a conjectural statement. Its objective is the establishment of a relationship between one variable or situation and another. The hypothesis in an appraisal is stated in the purpose of the report: to estimate a defined value. That value is traditionally the market value,

[9] Grissom, *supra* note 2, at 218.

[10] Richard U. Ratcliff, *Valuation for Real Estate Decisions* (Santa Cruz, CA: Democrat Press, 1972): 2–9.

but it may vary with the nature of the problem statement. For example, the estimation of insurable value may be needed in an indemnification conflict.

The hypotheses in market analysis are more flexible than in appraisal. In general, the conjectural statements in market analysis are concerned with the matching of supply and demand for a given or identifiable product. The need for an identifiable product in the context of a hypothesis (and the problem statement) of market analysis is why real estate market analysis must include the step of productivity analysis as well as the identification of supply and demand. Support for the issue of productivity analysis is identified in the appraisal process's identification of the property in the problem statement.

The problem situation and conjecture of the hypothesis direct the research to the data requirements. A major problem in real estate (as many other endeavors) is the availability and accessibility of data. The available data and the appropriate data may be mutually exclusive sets of information. The best available information (out of economic necessity) may have to be substituted. The issue of the data needed and available often directs the valuation techniques used in decision analysis. An appraisal example is the choice of units of comparison in the sales comparison approach, or the choice of capitalization technique in the income approach. A market analysis example is the use of an employment forecast to estimate demand, because a population forecast is not available at the time of analysis or does not appear to be realistic.

The nature of the problem, the formulation of the hypothesis, and the availability of data set the context of the research design. The research design concerns the research methodology, which is the evaluation aspect of research.

The fourth step in scientific method is the evaluation of methodological techniques. Once the problem is identified and a conjectural statement is proposed, a test of relationships is conducted. Those relationships can be tested by alternative methods. Examples are:

- Analogy
- Descriptive analysis
- Statistical analysis
- Observation
- Laboratory testing
- Cause and effect relationships

Both appraisal and market analysis include techniques that can be classified as analogy, descriptive analysis, statistical analysis, and cause and effect relationships. Most if not all of the valuation techniques and the issues of market research and market analysis fall into one of these research methodology categories.

The final stage of scientific method is the reconciliation of the data with the problem context. That is the fit of the solution to the problem.

§ 8.5 MARKET RESEARCH PROCESS

Market analysis is divided into three general scenarios, based on the nature of the problem and the context of the decision maker's needs.

(a) SITE IN SEARCH OF USE OR MARKET

The first scenario deals with the fit of solutions to the context of problems concerning a site in search of a use or market. In this situation, the analysis is concerned either with identifying appropriate support for a use or, upon accepting that a use is appropriate, with the delineation of a market to support the use.

The process of analysis begins by investigating the productive capacity of the site. This is done to identify the marketable attributes of a given parcel and to narrow the market delineation required in the investigation.

The identification of the productive capacity of a property in order to determine its market components is defined as productivity analysis. The logic process applied to a site in search of a use or market begins with the site attributes and works to the external features of the site and then of the market. If a valuation or investment analysis is required, then the market forms the context for a comparative analysis.

The logic process addressing the issues of a site in search of a use is depicted in Figure 8.3. Any number of uses is possible on a given parcel of real estate, because land is a factor of production to be used in the manufacturing of a good (products in agriculture, location, or a site in urban real estate). Because land is a factor of production, in the context of this scenario of market analysis, it is economically flexible. It may be the appropriate site for retail or residential, industrial or institutional use. The physical, legal, and locational attributes of the property establish the constraints that enable the appraiser to delineate the productive capacity of the site and direct its use.

Figure 8.3 Site in Search of Use or Market

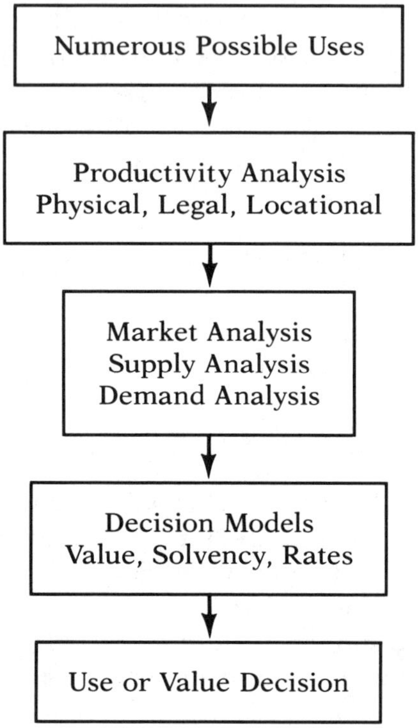

With the completion of the productivity analysis, the second phase of identifying the competitive supply and the effective demand for the package of attributes comprising a given site can be conducted. Supply and demand analysis is the essence of market research. Real estate market research must also identify the activities of the market in a spatial context. Linking the market analysis to the productivity analysis greatly aids the process of investigating real estate problems.

The data and patterns of market actions identified in the market analysis then establish the basis for the selection of the appropriate decision model. The analysis links the issues of the productivity capacity to market actions and directs the analyst to the application of the appropriate and available valuation techniques. As illustrated in Figure 8.3, the decision models occupy the third phase in the scenario of a site in search of a use or market.

The specifics of productivity analysis, market analysis, and the decision models link market activities to valuation techniques. This linkage is the basis for all of the general scenarios of the decision process.

(b) MARKET OR USE IN SEARCH OF SITE

The second general scenario in market analysis is a market or use in search of a site. The logic process of a market in search of a site is depicted in Figure 8.4. The second scenario begins the investigation of the broader level of the market. It is concerned with indications of what types of services or facilities the market in general is seeking. As illustrated in Figure 8.4, the analysis first addresses the elements of demand analysis (basic and general demographics), if use is the ultimate inquiry. If the appropriateness of a site is the objective of the analysis, a particular use may have been identified and the inquiry may be geared to focusing on the market's preferences for specific property attributes. In the latter situation, analysis would be concerned with delineation of the competitive supply.

Figure 8.4 illustrates that the second scenario begins with the market analysis (supply and demand issues) and then studies the macro/

Figure 8.4 Market or Use in Search of Site

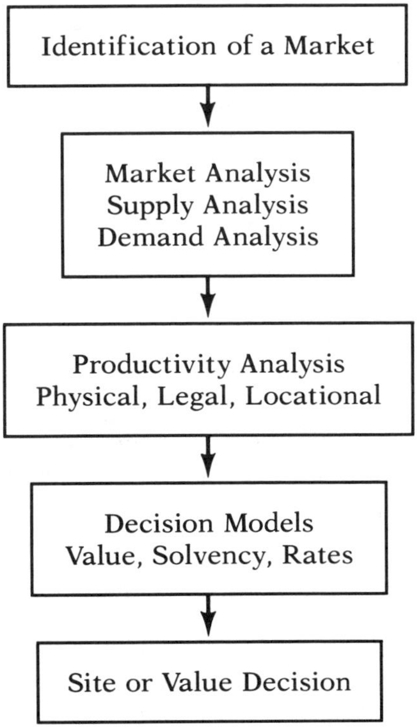

micro location concerns of the productivity analysis. This analysis extends to the investigation of physical and legal attributes. With the combination of market and product or site concerns, the appropriate decision models can be brought into play.

In comparing the first scenario to the second, an experienced analyst would see that the first scenario, a site in search of a use or market, represents the typical appraisal assignment. Most appraisers are asked to value a specific site, and, although the appraisal process as generally taught begins with city and/or regional data (a phase of productivity analysis), the essence of the valuation process begins with a specific site. As illustrated in Chapter 3, it is difficult to analyze the situs of a property without being site- or use-specific.

The second scenario, a market use in search of a site, is often the job assignment of specialists in market analysis. This type of assignment is only different in its emphasis on the traditional analysis tools; it is not a true difference in kind.

(c) REAL ESTATE AS ALTERNATIVE INVESTMENT ASSET

The third scenario, representing a general problem situation that confronts decision makers, is the consideration of real estate as an alternative investment vehicle. These decisions require more services than are offered in appraisal and market analysis. This problem context has received little attention in the literature and practice of those fields. Charles Wurztebach, former vice-president in charge of research and portfolio management for Prudential Realty Advisors, has identified, in several presentations, the lack of attention to the problem by pointing out the difficulty of getting appraisers to understand the need for valuation in a portfolio context.

In many aspects, the third scenario of market analysis is only a difference in emphasis as opposed to a difference in kind. The market support of real estate as an investment can be investigated for consideration of an individual parcel of real estate or for consideration of an individual parcel or multiple parcels within the context of a portfolio. The third scenario, especially in the context of portfolio analysis, is a growing area of opportunity, because of the increased influence of institutional investors in the national market and in many local real estate markets.

Figure 8.5 illustrates the logic format of the analysis of real estate as an investment alternative. The immediate concern is the identification of appropriate levels of return and risk. This is the equivalent of the

Figure 8.5 Real Estate as Alternative Investment Asset

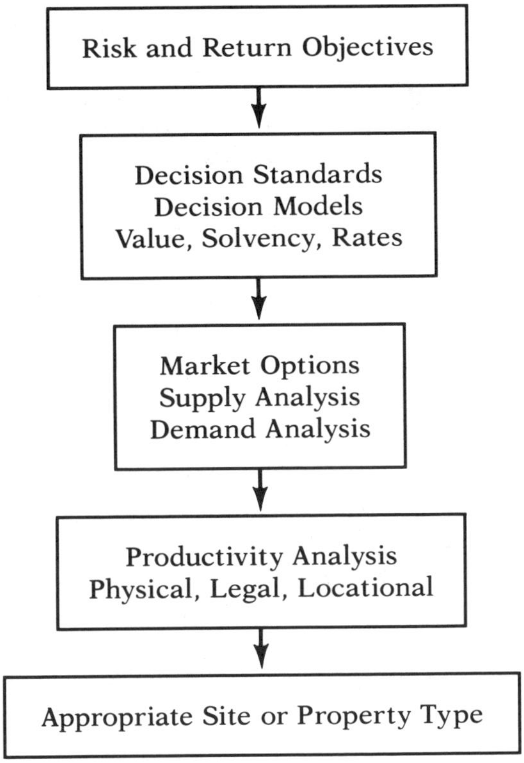

investment/appraisal levels of the previous scenarios. The decision models used by the investors must be identified, to establish the constraints on the problem issues that the appraiser is attempting to solve. The measures of returns and risk must be linked to standards of market performance and opportunity cost. The first level of the valuation analysis must address the alternatives to real estate. The second level must investigate the decision models used by the investors and the competitors. This leads to a concern for market activities of competitive supply and effective demand. A concern when real estate is included in an investment portfolio is the impact of geography (location). This leads to an inquiry of spatial issues and the micro-location concerns of the appropriate site within broader locational boundaries that can enable or at least influence the achievement of desired goals of returns and risk. Figure 8.5 depicts the investment scenario of market/appraisal analysis.

§ 8.6 REAL ESTATE DECISION PROCESS

The three scenarios illustrate the general problem situations that can arise in the analysis of real estate. Despite the possibility that any or all of the various scenarios may address the range of probable decision needs, only the first scenario represents the typical appraisal assignment. The second scenario is a situation that frequently arises in the general concept of market research. The third scenario is often a concern in an investment consulting situation.

The placement of the three scenarios into an overall real estate decision process is based on the context of value theory issues. These issues allow a process that is flexible enough to deal with the majority of problems that arise in real estate operations.

An understanding of all the assumptions in value estimation is beneficial to decision makers. As the discussion of Figures 8.1 and 8.2 indicates, the logical connections among market analysis, productivity analysis, and appropriate decision models can link to the highest and best use analysis. Highest and best use in the traditional appraisal process is where the value components are made explicit. This use can be achieved by documenting the levels of appropriate market support, measuring financial feasibility (via absorption projections), and conducting a synthesis of the property analysis in order to establish the physical and legal possibilities.

§ 8.7 CONCLUSION

Market analysis can be accepted as either an integral part of the decision process or a separate assignment. The nature of the assignment and the problem situation to be addressed in the report by the final decision maker are key elements. The purpose and function of the analysis best identify the appropriate fit to the problem context. Value theory, as well as valuation measures, is considered when the market analysis component is not only a requirement via regulation but also a central concern of the valuation process.

How can a market value be estimated or an investment decision finalized, without a consideration of supply and demand for a specific property type within a specific market's time frame? The linkage of value theory, highest and best use, and market analysis is the building block of a documented analysis.

Part Two

Market Analysis

Part One has established a process for analyzing real estate. Identification of real estate as a space–time product that has an economic function of converting space–time into money–time establishes the basis for a decision-making process.

The process requires linkage of the real estate product fundamentals to the income-generating capacity of a site. The analysis of fundamentals is demonstrated in the productivity analysis of the physical, legal, and locational attributes of a property. The product potential of the realty is then exposed to the competitive market, thus establishing the rental returns, value/prices, and rates that are appropriate for a given property. The market or actual returns are then protected over time, to establish the potential value.

In real estate, the projection of potential returns is difficult, because of low availability of data and information, a heterogeneous product, and the behavioral/emotional impacts concerning real estate as an asset. Alternative models to the standard DCF must therefore be considered. These include multiplier models, direct capitalization techniques, and yield capitalization models. The data accessible in any given situation can be linked to one or more of the alternative models.

The chapters in Part Two consider situations in which the decision-making process has been applied. The situations involve real estate securitization, appraising in markets with limited comparable properties, and the overall nature of appraisal. Other topics are: calculating property taxes with the value unknown, and asset management in a down market.

Nine

Real Estate Fundamentals and Securitization

§ 9.1 INTRODUCTION

This chapter investigates the fit of real estate assets to the securities market. Concern regarding this fit is a specific issue in general debates in economics and finance.

The dichotomy between value and market price or fundamental analysis (intrinsic value) and the random walk (or efficient market) theory is a continuing controversy. The concepts of value and fundamental analysis are based on predetermined criteria that evoke rational economic responses to the product and market attributes of an asset; market prices and efficient market concepts are more concerned with market participants' access to information and the responses of the market players to the expectations of others. The levels of price and market activity under these two concepts are often guided by "animal spirits"[1] (speculative expectations).

[1] Joanne Lipman, "Troublesome Issues: Real Estate Securities, Increasingly Popular, Can Pose Big Problems," *The Wall Street Journal,* Southwest Edition, March 4, 1986, p. 1.

Whether market participants are guided by their own perceptions of value or those of others is the central concern of current debate. To trace the origin of these perceptions necessitates a distinction between market and investment value and, consequently, a reconciliation of value perspectives that are in conflict in the negotiations of the market. Whether the directive forces are internal or external, the question must be asked: Was attention paid to the basic fundamentals of the asset?

The dichotomy in the appropriate level of attention to fundamentals is illustrated by real estate industry figures such as Harold Ellis, Jr., of Grubb & Ellis, and David Shulman of Salomon Brothers. Ellis has criticized Wall Street promoters for lacking any understanding of the underlying concepts that motivate property decisions, development, and investment. Shulman supports claims that broker-dealers do not need to know everything about the properties they peddle—"just the numbers."[2] Knowledge of the numbers about the property, as well as an overall knowledge of markets, has not always been an overriding concern in real estate transactions. Recent events attest to a lack of fundamentals; there is argument for the dominance of animal spirits in the market. The neglect of the relationship of the product to the financial structure has fostered several concerns. Will securitization of real estate compound the situation further? Can any market activity continue, when the fundamentals of the product are ignored? If so, will this activity allow a proper allocation of resources and will the system continue to support an improper allocation? These concerns lead to the identification of several issues that are related to the securitization process.

The objective of this chapter is to investigate the nature of the securitization process and consider the issues that can evolve in relating the security market to the real estate market. Because the basic link between securities and real estate is the treatment of both as investment contracts, the comparison of the two vehicles can be framed in the investment context of risk and return trade-offs.

Both assets' values are based on yields reflecting periodic returns and asset growth. The typical stock model is:

$$E(r) = \frac{D_t + (P_t - P_{t-1})}{P_t}$$

[2] Kenneth Lelen, "Wall Street Bullish on Real Estate, Bearish on Wall Street," *Real Estate Times*, March 31, 1987, p. 32.

where:

$E(r)$ = expected return
D_t = current dividend
P_t = current price of the stock
P_{t-1} = previous purchase price

This is the basic yield calculation discussed in Chapter 7. The expected return in real estate is:

$$Y_o = \frac{NOI_i + (V_1 - V_o)}{V_o}$$

where:

Y_o = yield or expected return
NOI_i = current net operating income
V_1 = future resale price
V_o = present value

These formulas show that the value of both real estate and securities is based on income to be received over time and capital gains or a growth in value (the change, over time, between the price paid for the asset and the price at which it is sold). Any possibility of difference in the two assets as investments must be connected to the basis or source for generating the income, the risk related to the generation, and the projection of the income. A major difference is the varying institutions that control and direct the interaction of people trading stocks and real estate.

To address the relationship of real estate fundamentals to securities, it is appropriate to review the basic nature of real estate fundamentals and of securities, and their respective markets, and to conduct an investigation of their history of market interaction. The historical investigation will offer insights to the levels of compatibility and conflict between the real estate and securities markets.

§ 9.2 NATURE OF REAL ESTATE FUNDAMENTALS

What is the fundamental nature of the real estate product? Fundamental analysis is defined as the evaluation of an enterprise and its investment attractiveness, based on its financial structure and its competitive position. The basis of earnings and the intensity and involvement of management must be compared against similar investment types.[3] Fundamental analysis evaluates changes in relevant underlying factors and equilibrium relationships. Fundamental analysis in real estate can be divided into three categories: (1) macroeconomic analysis, (2) market analysis, and (3) specific property or site analysis. The first category is concerned with conditions that influence the general economic environment: interest rate, general levels of employment, land policy changes, and so on. The second category is concerned with the market activity for specific types of property or investment alternatives. Key factors of concern are competitive supply of and demand for the asset, returns, and rents, all of which are usually based on a market standard. On the level of a specific property, the factors of concern are the relationship of the prior two categories to a specific parcel of real estate, and the consideration of the site's unique attributes as they may alter the expectations of the prior categories. These issues were identified in the productivity analyses in Chapters 2 and 3.

Real estate is an area of business in which the overall business strategy has to be linked to identifying and defining the product. The ultimate goal of all three levels of fundamental analysis is to estimate the productivity of the real estate project. The basis for this productivity is the net advantage or benefits that flow from the control and use of the property. For most types of properties, even owner-occupied buildings, these benefits can be measured as rental income flows for the purpose of economic analysis. In fact, the basic concern of fundamental analysis is the projection of valuation based on the expected income stream.[4] Real estate productivity has been referred to as a flow or stream of net benefits.[5]

The key to the analysis of the cash flow is the emphasis on future expectations. The future connotes uncertainty and risk, if the variation of the projection can be quantified. To make projections—and definitely to quantify them—certain factors that form the expectations regarding income must be delineated. In real estate, this must begin with

[3] Ben Branch, *Investments: A Practical Approach* (Chicago: Longman Financial Services Publishing, Inc., 1985): 547.

[4] *Ibid.*, at 159.

[5] Richard U. Ratcliff, *Ratcliff Readings on Appraisal and its Foundation Economics*, Edited by James A. Graaskamp (Madison, WI: Landmark Research, Inc., 1979): 486; John H. Miller III and Richard M. Betts, "The Impact of Securitization on Real Estate Appraisal," *The Appraisal Journal*, 54:4 (October 1986): 524.

the site analysis, because the flow of benefits is linked to the capabilities of the subject property to service the needs of humans. (See Chapter 5.) Each property represents a unique package of productivity features, and different potential users place different utilities on the property's varying features. Fundamentally, this broad range of variance is offset by grouping the properties and investors in a manner that links attributes to user types. To achieve this, the physical, legal, locational, and market attributes of a property have to be identified, because real estate as a commodity or asset has economically flexible uses and the flexibility can direct a site to compete in different market segments. The different markets suggest the possibility of different rents and different values for any given property. The same flexibility is possible in the identification of buyers/users in any given market.

The significance of real estate fundamentals is that the physical, legal, and locational attributes of a property influence the potential returns and hence the value of the property. These attributes are also a potential source of risk in a real estate investment. Examples are: loss in rental income that can result from foundation shifts and related soil problems; litigation exposure, expense, and lowered property revenue because of clouds on the title; and tenant loss resulting from a recent change in neighborhood use. The latter is especially important if the external use functioned as a draw for the subject parcel. The significant point is that the property attributes on a microlevel have a relevant impact on the real estate return. These factors, along with the supply and demand for similar type properties, can alter the income potential for a parcel of real estate. The question then is: Is the income potential of the real estate relevant to the securities market? If so, can variations from expectations be forecast without knowledge of the fundamentals, or can real estate fundamentals be ignored in the market for investment contracts? To gain insights into these inquiries, it is necessary to investigate the nature of securities and the securitization process.

§ 9.3 NATURE OF SECURITIZATION

This section investigates securities as a product. Securitization has been defined as "the process of dividing real estate interest or other business interest into securities traded in an organized market."[6] In this process, real estate ownership and financing are segmented and

[6] Branch, *supra* note 3, at 159.

placed with several institutions through the capital markets. This definition leads to three major perceptions of securitization:

1. Securitization enables an alternative form of ownership to the traditional legal estates in realty and the creation of a market for these interests;
2. Securitization offers an alternative form of financing with separate capital markets;
3. Separate and distinct market strata or layers can be structured.

The expectations of market participants for a security have much to do with its delineation as a product. It can be a process for restructuring ownership, a financial tool, or an alternative investment—the traditional description of a security. Securities are a general term for bonds, shares of stock, and other financial instruments. In essence, they are investment contracts or legal contracts of ownership often characterized by obligations to receive specific returns over time.[7]

The ownership issue of securitization can be addressed on two levels. Ownership as traditionally held in real estate is no longer a matter of direct sole ownership of an asset (unless one entity buys all of the interests available). The various estates in realty entail title and/or possession of the asset, as well as claims to the returns. With securities, ownership is represented by pieces of paper or entitlements. These entitlements are only claims on returns, with a voting interest in the policies of assets management. The pieces-of-paper ownership can become a separate market (a secondary market or a totally separate market). This separation of the ownership interest and active management from the asset has the potential of obfuscating the concern with fundamentals, which can lead to the valuation errors as defined by Lorans (see the discussion on market efficiency in § 9.5). The potential for valuation error arises from the passive investors' view of the securities transaction as the primary economic activity, rather than the production, management, and distribution of the real estate. Little or no thought is extended to the real asset's function or performance.

On the second level, securitization can be used in both the debt and equity markets. The offer of an alternative source of financing has created a major interest in securitization. Other people's equity or debt

[7] Bill Kuntz, former Director of the Texas Securities Board, stated in 1983 that the definition of securities as an investment contract was the basis for a move on the part of some regulators to bring all real estate contracts under securities regulation.

money is readily available to reduce the cost of capital to developers, investors, and lending institutions. Funds developed from the securities process can save a few points when compared to traditional financing,[8] an important advantage on multimillion-dollar loans. The process also affords a higher degree of liquidity than the standard debt–equity relationships in real estate.

The liquidity and ready availability of capital in securitization are best exemplified by a blind-fund real estate syndication in which shares in an issue are sold without any specific properties being identified for purchase by the originator. These shares can be sold in debt or equity markets. For borrowers who approached banks or insurance companies in the recent past, asking for loans on real estate to be issued that day to cover the possibility that a tract or two might be purchased in the future, the probability of a bank loan was slim but the availability of Wall Street funds was extremely high. Currently, the probability of Wall Street funds is at par with the availability of bank loans.

In an industry where a deal is determined by the availability of financing, the securities market as a source of capital could be perceived as unlimited in the short run. The potential for overleveraging properties and the temptation for poor underwriting as it relates to the capital investment in the underlying real estate asset can expose the securities buyer to high levels of financial and business risk. Before a financing tool can appropriately be offered, a workable hedging process must be developed. The alternatives will be discussed later.

The nature of real estate and securities as products influences, in part, the separate cultures of their markets and the range of potential ways in which they can interface. The history of the interaction between these two assets should enable further insights to the comparison of the risks and returns that are characteristic of either real estate or securities, or both.

§ 9.4 PRODUCT AND MARKET STRATA

According to Shulman, the profit in the securities market is based on short-term volatility. This is contrary to the longer-term investment nature of real estate. To mold real estate investment to this short-term format, the market perspective has to change from one concerned with people's expectations toward ownership interest or positions in

[8] Lipman, *supra* note 1, at 1.

real property, or even toward full ownership of real estate, to a mere game of gambling on human nature. The object of investment will be a security interest—an investment contract. As Wall Street has shown, when the market indicates an interest in some characteristic of an investment, a contract can be manufactured to meet the market preference. A new product can be quickly produced and entire new markets for that product can be created. Often, the preference is the issue addressed by the new product, not the underlying assets of which the security represents an equity or debt interest.

As an example of the various market strata involved in a security issue, a large syndication firm asked a security house to finance a $135 million office building leased to a large national tenant.[9] The loan on the structure was segmented into a credit transaction and a real estate transaction. Two investment contracts (securities) were created. The first contract was a private debt offering in which the national tenant's lease payments were passed through to the investors. That note was divided into two parts, with different maturities and coupons. The price on these debt instruments was close to the AA-credit corporate borrowing rate for the national tenant.

The balance of the funds was raised by using a zero coupon bond (a zero) backed by a first mortgage lien on the property. The beginning balance of the loan will grow over 10 years, and the investor will be repaid with the sale or refinancing of the property. The zero investor's risk is supposedly minimal, because low loan-to-value ratios were used under conservative assumptions. This applies to the initial and terminal loan positions.

The zero was priced at 250 basis points above the comparable term Treasury bill. It was then sold to a savings and loan association (S&L). The original syndicator's loan-to-value ratio was 90 percent with a coupon 25 basis points better than available bullets (short-term loans) at the time.

The S&L financed the zero by creating a zero coupon certificate of deposit (CD), pocketing the spread. Furthermore, the security house structured the transaction to allow the syndicator to sell another zero, subordinate to the first zero. This in effect resulted in 100 percent financing. Traditionally, the syndicator would have raised $100 million to $110 million maximum. The security issue raised $120 million initially and $135 million finally, plus the additional funds created by the S&L.

[9] *Ibid.*

The concern is with the actual level of risk, totally and to the segmented positions. What is the source of the assumptions? What are the comparable investments' returns and the estimates of value on which all of the financial instruments are based? What is the underlying collateral of a parcel of income property, if the income stream is severed from the fee? What is the risk associated with the terminal value estimate?

Unfortunately, security issuers are manufacturing a property to play on the perception of the safety of a tangible asset, at a time when the historical benefits in real estate have been diminished. Much of the growth potential in real estate can be tied to one of two factors: inflation, which currently is not sufficient to create the demand for a hedge, or a price increase resulting from inelastic supply and a rapid influx in demand. This can best occur in the spatial context (specific location) offered by real estate. Furthermore, the tax advantages of real estate, received in the form of higher after-tax cash flows or more cash at sale via the capital gains preference, have been reduced. Many of the benefits traditionally identified with real estate assets are not currently available. Who could possibly gain from the current move to infuse capital into the real estate industry? The answer is: the democratic process. In the short run, the securitization process will allow the sharing of the outstanding debt on the overbuilding in the United States. An example of this debt restructuring was Hall Financial Group's effort to restructure $500 million of loans held mostly by savings and loan associations, to avoid bankruptcy or foreclosure.[10] If a property cannot adequately support the current debt structure, will another level of debt sufficiently isolate it in the long run, if the local economy influencing the properties in the portfolio is not strengthened? This move may have allowed Hall the holding power to survive until the economy turns around. However, for the issue to sell, the investor's objectives must include a willingness to accept a risky long-term capital gain in lieu of a current return. Unfortunately, there are numerous investment alternatives like this on the current market. Under the Hall security offer, the debt restructuring may lower periodic cash outflow, but will the properties' economic life be adequate to support the retirement of the new debt? The general concern is: Will the separate financial market of the security interest (either debt or equity) have to be linked to the fundamentals of the realty market?

The lack of direct control that can result in securities markets raises questions regarding regulation. The protection for the loss of control

[10] *Id.*, at 12.

supposedly derives from the Securities and Exchange Act of 1934. However, much of this control is concerned with disclosure, not merit. Therefore, the next concern must be with the basis for collateralizing the alternative source of financing, if it is debt, or establishing the ownership rights, if it is equity money. Collaterization is a concern of the capital structure, whether the offer is debt or equity money. The similarity of the process has caused Hamilton to state that the financial revolution is breaking down the distinction between debt and equity capital.[11] Because the concern is the selling of investment contracts to raise money, the objective should always be collaterized, whether by mortgage pools in this decade or mortgage bonds, as in the 1920s.[12] Both of these instruments have a stream of income and a known maturity value. More recently, securities issues have expanded to equity offers structured to vary with the investment attributes desired by different investors. The collateralization process requires matching the securities market objectives with the underlying real estate market or property attributes.

§ 9.5 NATURE OF SECURITIES MARKETS AND REAL ESTATE MARKETS

A market is defined as the sphere through which supply and demand operate.[13] The institutions guiding the format of the sphere influence the capacity for supply and demand to interact. The institutional variations between real estate and securities markets are best characterized in three distinct areas. One is the *working methods of the professionals* that have evolved over time. "Real estate is a relationship-bound business, while the securities industry is an anonymous system of buyers and sellers."[14] Equity and debt institutions, techniques, and personal relationships have developed over time in both industries. Institutional factors—cultural, economic, political, religious, psychological, physical, and social phenomena—exert a continuing influence on economic

[11] Adrian Hamilton, *The Financial Revolution* (New York: The Free Press, 1986): 5.

[12] John McMahan, "The United States Real Estate Capital Market: Historical Perspectives, Emerging Trends and Future Directions," *Real Estate Issues*, 12:2 (Fall/Winter 1987): 13.

[13] Roger L. Miller, *Intermediate Micro-Economics* (New York: McGraw-Hill Book Co., 1978): 75.

[14] Lelen, *supra* note 2, at 32; quote is attributed to David Shulman of Salomon Brothers.

behavior.[15] Physical factors with economic significance do not exist in securities exchanges. Furthermore, real estate is itself an institution that incorporates religious, psychological, political, and social attributes that alter the "pure" economic yield models that are implemented in securities analysis. The contrasts among these institutional features are a major influence on the perception of the efficiency of each market.

The factors delineating the variation between the securities market and the real estate market are listed in Table 9.1.

Institutionally, the securities industry has had more receptivity to change, partly as a result of the more direct economic nature of the securities market and the lack of more eclectic institutional influences. Given its more direct economic character, the securities market has had the ability to be more flexible in the delivery of a product to fulfill a possible need or demand. That ability, combined with the anonymous nature of the market personality, requires that a rigid system of disclosure be instituted in the securities market.

A *system of disclosure* is the second aspect of deviation between the real estate and securities markets. The securities market has a disclosure system available that allows investors/consumers to make comparisons between alternative issues, based on transaction information published daily. In general, real estate does not have a disclosure system that allows a comparative capability; limited disclosure systems have resulted from institutional factors, such as the perception in Texas that private real property rights include the right of privacy. The mix of civil and property rights suggests that it is the right of the fee simple owner not to disclose the purchase price or terms of conveyance.

The final difference in the structure of the two markets is in the *methods of valuation*; in each market, they are linked to the working relationships and disclosure systems outlined above. However, there may be a difference in emphasis in the application of these models. Shulman is of the opinion that real estate emphasizes a long position, or a gain to be received in the future. "Real estate likes to make money over the life of the asset. On the other hand, Wall Street makes money on the volatile changes in price or spread over very short periods of time."[16] A short-term investment horizon is often used in security valuation. This short horizon and the volume and frequency of data enable

[15] Raleigh Barlowe, *Land Resource Economics* (Englewood Cliffs, NJ: Prentice-Hall, 1986): 310.

[16] Lelen, *supra* note 2, at 32.

Table 9.1 Comparison of Real Estate and Securities Markets

Real Estate	Securities
Inefficient conditions	Efficient conditions
Limited information: Data poverty Proprietary and unavailable data	Adequate to plentiful information: Data abundance Public data sources and a broad range of data sources
Active and passive investors	Generally passive investors
Limited funds	Relatively abundant funds
Limited potential for diversification, because of the magnitude of individual investments and limited funds	Numerous vehicles for diversification potential
Illiquid	Liquid
Infrequent transactions	Numerous transactions
Limited potential for comparative indices to represent the market	Alternative index options as market and trend indicators
Physical/Real assets	Legal contracts/Financial assets
Lumpy investments—all or none of the legal interests must be purchased by the investor	Fungible, ubiquitous, and fractional interests are available
No short sales, only long positions	Short sales possible (profit in market declines) Long and short options
No direct hedge potential, except inflation	Direct hedge potential
No transfer of rights without delivery of deeds	Margin trading—sale of commodities without ownership

the calculation of security return with more certainty than for real estate. At least, it is a better documented measure of risk. Although using a similar formula, real estate is subject to a higher degree of uncertainty, partly because of the limited data and the length of the forecast term for the typical investment.

The market differences between real estate and securities are a source of both potential problems and benefits, in the combined market offered by real estate securitization. The securitization attempts in real estate in the 1920s ran into trouble because of their failure to link the financing via securitization to basic fundamentals of supply and demand in the real estate market. A specific example is the Florida real estate bubble in the 1920s. Initially, the real estate market fundamentals were evident reasons for investment. Population was steadily growing and housing was in short supply.[17] Based on this supply and demand imbalance, land prices began to soar. The availability of terms based on readily available financing fueled the price rise. One source of financing was securities sales using mortgage bonds. Price rises continued until potential buyers were driven out of the market. With limited demand, activity dropped. As the market demand softened, speculators began dumping their product on the market, further driving down the value of the collateral supporting the securities. With the collateral value driven down because of market fundamentals, the funds available to support coupons to the bonds were not forthcoming, driving their value down further. These same problems have occurred in the traditional financial institutions in real estate, so the securitization process was not the lone causal factor. However, the situation illustrates a major difference in the institutional parameters of the real estate and securities markets. That difference is that the securities market, in offering liquidity to the traditionally illiquid real estate market, may be contributing to increased volatility in the product and a disruption in the tendency to move to equilibrium. (This is discussed further in § 9.9.)

A key concern with the changes in ownership and financing represented by the securitization process is the alteration of the real estate product as it relates to basic fundamentals of value and to market activity. This activity can be either for the real estate or for the created security interest as a separate market stratum is developed. Confusion arises as to whether trading is concerned with the asset itself, a fractional interest in the asset, the derivative interests of the underlying asset, or a separate and distinct market for the security contract. These problems in ownership and financing are not unique to real estate; they reflect the problems experienced in oil, corporate transactions, currencies, and numerous commodity futures. They have been identified as a refusal to "look at the fundamentals" of the asset. The key concern is to identify the asset and then delineate the fundamentals

[17] Burton G. Malkiel, *A Random Walk Down Wall Street* (New York: W. W. Norton & Co., 1985): 37.

that are its characteristics. This latter concern forms the basic format of this investigation, along the lines of a historic analysis of economic relationships.

§ 9.6 HISTORY OF SECURITIES AND REAL ESTATE MARKETS

The current movement for securitizing real estate is not the first time the issue has been proposed. The 1920s witnessed a failure of a similar proposal, as did the 1970s. The reasons for these failures and the nature of the proposals in the 1980s are investigated briefly here, to suggest lines of future research and the identification of trends (or cycles). An understanding of these historical patterns enables insights for comparing and contrasting the structures of the real estate and securities markets. The difference may suggest an appropriate strategy for dealing with the securitization process and the economy as a whole.

The difficulties experienced in the 1920s contributed to limited efforts to securitize real estate in the decades of the 1930s through the 1950s. This inactivity can also be accredited to the economy's condition in the 1930s, the war in the 1940s, and the concern with production of real goods to remedy shortages in the 1950s. Apart from the traditional transactions, this era experienced the development of real estate syndication by such pioneers as Lawrence A. Wien and Harry B. Helmsley.[18] Wien thought up the syndication idea in the late 1940s, with the objective of achieving a yield of 12 percent while avoiding the high corporate income tax. The tax statutes at that time led Wien to seek a partnership that was not engaged in business but merely receiving a fixed return on capital through a conduit, which allowed investors to pay only an individual income tax.[19] The syndication format was used by William Zeckendorf over several decades. In 1951, his company, Webb and Knapp, went public. Zeckendorf credited this move with enabling a level of liquidity that Webb and Knapp as a real estate company had been lacking.[20] To further increase his liquidity, Zeckendorf developed a technique that, in essence, securitized the real estate product as well as the capital structure. It was termed "the Hawaiian technique" in the industry.

[18] Jim Powell, *Risk, Ruin and Riches* (New York: Maxwell Macmillan Co., 1986): 123.

[19] *Ibid.*, at 127.

[20] William Zeckendorf and Edward McCreary, *Zeckendorf* (New York: Holt, Rinehart and Winston, 1971): 4.

The 1960s were a period of active interest in stock markets, especially in the early part of the decade. An interest in real estate investment trusts (REITs) developed. The REITs enabled smaller investors to get involved with real estate and to receive a sufficient level of liquidity, given a REIT's legal requirement to pay out a major portion of its current income. (The current distribution rules are 85 percent of the REIT's ordinary income and 95 percent of its capital gain income.[21]) In the 1970s, REITs, specifically mortgage REITs, suffered difficulties. These difficulties, again reflecting the economic fundamentals of supply and demand in the real estate market, had extended impacts on the securities exchanges. The overall problem was the real estate cycle of overbuilding, encouraged by available financing. As the cycle heated up, REITs, which were by mandate required to hold 75 percent of their assets in real estate or real estate related instruments, cash and cash items, and government securities, found limited investment opportunities. Furthermore, they leveraged themselves ten-to-one, with bad construction loans. Marginally sound investments resulted, and these poor or nonexistent real estate projects lowered the REITs' income distribution or dividend payments. The lower dividends made the REITs less desirable, and security purchases fell off. The contradilution benefits of the early 1970s diminished, and the funds coming into the REITs declined.[22] The solvency problems were accelerated by the fact that many banks created REITs and transferred many of their marginal and bad loans to the REITs, to avoid audit problems with the bank examiners. An adverse risk pool was created. This pool could not generate the returns needed to comply with the distribution requirements, and the security cash flows declined even further. The equity REITs, which invested directly in real estate, did not suffer from the underlying collateral problems that the mortgage REITs experienced. However, the security buyers did not distinguish between the two, and there was some rub-off in the flow of equity dollars from investors. The same solvency problems occurred for many of the equity funds. The Tax Reform Act of 1976 substantially amended the REIT provisions, but the market did not readily accept this financing vehicle again until the mid-1980s.

[21] Peat Marwick, "MLP–REMIC–REIT: Similar, Different, or Overlapping?" 87-1, *Developments for Real Estate Executives* (March 1987): 7.

[22] Stephen E. Roulac, *Modern Real Estate Investment: An Institutional Approach* (San Francisco: Property Press, 1976): 192–193.

During the 1970s, the securities market was in the doldrums, except for the blue-chip stocks. Competition for the blue chips by institutional investors resulted in overpriced stocks. Many investors were driven out of the stock market and created a demand for alternative investment vehicles. Real estate, as an alternative, offered the benefits of an inflation hedge, real growth, and tax advantages. The high starting cost of getting into real estate was offset by the use of syndications and security issues. These various equity pools were attracted by the relative benefits of leverage in the debt markets; their availability of capital did much to spur investor interest in real estate. The amount of equity funds flowing to real estate was further heightened by regulations influencing the fiduciary responsibility of pension funds to invest in a manner that would increase the wealth under their control (Employment Retirement Income Security Act (ERISA), 1974). Faced with the fiduciary responsibility to increase the value of the pool of funds under their control, pension fund directors looked for investments that were experiencing rapid growth in value. Real estate has been one of those assets. In fact, given the diversification risk concerns of the pension investors, various groups projected that up to 20 percent of pension portfolios would be in real estate. This percentage expectation mellowed, given the real estate market of the latter 1980s and the early 1990s. The forces encouraging securitization in the 1970s continued into the 1980s with the enactment of tax laws that allowed rapid depreciation of buildings and the benefits of capital gains tax.

During this same period, corporations discovered that real estate is a dynamic asset that can enhance the value of a firm. These players, along with the institutional groups discussed above, began to alter the character of the real estate market participants. An increase in the institutional component and a change in the decision process of the market players have resulted. The trends and occurrences leading up to the current interest in real estate securitization are the result of the perception, by people experienced in securities markets, that real estate is another market that can be brought under the umbrella of financial institutions. Real estate people see an alternative form of financing that offers a very liquid flow of capital into real estate. Given the history of liquidity problems in real estate, securitization is seen as a continuing source of capital.

The real estate capital market continues to evolve. Indications are that the traditional sources of capital, the capital instruments, the capital and investment intermediaries, and the investments have been changing. These changes are best identified by a comparison of Figures 9.1 and 9.2.

Figure 9.1 Traditional Real Estate Capital Market

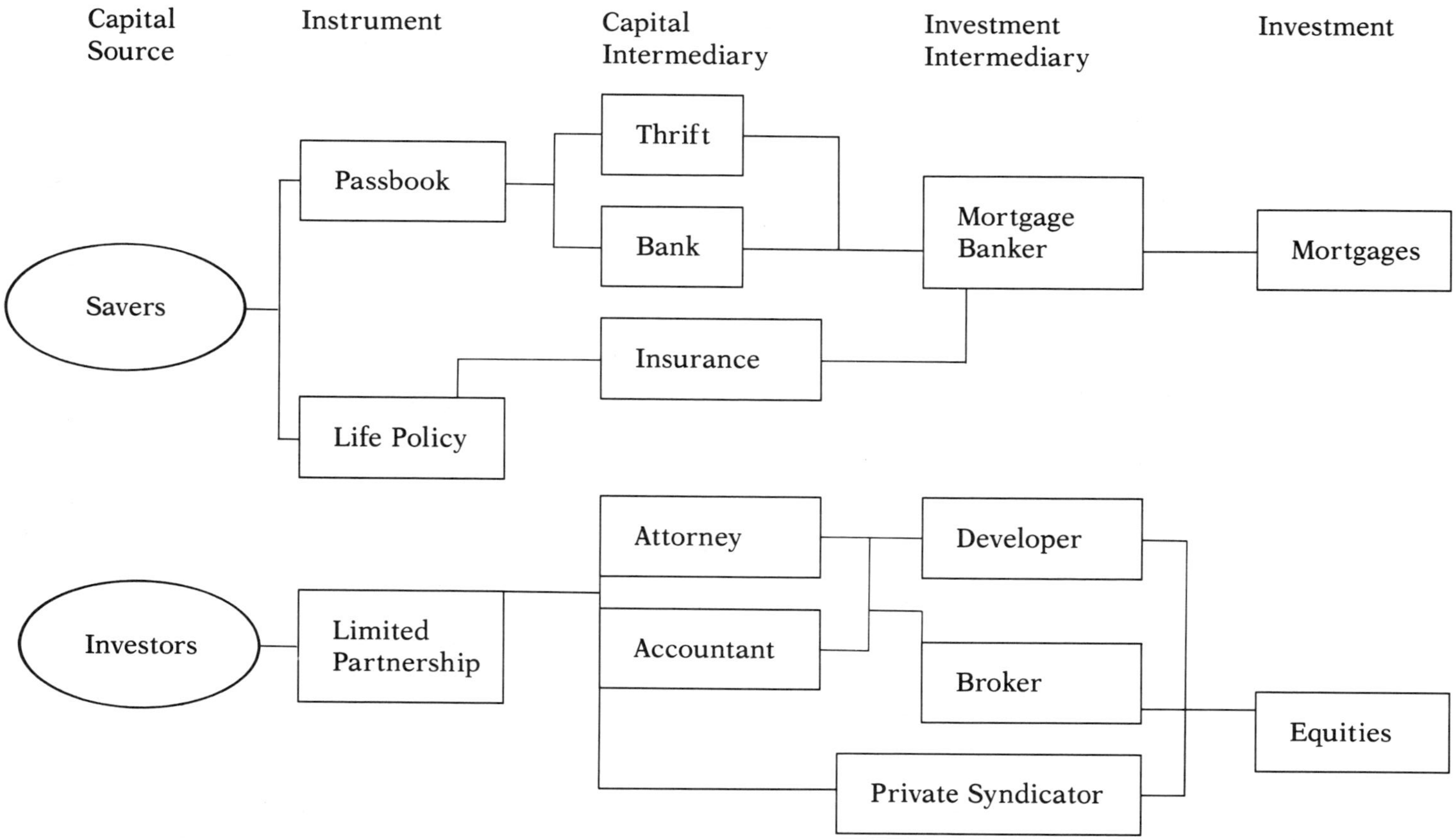

Source: Real Estate Center, McMahan & Associates.

Figure 9.2 Emerging Real Estate Capital Market

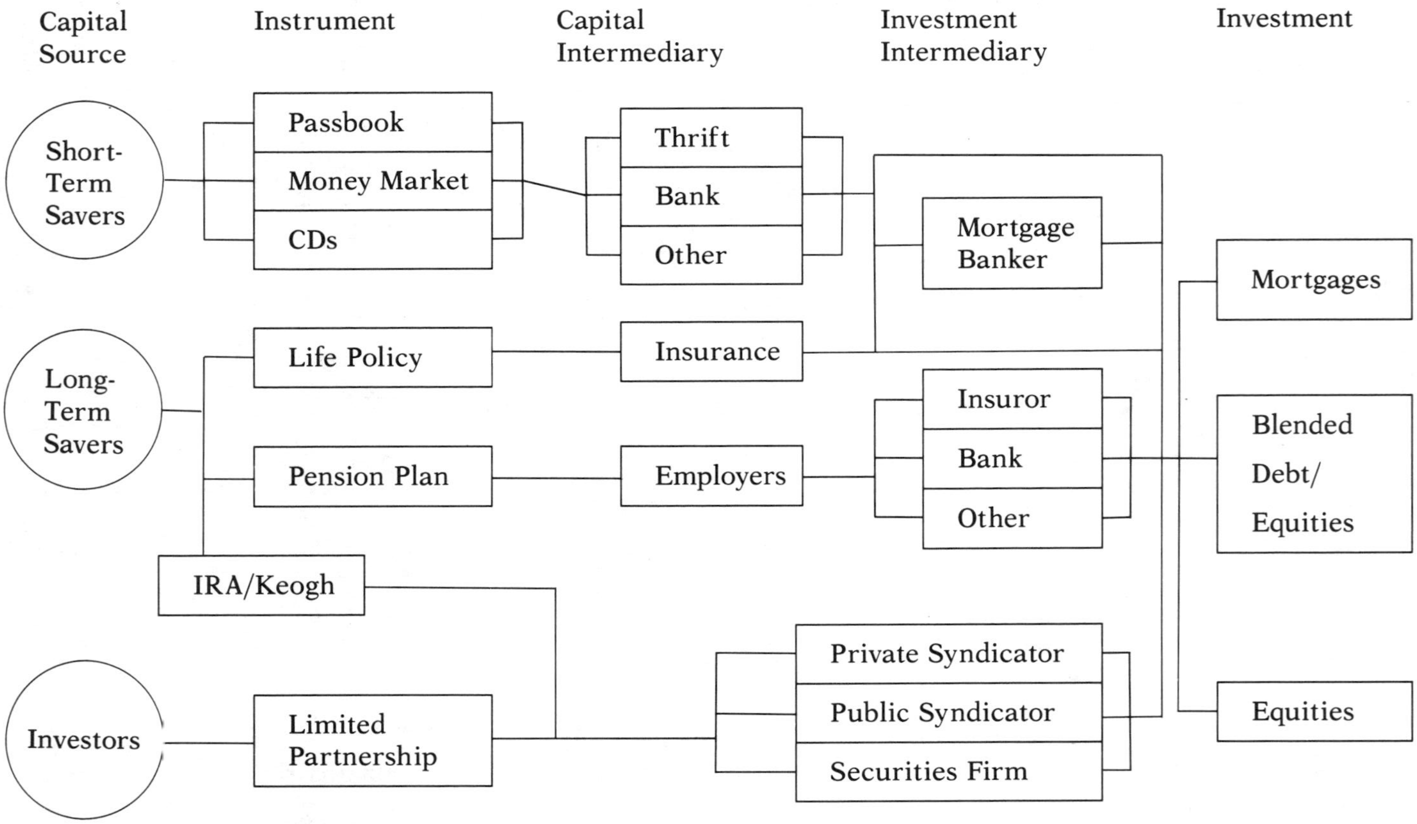

Source: Real Estate Center, McMahan & Associates.

As Figure 9.1 illustrates, the real estate market has traditionally been composed of savers and investors as the originating sources of capital. Savers, in general, had the opportunity of using passbook savings accounts offered by thrifts or banks, and various life policies via insurance companies. These instruments generated funds used in mortgage pools. Investors were tied to limited partnerships via accountants, attorneys, and private syndicators that generated equity funds for developers, brokers, or investment groups. Over the period from 1970 to 1986, the forces of inflation, tax legislation, financial deregulation, absentee ownership, "spread" financing, international investment, and securitization led to changes in real estate capital markets.[23] These changes will continue into the 21st century. The overbuilding, and the changed financial institutions, of the 1970s, 1980s, and early 1990s have established a real estate market structure and an overall economy that will heavily influence markets during the next 50 years.

A result has been an emerging capital market characterized by a segmentation into short- and long-term savers. This segmentation of savers is linked to the creation of alternative saving/investment instruments and the entrance of alternative capital intermediaries. These events occurred along with the introduction of pooling or aggregated investment opportunities, such as public syndications and securities firms. The relationships of the development of funds in the emerging capital market are indicated in Figure 9.2.[24] Of interest along with the emergence of security operations are the blended debt/equity investments that have appeared; their blend of debt and equity instruments is a concern of the risk considerations discussed in § 9.11. The changing capital markets tend to suggest that real estate markets in the near term will be linked more directly to other capital markets, probably via institutional investors such as pension funds and international capital movements. The attitude of pension fund managers toward guaranteed investment contracts (GICs) can directly influence mortgage availability and cost.[25] The capital linkages will force a direct connection or comparison of real estate markets with one another, via property portfolio concerns. The linkage of capital and diverse real estate markets will contribute to greater volatility in the real estate and real estate capital markets.[26] The volatility will, in turn, create greater

[23] McMahan, *supra* note 12, at 12–14.

[24] *Ibid.*, at 19.

[25] *Id.*

[26] *Id.*

difficulty in finding available long-term financing. Shorter loan and investment terms can be expected; they will contribute to more volatility, which will contribute to the difficulty of reaching market equilibrium. McMahan identifies this currently with the new building that is occurring despite the existence of 20 to 30 percent vacancy. Periods of continued overbuilding and soft markets could follow. Frictional vacancy may soon be redefined to be 10 percent rather than the traditional 5 percent.[27]

Finally, as with the divorce of capital from real assets, there will be a separation of production from investment. As the traditional investment builder continues to become a merchant builder, an understanding of the structure of both the real estate and the capital markets will be needed.

The changes in the real estate, capital, and securities markets have given no evidence of a buffer that will reduce risk by combining the real estate market and the securities market. In fact, as discussed in § 9.11, the overall risk in the system might be increased. Furthermore, history has not given insight to the key concern that may clear up the illusion: Is there a need for a relationship between the activities of the security market and the fundamentals of the underlying asset? This requires an investigation of real estate and securities products and markets.

§ 9.7 NATURE OF PRODUCTS AND MARKETS

What benefits can securitization bring to real estate? The key benefit is the ability to develop new product and improve liquidity. When financial and investment entrepreneurs identify an investment characteristic that the market favors, they manufacture that product or a reasonable substitute. Traditionally, real estate has been held in a fee simple estate and the total property has been controlled by equity investors with full risk exposure. However, an investment vehicle that has a variable income return, a long-term capital gain, and high illiquidity risk is not the option sought by all investors. Financial markets have identified that investment objectives vary and have delivered alternatives. Therefore, if an investor seeks a fixed income return with limited risk, he or she can purchase a broad array of bonds. If growth in value is important but the investor is also concerned about periodic

[27] *Id.*

income, options are available in the stock market. Some convertible bonds even allow an investment product that offers a fixed income with conversion to stock benefits over time. Financial markets have illustrated over time that, if a need or preference can be identified, a matching product can be delivered.

One of the best examples of combining the product variety of the securities market with the fundamental attributes of real estate was accomplished by William Zeckendorf's Hawaiian (or "pineapple") technique,[28] mentioned earlier. The essence of this technique is to stratify and segment alternative interests in a parcel of real estate, creating different financial interests and products for different investor markets. For example, a tract can be divided into separate fee interests within one overall proposed project. The air rights can be sold off in one or two of the separate tracts. Ground rents can be established on the surface estates, whether or not the tract is held in fee. The air rights on all tracts can be leased out or built on—or both—by the owners. The buildings within the air space and the fee estate can be leased out and/or subleased. If a legal estate can be created, financial interest can be developed in both equities and mortgages. In fact, the leasehold estates and the mortgages are investment contracts; they are securities. The relevance of the Hawaiian technique is that it showed how more financial products, beyond the traditional tract of real estate, can be manufactured. A panoramic market open to a broader range of investors can be introduced. Its synergistic effect is that the sum of the parts of the created estates and interest exceeds the value of the initial fee simple estate. In the above example, real estate fundamentals were used to aid in the development of the securitization process. The securitization movement can be used to create even more investment product on both the equity and debt sides of the market.

An interesting development in the securitization evolution has been the construction of vehicles to offer ownership or financial interest in intermediaries that, in turn, own real estate or obligations secured by real estate. Besides the REIT, discussed above, the master limited partnership (MLP) and the real estate mortgage investment conduit (REMIC) are available. The MLP is not a legally defined entity; it is essentially a publicly held limited partnership in which interest are freely transferable on an established securities market. The MLP has

[28] Charles H. Wurtzebach and Mike E. Miles, *Modern Real Estate* (New York: John Wiley & Sons, 1987): 94–96.

all the traditional partnership characteristics, as well as the liquidity created by a security traded on an established market.[29] A problem with the MLP is the marketability of the share and the headache of recording transfers of partnership interest for tax purposes. Liquidity for investors has been created by a sales mechanism similar to syndication or security interest: properties can be divested on the basis of maximum value per share rather than aggregate value.

The REMIC is an entity that is generally not subject to tax; investors are taxed on their allocable share of the REMIC's income. The income is derived from the purchase of mortgages or mortgage-backed securities (MBS), which are then capitalized by sales to investors by transforming the pool of mortgages or MBSs into a series of securities that have investment features quite different from the original pool.[30] The scope of the structure and operation of the REMICs, REITs, and MLPs is complicated; however, these entities must be addressed, because their further development will result in a range of real estate security choices.

The REMIC offers, generally, an interest-type fixed-income investment derived from large pools of mortgages or mortgage-backed securities (which are frequently guaranteed). REMICs offer limited high-side potential but reflect a relatively low risk.[31]

REITs are of two classes, mortgage REITs and equity REITs. Mortgage REITs are similar to REMICs in risk–return trade-off. Equity REITs own real estate directly and thus are exposed to the up-side and down-side potential of real estate market risk and return. The limitation on the risk–return relationship is that it is subject to the restrictions on assets, management, and operations.

MLPs, which have no restrictions on assets, types of activities, or income sources, are the most volatile of the securitization modes. An MLP as a real estate owner, developer, or manager could generate significant income or loss.[32] The returns must be sufficient to cover exposure to this level of risk. MLPs are currently being scrutinized by the Treasury Department. The IRS advocates the treatment of MLPs as corporations. The scrutiny of MLPs began in 1987, after the Tax Reform Act of 1986 established three types of income: active, passive, and portfolio. Many investors had purchased shares of limited partnerships that

[29] Peat Marwick, *supra* note 21, at 1.

[30] *Ibid.*

[31] *Id.*, at 8.

[32] *Id.*

had positive cash flows (passive income), to offset their passive losses. The Act impacted the marketability of some MLPs that had, in effect, created a fourth type of income—limited partnership income. To prevent the creation of MLPs solely for tax shelter, the passive income from publicly traded partnerships (PTPs) cannot be used to offset passive losses from MLPs. The PTPs are perceived to be similar to mutual funds: the losses can be viewed as passive and the income is viewed as portfolio.

The securitization movement has responded to the fundamentals of investment strategies and has developed a range of investment alternatives based on modern investment concerns of return and risk tradeoffs, given the four types of incomes. The submarkets of investors will select the balance of risk–return trade-off that is appropriate; the significance of the securitization process is that it has allowed the introduction of new products and the segmentation of markets.

§ 9.8 BENEFITS OF SECURITIZATION

The other advantages that securitization can offer are:

1. Geographical constraints characteristic of real estate markets can be overcome;
2. Opportunities that exist because of the location dimension of real estate can be diversified.

The real estate market has traditionally been defined by its physical fixity and thus its exposure and/or sensitivity to external forces in the immediate proximity of any site. The portfolio nature of pooled properties in any of the investment vehicles discussed in § 9.7 enables a reduction in risk and a potential increase in return that is not possible in the traditional freehold ownership of a singular property. Furthermore, the broader access to capital offsets the typical geographical concerns of capital-rich and capital-poor areas or cities that have been the nemesis of real estate in the past. Therefore, securitization enables the application of concepts of arbitrage that previously could not be applied directly in real estate. Arbitrage is the sale of overpriced stock to purchase underpriced stock, in the expectation that the former will drop and the latter will rise. The end result is that an overall market rate of return is maintained and risk exposure is reduced. This result can be achieved in real estate but requires a shifting from one geographical market to another, or from one property type to another, or both. Achieving this mobility of investment opportunities requires a high degree of liquidity that is often lacking among land-rich, highly levered real estate entrepreneurs.

Securitization may offset this problem; historically, it has offered both liquidity and mobility. At the same time, securitization may offer a lower cost of capital than traditional equity and debt sources in real estate. The experiences of syndications during the period of high institutional capital cost illustrate that public and private issues for equity dollars can offer a lower cost of capital. This reduced cost of capital is the result of the broader markets, the ease of transferability of ownership interest, and the returns acceptable to equity investors, given their perception of risk. This ability of equity markets to offer lower capital cost changes within distinct capital markets. However, to alter established institutional patterns, the availability of alternative sources must go a long way in influencing the cost of capital at any given time.

The nature of the product, the availability of capital, and the formation of market institutions are the bases for the structure of a market. The market structure establishes the context in which the market decision maker must act. The concerns are then: Do the participants make their decisions based on the fundamental elements of the spheres or influences of the market, or do they respond to the perceptions of the players in the market? Is the market based on basic economic principles or on psychological concerns? In Malkiel's terms, is the market built on a firm foundation or is it a matter of building castles in the air? A firm foundation would suggest that real estate has a firm anchor called intrinsic value, which is determined by careful analysis of present conditions and future prospects (including the items discussed under real estate fundamentals). When market prices rise above this intrinsic value, a selling opportunity arises; when prices drop below this value, a buying opportunity develops. Investing, then, is a dull process of comparing an investment's offering or actual price with its firm foundation of value.[33] The firm foundation theory stresses that value is the present worth of the benefits received from ownership. In investment real estate, these benefits generally occur in the form of periodic income flows and the change in property value upon resale. Usually considered in both of the components of value is a projection of growth, that is, future expectations.

[33] Malkiel, *supra* note 17, at 20–22.

The castles-in-the-air approach suggests that investing—and hence, value—is a psychic concern.[34] If psychic values are the essence of forecasting or decision, then analysis of the actions of the crowd is the key factor in real estate investment. John Maynard Keynes best characterized this perspective of the market when he suggested the beauty contest dilemma. Keynes described the stock market as analogous to entry in a newspaper-sponsored beauty contest in which the objective was to pick the beauty winner from a set of photographs. The reader, in order to win, had to pick the beauty contestant who received the most votes from the other readers. The streetwise player would recognize that a personal perception of value was irrelevant. To win, it was necessary to pick the photo with the most general perception of value. Because other players would also recognize the validity of this strategy, the game would be to predict the average opinion of the average opinion. The securities market has long been characterized by this process. The real estate market, in general, only began to be characterized by this process in the past decade. Until the 1970s, the order of the real estate market was best characterized by the question: What is going on? In the later years of the 1970s, the question was: What do you think is going to happen? Since the early 1980s, the question has been, What do you think people think is going to happen? The market has evolved, over time, from being oriented around current activities to being expectant of change; hence the importance of information and the reactions of markets to expectations. The nature and structure of a market are characterized by the efficiency with which the market reacts to and processes information. The efficiency level of information use is the basis of expectations. Expectations lie at the heart of the castles-in-the-air theory of markets, the premise of which can become the "bigger fool theory."

§ 9.9 EFFICIENT MARKETS CONCEPTS

The relationship of fundamentals to player expectations leads to the efficient markets concepts. Efficient markets, often referred to as the random market theory, is a pet concept of many academics. The

[34] The behavioral approach promulgated by Ratcliff is supported by the theory of hedonic models; see Lancaster, "A New Approach to Consumer Theory," *The Journal of Political Economy* (April 1966): This same concept is applied in finance as the new equilibrium theory of Ibbotson.

hypothesis of the theory states that a market is efficient if prices "fully reflect available information."[35] Informational efficiency is not an absolute; it is a matter of degree. The stratification of the degrees follow three forms, as follows.

1. Weak form efficiency—the information set capitalized is limited to past market prices. Knowledge of past market transactions will not help the investor to make abnormal returns in the future; hence the title, "the random walk theory." The theory states that trying to predict the market based on past transactions is like trying to forecast the trail a drunk would take in an open field. The analysis of past prices is the basis of the appraisal process in real estate, but appraisal does not attempt to indicate the possibility of abnormal prices. At best, it indicates a value based on the market norm, which is the tendency of an efficient market.

2. Semistrong form efficiency—an investor cannot beat the market, even if public information beyond price history is considered. This process in real estate is illustrated by the potential for gain based on having surveyed the market in an area where a new highway has been announced. The investor may have difficulty in profiting from this public information because owners of land, other investors, and speculators all have access to the same information.

3. Strong form efficiency—investors are unable to benefit in terms of above-normal prices, even with the knowledge of all information, public or private. An example is insider information in the stock market.[36]

As may be noted above, the definition of efficient markets not only illustrates the influence of information on price structure but it includes Jensen's contribution of considering the possibility of making above-"normal" returns.[37] If the market is efficient, it is impossible to make economic profits by trading on the basis of the varying degrees of information (past prices, and public and private information). The

[35] George W. Gau, "Efficient Real Estate Markets: Paradox or Paradigm?," *American Real Estate and Urban Economics Association,* 15:2 (Summer 1987): 2.

[36] In an appraisal of land in Austin, Texas, the sales ranged from $5,000 to $65,000 per acre. I was attempting to contact a developer to confirm a sale across the street. At that time the data suggested a value of $20,000 per acre for that site. Before I could ask any questions, he stated that he had heard I had valued the property at $20,000 per acre. I was alone in the room. That is efficiency! He then proceeded to try to persuade me that the property was worth more. Fundamentals at the time and now suggest otherwise.

[37] M. C. Jensen, "Some Anomalous Evidence Regarding Market Efficiency," *Journal of Financial Economics,* 6:2 (June–September 1978): 95–101.

reason for this inability to capture a profit is that probable buyers in the market quickly capitalize the information into their offer price. The competitive price of the transaction changes, and an individual investor trading on the information cannot earn superior returns as compared with other assets that have equivalent risk.

The problems with the application of the Jensen perspective of efficiency in commercial real estate markets are that, because real estate is a heterogeneous product, direct risk–return comparisons are difficult, and real estate at any one time and in any given area is characterized by an inelastic supply. The inelastic supply, which may give a monopoly potential to a single parcel of property, can result in an economic rent being paid. This "abnormal" return can draw marginal properties into competition with the more fundamentally desirable properties because of a perceived demand. These properties are truly marginal in the Ricardian rent sense. (Ricardo stated that, as land rent rises on the "best" tracts, marginal land is brought into use.) The direct result is an oversupply of competitive properties. As markets tighten up, these properties are not desirable; they distress the value of fundamentally sound properties. (Despite the supply problem, there *are* still marketable properties.)

There seems to be a shortage of persons who are knowledgeable on these fundamentals. Fundamentals cannot be directly valued for most assets.[38] Research in the stock market by Kenneth French and Richard Roll has shown that (1) market prices (they used the term value) diverge from fundamental values and (2) much of the volatility in the market is self-generating.[39] This research would suggest that markets are not sufficient in the sense that they rationally reflect fundamentals. Summers illustrated this by identifying valuations as being different from rational expectations of the present value of future cash flows by a multiplicative factor of $(1 + u_t)$. The symbol u_t represents random shocks to market transactions. The shocks are market variations linked to past disturbances. This concept would modify the weak form theory of efficiency, because it indicates adaptive expectations—the forecasting of future expectations based on the modification of past occurrences. This reliance on past information (especially price

[38] Lawrence H. Summers, "Does the Stock Market Rationally Reflect Fundamental Values?," *Journal of Finance*, 41:3 (July 1986): 599.

[39] Kenneth R. French and Richard Roll, "Is Trading Self-Generating?" Center for Research in Securities Prices, University of Chicago, Working Paper No. 12 (February 1984).

behavior) seems to contradict the random walk theory discussed above. Summer named this variation "valuation error." Valuation error recognizes that markets may react to information but not necessarily incorporate that information into a rational value estimate. Keynes recognized this same issue in delineating between speculation and enterprise. Speculation is the activity of forecasting the psychology of the market. Enterprise is the activity of forecasting the prospective yield of assets over their whole life.[40] The variations between the concepts are the issues for the basis of estimating asset values. A key issue is time. Speculation is driven by a short-term horizon; enterprise is long-term. The time element opened the recognition of preferences for form of returns. The speculator desires short capital appreciation. The active management involved with an enterprise is often seeking income.

Keynes recognized that the securitization process encouraged the evolution of the market to speculation; it was to be a market characterized by owners who do not manage and have no special knowledge of the circumstances or the business fundamentals underlying the valuations of an investment.[41] The more the market is represented by these uninformed investors, the more the fundamentals are ignored by the professionals, because the market pattern becomes a matter of anticipating possible changes of the market psychology. This pattern often entails foregoing the mathematics of investment—an inevitable result of structuring investment markets to achieve "liquidity." Keynes best summarized the situation by saying that markets are sometimes driven by animal spirits unrelated to economic realities. This analysis is consistent with the experimental evidence of Tversky and Kahneman that subjects overreact to new information in making probabilistic judgments.[42] In real estate, this overreaction has often occurred as a valuation error in which the investors recognize the fundamentals but fail to discount a "ripening" period in order to receive acceptable returns. In essence, in real estate there is a tendency to pick things too green. The valuation error will continue as long as investors are responding to market forces that are influenced by average expectations. These expectations often are the result of a human preference for an action that is guided by a spontaneous optimism and fueled by a speculative

[40] J. M. Keynes, *The General Theory of Employment, Interest and Money* (New York: Harcourt Brace Jovanovich, 1964): 158.

[41] *Ibid.*, at 153.

[42] Amos Tversky and D. Kahneman, "The Framing of Decisions and the Psychology of Choice," *Science*, 211 (January 1981): 453–458.

confidence and the state of credit. Securitization, by its character, tends to contribute to and result from both, because of the liquidity of the security market, the profitability linked directly to volatility, the lack of entry constraints, and the availability of funds. These factors direct returns to passive investors and lower the cost of capital through financial pools.

An understanding of market efficiency is important because it shows that activity need not be directly linked to the underlying fundamentals of the asset. Real estate is not different from an industry, firm, or business enterprise that has been publicly sold. History has shown that an asset's market can function independently of its capital market. The problem is that the real estate securities market can and will be efficient where the market for real estate, and especially commercial property, will not. The misunderstanding by investors that the securities issues are not directly related to the real estate collateral contributes to the risk/security illusion. If one is an efficient market and the other is not, increased volatility in real estate returns can be expected. The confusion for risk illusion and valuation error is illustrated by Wofford and Moses where REIT returns and Betas (market sensitivity/risk measures) are used for the real estate measures.[43] This tendency will contribute to the valuation error and the further removal of the capital formulation of real estate and the direct real estate market. This point is not sensitive as long as speculative confidence and the state of credit are strong. If either confidence or credit is weakened, then, as current real estate market experience has shown, expectations can diminish until fundamental analysis is the only available method remaining to allow any investment decision activity at all. This experience would tend to comply with value theory and financial theory; in the long term, markets are efficient.

Securitization as a form of financing is fundamentally linked to the current and potential income productivity of the real estate that is the collateral of the issue. This is what was referred to earlier as "seeing the numbers" of the real estate. However, as has been shown, the numbers cannot be isolated from the physical, legal, and locational dimensions of the real estate. If this isolation does occur, the risk of the investment cannot be appropriately assessed without segmenting the component parts. Furthermore, the equation of exchange discussed

[43] Larry E. Wofford and Edward A. Moses, "The Relationship Between Capital Markets and Real Estate Investment Yields: Theory and Application," *The Real Estate Appraiser and Analyst*, 44:6 (November–December 1978): 51–61.

earlier illustrates that the attempt to create a separate market stratum with the security issue may be an illusion. At best, it is a short-term imbalance that will seek a return to equilibrium.

§ 9.10 NEED FOR INFORMATION

Traditionally, the real estate product market and the financing involved have been the concerns of persons directly in contact with the properties and markets. Even with this direct involvement and active participation, economic problems have occurred because of misunderstandings and limited information. If the financial sector of real estate becomes more and more controlled by the securities market, then there is a growing need for information and sources of information that allow not only the accumulation of facts but also comparative analysis. Given the anonymous system of the securities market, it is important that quality information be available in order to make investment decisions.

Sources of information on the underlying real estate are presently limited. Information is available on the securities, REITs, and REMICs, and on limited portfolios held by certain institutions. The same quantity and quality of information do not exist for the real estate collateral. Real estate is in a state of data poverty. The uneven availability of information may be a signal into the securitization problems that can be expected to occur in the coming years.

Efforts to enhance the information needs of real estate securitization are seen in the ratings system developed to analyze commercial real estate debt. Moody's, Standard & Poor's, and Duff and Phelps have created rating systems to aid in the development of the commercial market-backed securities market. In the ratings procedure, the relationship between the securities market and the real estate market's different orientation is identified. Under the traditional financing procedure, the underwriting process affords a method to identify and control risk. The rating system attempts to offer an equivalent tool in securitization. However, to achieve a desired AA rating, the investment house has two alternatives: to offer a prime parcel of real estate as collateral, and to insure or, more specifically, guarantee the issue. The investment houses have chosen in most cases the route of guaranteeing the issues.[44] The shifting of risk to a third party, without

[44] Leon Shilton, "Credit Ratings Still a Stumbling Block to Commercial Debt Securitization," *Real Estate Times*, August 1, 1987, pp. 7, 30.

first understanding the source of the risk or establishing an appropriate method of measurement linked to the causes for variation, can lead to problems. They are the same problems as those currently existing for the S&Ls and other lending institutions. A contributing factor to the current problems being experienced by financial institutions is that mortgage insurance buffered the individual lenders from feeling the full cost of their loan decisions. This separation of "who benefits" from "who pays" can be an even more costly occurrence to the overall economy, with the securitization of real estate. A decision to guarantee an issue, as opposed to the appropriate analysis of the collateral, is not only a matter of shifting risk. A major issue is the overall cost—and the identification of the ultimate payor. The choice to guarantee the issue can be partially attributed to the lack of information on specific property, the perceived cost of such information, a lack of knowledge regarding relevant attributes, and a preference to do business in the familiar manner of the securities market (not the real estate market).

The nature of the real estate product, the securities, the market for both, and the manner of doing business in both markets have set the environment for the concerns identified in this chapter.

The key to all of the trends toward securitization is to determine whether the fundamentals of real estate value, return, or productivity are relevant to the market for commercial paper or the investment contracts for which the real estate is collateral. Failure to delineate the separate markets and to fully understand the risk exposure in the combination can lead to an illusion of security and limited risk exposure.

§ 9.11 THE RISK/SECURITY ILLUSION

The major issue of concern that should arise in the securitization process is the false security or limited risk illusion that seems to accompany the use of real estate as collateral. According to Leon Shilton of Sean Trebor Co. and Fordham University, Wall Street has ignored the four major elements of real estate analysis, even in the rating techniques.[45] Appropriate analysis of the following elements could reduce risk exposure and make the security illusion a reality:

1. The underlying demand for real estate space that is a function of a city's economic base;

[45] *Ibid.*, at 30.

2. The relative attractiveness of a given parcel of real estate in the local inventory;
3. The debt and equity structure of the deal;
4. The productivity of the property—the physical, legal, and locational attributes of the property, in terms of its capacity to generate income.

These issues would relate the real estate asset to the purchase of the security. The quality ranking of the security would be tied to the quality and productivity of the real estate. Shilton states that this has not been done. Yet, many investors perceive their investments in real estate securities to be investments in the underlying real estate assets. Securities are priced in their own market, and the real estate securities market is based on its own set of economic and psychic factors. Similar occurrences involving various industries can be found in the stock market. The purchasers and users of industrial plants and companies are often a distinct market from the investors in corporate stock. There are times, however, as in the case of corporate takeovers, when the two agents from the market clash. In this example, the industry-oriented buyer may be bidding against purchasers interested only in flipping the company for a speculative profit. This same scenario is played out in real estate markets, but, unlike some of the more generic financial markets, the perception of real estate as a sound, tangible investment can create an illusion of security that does not exist. The security illusion possible in real estate securitization mirrors the situation that exists in the general economy. As Drucker points out in his discussions of the changing world economy, "Capital movements rather than trade (in both goods and services) have become the driving force of the world economy. The two have not quite come uncoupled, but the link has become loose, and worse, unpredictable."[46]

The statement of unpredictability indicates increased risk in the analysis of market trading. This risk is the result of the financial components' no longer being linked to the physical asset. Standard economic logic has promulgated such a relationship, even if synergism is considered. Macroeconomic and microeconomic examples of the relationship of capital markets to real assets are offered to establish this point. A macroeconomic model that incorporates the concerns of the

[46] Peter F. Drucker, "The Changed World Economy," *Foreign Affairs* 768.

financial components, the expectations of the participants, and the supply and demand for a product is called the "equation of exchange":

$$MV = PQ$$

where:

M = quantity of money
V = velocity, or number of times the money is spent in a given period; this variable considers the impact of expectations
P = prices—average level; this variable considers expectations
Q = quantity of goods produced

This model is based on prices of goods being currently produced. Real estate transactions often involve goods that are being exchanged but are not currently produced.[47] Wallace Smith described the process by which this model can be adjusted to deal with time issues that are relevant in real estate. The basic model is appropriate;[48] the purpose here is to show that a hypothesized relationship exists between financial markets and real assets. Given Drucker's observation that the capital markets are uncoupling from the asset markets, the equation of exchange would not hold. It would become $MV \neq PQ$ (the monetary sector is not equal to the product sector). The concern is that, if this is a tendency in the general economy, then is securitization in real estate an example of this uncoupling or is it a vehicle by which the uncoupling will be speeding up? If the uncoupling is indeed occurring, does the collateral for any security, real estate or not, back it up?

A microeconomic example of this principle (to equate capital structure to asset worth) is exhibited in the context of the corporate balance sheet. The objective of the balance sheet is to equate the assets of the company to its capital structure. The debt and equity, in the form of loans, bonds, preferred shares, and common stock, often tend to exceed the current cash and fixed assets. This excess is termed goodwill. It is the product of the synergy formed by the operation of a going concern and the present value of investors' expectations of future returns. The underlying assets do not reflect this attribute (unless they are valued at current market value rather than book value), but the

[47] Wallace Smith, *Housing: The Social and Economic Elements* (Berkeley: University of California Press, 1971): 69.

[48] *Ibid.*, at 70.

debt and equity components immediately incorporate these expectations. Unfortunately, if the expectations are incorrect, the goodwill is eroded and the collateral does not cover the capital investment. The separate market for the security interest enforces the imbalance in the balance sheets. What is the risk exposure in real estate investments, if the financial interests are removed a farther distance from the underlying asset than currently exists in the market?

The increasing uncoupling of capital and real asset markets has resulted in neglect of the basic fundamentals of supply and demand for the product. An example is the disregard of lenders and underwriters to fully scrutinize real estate collateral because, in part, any poor real estate decisions would be bailed out by the final mortgage insurer—often, a government agency. If abuse like this can occur on the debt side of the capital equation, what will be the impact of equity investors that have become concerned with the ebbs and flows of the securities market, while simultaneously ignoring the status of the real estate industry? The investors feel safe, given that the securities issue is guaranteed and collateralized with a real, tangible asset. The reality is that an empty office building has no value, except perhaps negative value because of the cash outflow in its operation. The illusion of security comes because of the tangible nature of the real estate. However, this tangible asset is increasingly being uncoupled from the capital supporting it.

Real estate does not have an inherent or intrinsic value. The price or value is based on the willingness of users to purchase the property. The availability of real estate is often contingent on getting financing. The influx of security market capital is fueling the industry at a time when the nation is more overbuilt than at any other point in history.[49] Even when this capital is used for existing buildings, other capital is freed up for more construction. This increasing supply is often used as an indication of an active market, with real estate—and especially the securitization process—being driven by Say's Law. Say's Law implies that supply creates its own demand. Unfortunately, the 20 percent level of vacancy in many office markets shows that this law is circumstantial. With the creation of a nationwide development profession, the potential for overbuilding will continue as long as the funds are available. The developer must build or die. The overall real estate market is in bad shape and the possibility of its continuing on this path is heightened by the fact of more capital infusion. If savings and loans and

[49] Lipman, *supra* note 1, at 1.

other institutions, with their supposedly stringent underwriting guidelines, cannot offset the losses, then how can an alternative financing system be expected to overcome the problems traditionally experienced in the real estate market? The system is *contributing to* the uncoupling of the financing from the product and is characterized by passive investors whose only management guidance is offered by securities salespersons. Thorstein Veblin, in *Theory of Business Enterprise,* states that the businessperson was not the motivating force behind the capitalist system but was more a saboteur of the system.[50] According to Veblin, the aim of the businessperson or, more precisely, the speculative investor, is not to produce anything; the aim is to create a profit. The profit-lacking innovation of new "real" product for which there is an effective demand can only be obtained at the expense of the other factors of production. At best, the product created may be a financial instrument that adds to capital flows away from real product production, regardless of the level of technology. Therefore, according to Veblin, the objective of the businessperson is not to help make the goods but to cause breakdowns in the regular flow of output so that values fluctuate. The speculator could then capitalize on the confusion to reap a profit. On top of the actual production apparatus, the businessperson can build a superstructure of credit, loans, and make-believe capitalizations.[51] Without appropriate underwriting and risk management, these same actions may lie at the heart of the new financial revolution. The objective seems to be the control of legal/economic possession and not the use or physical/economic possession of a good. The latter form of possession is the basis for a perception of security (less risk) in real estate ownership.

§ 9.12 PROPERTY RIGHTS AND SECURITIZATION

The uncoupling of the financial and realty markets will open up issues concerning property rights. The traditional freehold and leasehold estates can be commingled under the securitization process. Conceptually, the estate should be a freehold, fee simple, prorated, divisible part of the whole, if the security interest is an equity stock. The securitized debt position is an interest in the secondary market that has existed in

[50] See Robert L. Heilbroner, *The Worldly Philosophers* (New York: Simon and Schuster, 1980): 231.

[51] *Ibid.,* at 232.

the issues offered by the Federal National Mortgage Association (FNMA; "Fannie Mae") and the Government National Mortgage Association (GNMA; "Ginnie Mae").

The major issue involving property rights under securitization is the legal status of fractional interest exceeding the fee simple estate, as illustrated in the Hawaiian technique mentioned earlier. Securitization is concerned with the value per share. This new concept in real estate can only hold if the finance theory of value additivity is applicable to real estate. Existing legal and economic premises would tend to suggest otherwise. The principle of value additivity states that the overall value (hence, the value per share) of a corporation is the sum of the present values of its component parts. The principles in real estate contrary to value additivity are the impacts of plottage and plattage,[52] the concepts of marginal productivity that are linked to a product constrained by physical size, and the appraisal standard that market value is not the sum of the value of component parts.[53] The legal/economic dimension of property rights is an area of potential difficulty in mixing the activities of the real property market and the securities market. A future problem that could result from this mixture is a combination that is currently seen in real estate foreclosures and in corporate takeovers. A real estate investor acquires what he or she thinks is the controlling interest in the securities market and then gets tied down in a legal suit over the value of the real estate equity—or, worse, in litigation as to how the equity is defined.

This problem of property rights is further complicated by the concerns of a proper recording system for both the transactions of real estate and the securities interest. Many of the securities markets are handled in compliance with Securities and Exchange Commission (SEC) procedures. However, state regulations also come into play, both with the initiation of security issues and with the selling of issues within various states. In a merit state, in order to offer a public issue, the prospectus must be reviewed by analysts of the state and be judged to be a meritorious security offering. Many states are full disclosure states, as is the SEC. A full disclosure state requires that all relevant information be disclosed. For example, a prospectus may have on its cover, in bold letters, the statement: **WARNING: THIS COMPANY**

[52] Peter F. Colwell and C. F. Sirmans, "Area, Time, Centrality and the Value of Urban Land," *Land Economics*, 54:4 (November 1978): 514–519.

[53] American Institute of Real Estate Appraisers, *Professional Ethics and Standards* (Chicago: AIREA, 1985): 24.

HAS NO ASSETS OR EARNINGS AND WILL BE UNABLE TO PAY DIVIDENDS IN THE FORESEEABLE FUTURE. THE SHARES ARE HIGHLY RISKY.[54] The above warning is possible in a blind-pool securities offer, where the issuers may market a project idea before it is completely formulated. Another scenario is where properties in the portfolio have not been identified at the time of issue and then may never get acquired. Finally, the possibility exists for properties to be acquired but to have no value because of an oversupply and very limited demand for an asset in its local market. All of this information may be unavailable to the investor because of the nature of security and realty recording systems. The end result is that an expansion of the exposure to risk is avoided because of the risk illusion that exists in the perception of real estate as a tangible asset.

§ 9.13 CONCLUSIONS AND OUTLOOK

Securitization lends liquidity to real estate markets. Liquidity offers more available funds for real estate and thus lowers the cost of capital. The secondary market for mortgages and the stock issues they generate have lowered the interest rate in the short run, despite the deficit, partly because the mortgage funds are competing with Treasury bills with similar terms. The current overbuilding in the real estate market may be aided by the liquidity objectives of securitization. The stock market tends toward the refinancing of existing assets rather than new capital development. Perceptions of risk in start-up enterprises and speculative preferences for short-term appreciation are partly responsible. The trend will aid a segment of the economy that represents one-half of the nation's wealth and 15 percent of the gross national product.[55]

Even as securitization is affording liquidity to an overbuilt real estate market, the entire economy is currently undergoing a structural change, exemplified by the uncoupling of the capital market from trade in goods and services. Concern with capital movements, exchange rates, and credit flows—as opposed to the production and flow of goods and services as the driving force in the economy—has resulted in two economies that seem to act independently (or increasingly so). Capital movements unconnected to trade greatly exceed trade finance, even after accounting for transactions that involve movements from one pocket

[54] Malkiel, *supra* note 17, at 54.

[55] Drucker, *supra* note 46, at 781–782.

to another.[56] Historical evidence has shown that this is not a problem until it is necessary to identify the fundamentals of the collateral. Securitization in real estate (both equity investments and debt investments in mortgage backed securities) is representative of this uncoupling activity's occurrence in the real estate sector. The potential is for two distinct markets, one for real estate securities and one for real assets. The flexibility and policy implications involved in value definitions used to establish transactions will separate even further the "real" from the financial or "symbolic" market. The potential for a chasm between the two markets is tied to this fuzzy construct of value. Value theory states that the basis of worth is the ability to exchange or transfer the property, a scarcity of supply, the presence of effective demand, and a use for the property. Both real property and securities have the characteristic of transferability. As discussed earlier, they are transferred under two distinct institutional systems that have had difficulty in meshing before and may again. Both real estate and securities are subject to elements of supply and demand; their markets can reflect players with different objectives and needs who are often working against one another.

The most significant variable of value that indicates a difference in the real estate and securities markets is use. The sole purpose of use for securities is as an investment contract. The objectives of the investors may vary, but the function of the securities market is consistent. The real estate product (and hence its market) is totally contingent on use, even if that use is at a future date. Real estate, though physically fixed, is economically flexible; with modifications, a parcel can be converted to another use. Therefore, the fundamentals of the real estate investment are the basis of its market performance.

The current uncoupling of real and financial assets, of which the current securitization move is a part, can create a state of imbalance in the economic system that cannot continue indefinitely. After the current restructuring of the economy is completed, economists assume that the real economy and the "symbolic" economy will come together again. The concern is whether the recoupling will be easy or hard. Although perceived to be a new phenomenon, the conflict in the relationship between capital and real estate markets has occurred before. Each time, the landing has been hard for both parties. The pattern currently observed in the securitization process will lead to still another head-on collision. The alternative to this outlook is for the securities issuers to recognize the importance of the fundamentals

[56] *Id.*

underlying real estate as an asset and to consider the risk and returns of the securities as they relate to the real estate product. Alternatively, consideration should be given to operating as if the current uncoupling is a short-term phenomenon. The fundamental strengths of the real estate asset must set the framework for the capital structure, and the use of securitization must be based on an understanding of risk other than financial risk.

Ten

Appraising without Comparables: An Expanded Concept of Appraisal Practice

§ 10.1 INTRODUCTION

"You can't do an appraisal without some damn comparables." This quote was overheard in an appraisal office prior to the economic downturn of 1983–1984. The statement reflects the common perception that an appraisal cannot be made without comparable sales ("comparables"). Throughout the country, with increasing frequency, appraisers must do appraisals without comparables; under varying circumstances, appraisers have been appraising without comparables for many years. The problem of a lack of comparable sales is not new. In fact, the appraisal process as it was established in the 1930s was set up to relieve the reliance on sales transactions.

§ 10.2 NATURE OF APPRAISAL PROBLEM

The appraisal report was established as a tool to aid decisions in real estate. Despite a lack of comparable sales, people must make real estate decisions, usually requiring a choice based on economic, physical, and financial limitations. Any choice must deal with alternatives and expectations, and these vary with the choices that can be identified. At the same time, the alternatives and expectations direct the choices that can be made.

Appraisal enables the comparison of alternatives via the principle of substitution. This principle states that a purchaser will pay no more for a good than the cost of acquiring a similar property, and puts rational constraints on the exchange of real estate. The consideration of alternative properties injects the realities of competitive supply and enables inference about buyer behavior.

Appraisal also considers the principle of anticipation, which states that value is the present worth of future anticipated benefits that flow from control of or access to an asset. The consideration of buyers' expectations requires recognition of the reasons for a property's being in demand. The purchase price of a property illustrates the price that a buyer places on the expected benefits of ownership and possession.

The traditional appraisal process emphasizes the principle of substitution, partly because market value predominates as the criterion for making real estate decisions and because of the simplicity of applying the sales comparison approach. Market value is a court-defined concept. Sales comparison is a preferred method of courts and other legal bodies. With this weight of legal enforcement, the principle of substitution has enhanced its application in many nonlitigative economic decisions. A standard or precedent can be identified for a decision. Finally, there is a logical assumption that people tend to shop before making large purchases. After making comparisons, they will purchase the property that offers the most benefits for the lowest price.

The principle of anticipation has historically received less emphasis in the traditional appraisal process because of a concern regarding estimating expectations. The expanded concept of appraisal offered here emphasizes the expectations of the principle of anticipation within the constraints of the principle of substitution. The valuation techniques based on the combination of these basic principles allow simulation of the market when transactions are limited or nonexistent. Simulation of market activity is necessary when normal market activity for a good is stifled because of generally unfavorable economic conditions. In these down cycles, decisions concerning real estate must often address issues of supply and demand for the product. If these decisions require a value, an appraisal often must be furnished regardless of the availability of sales data. Decisions concerned with market supply and demand are more crucial in down periods than in a favorable economic environment.

The techniques for simulation offered here have developed over time; appraisers have had to deal with a multitude of situations in which comparable sales have been lacking. To show the general applicability of the proposed process and its practical application, it is necessary to delineate the situations in which appraisers experience valuation with limited comparables.

§ 10.3 APPRAISAL SITUATIONS CHARACTERIZED BY LIMITED COMPARABLES

In normal markets, limited or poor quality data are not unusual, because of the unique nature, infrequent transactions, and spatial dimension of real estate. The heterogeneity of the real estate product, the illiquidity of the asset, and the restrictive market structure have caused appraisal to evolve into the ad hoc process used today. The nature of the general real estate product and market has always been characterized by limited data.

A lack of comparable sales data confronts appraisers most frequently in two general situations: (1) the appraisal of a special-purpose property for which a market value is requested, and (2) the valuation of marketable properties that have unique locations or are experiencing tough economic times. This chapter shows why a lack of comparable sales is a key characteristic of real estate analysis and why an ad hoc appraisal process has evolved rather than a general equilibrium model, as is often devised for other assets.

(a) SPECIAL-PURPOSE PROPERTIES

Special-purpose properties, by their nature, indicate why comparables are difficult to find. Unique property types for which market value is needed might include a girl scout meeting hall, a cheese processing plant, a beef processing plant, a church with a bowling alley, a golf course, a barrel manufacturing and cleaning operation, a distillery, a grotto, air rights, a cave, and a theme park. These properties, among others, might involve a decision requiring a market value, for a transaction of the property, financing, or condemnation. These actions require a market value by law or institutional regulation, even though the properties, by their nature, cannot be characterized as readily marketable.

(b) LOCATION-RELATED PROBLEMS

Neighborhoods or properties that typically have limited markets because of location are: rural areas and small towns, economically depressed areas, CBDs, areas in transition, and areas experiencing rapid growth (the suburban fringes of major cities). In rural areas and small towns, and in depressed economies, the lack of comparables is immediately obvious. The lack of sales in CBDs and expanding areas may not be as clear. A built-up urban area will have many existing properties, but no sales may have occurred within a reasonable market period. A prime example is the CBD of Kansas City, Missouri, where no new office building was constructed from the late 1950s until recently. Although little activity or change had occurred in the CBD to support a market value estimation, situations arose that required decisions based on value estimations.

Another location-related situation is the appraisal of properties that have historically experienced a changing or cyclical market that cannot be identified in a timely manner. These are areas in transition, whether in the built-up core of the city or in the expanding and developing urban fringe. These appraisal situations arise because of a change in highest and best use of a property and the lack of a developed market. The subject property may be the only one in the area that is changing its use. There may be comparables within the city or the extended neighborhood but no directly proximate comparables.

(c) NEED FOR SIMULATION

Besides the spatial aspects of real estate that may limit market comparison techniques, there are timing issues that create comparable data problems. For the appraiser or the land economist, these problems result from the difficulty of comparing one market environment and its set of economic activities to another that has a different set of economic activities. A time adjustment implicitly contains many economic variables. These variables need to be explicitly analyzed, to appropriately use older comparable sales in changing economic situations. A lack of comparables can result from slow economic activity, rapid economic expansion, or economic conditions that are not "normal." Rapidly expanding areas have data problems similar to those of developing fringe areas. The subject property may simply be the first in the area.

The identification of a "normal market" is difficult. Obvious deviations are the Great Depression of the 1930s and the recessions of the

1970s and 1980s. There was a "hot market" in the early 1980s and a slow to stagnant market in the late 1980s in some parts of the country. Other sections experienced a slow or recessed economy in the early 1980s and "hot markets" in the late 1980s and early 1990s. The term used to reflect this type of comparison is a market "correction." What this means remains to be discovered.

The lack of comparables can be a consequence of overbuilding, limited or declining demand, recession, or failure of properties to meet owners' and investors' expectations. The change from a "normal" market has required a rethinking of the standard approach to appraisal—not regarding its methodology, but directed toward its emphasis on existing models. The traditional emphasis in appraisal has been on analysis of a dependent variable, the selling price, which is the end product of the transaction.[1] In the absence of price as the end product, as is characteristic of the real estate owned (REO) by numerous savings and loans and the Resolution Trust Corporation, an alternative can be an emphasis on the transaction process itself. Ratcliff termed this method of valuation as simulation. Appraisal normally is concerned with the value conclusions of the investors or purchasers involved in a given market. Appraisal is not concerned directly with the logic and accuracy of the methods employed by the market participants. Simulation attempts to replicate the market process itself. This necessitates an economic analysis of the situation and an understanding of the calculus involved in the decision or negotiation process. These activities require an understanding of why certain parcels of real estate have value, the difference between price and value, and the relationship of value theory to valuation theory. A linking of these fundamentals facilitates making market value decisions in a limited-activity market. The lack of comparables is often directly tied to the existence of a problem and the need to make decisions concerning non-liquid assets.

The current market, characterized by overbuilding, guarded capital availability, declining employment, and foreclosure activity, is not the first market in which these economic situations have been encountered. Research of economic cycles indicates that the problem of estimating market value without comparable sales has occurred before, and caused the development of techniques that could be used as alternatives to the reliance on comparable sales. The country's leading

[1] Richard U. Ratcliff, *Valuation for Real Estate Decisions* (Santa Cruz, CA: Democrat Press, 1972): 78–83.

appraisal organizations of today were founded in the Great Depression of the 1930s. The methods employed during the 1930s and subsequent periods will be investigated, with extensions to fit current situations. The decision models presented in Chapter 5 will be reviewed for their relevance to comparables and applied to examples of property types.

§ 10.4 HISTORY OF APPRAISING WITH NO COMPARABLES

The appraisal of real estate as a documented process has its roots only in this century. Prior to its becoming a formal method of practice, valuation of real estate was the opined expression of the judgment and experience of experts. The weight of an expert's decree is represented by a "war story" of two Texas appraisers.[2] One appraiser lives in Dallas, the other in west Texas. The Dallas appraiser was assigned to appraise the only service station in a small west Texas community. After strenuous and futile search of the market for several days, he called on his west Texas colleague for help. The west Texan told him to seek out a specific elderly lady in that community and ask her what the station was worth. Whatever amount she gave would be the value.

Appraisal has always been conducted to some degree without comparables. The economic growth in many areas of the country has spoiled the appraisal industry since World War II, but two significant periods were characterized by appraisal analysis with limited emphasis on comparable sales. These periods encompassed the volatile markets experienced during (1) the Great Depression of the 1930s and the turmoil of World War II, and (2) the recession of the mid-1970s. An investigation of the appraisal technique used and the decisions faced during these periods will lend some insight to the process of appraising without comparables.

To give these two major periods a proper perspective, some brief comments on the overall history of the appraisal process are in order. The theoretical basis for the sales comparison, income, and cost approaches to valuation lie in the works of the neoclassical economists. The founding neoclassical economist was Alfred Marshall, who established a long-term concept equating normal value (market value) to normal cost (theory of distribution). Marshall was the first economist

[2] The alleged parties involved in this event were Ed Compere, MAI, of Abilene, and Karel Clettenberg, PhD, SRPA, of Dallas. (Narrated to the author at AIREA course in Orlando, FL, 1990.)

to offer methods for estimating value, not just a theory as to what value is. His work was published originally in 1890.[3] Arthur J. Mertzke linked Marshall's general theories of valuation to real estate in 1920, and emphasized a theory of equivalence among the three approaches that is the basis of current appraisal practice.[4] Despite the availability of three approaches and the pronouncement that they should indicate similar if not equivalent estimations of value, the sales comparison approach was perceived to be the most objective (or least subjective) indicator of value. A comparison of the sales of similar properties directly addressed the price that would be paid for substitute properties.

(a) THE 1930s

In the 1930s, market price lost the central position in valuation,[5] for several reasons. The dominant reason was a change in the market environment. The rapid gyrations in market prices during the 1930s and the war years eroded the ability to consistently apply the market price technique and weakened its credibility among decision makers. McMichael and Bingham had earlier stated that "sales can never be more than sign posts to mark the way towards a correct conclusion."[6] For this position to be taken, there had to be a belief that value and price did not equate. This perception began to spread among appraisers, if not economists, during the 1930s.

Other reasons for the erosion of the sales comparison approach during this period were the development of a separate identity for appraisers (distinct from brokers), the increasing occasions for valuing real estate (especially at a time when the market was gyrating and stability was sought), the recognition of varying concepts of value used for different purposes, the collapse of markets, and the increased encroachment of government in real estate activities. The combination of these factors coincided with conjoined academic and government efforts that established policies of appraisal. Frederick Babcock's work in 1932 established the income approach as the central premise of value.[7] The

[3] Alfred Marshall, *Principles of Economics*, 8th Edition (London: Macmillan Press, 1979).

[4] Paul F. Wendt, *Real Estate Appraisal: Review and Outlook* (Athens: University of Georgia Press, 1974): 218. See also Arthur J. Mertzke, *Real Estate Appraising* (Chicago: National Association of Real Estate Boards, 1927).

[5] Wendt, *supra* note 4, at 89.

[6] Stanley L. McMichael and Robert F. Bingham, *City Growth and Land Values* (Cleveland: McMichael, 1923).

[7] Frederick M. Babcock, *Valuation of Real Estate* (New York: McGraw-Hill, 1932).

force of government endorsement was added when Babcock was made director of the newly formed Federal Housing Administration (FHA). Babcock's techniques were based on Irving Fisher's work, developed in 1906. Fisher's work, in turn, was the mathematical formulation of the discounting process suggested in Marshall's earlier publications.

Babcock distrusted the use of market price as an indicator of market value. He broke with other economists of his time, stating that price and value were not equivalent. He accepted the concept of value as a long-term phenomenon, partly to enable the justification of decisions made prior to the collapse of the real estate market. Given the numerous problems experienced during the collapse, Babcock held that multiple value concepts were possible, depending on the problem situation experienced. The government's decision needs greatly increased the value concepts that were used to address the real estate decisions as envisioned by bureaucrats during this period. Based on his own perceptions, Babcock developed seven valuation methods. One was the direct sales comparison approach, which he placed sixth on his list. The other methods can be grouped into income and cost models. Babcock's methods were:

1. Income method—commercial rentals (similar to the traditional income approach);
2. Income method—business profits attributed to real estate (income observed is the result of a business operation, the bulk of which is attributed to the real estate; much like a hotel or other space-intensive activity, the product of the business is selling space and related services);
3. Income method—business profits distributed between real estate and chattel (a restaurant, or certain manufacturing facilities);
4. Income method—business profits distributed between real estate and business (the real estate is necessary but not primary in the production of income or profits, which differentiates it from method 2; an example is a cheese processing plant, where the income from the operation is distributed among the labor, capital, management, and real estate involved in the operation of making cheese);
5. Replacement cost method—business profits (income to the real estate is minor or indistinguishable; an example would be a meeting hall, paper mill, or railroad right-of-way);
6. Direct sales comparison approach—amenities returns (this method is used when there are many market evidences);

7. Replacement cost method—amenity returns (used when no market data are available and income is not applicable; examples are a church, state capitol building, and so on).

Babcock's income models illustrate the use of the theory of distribution. The activities linked to the generation of income are identified in each of the separate models. The income is then distributed to the contributing factors.

The emphasis on the income approach during this period was tied to a down market, a suspicion of sales data, a theoretical preference for the rental approach, and an extension of the principle of substitution to rents as well as sales. The substitution principle for rents is based on the truism that, even in a down market, space is needed. If it cannot be purchased, it can be rented.

The government agencies involved with real estate during this period exhibited a preference for the cost approach. Their conceptual preference was linked to a long-term "normal" value premise. The practical reasons for government preference of the cost approach were that it had an objective base, it could be easily verified, and the process could be reproduced.

An emphasis on approaches other than the market approach and a perception of the difference in price and value contributed to the evolution of the requirement of the three approaches to value. The theory of equivalence developed by Mertzke was institutionalized by the profession and the government during the decades from the 1950s through the 1970s.

(b) THE 1960s AND 1970s

Some professional and academic attacks on the process, as it had become entrenched, were launched in the 1960s. Many of the issues identified by Ratcliff, Wendt, Kinnard, Smith, and others who formed the contemporary school of appraisal thought are still being debated today. The conflicts between the traditional and contemporary schools offered some techniques of valuation that can be useful in appraising without comparables. The suggested techniques resulted from another down real estate market, which occurred in the mid-1970s during a period of disintermediation (the loss of funds coming into lending institutions such as banks and savings and loans). The lenders' loss of funds during this period can be attributed to short-term government bonds that were offering returns above the interest rate being paid on savings accounts. Savers would withdraw their savings from a passbook account paying 6 percent and invest in a 90-day government note at 9 percent. A shortage of funds for real estate and a continuing rise in interest rates were the results.

At the same time, real estate was being overbuilt because of tax-law advantages, cheap loans (previously), and erroneous perceptions of the market. When properties lacked demand or sufficient tenants, the owners often incurred more debt. Properties became distressed because debt service exceeded income. The forces of recession, inflation, and disintermediation caused a distressed real estate market. Limited transactions were available for using the market approach. If sales were used, they were not comparable because they had occurred in the immediately preceding market, which was not under the duress of a down market at the time of sale. It became necessary to adjust for the subject's distressed position or the unrealistic expectations. Unfortunately, the more sales have to be adjusted, the less comparable they are. As Marshall had pointed out, sales are the most appropriate indicators in the short run.[8] The longer the time lapse since the sale occurred, the less likely it can be used as a market indicator.

As in the 1930s, the alternative methods to pursue were the cost and income approaches. Unlike the 1930s, however, the cost approach was not considered appropriate. The 1930s depression had declining costs of producing many goods. The 1970s were characterized by inflation. Cost as a measure of value was considered inadequate for distressed property. Its premise as a measure of value based on the construction of an alternative structure of equal utility was rendered inferior because cost during an inflationary period greatly exceeded possible selling price. The market for improved property lagged the markets for the factors of production (labor, capital, materials, and land). The difference between cost new and existing facilities necessitated large depreciation adjustments. To adjust the difference between cost new and remaining value, an extension of the concept of economic obsolescence was applied as a measure of loss due to factors, external to the property, resulting from overbuilding and insufficient demand. The problem with adjusting cost for obsolescence because of external factors was that the economic downturn experienced in some sections of the country was not local.[9] This caused appraisers to debate whether the

[8] Marshall, *supra* note 3, at 298–313.

[9] Judy Baumgarten, "Market Value When There Is No Market," *The Appraisal Journal,* 46 (January 1978): 79–89.

deduction for depreciation was appropriate. The Society of Real Estate Appraisers identified economic obsolescence as locational obsolescence. The cost approach was not considered a valid measurement technique because of the lack of clear identification of the neighborhood (its size dimensions) affected by external obsolescence. The issue of whether cost of replacement was a rational premise in an overbuilt environment was also debatable.

Thus, the income approach became more important during this period. Given the lack of sales, the income approach was seen as the approach in which it was least difficult to reflect the probable logic of buyers' and sellers' actions.[10] The income approach was perceived to be appropriate because people would not buy during this period unless they could hope to turn a property around. This complied with the principle of anticipation and was consistent with the notion of the 1930s, that value and price are not the same. The difference in the technique used in the market of the 1970s was that the income was explicitly calculated and was forecast on a year-by-year basis. Babcock had concentrated on the sources and nature of the income in his numerous approaches; contemporary appraisers emphasized a year-by-year analysis of the flow of funds.

The discounted cash flow (DCF) model was encouraged in the context of an "as is" appraisal.[11] Paul Wendt suggested that an after-tax format was most appropriate in estimating highest and best use (and market value).[12] The annual DCF method on an "as is" basis required the rethinking of previously held valuation presumptions. The presumption that a proposed project would be completed according to plans and specifications had to be questioned. Assumptions for forecast of a year-by-year income flow included the need to identify a normal occupancy level, sufficient demand, reasonable projection periods, and the appropriate competition. Other areas of concern in the income analysis were the limited attention given feasibility and market analysis, and the optimism of the future (in a down market). The optimism was a result of the limited analyses and of the tendency in real estate to take a two-year trend and project it over a decade.[13]

[10] *Ibid.* at 80.

[11] *Id.*

[12] Paul F. Wendt, "Highest and Best Use—Fact or Fancy," *The Appraisal Journal,* 40 (February 1972): 165–174.

[13] Paul A. Howcroft, "A Review of Appraisal Practices and Methods of Analysis," *The Appraisal Journal,* 46 (July 1978): 421.

The economic problems of the 1970s indicated that actual cash flow rather than "normal" income was the issue to be investigated and that the forecasting of cash flow had to be linked to an overall economic analysis. Appraisal had to be recognized as market analysis.[14] Absorption periods, capture rates, and management skills had to be acknowledged, and the appraiser had to investigate the presumptions of the appraisal and develop models in an attempt to predict or estimate year-by-year activities.[15] The challenges were to develop a process for understanding how the market participants make their decisions and to create models for using the decision makers' criteria.[16] Baumgarten suggested that the primary objective was to make these processes explicit. Howcraft promulgated that sophistication was secondary to creating the best predictive model based on the decision makers' criteria and/or actions. If decision makers were using gross income multipliers (GIM), then that was the appropriate model. Ratcliff offered a format for making the suggestions of these authors functional when he termed the process to be a matter of simulation, not market inference.

Because value is a concept, it can be simulated. The suggestion of simulation enables an emphasis on the process of the creation of a transaction price and takes the emphasis away from the interpretation of the price artifact. The distressed periods of the 1930s and 1970s showed that appraisal is possible without a reliance on comparable sales. As noted earlier, the origination of the appraisal profession as it exists today is traceable to a depressed market. These periods illustrated that pecuniary value can be estimated without a normally active market and that, during periods of abnormal markets, the emphasis in appraisal shifts from interpretation of the end product (value) to the appraisal process itself. These insights from history, and the fact that markets change and can be characterized by cycles and trends, suggest methods to aid in the current problem situation.

§ 10.5 CHANGE IN EMPHASIS OF APPRAISAL PROCESS

During normal market periods, market inference or direct sales comparison was the mode of operation. Since World War II, the market

[14] Ratcliff, *supra* note 1, at 15–48.

[15] Howcroft, *supra* note 13, at 419.

[16] This emphasis is promulgated in the previously cited works of Ratcliff, Baumgarten, and Howcroft (*supra* notes 1, 9, and 13).

comparison approach has been the central premise of the appraisal process. In 1956, Wendt stated:

> Market value should be viewed as the central concept in real estate valuation. The doctrine of a willing buyer and a willing seller encourages the establishment of hypothetical market values and nurtures elements of flexibility in the appraisal process. Market prices are the most reliable indicators of market value and the market-comparison method should be the preferred approach to its estimation.[17]

The significance of this quote is twofold: (1) the market comparison approach is central to appraisal because the value premise that is most appropriate is market value, and (2) the essence of market value is the doctrine of willing buyers and sellers. The first issue is important because, if the direct sales comparison approach is to receive priority without a challenge, then market value has to be the value that is sought by the decision maker. However, as Friday stated, "The market has not now, nor has it ever had a monopoly of pecuniary valuation."[18] In fact, value may not be the necessary criterion on which to base many asset decisions.

The alternative real estate asset decision models presented in Chapter 5 can be classified in terms of decision criteria as value models, solvency/income models, and rate models. The various classes of models are related. The income models are related to the value models via the rate concepts, and the rate models are contingent on value and income calculations. Despite these interrelationships, different decision makers have varying preferences as to an appropriate model for their needs. Investors have a tendency to rely on rate models—either the direct ratio models or the yield models. Lenders use value models (loan-to-value ratios), solvency models (debt coverage ratios), and yield models (effective interest returns). When dealing with non-income-producing properties, lenders often rely on solvency models; they may wish to match the home purchaser's disposable income to the principal, interest, taxes, and insurance (PITI) payments. Government agencies and other litigants often rely on value models. The final decision criteria of rate, value, or solvency cannot be determined without input or reliance on the other decision concepts.

Given the number of income and rate models, why is there an emphasis on market value as the central decision criterion? The answer, in

[17] Wendt, *supra* note 4, at 227.

[18] David Friday, "An Extension of Value Theory," *Quarterly Journal of Economics*, 36 (1922): 197–219.

part, is that exchange value is an objective value: more than one party is involved in its determination. This was the second issue identified by Wendt—the doctrine of willing buyers and sellers. Another contributing factor is the court-established precedence of the concept of market value as being the criterion by which to settle debate. Judicial rulings have had a heavy impact on the appraisal process in this country. The need for a market value definition, as enforced by law, resulted from condemnation; the issues of willing buyers and sellers (neither under duress to act, both with full knowledge, and so forth) did not exist in the litigated cases. Therefore, the courts and decision makers found it necessary to create the attributes necessary to simulate the conditions of a normal, active market. Given the objective nature of the market value/value-in-exchange concept, the support of case precedent, and the fact that, as a conceptual model, it can be constructed even if the actual situation is different, market value can be the appropriate concept for some situations in a down or inactive market.

The problems in an inactive or limited market as experienced today are that price is an insufficient criterion on which to base value, and there are limited or no indicators of price on which to make value estimations. If limited data do exist, the sales are not comparable, they are not at arm's length, or the data are so eradicated that a pattern cannot be identified—yet a decision must be made. A final decision in this context may be more significant than in a more clear-cut market situation. Emphasis is diverted from the conclusion of the process (estimation of a value based on analysis of market prices) to the appropriate application of the process. The process and its methodology are important concerns in an unstable market. Emphasis now is on the documentation and analysis contained in the report, as well as on the final value conclusion. Theory is important when information is scarce.

If prices by which to estimate value are not in evidence, then the process by which price is determined must be understood and explicitly documented. The use of transaction prices allows the implicit consideration of market behavior. The motives behind a sale are secondary to the conclusion of the transaction, which is represented by the actual price paid. This price becomes the basis for predicting prices of other assets. The loss of the "price artifact" directs the concept of the market value appraisal to a process of behavioral analysis, an economic forecast under conditions of uncertainty.[19] The behavioral approach or economic forecast necessitates the delineation of the concepts of price and value and of the relationship between value theory and valuation theory.

[19] Ratcliff, *supra* note 1, at x.

Numerous articles have explained the difference between value and price.[20] The significant difference for appraisal is that price is a historical fact, an actual occurrence.[21] Value is a potential price;[22] it implies a hypothetical event that is to occur at a future time. Even if comparable sales are available, the raw prices did not constitute value; an adjustment process was necessary. The prices plus or minus the adjustments became the basis of the value estimate, and the adjustment process involved analysis and documentation, which, in turn, involved judgment. The adjustment process was based on observation, comparison, and preferences of the market (the behavioral analysis of willing buyers and sellers, alluded to before). The basis of this behavioral approach lies in value theory. Value theory is concerned with the basis of worth to an asset; it answers the question: Why does something have worth?[23] Assets have worth because they have a use (or a potential use), they are limited in supply, there is an effective demand for them, and they can be transferred or exchanged. The latter two attributes imply that others will want the assets and can have them.

The appraisal process is concerned with identifying these attributes of a property. When comparables are in ready evidence, these attributes do not necessitate the degree of scrutiny that is required in a down market. The issues of supply and effective demand are implicit in the transaction prices, and use analysis delineates the appropriate comparables. However, the existence of comparables again suggests that the existing use is an appropriate use. Because the ability to exchange the property is directly evident in the comparables, the need to emphasize value theory is given secondary treatment (if any) because the prices implicitly represent the value concerns.

The place of value theory in an active market would be to explicitly abstract the determinants of value from the comparable prices. In a down market or one characterized by oversupply and limited demand, the process, with its emphasis on value theory, becomes the central

[20] Classic examples are: Babcock, *supra* note 7; Wendt, *supra* note 4; Robert H. Plattner, "Value and Price," *The Appraisal Journal,* 53 (October 1985): 516–523; Terry V. Grissom, "Value Definition: Its Place in the Appraisal Process," *The Appraisal Journal,* 53 (April 1985): 217–225.

[21] Ratcliff, *supra* note 1, at 53–66; Halbert C. Smith, Jerry D. Belloit, *Real Estate Appraisal* (Dayton, OH: Century VII Publishing Co., 1987): 6.

[22] Grace Milgram, "A Land Price Index for the San Juan Metropolitan Area," in *Urban Land Markets: Price Indices, Supply Measures, and Public Policy Effects* (Washington, DC: The Urban Land Institute, 1980): 27–38.

[23] Grissom, *supra* note 20.

point of analysis. Adam Smith's creation of a theory of distribution along with a theory of value was not accidental. The theory of distribution is concerned with the returns to the factors of production: land receives a rent in the production process, labor receives a wage, capital receives a yield, and entrepreneurs realize a profit. The relevance of this to appraisal is that, if the price represents the end product of the production process (value theory), then the analysis of the factors of production and their returns represents the components of the appraisal process (the theory of distribution). If the end product, price, is not available as an indicator for a value estimation, then the process of analyzing the component parts can be used to simulate the value estimate.

The ability to link value theory to the valuation techniques is the essence of appraising in an inactive market. Valuation theory is concerned with the techniques, approaches, or methods of estimating worth in an asset.[24] In a down market, decision makers seek valuation methods. However, the valuation methods cannot be effective without an understanding of their link to value theory. This linkage should exist in the appraisal process, regardless of the market's status. It is the essence of the issue in a down market because the value components, which are implicitly considered in the prices paid in the market, are not available; there have been no transactions. The value components must be explicitly identified in the valuation techniques of the appraisal process.

Consideration of the value components directly in the valuation techniques has varied over time because of the different problems and market environments that appraisers have experienced in various time periods.

§ 10.6 CONTEMPORARY SETTING FOR PROPOSED METHODS OF VALUATION

Appraisal without comparables does not occur only in down markets. Certain areas of the country, especially smaller urban regions and rural communities, are constantly exposed to the pressures of having limited or nonexistent market data. Single-family homes could qualify as special-purpose properties in Harlan, Kentucky. Harlan is known by many as a place of violent strikes, involving owners, coalminers, and the National Guard in the 1930s. Harlan sits in the heart of the Appalachian Mountains and has few level sites. A level spot is called a

[24] *Id.*

"house seat" if there is sufficient terrain to accommodate a house. In that area, depth tables are often used to quantify an appraiser's belief that larger lots are worth more than smaller lots (with diminishing marginal contribution attributed to the rear footage). By contrast, in Atlanta, to appraise a home converted to a duplex, an appraiser can find, in close proximity, other sales of single-family homes converted to duplexes. In either situation, the appraisal process is carried out. In areas or times of limited data, judgment is often emphasized more than the ability to quantify value adjustments and estimates. The places and times of limited markets give insights to the appraisal process, but a subjective or judgmental process is required because data are lacking in both frequency and quality. The lack of data is partly attributable to the nature of both real estate products and markets.

In areas or times of limited markets, the process itself is emphasized. This approach is no different from that of any other social or behavioral science. The sophistication of the process versus the inconsistency of the data is addressed by Milton Friedman in his *Essays on Positive Economics.*[25] The paucity of real estate empirical data forces an emphasis on the process of analysis. This was witnessed in the down market of the mid-1980s, when emphasis was on the Federal Home Loan Bank (FHLB) memoranda R-41b and R-41c and on the proposed Real Estate Appraisal Reform Act of 1987 (the Bernard bill). R-41b, dated as of 1982, was not a general concern of appraisal until approximately 1984–1985. R-41b was replaced with R-41c in 1986. Both of these institutional formats, which were terminated in December 1987, have had a continued impact on the appraisal process, through the Federal Institutional Reform, Recovery and Enforcement Act (FIRREA, 1989). FIRREA sets forth the Resolution Trust Corporation standards and policies on the requirements of an appraisal. These standards and policies went into effect in September 1990.

These memoranda and Acts were and are in effect during a period characterized by undue stimuli on both the high side and the low side of a "normal" market. The concerns on the high side were speculative markets and the unreliability of the comparable sales data. The low side was concerned with whether foreclosure sales represent arm's-length transactions and with the change in market conditions between the last sales and the date of appraisal. This is value from the standpoint of time, not price as a point estimate; in this context, value must be based on market analysis. Market analysis that investigates the

[25] Milton Friedman, "The Methodology of Positive Economics," in *Essays on Positive Economics* (Chicago: University of Chicago Press, 1966): 3–46.

interaction of supply and demand must be more explicit than mere indications illustrated by previous sales. An estimation problem needs to be resolved, especially if the sales from the past are not representative of the current or forecasted market. The regulation that requires the use of all three approaches as backed by market analysis and documentation is FIRREA. It further requires an emphasis on discounted cash flow (DCF) to estimate a required "as is" value.

The problems of the 1930s, the 1970s, the appraisal process in general, and the regulation scenarios of the 1990s suggest that the concern of the appraiser is not only the estimation of value but the application of the appropriate analysis process. Numerous models are available to address real estate problems. The majority of them are not value models (although they are related). Among the value models, only three general approaches—market, cost, and income—have been identified in both theory and practice. The dilemma in a down market is that the preferred model in a normal market is not easily used. The 1930s emphasized the use of the cost and income approaches. The 1970s witnessed a disenchantment with the cost approach (in part because of inflation), a preference for the income approach, and an emphasis by a minority on the use of discounted cash flow. The 1980s followed the technical leanings of the 1970s. The expectations for the 1990s will be a compliance with FIRREA and an increased emphasis on DCF, as supported by cap rate analysis, to achieve desired expectations. Market analysis will be emphasized in terms of value, solvency, and rate comparison. Market analysis will also employ more data analysis than the minimal comparable sales with the use of computer statistical programs.

§ 10.7 PROPOSED METHODS OF VALUATION—ALTERNATIVE MODELS

As noted earlier, the alternative models for valuing real estate in a market of limited comparables have their roots in the techniques of the 1930s and 1970s. Many of the models are different now because of changes in emphasis in the 1980s and early 1990s. The emphasis is now on the process of trying to simulate the mental calculus of the market participants or, more specifically, the probable market participants. An identification of the probable buyers, based on market analysis, begins with the property. The property's specific attributes can appeal to specific types of investors or consumers. The appraiser's function is to identify those investors and consumers. For example, if the basic source of income to an apartment project has been from tax shelter, who would be a likely purchaser? Recent changes in the tax laws have ruled out numerous participants. However, if the property is to be sold, a purchaser who can still place value on the tax shelter must be found. The likely candidates are persons or entities that have other passive income sources to shelter. Though few and far between, they do exist in many areas of the country. Because this type of investor will view real estate from a portfolio perspective rather than on a project-by-project basis, identification of how that probable buyer makes purchase decisions becomes important. To an investor—especially one with a portfolio—the rate models identified in Chapter 5 are probably the models of preference. If after-tax yield rates are the choice, the appraiser will identify the appropriate yield returns desired by this type of investor. The estimation of a buyer's or market segment's yield can be a complex issue. (The process of estimating a probable investor's yield is discussed in § 10.8.) At this point, it is important to recognize the interrelationships of yield and value concepts. Rate models equate to the value models. The yield rate can be used to discount the forecast cash flows, in estimating the present value of the property. The present value can indicate the probable selling price (especially in a buyer's market). If the seller has some negotiation skills or a strong bargaining position even though it is a down market, then the above calculations represent only the buyer's retention price.[26]

Before a simulated market transaction can be forecast, the seller's retention price has to be simulated. In a down market, the refusal of a seller to sell might be related to the outstanding debt on the property. If the market has fallen to a level where not only is equity eroded but the probable selling price will not cover the existing debt, then the seller's retention price may be higher than the market price, because the capital structure lags the market perceptions of the property's potential. The existing capital structure was based on previous market perceptions. Otherwise, the reason is sentiment or ignorance. In either of these cases, the property is not effectively on the market. The way to simulate the selling price based on outstanding debt is to find out the amount of debt and add to it all the relevant costs of closing and transferring the property. If the market is only slightly down or if the property has limited competition, then some return might be considered in

[26] Howard Raiffa, *The Art and Science of Negotiation* (Cambridge: Harvard University Press, 1982): 44–65.

the seller's retention price. If the market is poor, the objectives are to minimize liability on the part of the seller and to limit out-of-pocket expenses. The probable selling price of the property should fall within a range between the buyer's and seller's retention prices.[27]

The simulation techniques are quantitatively the same as the traditional appraisal models. The difference lies in the direction and intensity of research. More emphasis is placed on how people make decisions rather than what their decisions are, because no transactions have transpired in the current market.

Another aspect of the simulation approach is its effort to make explicit the decision criteria and concerns of the market participants and the attributes of the property. The income approaches range from the gross income multiplier as the most implicit model to the DCF model as the most explicit. (For detailed discussion, see Chapter 5, text relevant to Figure 5.2.) The most direct ratio model, the gross income multiplier (GIM), assumes that the vacancy level, operating expenses, and financing are the same for all of the comparables and the subject. The variation in the multipliers observed in actual appraisals can be explained, in part, by the variation in these items as they differ among comparables.

The direct cap rate model makes explicit the levels of vacancy and operating expenses experienced by the comparables, the subject, and a general market level. This model assumes that the financing and physical components are similar in each of the properties being considered. The direct or ratio models, using mortgage-equity techniques, can allow for variation in financing or in the physical relationships of different properties. These models go a step further in making the criteria that influence transactions more explicit.

The yield models identified in Chapter 5 consider the impact of time, the holding period, and the buyers' and sellers' expectations regarding the values paid and received in various transactions. The explicit consideration of these factors relates the income valuation techniques to the underlying premise of value: the present worth of future anticipated benefits. The yield models, like the ratio models, achieve the explicit consideration of the value parameters through the modification

[27] Value concepts in the transaction process are discussed in Raiffa, *ibid.*, Ratcliff, *supra* note 1, and Grissom, *supra* note 20. Additional sources are Norman Miller and Peter Rice, "A Note on the Differentiation of Market Participants by Search Costs," *Journal of Economic Letters* (Fall 1981); The American Institute of Real Estate Appraisers, *The Appraisal of Real Estate*, 7th Edition (Chicago: Appraisal Institute, 1978): 27–31.

of either the income flow or the capitalization rate. These relationships have been identified in the literature.[28]

The DCF model, given its explicit input format, might be the most appropriate model to simulate probable buyer behavior. Despite this intuitive appeal, much of the data needed to construct and fully document a cash flow are not available. Another concern is that certain components required to develop a DCF, such as debt service, are based on the loan, which is based on value. Value is the end result of the appraisal process. Therefore, the income approach suffers from a situation similar to Hirschliefer's dilemma in which the value cannot be estimated without knowing the capital structure, and the capital structure cannot be known without knowing the value. The rate modification simulation models offer a format for circumventing this dilemma and allowing the estimation of value using only the capital structure parameters (loan-to-value ratio, interest rate terms, etc.). The utility of this method was supported by Roger Cannaday, Peter Colwell, and Robert Gibson, when they stated that yield capitalization models are DCF models.

This investigation of the factors explicitly considered in the income simulation models shows that the factors and the models can be used to analyze the activity witnessed in the market and to enable more documentation of the variation that must naturally exist in a market comprised of heterogeneous products with attributes of both real and financial assets.

§ 10.8 INCOME SIMULATION

The discussion to this point has suggested that the income approach is an acceptable approach for market simulation, if the emphasis is on the process of illustrating buyer behavior. In 1972, Ratcliff said that the income approach did not reflect market value and that it was a simulation approach in that it simulated investor behavior for income property. Land economists from Richard Ely (1922)[29] to James R. Markusen

[28] Roger E. Canaday and Peter Colwell, "A Unified Field Theory of the Income Approach to Appraisal—Parts 1, 2, and 3," *The Real Estate Appraiser and Analyst,* 47:1,2,3 (First Quarter; Summer; Fall 1981): 5–10; 29–43; 25–37. For another article addressing these points, see Robert A. Gibson, "Ellwood Is Discounted Cash Flow before Taxes," *The Appraisal Journal,* 54 (July 1986): 406–415.

[29] Richard T. Ely, *The Elements of Land Economics* (New York: McGraw-Hill, 1922).

(1979)[30] and Ko Wang (1990)[31] have used the income approach as the format for valuing real estate. The premise has been that value is the present worth of future benefits. The concern has been: is this an exchange value? Ratcliff was of the opinion that it is only a simulation. The income approach can be removed one step from the market for assets, because the income approach is not only an approximation of investors' actions; it is the simulation of one market for another. In the income approach, the distinct market for user space (the rental market) is used to illustrate values in the market for asset ownership. That is, data from the leasehold estate are used to measure a freehold estate. The freehold estate is the fee simple absolute estate represented by the general market value estimate. At best, only a leased fee estate is valued. Therefore, the value based on the analysis of leases and the capitalization of rental incomes is a simulation of a real asset's worth. The market for rental space is a separate and distinct market from the market for real assets. As such, there is an element of risk and an illusion of security in the valuation process, and these are not fully considered in the appraisal process. The introduction of risk into value estimation in the 1990s may be the major contribution to the process because it shows that a component of variation must be expected when comparing the demand for and supply of space as the basis for the value estimation of a real asset. No asset value can be measured directly, but, in the case of income real estate, a totally separate market unit of comparison—the rent paid for the use and possession of the space—is observed to arrive at the value of all the legal rights that comprise the asset.

The income approach as used in previous slow market experiences must be altered in current situations. These alterations require modifications and behavioral input. The models can be differentiated by the degree to which inputs are made explicit. The more explicit models allow for an increased ability to simulate buyer calculus. The change in emphasis in using the income models is accomplished with an improved understanding of consumer behavior and an awareness of the types of externalities that affect segmented real estate markets and the price

[30] James R. Markusen, "Elements of Real Asset Pricing: A Theoretical Analysis with Special Reference to Urban Land Prices," *Land Economics*, 55 (May 1979): 153–166.

[31] Ko Wang, Terry V. Grissom, and Su Hun Chan, "The Functional Relationships and Use of Going-In and Going-Out Capitalization Rates," *The Journal of Real Estate Research*, 5 (Summer 1990).

structures that develop. The use of the income models and the explicit expression of externalities that impact buyer behavior must reflect the underlying utility functions of the possible market participants. This reflection can be accomplished by profiling the probable buyer for a given property (or more specifically, a given set of property attributes). The simulation can be further improved by noting characteristics of the seller. In a behavioral format promulgated by DeLisle,[32] the following steps were suggested:

1. Identification of a need or needs of the parties involved (establishing the possible bargaining positions of the players);
2. Intention to purchase or sell (indicating probability of negotiation or transaction zone overlap);
3. Specification of evaluation criteria (choosing the appropriate valuation model);
4. Search for alternatives (comparing rentals, investments, properties, and so on);
5. Selection of alternatives;
6. Implementation of choice (reconciling information, data, and techniques);
7. Monitoring and feedback (testing value conclusions and models against market activity or performance).

This interfacing of consumer behavior research with the appraisal process prevents the income simulation from being only an application of investment models. In a recent experience concerning an apartment project, the subject property had a 10-year experience that reflected a 97 percent occupancy level. The current market rate of vacancies for comparable properties within the immediate area was 30 percent. The economic rent required on the appraisal form would have driven the net operating income (NOI) thousands of dollars below the actual NOI. Furthermore, since the subject was an older performing property, it tended to have a higher than normal maintenance expense and needed an allowance for reserves for replacement. The appraisers' use of the

[32] James. R. DeLisle, "Behavior Theory and Residential Appraisal," *The Appraisal Journal*, 53 (October 1985): 493–506.

low rents, combined with the higher actual expenses, penalized a quality property in a down market.

A higher-quality property that is penalized in a down market can still receive a premium over and above a market value, if the property has above-average management. According to the theory of distribution, the management contribution can be compensated based on the return generated to the property above and beyond the current market standard represented by a 30 percent vacancy. The market standard (30 percent, in this case) represents the loss in productivity of the property in the context of competitive properties. The analysis of the subject property, in comparison to the competitive properties, is guided by the principle of substitution: similar properties will trade at similar prices. Real estate, however, is management-intensive; the individuals involved with a parcel of property can make or break a property's value. However, as the difficult market times have illustrated, returns, if not values, are often influenced by the management teams controlling the property. The significance of these issues will become more apparent in the asset management skills that will be required of real estate professionals in the 1990s. For example, for many loans made during a prosperous market period, the value created by management skills was credited with contributing to the market value of the real estate. Application of the theory of distribution might have more clearly identified an appropriate allocation of compensation to the contributing factors of production. Entitlements to several properties resulted from contractual leases that created value over and above a fee simple interest. These contractual agreements were often the result of management, negotiating, and entrepreneurial skills, rather than property attributes. Appraisers often limit their analysis to the property's physical attributes, comparing the physical components to those of another property. The income simulation has to make these nonproperty aspects explicit. If it does not, it offers no more than the use of antiquated comparable sales.

The use of the income approach as a simulation tool is not limited to the estimation of a value. Because the constructs of many income models enable appraisers to make decision aspects explicit, the models can be turned around to gain information. An example is the concept of yield capitalization, discussed above. If the cap rate is implicitly composed of the yield rate and the expectations of property change over time, then previous rates from sales can be used to interpret investors'/buyers' expectations of the future. The derivation of market expectations of change is calculated as follows:

$$R_o = Y_o - \Delta_a$$

where:

R_o = overall cap rate derived from the most recent sales possible;
Y_o = overall before-tax yield desired at time of sale, based on market experience or on alternative investment opportunities;
Δ = change (percent) expected over the holding period;
a = annualizer that converts the total change over the holding period to an annual change

The cap rate formula can be turned around to isolate the expectations of change:

$$\Delta = \frac{Y_o - R_o}{a}$$

The abstraction of the expected annual change can be used to simulate the probable buyers' expectations of change in the market. These expectations can then be compared to actual performance or reconciled with current and projected economic data, to strengthen the appraiser's interpretation of the market.[33]

This universal or yield capitalization formula can be used to calculate the overall yield (Y_o) from cap rates, by reversing the formula to read: $Y_o = R_o + \Delta_a$. In this context, the yield is a historic measure of return or a retrogressive yield. The cap rates can only come from older sales, given the market environment that this chapter has addressed. The measure of annualized change (Δ_a) has to be derived from the observation of past sales. The annualized change (Δ_a) is the time adjustment extracted from previous transactions.

Even when comparables are available, most appraisals have to estimate value with the use of historical observations. In fact, most economic analysis can be compared with navigating by looking out the back window. Past data must be adjusted with a degree of economic logic, if data do not exist; hence the importance of value theory.

Y_o is the overall yield or discount rate that illustrates the cost of capital to the property. This capital cost can be all equity dollars, all

[33] Terry V. Grissom and Ko Wang, "Market Segmentation Using Capitalization Rates," Real Estate Center, Texas A&M University, Austin, Technical Report, August 1987.

debt, or a combination of both. Because Y_o is a measure of the cost of capital, and given a lack of current comparables, then the capital rate may have to be built up. This is where theory is directly applicable in the valuation process. The Akerson format for calculating the cap rate, discussed in detail in § 5.7, is illustrated below:

$$\begin{array}{lll} M \times R_M & = MR_M & \text{(the weighted equity position)} \\ +(1-M) \times Y_E & = +(1-M)Y_E & \text{(the weighed debt position)} \\ \underline{-\ M \times P \times SFF} & = \underline{-\ MPSFF} & \text{(the return from mortgage amortization)} \\ = Y_o & = Y_o & \end{array}$$

where:

M = loan-to-value ratios (can be obtained from lending institutions)
R_M = mortgage constant rates (based on current interest rate and available financing terms; information can be obtained from financial institutions)
Y_E = equity yield rate
P = percentage of mortgage to be paid off during forecasted holding period
SFF = sinking fund factor at the Y_E rate; used to annualize the equity build-up because of mortgage amortization

This formula can also be turned around, using the cap rates from older sales, to estimate the equity yield desired in the past or to abstract the actual yield derived on previous transactions. Given that:

$$Y_o = R_o + \Delta_a$$

the reversed formula is:

$$Y_E = \frac{Y_o + MPSFF - MR_M}{1 - M}$$

The difficulties with this format are that the sinking fund is based on an unknown yield rate, and R_o and Δ_a are abstracted from the market, which is comprised of old sales. This format is only preferable to using comparables adjusted for time because of the theory that the cap rate is constant over time and that the expectations abstracted illustrate a future perspective that may include the current market period. The dynamics of the market may make this approach useless, despite its technical appearance. Ellwood offered a similar technique that could be used in inactive or stable markets—those with no expectation of appreciation or depreciation in overall value. Again, the format is dependent on past transactions and is calculated as follows:

$$DA = \frac{R_o}{I} - 1$$

where:

DA = Differential additive; as termed by Ellwood, the ratio difference between the return to the overall property and the return on the debt
I = Nominal interest rate

The differential additive is then used to calculate the equity yield, using the following formula:

$$Y_E = \frac{DA + (1 - M)}{(1 - M)} \text{ (I)}$$

Where:

Y_E = Equity yield, which may be equated to an equity dividend, given no expectations of appreciation in terminal value

An example would be a property with a cap rate of 10 percent, an interest rate of 8.5 percent, and a loan-to-value ratio of 75 percent. If M = .75, then 1 – M = .25 and:

$$DA = \frac{.10}{.085} - 1$$

$$= .176471$$

Then:

$$Y_E = \frac{.176471 + .25}{.25(.085)}$$

$$= .145$$

As each of the models illustrates, historic yields can be calculated, but they need to be adjusted to reflect current economic conditions, to arrive at an appropriate measure to use in the current market. An alternative process enlists the principle of substitution, in looking at alternative capital market investments. Alternative investment yields can be tracked through a number of sources—publications of the Board of Governors of the Federal Reserve, especially *The Federal Reserve Historical Chart Book,* which gives information on stock and bond interest rates and mortgage interest rates; *The Wall Street Journal*; *Barron's*; and other general financial publications. Specialized publications that furnish information on returns to real estate include *The Frank Russell Index, Pension World, RERC Trends,* and information services available through accounting and real estate firms such as Kenneth Leventhal, Price Waterhouse, Landeauer, Peat Marwick, Real Estate Research, and Cushman and Wakefield. Data gathered from these general sources of capital market activity can be compared to releases circulated by local bank and thrift activities, noninstitutional lenders, and international activities. The estimation of alternative yields, cap rates, and capital returns that reflect investors' options and desires will benefit from this research. The comparison of previous periods' yield rates to current rates (both available from these services) enables the appraiser to maintain an updated schedule of the rates used in real estate transactions during various time segments.

Another useful method for documenting desired yields, cap rates, and lenders' terms is to survey local or probable buyer types as to their desired or expected returns. The publications listed above tend to use this method. Their national or regional findings can be compared to those on local investors/buyers. Furthermore, expected returns can be compared and contrasted to the historical returns abstracted, for an indication of economic changes and a measure of risk. The survey can also be used to document perceptions of risk among various property types. If there are no current sales, then the transaction process itself must be simulated.

Emphasis on the simulation of market behavior, using the income approach in a down market or in any market that is lacking in comparables, has resulted from several experiences:

1. It allows explicit consideration of buyer and seller behavior;
2. It allows explicit analysis of the property over time;
3. It explicitly considers the economics of the property;
4. It allows accessible data in an inactive market (people need space and will rent even when they cannot buy).

§ 10.9 LAND VALUATION

The valuation of vacant land is identified most strongly with the direct sales comparison approach. In general, land has no reproduction cost and usually does not rent if it is vacant (pasture use is limited in most urban areas). How can land be valued in a market that has limited or nonexistent comparables, such as a down or overbuilt market?

The Appraisal of Real Estate, published by AIREA, indicates five procedures, other than the sales comparison approach, for valuing raw land. They are:

1. Ground rent capitalization
2. Subdivision development
3. Allocation
4. Extraction
5. Land residual

The first technique is as direct as the sales comparison approach: the rent received for the use of the land is capitalized into a value. The problem is that current data are as difficult to obtain as sales in a down market. Adjustments to prior returns may be suspect as large adjustments to prior sales. However, the technique can be useful because economic rents can be calculated and discount rates, if not cap rates, can be built up.

The subdivision development method has been heavily applied in recently active markets, to enable financing of proposed projects. Its use in a down market has to be carefully scrutinized because the absorption period will be long and the discount rate must reflect the risk in an overbuilt market. This technique can be applied in limited markets. As an example, evaluation was needed for a large acreage tract in an area in which the terrain prevented direct comparables. The neighborhood had several lot sales, but no large-tract sales. Based on the values of lots and a tracking of market activity over time, a subdivision plan was developed on the subject site. The costs of development were deducted over time, and the revenues were discounted to arrive at the contributory value of the land. The subdivision development method is based on the theory of distribution, discussed earlier.

The allocation or abstraction method is based on a comparison with an active, comparable neighborhood or with trends observed over time. Allocation can be established based on the principles of balance and contribution (distribution). These principles state that the land component makes up a certain percentage of a property's value. This percentage is applied to the overall value, to arrive at the land value. Appropriate amounts for profit and overhead must be deducted (as in the subdivision development method), to arrive at the logically documented land value. The problem with this technique in a down market is that it extrapolates trends from the past. Like the market approach, this extrapolation is subject to criticism because the relationships may have changed. The method also depends, in some cases, on an active market for improved properties. Given that requirement, this method can often be used in the early phases of a down market.

Extraction is a variant of the allocation method. The land value is calculated by deducting the contribution of the improvements from the sales price of an improved property. This method is difficult in a down market, except in the early phase, given that raw land tract transactions curtail before improved property sales.

The land residual technique, an income approach, is a useful valuation technique in a market with limited sales. It illustrates the advantages of the income technique in a down market, and it is useful in a market of limited activity because it addresses the basic economics of land value. To have value, land must have a use. The land residual method quantitatively tests the highest and best use alternatives of any given site. Because of the economic flexibility of land, alternative uses can be conducted on any site. The model traditionally allocates the rent of the proposed use to the improvements (allowing for a reasonable return); the remaining income is then attributed to the land and capitalized into a land value. An improvement on the traditional model is the consideration of the capital structure in the context of the land residual model. The integration of the capital structure into the traditional land residual model is linked to the development of the market revenue investment (MRI) technique or the financial feasibility model.[34]

As an example, a site to be appraised is in a market that has had no comparable sales for two years. The area is experiencing moderate transition. The analysis of the physical and legal information suggests the development of a free-standing retail building. This use is supported by the income and demographic profiles of the neighborhood. There are limited retail facilities in the immediate neighborhood. Many of the retail purchases by local residents are conducted in other areas of the city.

[34] Two sources that develop this model are Terry V. Grisson, "Appraisal Models and the Feasibility Process," *The Appraisal Journal*, 64 (April 1986): 214–224; and Stephen A. Pyhrr and James Cooper, *Real Estate Investment, Strategy, Analysis, Decisions* (Boston: Warren, Gorham, & Lamont, 1982): 256–260.

The site can support a 20,000-square-foot building with a net leasable area (NLA) of 18,000 square feet. The currently documented comparable rental in the area is $15 per square foot of NLA. The following information is available for the proposed structure:

PGI = potential gross income, or rent at 100 percent occupancy; rent is $15 per square foot for 18,000 square feet, or $270,000

VR = vacancy (VAC) rate; market shows a 5 percent rate, or $13,500, for the subject building; VAC = PGI × VR

OE = operating expenses; estimated at $3.50 per square foot (NLA), or $63,000, based on the investigation of several comparable rental properties

DCR = debt coverage ratio; 1.2 from local lenders

NOI = net operating income; NOI = PGI − VAC − OE

DS = debt service or $\frac{\text{PGI} - \text{VAC} - \text{OE}}{\text{DCR}}$

CTO = cash throw-off to equity, or NOI − DS

Using the above information, the income flows to the debt and equity components of the project can be estimated:

$$\text{DS} = \frac{\$270{,}000 - \$13{,}500 - \$63{,}000}{1.2} = \$161{,}250$$

$$\text{CTO} = \$193{,}500 - \$161{,}250 = \$32{,}250$$

The capital flows are now placed within the value model, given the following information:

R_M = mortgage constant of .12343, 12 percent payable monthly, 30-year amortization

R_E = equity dividend of 6 percent, derived from comparable investment alternatives that offer a cash on cash return (Treasury bonds, money markets, etc.); the recapture of the investment is to be separately calculated in the resale of the property

The model takes the form of:

$$JV_o = JV_M + JV_E$$

where:

$$JV_o = \text{Total project investment value}$$

$$JV_M = \text{Justified mortgage value or } \frac{DS}{R_M}$$

$$JV_E = \text{Justified equity value or } \frac{CTO}{R_E}$$

$$JV_o = \frac{\$161{,}250}{.12343} + \frac{\$32{,}250}{.06} = \$1{,}843{,}908 \text{ (rounded to } \$1{,}845{,}000)$$

The land value is estimated by deducting the cost of the proposed improvements from the justified investment value. The cost of the proposed improvements was $1 million (20,000 square feet at $50 per square foot):

$$V_L = JV_o - V_c$$

where:

$$V_L = \text{land value}$$
$$V_c = \text{cost of proposed improvements}$$
$$V_L = \$1{,}845{,}000 - \$1{,}000{,}000 = \$845{,}000$$

The land value is estimated to be $845,000, based on the proposed highest and best use. With a lot size of 42,250 square feet, the price per square foot is $20. Sales from two years ago indicated prices around $27 per square foot. This would indicate a 25.9 percent decrease in the market of the site.

This method simulates the investment calculus of probable investors and explicitly considers the economics of the land in a market context that is subject to institutional constraints during any given decision period. If the institutional parameters and constraints change, the value estimate of the property changes. This relationship is a business and financial risk concern that is not usually considered in a traditional appraisal based on past sales. In the proposed model, alternative rates (DCR, R_M, R_E, and other variables) can be considered. The consideration of these variables and the resulting value estimates will reflect the uncertainty of estimating values in a market of limited transactions, underscore the application of the principle of substitution to factors other than sales, and enable decision makers to consider a range of rational concerns and their possible effect on the value and operation of a property. Continuing with the example, a change in the DCR to 1.5 from the current 1.2 guideline would lower the DS to $129,000 and, consequently, would raise the CTO to $64,500. The value estimate would then be $2,120,000, or about a 15 percent variation from the estimate using the more liberal lending policies. This approach assumes that the lender is the only participant that may identify a change in the economy. If the lender increases the debt coverage ratio, the action may be representative of an expectation of increased risk from investing in this property type. The equity investors may have the same perception or expectation. If the equity investors respond and the equity dividend is raised to reflect the risk loading to, say, 8 percent, then the value will remain constant at approximately $1,845,000. If only the lender alters the rates because of activities in the capital markets, the signal to the appraiser may be that syndications are the evolving financing/ownership vehicle. The value estimate may be secondary to an understanding of the market structure and players—a factor that should improve the forecasting or interpretive abilities of the appraiser or decision maker.

Many appraisals of raw land observed during the current down market have identified the highest and best use of the land to be for speculative holding or future development. For appraisals, past sales are then used and discounted for long marketing terms. The residual technique, if not acceptable as a valuation method, can at least function as a test of the reality of future development. Many alternative use scenarios in a down market illustrate negative values.

As in the appraisal of improved properties in a down market, land valuation must emphasize the analysis of the process as an aid to decisions. The emphasis of the appraisal is not on the estimation of value alone.

§ 10.10 COST APPROACH

Graaskamp has asserted that there is not an equivalence among the three approaches to value; they are a hierarchy of valuation techniques.[35] He identifies the market approach as a matter of direct inference, if the objective is to estimate the probable selling price. He agrees with Ratcliff that the income approach is only a simulation of market

[35] James A. Graaskamp, *The Appraisal of 25 North Pinckney: A Demonstration Case for Contemporary Appraisal Methods* (Madison, WI: Landmark Research, Inc., 1977).

activity, and declares the cost approach to be a normative approach for estimating value. "Normative" implies that the cost approach is not a realistic or practical method of estimating value, but is an authoritative standard that serves to guide, control, or regulate proper appraisal procedure. This normative role evolved from the neoclassic valuation theory, which stated that, in the long run, "normal" value tends to equate to normal cost. This equating of the theories of value and distribution says that, in the long run, cost is the measure of value because it considers a return to all the factors of production. Furthermore, the productive factors will not be placed in the development of certain assets unless all of them receive an adequate return—at least in the long run.

As traditionally applied, the cost approach failed to reflect this theoretical premise; only physical or material capital and land were considered as cost components. The financial capital and entrepreneurial returns were not considered.[36] Concern for the consideration of developers' profit and its appropriate measurement has been a recent outgrowth of the financial regulatory agencies.[37]

The speculative and stagnant markets of the 1980s introduced a scrutiny of the cost approach that runs contrary to the thinking of the 1930s and is more conceptually aware of value theory than the thinking in the 1970s. As a measure of value based on the theory of distribution, the cost approach has been incomplete. The need to introduce the various forms of depreciation into the calculation, thereby enabling cost to approximate value, has made this approach ineffectual in many ways. In certain periods of the 1970s and 1980s, it was necessary to calculate extensive measures of external obsolescence, which was attributed to the general state of the economy. External obsolescence (or locational or economic obsolescence, as it was once called) should be specific to the property and not the result of general externalities. Its application will be used in the analysis of properties and markets in the 1990s. Economic obsolescence will become an adjustment to offset the difference between high cost measures and low market prices. It must be used to offset the developer's (or entrepreneur's) profit.

In the context of market value, the place of cost analysis is to support the economic logic of the market transactions. Cost analysis can

[36] Two articles by Kahn address the issue of factor return within the cost approach. Sanders A. Kahn, "The Entrepreneur—The Missing Factor," *The Appraisal Journal,* 31 (October 1963): 472–476 and "The Entrepreneur Revisited," *The Appraisal Journal,* 41 (January 1973): 113–118.

[37] Based on discussions with James Crow and Roger Tegenkamp, who were with the Federal Home Loan Bank at the time of the discussion.

even be used for market segmentation and the determination of probable uses. Cost estimations reflect the capital outlay that is required for an asset, but this is not the asset's value. The cost is the basis for a feasibility measure and can be used to illustrate the impact of future competition. Cost is the basis of the supply curve or competition measure in the market analysis. The relationship of current transaction prices or investment value to a cost measure is indicative of the cost of capital and of the cost of additional supply in the market. A comparison of cost to value can be used to influence the probability of new construction. In essence, a cost measure is not value or a value approximation. It can be used to aid market analysis and to test the economics of various market situations. This is not to say that cost is not appropriate or even necessary in the context of estimating value in use or as a market value proxy for special-purpose properties. The problem is: How can cost be used as a proxy for value in exchange, in a general market context?

§ 10.11 CONCLUSIONS

Appraising without the benefit of comparables has been a dilemma since the infancy of the appraisal process. Both time and location may be involved. Rural areas, the developing suburban fringe, small towns, and inner cities in transition are often the locations with no comparables. The time is either a period of speculation and rapid growth or one of down, depressed markets. Many currently active segments of the United States are expected to be heading toward down markets, because of overbuilding and liquidity problems.

During the slow economic periods of the 1930s and 1970s, emphasis was placed on variations of the cost and income approaches. The ability to achieve alternative forms of valuation is linked to an understanding of value and valuation theory. The theoretical underpinnings of the appraisal process, if properly understood, enable the direct incorporation of economic logic (both market analysis and feasibility analysis) into the appraisal process.

The history of down markets has revealed that the essence of the situation is to make an economic decision. If the information on sales is not available to directly address the problem, then emphasis must be placed on the analysis contained within the appraisal process itself. Estimation of a value is not the only concern; the analysis of the situation must also be documented. Because the artifact of the sales price is not available in all times and areas, the process by which the price would have been established must appear in the appraisal instead. The transaction price is simulated. Each of the down markets has emphasized the income approach to varying degrees. The support for this method in each period was that people buy in a down market because they have expectations of future benefits. The principle of anticipation, the heart of the income approach, can be explicitly identified to varying degrees in the income techniques.

When the direct information contained in sales is not available, the appropriate procedures for simulating the market are the techniques that most explicitly elaborate the criteria involved in the possible purchase decision and/or the method that best resembles the decision process of the probable buyer. To achieve these insights, the appraiser must profile the probable buyers for a specific property or the buyers who best match up as purchasers of particular sets of property attributes.

Because simulation is the best method (without comparable sales), appraisers must develop market insights. These insights can be achieved by constructing a thorough data base, which will require collecting and observing sales and rents (and cost) over time. The data from the past can indicate the preferences for various attributes and the differentials paid at different times. These indications from various market segments can be modified to comply with different economic phases. Perhaps the approach to take is to first analyze the market data (rents, sales, and so on) and then consider the economic and regional factors that alter the status quo. As an example, probable selling prices of houses would decline if interest rates were to increase.

Interest rate forecasts are readily available, but development of a thorough data base has been lacking in real estate investment and appraisal. Traditionally, appraisal and investment analysis has been practiced as an ad hoc process: one appraiser solves one problem for one particular property in the short term. Appraisal in the future must be a matter of ongoing economic and market analysis; trends and cycles are different, and both are constantly in motion. The ability to appraise during periods of limited comparables must be guided with a broad view. Preparation, the key to a professional approach, can be learned from W. C. Fields. When asked by a friend why he kept one entire room of his house filled from floor to ceiling with cases of gin, he stated, "Prohibition caught me once, it won't catch me again."

Eleven

Financial Decisions and Asset Management in a Down Market

§ 11.1 INTRODUCTION

This chapter introduces two general models to help real estate professionals work out difficulties with problem properties. The first model is a mortgage instrument termed the inside-outside wraparound. The second model suggests an alternative to the traditional valuation process used in the loan underwriting industry and is offered to aid in solving the collateralization problem of equating financial contracts to property values.

The presentation of these two models is in the context of two case studies that are based on actual consulting experiences.

Although the models proposed are practical models, the basis for their development is theoretical. When Adam Smith developed a theory of value, he also developed a parallel theory of distribution. The theory of value is basically concerned with explaining why an object has worth; the theory of distribution is concerned with the recognition and pricing of returns to the various factors of production. The delineation of these factors and of their returns has evolved over time. The current theory of distribution considers the determination of:

1. *Rents* to land and other resources
2. *Wages* to various kinds of labor
3. *Interest rates* on capital assets
4. *Profits* as a return to entrepreneurship and risk taking.[1]

§ 11.2 PROBLEM AND APPROACH

Understanding the link between the theory of value and the theory of distribution enables an alternative approach to dealing with the current economy. Valuation cannot get around the fact that a good's price is determined by what someone will pay. However, a circular process exists between the two theories: the worth of a commodity is influenced, in part, by the cost of producing it, and the allocation of factors of production to a specific good is influenced by the price someone will pay. This means that the price (cost) of the factors of production influences the price asked, if not paid, for a commodity. At the same time, the price of the factors of production is influenced by the general market of producers competing for the productive resource.

The implications of the related theories are: (1) because the perceived return to real estate is high, a site gets developed; and (2) a site must be developed because a high price is paid, based on expected returns in a competitive market.

The drive to produce the real estate forces up the price of construction labor, architectural fees, materials, the interest rate, and so on. Because the costs of capital and other goods are high, the return and the value estimate of the real estate are often high.

The relationship of the commodity to the factors of production holds, if supply and demand for the goods in all markets are in equilibrium. Smith recognized this as possible in the long run. He called this long-run value the "natural price."[2] Today, it is called market value.

The problem is that, in any given period, supply and demand for the commodity and the factors of production may not be in equilibrium.

[1] Paul A. Samuelson, *Economics* (New York: McGraw-Hill, 1967): 509.

[2] Adam Smith, *The Wealth of Nations* (Indianapolis: Bobbs-Merrill, 1961): 44–52. This is a paperback reissue; the original printing was in 1776.

This disequilibrium is represented by a short-term market price that may be above or below the long-term market value.

This is the general nature of the problem currently facing many parcels of real estate. There may be an oversupply of many types of properties but there is an undersupply of available financial capital. The uncoupling of these two previously related assets has led to insolvency and an erosion of value.

In practice, the value erosion can be rectified with creative valuation and policy or with "accounting book" procedures. The real return of the asset's value is not possible until the market turns around. What is needed in the interim is a structure for the relationship between the real estate and contractual debt that will allow solvency to be achieved.

A schematic of many current real estate problems is illustrated in Figure 11.1, which represents the value situation over time. In time 1, a value or purchase price (V_o) is set in the market. This overall value sets the basis for the initial debt and equity positions (V_M and V_E respectively). Over time, two things occur, as depicted in time 2. The first occurrence is the pay-down of the mortgage to position V_b. The second occurrence involves three possible situations (in a down market, all three situations consider a loss of value). The first situation is a

Figure 11.1 Resale Scenarios in a Down Market

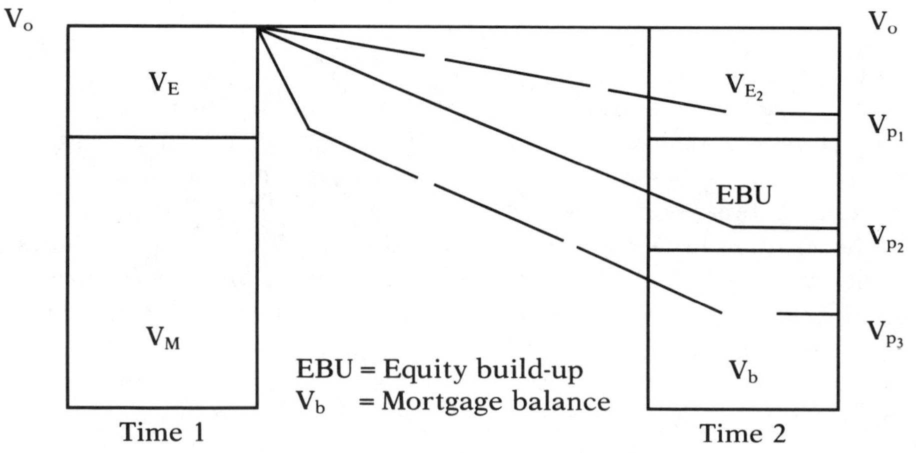

V_o = Purchase price
V_M = Original mortgage value
V_E = Original equity value

V_{P_1} = Resale: V_E remaining
V_{P_2} = Resale: EBU remaining
V_{P_3} = Resale: less than V_b

drop in the current market price to V_{P_1}. This price drop involves a loss in original equity—a problem for the owner only at the time of resale. The lenders may be concerned with default, given the decline of the loan-to-value ratio, or with the failure to comply with regulatory requirements of loan-to-asset or collateral ratios.

The second situation involves a decline to V_{P_2}. There is further erosion of the original equity and a partial loss occurs in the equity build-up component of the investment. The lenders still have the same concerns, but the potential for default may now depend on whether the value decline is at a more rapid rate than the amortization rate of the mortgage pay-down. If so, the investor's best option is not to expose the property to the market.

The final situation is depicted by V_{P_3}. All equity components have eroded, and a portion of the debt position is lost. Any attempt at resale in the market depicted by V_{P_3} will result in an inability to repay the mortgage balance due at sale, unless the seller has other sources of liquid capital. In all three situations, the current market price is a problem only if the owner decides to sell. If no sale is contemplated, the value erosion is only a "book" loss.

The best advice in a down market is not to sell. Unfortunately, in a down market, people are forced to sell for various reasons (loss of jobs, financial overextension, decline in income, and so on). The problem is basically the inability to make the debt payments because of a lack of personal income, for owner-occupied residential property, or insufficient rental returns, for income properties. Both are usually the result of an imbalance between supply and demand. Foreclosure does not occur until payments are missed. Unfortunately, lenders will not negotiate as long as payments are being made, and when the payments are no longer being made, institutional constraints prevent many problems from being worked out.

Eventually, institutional and bureaucratic constraints may be alleviated, but usually not until there are many dead bodies and the real problem is delineated. A current general problem is the difference between the outstanding mortgage balance (V_b) and the lower market price (V_p) less selling expenses. (See Figure 11.1, time 2.) This difference would be the deficiency at the time of the foreclosure sale, or the unsecured debt if the lenders choose to work out the problem.

The problem in a work-out is to overcome insolvency. If markets are rational, an assumption that the V_p is based on the current rental for that type of property is acceptable. The rental supporting a value of V_p would be below the existing debt service.

The issue is to determine how the unsecured debt contract (the uncollateralized portion of the current mortgage balance) can be worked out to achieve solvency. Mechanically, there is a need to amortize the difference between the mortgage balance (V_b) and the market price (V_p). The point is to allow the borrower to do this over time.

§ 11.3 SUGGESTED MORTGAGE MODEL

The suggested mortgage model is called the inside-outside wraparound mortgage. The model involves the wrapping of the uncollateralized debt difference between the current market price and the outstanding mortgage balance. The terms can be linked to the current market's interest rates for mortgages and unsecured personal or business loans. The market has shown that the price of realty varies over time; it is not unreasonable, therefore, to expect the return on the related debt capital to fluctuate accordingly. Lenders have accepted this premise on the up side with variable rate mortgages, income participation, and equity kickers. It is justifiable to accept the premise on the down side. The premise involves the nature of business and market risk.

The terms could be as follows; the mortgage on the real estate can go at the current lowest mortgage rate, based on the remaining or current mortgage term. The lowest rate is justified because the real estate is at or near the bottom of its down cycle. Therefore, little or no value erosion is expected to continue, and down-side risk is at a minimum (unless the property is saddled with a negative amortizing mortgage; in this case, the solvency actions are all the more important). Because the real estate is at a currently expected base value, a nonrecourse loan could be extended (if the real estate's income is not perceived as appropriate to carry the loan, the loan as it was structured should have not been made in the first place). The amount of this loan is determined by either the market price at a high loan-to-value ratio, or the current contract rental less allowances for operating expenses. The V_p is modified to V_{PM} if there is not a net lease arrangement. With a net lease arrangement, all rent can go to the debt service.

Wrapped around this collateralized real estate loan is an uncollateralized business or personal loan. This loan is for the amount of the difference between the outstanding mortgage balance and a mortgage based on the current market price ($V_b - V_{PM}$). This loan should also be for the balance of the original mortgage term or the equivalent current term. The interest rate charged should be commensurate with the rate on longer-term business and personal loans. The rate can vary with the lender's risk perception of the borrower. Because this debt is not collateralized, it should seek recourse against the borrower's nonexempt assets.

(a) MORTGAGE CASE

An income property originally valued at $175,000 and mortgaged for $131,250 has an outstanding mortgage balance (V_b) of $130,006.35 at the end of 1.5 years. The existing obligation is at 9.5 percent. The original mortgage term was 30 years. The mortgage, based on the current rental or market price (V_{PM}), is $100,000. The V_{PM} loan is amortized at a rate of 8.5 percent for 28.5 years. The difference leaves an unsecured debt of $30,006.35. The unsecured loan is charged a 12 percent rate for the remaining 28.5-year period of the original mortgage. A 10-year period is projected before the turnaround is expected. The periodic payments and yield to the lender are calculated as follows:

Loan Class	Amount	Yearly Cash Flows during Term	Percentage Change	Cash at Balance
Unsecured	$ 30,006.35	$ 3,724.69	7.92%	$ 27,630.60
Mortgage	100,000.00	9,335.12	13.09	86,906.78
Total or Percentage	$130,006.35	$13,059.81	11.90%	$114,537.38

The effective annual yield to the lender is 9.27 percent. This is higher than the current mortgage yield of 8.5 percent and approximates the rate of 9.5 percent of the original loan. The wrap also limits a down-side potential loss to the lender. The potential loss is the $30,006.35 of existing debt over the current market price. The likely or actual loss is the difference between the original yield and the effective wrap yield (9.5% – 9.27%), applied to the original loan amount of $130,006.35.

The loss is:

$$(.095 - .0927) \times \$130{,}006.35 = \$2{,}990.01 \text{ per year}$$

Discounted at the opportunity cost of 9.5 percent, the bank loss is $18,773.70. The possible loss via the wrap is less than the known loss at foreclosure, so this is a rational tool for lenders.

The $18,773.70 is still only a possible loss to the lender because, as the market improves, at the end of 10 years the loan can be linked back to the real estate. This linkage can be conducted like a refinancing effort (with the hope that many of the bogus administrative charges are not applied).

The underwriting position is that, in 10 years, the property will be worth $155,000. This future value represents only a 4.5 percent straight-line increase per year or a 4.48 percent per year compounding increase. The value in 10 years may not reach the previous high market price of $175,000, but the property value easily supports the outstanding mortgage balance of $114,537.38. The loan balance is only 73.9 percent of the expected future value.

(b) BENEFITS OF INSIDE–OUTSIDE WRAPAROUND MORTGAGE

Although there are institutional constraints against the proposed model, the efforts to alter those restrictions are more than offset by the benefits. The borrower is relieved of a heavy personal liability. The personal monthly debt carried by the borrower is reduced from $1,103.62 to $310.39. The $310.39 may still be painful to the borrower in a down market, but the payment is more feasible and less subject to default than the higher debt service payment.

The lender, as indicated above, reduces the risk of default, reduces the eventuality of foreclosure, retains an active loan, minimizes the loss, and actively defers the possibility of a loss.

Both the lender and the borrower remain solvent and in business.

§ 11.4 VALUATION/UNDERWRITING MODEL

The theory of distribution also enables an alternative process for evaluating and underwriting realty. As with the wrap loan, many real estate problems are multileveled. By looking at each layer of the problem and thus creating an alternative perspective of the collateral, several "assets" can be identified as being potentially involved in any given real estate deal.

Lenders have traditionally dealt with the varying risk contingencies of a real estate loan. These contingencies may, in essence, be considered as different factors, resources, assets, or commodities themselves, and they may have contributory values and risk levels that differ from the real estate product. Lumping a composite asset into one residual product may explain why many people in financial distress often expected to be bailed out by the real property.

An example of this misperception is a clothing store business that failed. The business owners counted on selling the converted residence in which the store was located for enough to pay off all the debt. The real estate was not sufficient collateral. The real assets covered the mortgage. Some equity in the real estate was available to pay some of the business debt.

In periods of inflation, reliance on real estate (although irrational) may not be an unreasonable practice. In the current down market, this has become a fatal practice, leading to a dumping of properties on the market, often through the foreclosure process.

The proposed alternative valuation and underwriting process requires the identification of the appropriate assets and the assets' operating risk level. The following case study is offered as an application of the theory of distribution. As a twist on the distressed example of the wrap mortgage, the valuation case involves the refinancing of a successful property that is penalized by institutional procedure in a down market.

The property is an apartment complex located near a major state university. It has had a successful occupancy rate of 98 percent for a proven 10-year operating history. Two of the good operating years have occurred in a distressed economic period. By appraisal standards (especially in order to fit the Fannie Mae form), the property must be compared to various market standards (one standard is a market vacancy of 33 percent), and the property must be appraised using a concept of market or economic rent (the contract or actual rent has been above the market level for the past four years).

A factor in the success of the project has been its high standard of maintenance and repair, which has resulted in above-market operating expenses and reserves for replacement. Despite the fact that economic rents are used in appraisal, appraisers often weigh the actual expenses over market standards (if they are higher), perceiving a problem with the property or its management. The net result of using a market standard for rent and an above-market standard for expenses is a lower net operating income (NOI) than may actually exist. This is a problem when determining the property's value for loan purposes, because the lender often uses a debt coverage ratio as the decision criterion on the loan. The debt coverage ratio bases the amount of financing on the ability of the property's income to carry the periodic debt.[3]

The guidelines of the traditional approach reduce the income solvency and the value. The reduced solvency lowers the basis for refinancing the property. The result is that a property with superior performance is penalized in the financial and real estate markets.

[3] Wayne E. Etter, "Evaluating an Income Property," Real Estate Research Center, Texas A&M University, Austin, Technical Report (June 1988): 3.

Traditional appraisal or underwriting is based on the concepts of "typical or average" management, expenses, performance, and so on. These assumptions of mediocrity are rational in terms of seeking a conservative picture of any decision situation. But a conservative picture may not be an appropriate objective. Perhaps the objective should be: What is the actual situation or problem? In terms of the case study, an appropriate inquiry is why the property is performing better than the market. The theory of distribution can aid this inquiry. Distribution enables an investigation of all the levels that make up a property—or, more correctly, a business enterprise.

Babcock, in developing valuation techniques in the 1930s, established seven methods (see § 10.4(a)). He delineated between properties that are income properties and properties that are used in the production of an income. The latter category necessitates that the business profits be allocated between real estate and the business.[4] In Babcock's taxonomy, an apartment was classified as an income property; it is a property generating a return for the privilege of space occupancy. In the allocation technique of realty used in the production of an income, he gave an example of a movie theater, where the space use is more like a license to participate in an activity but the real estate is still an integral part of the business.

This apparent digression on the relationship of real estate to the activities housed is necessary for an understanding of why one property is performing better than the market (especially a down market). The success can be traced to the development of a monopoly perception for any given property. Attributes of a specific enterprise are recognized as unique, in an otherwise competitive market. Monopoly in real estate is often established by its location. In this case, comparable analysis revealed no locational pattern of preference. No physical property attributes other than maintenance could be identified to explain consumers' preference for the subject property.

A second explanation for superior performance is that the property is perceived as a monopoly because the project is being marketed as something more than space. In this case, the management was selling a concept of life-style associated with tenancy. The life-style was not a cost factor for management but resulted from the congregation of students; a social experience was being offered. The life-style was a commodity

[4] Frederick M. Babcock, *The Valuation of Real Estate* (New York: McGraw-Hill, 1932): 168–174.

over and above the shelter offered by the property. It was not a cost, because the management offered limited recreational events.

A monopoly may be the result of superior marketing and management. If this is the case, then the traditional appraisal form is limited. The superior returns may not be solely related to real estate; they may be the result of management or entrepreneurial effort. If this is the case, then comparison based on the assumption of average management is inappropriate to the problem situation.

The implications of an alternative perspective of the problem are illustrated by the analysis of the example property under a traditional appraisal format and a format considering the theory of distribution.

§ 11.5 VALUATION AND UNDERWRITING

There are several different models for the valuation of a property. Each approach is examined now in turn.

(a) TRADITIONAL APPRAISAL APPROACH

The property, located near a large university, has 103 units containing a leasable area of 51,500 square feet. The actual rental return averages about $.65 per square foot. The typical return to the comparables in the area is $.53. Typical vacancy in the area is 33 percent. The subject is 2 percent vacant. The subject has an expense ratio of 50 percent of gross income. Five percent of the gross is allocated to management. The management return is included in the 50 percent expense ratio. The market trend is 4 percent for management, out of a total of 38 percent for the overall property expenses. The debt coverage ratio (DCR) for refinancing is 1.2, the interest rate is 9.5 percent monthly, and the amortization term is 25 years. A desired equity dividend is 6 percent (cash on cash return).

Based on the synthesis of the subject and market data, the following value is estimated for the subject property:

Gross income: 51,500 sq. ft. @ $.55 per sq. ft. per month × 12	$339,900
Less: Vacancy and credit allowance of 20%	67,980
Effective gross income	271,920
Less: Expenses at 43% of Gross income (GI)	146,157
Net operating income (NOI)	$125,763

The financing and market value are determined as follows:

$$\text{Debt service (DS)} = \frac{\text{NOI}}{\text{DCR}}$$

$$= \frac{\$125,763}{1.2}$$

$$= \$104,802.50$$

The debt service divided by the mortgage constant (capitalization rate of the debt component) equals the amount of the possible refinancing mortgage. The mortgage constant (R_M) can be found in any set of mortgage tables or developed with a financial calculator. R_M is based on monthly payments of 9.5 percent interest, amortizing over a 25-year period.

The mortgage constant is .104844. The refinanced loan amount (V_M) is:

$$V_M = \frac{\text{DS}}{R_M}$$

$$= \frac{\$104,802.50}{.104844}$$

$$= \$999,607.99$$

The equity amount is:

NOI − DS = CTO (cash throw-off or equity income)
$123,763.00 − $104,802.50 = $20,960.50

$$\text{Equity amount} = \frac{\text{CTO}}{\text{Re}}$$

$$= \frac{\$20,960.50}{.06}$$

$$= \$349,341.66$$

The value of the property based on a traditional analysis is:

Debt amount	$ 999,607.99
Equity amount	349,341.66
Market value	$1,348,949.65 (rounded to $1,350,000)

(b) ALTERNATIVE MODEL—REAL ESTATE MARKET VALUE

The suggested valuation technique involves two income appraisal analyses: a straight market appraisal without the judgmental modifiers used in the traditional approach, and a technique that is property-specific. The property-specific technique approximates an accounting or investment analysis approach.

The market approach would establish the basis of the property that must be the competitive worth of the asset in an oversupplied or down market. The investment analysis investigates the actual performance of the subject property and implicitly considers the contribution of management (or any other special attribute unique to a property). A comparison of the two approaches enables a test of the property's performance against the current market situation.

The straight market worth is delineated first:

Gross income: 51,500 sq. ft.	
@ $.53 per sq. ft. per month × 12	$327,540.00
Less: Vacancy @ 33%	108,088.20
Effective gross income	219,451.80
Less: Expenses @ 38% of GI	124,465.20
Net operating income (NOI)	$ 94,986.60

The financing for the real estate is:

$$\text{DS} = \frac{\text{NOI}}{\text{DCR}}$$

$$= \frac{\$94{,}986.60}{1.2}$$

$$= \$79{,}155.50$$

$$\text{Mortgage amount} = \frac{\text{DS}}{R_M}$$

$$= \frac{\$79{,}155.50}{.104844}$$

$$= \$754{,}983.59$$

The equity value is:

$$NOI - DS = CTO$$

$$\$94{,}986.60 - \$79{,}155.50 = \$15{,}831.10$$

$$\text{Equity amount} = \frac{CTO}{R_E}$$

$$= \frac{\$15{,}381.10}{.06}$$

$$= \$263{,}851.67$$

The value of the property based on a straight market comparison is:

Debt amount	$ 754,983.59
Equity amount	263,851.67
Real estate market value	$1,018,835.26 (rounded to $1,019,000)

(c) ALTERNATIVE MODEL—INVESTMENT VALUE

The investment valuation process is based on the actual income performance of the property. The investment value calculation is conducted to represent the contribution of attributes that may vary from the typical market standards (management, in this case).

As stated originally, the subject is 98 percent occupied. The average rental is $.65 per square foot per month. The actual expense ratio is 50 percent. Both the rents and the expenses tend to be above market:

Gross income (GI): 51,500 sq. ft. @ $.65 per sq. ft. per month × 12	$401,700.00
Less: Vacancy @ 2%	8,034.00
Effective gross income	393,666.00
Less: Expenses @ 50% of GI	200,850.00
NOI	$192,816.00

The financial structure and value are calculated as follows:

$$DS = \frac{NOI}{DCR}$$

$$= \frac{\$192{,}816}{1.2}$$

$$= \$160{,}680.00$$

The mortgage amount, based on actual performance, is:

$$V_M = \frac{DS}{R_M}$$

$$= \frac{\$160{,}680.00}{.104844}$$

$$= \$1{,}532{,}562.67$$

The equity amount is:

$$NOI - DS = CTO$$

$$\$192{,}816.00 - \$160{,}680.00 = \$32{,}136.00$$

$$\text{Equity amount} = \frac{CTO}{R_E}$$

$$= \frac{\$32{,}136.00}{.06}$$

$$= \$535{,}600.00$$

The value of the property, based on the actual performance, is

Debt amount	$1,532,562.67
Equity amount	535,600.00
Investment value	$2,068,162.67 (rounded to $2,068,000)

§ 11.6 DECISION PROCESS OF PROPOSED VALUATION/UNDERWRITING MODEL

The application of the proposed model can concentrate on three of the model's aspects, to gain insight to the assets collateralized and the underwriting risk considered. These aspects are: the varying NOI produced under each scenario, and the alternative debt amounts and values calculated under the different assumptions of each analysis. The decision criteria are depicted in Table 11.1.

The classification of the decision criterion aids the underwriter. The traditional appraisal procedure would attempt to compare the superior performing subject property to a less successful group of market comparables. The principle of substitution requires upward and downward adjustments to the property, where the appraiser deems them appropriate. The end result of the adjustment process, using a high level of subjective judgment, is NOI of $125,763. The traditional approach would estimate an income of $30,776.40 ($125,763.00 – $94,986.60) more than if the real estate had been judged to be equivalent (not just comparable) to competitive properties.

The assumption of equivalence is a direct application of the principle of substitution. The rigid standard applied is that any other apartment complex is a direct investment alternative to the subject. In this case, the superior rent and inferior expense ratio of the subject are canceled out of the comparative process. A rigid application of substitution can apply because, in a down market of excess supply, the property could not be expected to perform any better than any of the competitive properties. The traditional benchmarks of a "normal market," such as a "typical return" or a "stabilized income," are not appropriate decision criteria, given the problem identified. Furthermore, a rigid application is reasonable, given the earlier observations that the property did not possess any significantly different physical attributes. By comparing the traditional appraisal procedure to a "rigid" real estate market value analysis, the lender would be loaning on $30,776.40 of income that is not supported by the performance of comparable properties. The excess income could disappear if other management were employed.

Table 11.1 Decision Criteria for Valuation and Loan Underwriting in a Down Market

	Alternative Bases		
Criterion	Traditional Appraisal Model	Equivalent Real Estate Value	Investment Value
NOI	$ 125,763.00	$ 94,986.60	$ 192,816.00
Debt amount	$ 999,607.99	$ 754,983.59	$1,532,562.67
Value	$1,350,000.00	$1,019,000.00	$2,068,000.00

The concern is whether the adjusted income concept used in traditional appraisal is appropriate in this type of market. In a "normal market," the variation between a specific property and the market standard is expected to be small. In the current economy, the traditional appraisal technique does not link an income projection representing a specific property's productivity to a value estimate based on the "market standard" of comparable property performance. If economic events have driven the temporal market standard down, then there must be a reason for superior returns for a specific property. If analysis indicates that the superior returns are not tied to the realty, the causal factor must be sought out. The traditional appraisal process of adjusting the subject for superior performance is not explaining the basis of value of an asset; it is only describing the fact of value. The investigative concern must be: If the return is not totally dependent on the realty, what is its source? Analysts asking this type of question not only describe the value but also are able to identify the risk related to the value estimate. The added dimension of insight (risk analysis) indicates the duration of the value source and the expectations of change in value.

In this case study, the excess income is attributed to the superior performance of the property's management. Therefore, a key question is: If the property goes belly-up, will the management contribution be redeemed in the market price paid or will the property's selling price be based on the operating standards of the comparable projects? If the project goes belly-up, the income to the property will be $94,986.60.

The income ($94,986.60) should be the basis for underwriting the realty in the first place. The property income is the basis for the two decision concerns of the lender. First, the lender is seeking a periodic income to cover the debt service. The more certain income is the typical income to surrounding properties. Second, the lender seeks an estimate of the potential sales price, if a default occurs. The likely selling price will be a value based on the comparable sales activity (which is $1,019,000, not $1,350,000). Therefore, the market value of the realty collateral is based directly on comparable sales.

However, the specific property is generating an income in excess of the market return to the real estate. This specific project can carry a higher debt service payment than the comparables. The quantity of that income stream can be measured because the income stream is no different than a security. Therefore, the income stream is potential collateral for debt. The basis for the excess income is the management. In the context of appraisal, management is property-specific. The basis for the future sales price is the realty. The real estate is constrained by market forces. If bad times injure the subject property, the management component of the project will not exist, but two distinct assets (or securities) will exist. The issue then becomes one of appropriately estimating the risk.

The counter argument should be that value over and above the realty contribution exists because of superior management. Real estate is management-intensive and requires much "sweat equity" to survive (if not succeed) in a down market. Management can make or break a project but should not be treated as an integral part of the real estate. Management is a separate asset or factor of production (distribution theory) that must receive a return. The appropriate combination of management and real property should create a value over and above its component parts.

With this perspective, the concern of the appraiser is to estimate the value of the combined factors. Traditional appraisal has accepted that the excess value is a residual return or economic rent attributed (via Ricardo) to the land.[5] Economists since Ricardo have recognized that any factor of production can be placed in the residual position. Later economists have concluded that returns over and above the wages to labor, market rent on land, and interest return to capital can be attributed to the entrepreneur as profit. Kahn, in applying this modern theory of distribution to real estate, recognized the failure to compensate the entrepreneur in the cost approach. This oversight results in the real estate's being overcompensated.[6]

To deal with the inequality in the ratio of assets to the financial structure, accountants have created the intangible asset of goodwill. Goodwill is defined as those elements of a business that cause customers to return to the business and that usually enable a firm to generate profit in excess of that which is required for a reasonable return on *all* of the other assets of the business.[7] Goodwill is usually measured by some excess profit or profit advantage technique.

As Table 11.1 shows, the subject property has excess profits over and above the standard market returns to the tangible assets. Under the definition of goodwill, the appraiser/underwriter must identify those

[5] D. P. O'Brien, *The Classical Economist* (Oxford: Clarendon Press, 1978): 37–49. *See also* Samuelson, *supra* note 1, at 517.

[6] Sanders A. Kahn, "The Entrepreneur—The Missing Factor," *The Appraisal Journal,* 31:4 (October 1963): 472–476; and "Entrepreneur Revisited," *The Appraisal Journal,* 41:1 (January 1973): 113–118.

[7] Glenn M. Desmond and Richard E. Kelley, *Business Valuation Handbook* (Los Angeles: Valuation Press Inc., 1980): 166.

elements (other than the real estate) that generate the excess profits. Some examples of the possible factors are advertising, a good reputation, and efficient operation. All of these factors are functions of the management.

Using the theory of distribution, the appraiser can estimate a value for the contribution of management or entrepreneurship by measuring the excess return to the apartment operation, over and above the operating income based on activity.

The underwriter must analyze the risk and returns of the total enterprise. The returns and their value can be measured for the total enterprise; the difficulty is the appropriate identification of risk. This difficulty, to a major extent, arises because of the intangible nature of the management contribution as an asset and the complexity in determining the management's economic life.

§ 11.7 MEASURING THE DISTRIBUTIVE VALUES

As Table 11.1 illustrates, the investment value, using the actual operating returns and losses of the project, supports a value of $2,068,000. This is a value contribution of $1,049,000 over the realty value ($2,068,000 – $1,019,000). Using traditional mortgage-equity analysis, the operation can support a loan of $1,532,562.67 (see Table 11.1). The loan, based on the investment or enterprise value, is $777,579.08 over the collateralized real estate loan ($1,532,562.67 – $754,983.59). The strength of this loan is based on NOI of $192,816 (investment or enterprise value). This income is $97,824.40 over the market rent supported by the comparables ($192,816 – $94,986). The basis for this return can be attributed to the management success of the project. It should not be attributed to the real estate, because the real estate will not generate the high investment return if the current management fails and the project must be sold against the competitive apartments (the "rigid" principle of substitution is in effect).

Therefore, rather than attribute $244,624.40 ($999,607.99 – $754,983.59) to the collateralized debt of the real estate (which will probably not be recaptured if the project fails), the lender might investigate the possibility of giving a business or personal loan based on the contribution of the management. The management component is important in any standard commercial or business loan. Management must be considered along with product, financing, market share, and marketing effort. The risk level and loan charges for a business loan vary with the lender's perception of the operation's success, the track record of the company, and its creditworthiness.

Given the above concerns, three issues are considered in the underwriting process:

1. The value difference between the investment value and the real estate market value. The difference is:

$$\$2{,}068{,}000 - \$1{,}019{,}000 = \$1{,}049{,}000.$$

At a loan-to-value ratio of 75 percent, the value differences could support a loan of $786,750 ($1,049,000 × .75).

Comment: The value difference of $1,049,000 could be the basis for a business loan. However, this value component fails to consider the risk exposure of the lender to the indeterminable economic life of the superior management. Management has shown the ability to beat the level of standard market performance, but has only done so in a down market for two or three years. The remainder of the operating performance occurred during a prior up market. Risk loading and discounting of this overall value are necessary to appropriately underwrite the contribution of the management.

2. The difference between the possible debt amount under the investment scenario and the amount of debt under the real estate market scenario. The difference is:

$$\$1{,}532{,}562.67 - \$754{,}983.59 = \$777{,}579.08$$

Comment: The actual performance of the property illustrates that it can carry a debt almost double that of the debt that can be supported by the underlying collateral value of the real estate. If the incremental income of $97,829.40 (see issue 3) is pledged as security for the loan difference, a yield of 11.935 percent to the lender would be indicated. This exceeds the 9.5 percent rate current in the market. However, the risk exposure of the 2.435 percent gain in return is not known. The risk surrounding the unknown term of the economic life of the successful management might be linked to the term of a typical business loan. The term of successful management should link to the mortgage term. The business of successfully selling living space may not be very different from selling any other durable good. Therefore, the risk concerns might be made more explicit in the analysis of the third issue.

3. The difference between the NOI of the actual production of the property and the NOI of the real estate based on market standards is the direct measure of the superior management. The difference is:

$$\$192{,}816 - \$94{,}986.60 = \$97{,}829.40$$

Comments: Several alternative decision options exist from this perspective.

a. The entire amount of the excess income can be used as the debt service payment for a business loan. In this example, the lenders have decided to make a loan for 10 years at 15 percent. The loan amount would be $490,983.12. This loan and the real estate loan of $754,983.59 gives a total loan package of $1,245,966.71. The weighted yield for the combined loan is 11.67 percent.

b. The excess income of $97,829.40 can be allocated between the equity and debt positions. The 6 percent equity return of $5,869.76 can be deducted from the income, leaving $91,959.63 for debt service. This will support a debt of $461,524.14 at the business loan terms. The combined loans are $1,216,507.73. The weighted yield for this loan structure is 11.59 percent.

c. The excess income can be allocated between an entrepreneurial return and additional debt. This entrepreneurial return is treated like the developer's return in the development of a subdivision. An 18 percent return is deducted from the periodic income stream ($17,609.22). The remainder of $80,220.18 is used to establish the loan amount. The business loan is $402,606.52, and the total loan is $1,157,590.11. The weighted yield to the lender is 11.41 percent.

In all three situations proposed above, the loan package is for a greater amount and affords a higher yield to the lender than the loan based on the traditional appraisal/underwriting perspective. The alternative loan structures also allow more capital to flow to the successful projects.

§ 11.8 BENEFITS AND CONCLUSIONS OF VALUATION/UNDERWRITING MODEL

In practice, lenders tend to recognize successful management and other non-real estate or intangible assets in the underwriting of real estate assets. However, as the traditional appraisal example shows, the benefits are all assigned to the real estate. If misfortune hits the project, as is possible in a down market, the secured collateral is only the real estate. The overvaluation to allow for the non-real estate factors results in accusations about the appraisers, the lenders, the parties in a transaction, and/or the appraisal and underwriting process. This is misdirected negative energy. The problems are the appropriate identification of the assets and the appropriate structuring and underwriting of the loans. It is hoped that the above models will contribute to addressing the appropriate issues.

§ 11.9 CONCLUSIONS ON ASSET MANAGEMENT IN DOWN MARKETS

Two models are proposed to aid management decisions in a down market. Both models are based on the theory of distribution, a concept concerned with the rewards and allocations between factors of production. The theory of distribution is a complement to the theory of value. Distribution helps in the valuation process by aiding in the appropriate identification of the assets involved in the problems experienced in uncertain markets. The model discussions show the options between solvency and value as decision criteria, because they link to different market environments.

The first model offers an alternative tool to refinance or restructure outstanding contract debt that exceeds the market price of the property.

The second model enables the identification of joint assets comprising a real estate project. The levels of the components of an enterprise aid in the valuation of individual projects in fluctuating markets.

Both models enable alternative perspectives in estimating risk and returns/values in down markets. The models are offered as tactical tools, to identify the potential for *solvency* to all parties involved in real estate financial relationships. Solvency rather than value may be the major concern until equity value can once more be accumulated.

Twelve

Tax Assessment Analysis: Loaded Cap Rate and Market Value

§ 12.1 INTRODUCTION

The concept of market value is used as the basis of many real estate decisions. Examples of these decisions are the purchase, selling, financing, taxation, and use selection of a given property.

A dilemma occurs in the valuation of properties for financing and property tax purposes: value cannot be estimated without knowing the capital structure (financing), and the financing cannot be established without knowing the value.[1] The same interrelationships exist between ad valorem taxes and property values (especially in jurisdictions premised on market value).

The problem with the tax situation is illustrated by the following situation. Typically, property taxes are deducted, in order to estimate net operating income (NOI). The NOI as a measure of property

[1] Suzanne R. Mellen, "Simultaneous Valuation: A New Capitalization Technique for Hotel and Other Income Properties," *The Appraisal Journal,* 51:2 (April 1983): 165–189.

productivity is then capitalized into a value by a market cap rate. If the purpose of the valuation is to establish ad valorem taxes, then inconsistency occurs. Taxes must be estimated to establish a value, in order to determine property taxes. This has often been achieved by using the existing assessed value (which may not be current market value) and/or historic taxes.

This inherent inconsistency can contribute to a biased indication of value if, in the interests of accuracy, the previous charge for ad valorem taxes, a fixed expense,[2] is used in the reconstruction of the operating statement.

The property tax dilemma, like financing, can be overcome by allowing for the tax impact on value within the rate structure.[3] Appraisers are often criticized for what appears to be an overindulgence in rate analysis rather than a use of the more generally accepted cash flow techniques. As the following examples illustrate, appraisers face problems of

Table 12.1 Reconstructed Operating Statements

Ad valorem tax rate: $2.00/$100 of assessed value
Assessed value: $1,000,000
Taxes: $20,000

		Typical Model		Loaded Rate Model
Gross scheduled income		$150,000		$150,000
Less: Vacancy and collection loss (15%)		−22,500		−22,500
Effective gross income		127,500		127,500
Less: Expenses:				
Taxes	$20,000		*	
Insurance	5,000		$ 5,000	
Management (10%)	12,750		12,750	
Maintenance	2,500		2,500	
Total expenses		−40,250		−20,250
Net operating income (NOI)		$ 87,250		$107,250

*Item to be determined based on market value; charge for taxes is included in overall rate.

[2] American Institute of Real Estate Appraisers, *The Appraisal of Real Estate*, 9th Edition (Chicago: AIREA, 1987): 446.

[3] *Ibid.*

interrelationships (simultaneous occurrences) and the availability of objectively documented data.

The comparative advantage of loaded rate analysis is illustrated in Table 12.1.

In the "typical" model of a reconstructed operating statement, the NOI is processed into a value indication by direct capitalization. For illustration purposes, an overall market-supported cap rate of 12 percent is used:

$$\$87{,}250/.12 = \$727{,}000$$

In the "loaded" example, the overall rate of capitalization is added to the effective tax rate to produce a rate inclusive of property tax (.12 + .02 = .14); thus, $107,250/.14 = $766,000.

Proof: The $766,000 value is the basis for the ad valorem taxes. The taxes are computed at the market value and charged against the property:

$$\text{Assessed value } (\$766{,}000) \times \text{Tax rate } (\$2.00/100) = \$15{,}320$$

Thus:

Gross scheduled income		$150,000
Less: Vacancy and collection loss (15%)		− 22,500
Effective gross income		127,500
Less: Expenses:		
Taxes	$15,320	
Insurance	5,000	
Management (10%)	12,750	
Maintenance	2,500	
Total expenses		− 35,570
Net operating income		$ 91,930

Therefore, a value based on the market-supported cap rate is:

$$\$91{,}930/.12 = \$766{,}000$$

By loading the capitalization rate with the effective tax rate, sufficient income is afforded to pay the tax burden based on a documented market value. Any prejudice in indicated value caused by reliance on previous assessed value or historic taxes is removed.

Loading the cap rate or discount rate is an essential requirement where precise measurement of expenses is required for testing feasibility and highest and best use.

§ 12.2 YIELD CAPITALIZATION

The loaded cap rate technique is also an appropriate expansion of capitalization models. To illustrate this expanded analysis, the Akerson format is employed to relate the mortgage-equity yield techniques to the direct capitalization rate claimed from the market.

☐ Yield capitalization example = 75 percent loan-to-value ratio, 10 percent interest rate payable monthly for a 20-year amortization period

Yield rate = 14 percent

Holding period = 10 years

Future expectations = 20 percent appreciation

Akerson band of investment (BOI) model:

Debt position (.75 × .11580)	.08685
Equity position (.25 × .14)	.03500
Equity build-up via amortization of mortgage (.75 × .26975 × .0517)	.01046
Basic rate (Y_o)	.11139
Expected change at resale (.20 × .0517)	.010340
Overall cap rate (R_o)	.10105

Capitalization: $87,250/.10105 = $863,434 (rounded to $863,500)

The cap rate is lower in the yield capitalization technique than in the direct ratio model, because of the allowance for an increase in value over a projected holding period and the consideration of financial leverage. A composite rate (Y_o or r = basic rate) illustrates the blended cost of capital, allowing for both debt and equity dollars. The expectations of a change in value (appreciation) over a holding period are illustrated as a percentage. All of the above factors (debt and equity capital, a holding period, and expectation of future value changes) have an impact on property value. These factors and the perspective of their inclusion in the valuation process differentiate yield capitalization from direct capitalization.

Property taxation is a concern in the valuation of property over time. This concern can be incorporated into the yield cap techniques and into direct capitalization. This is also done in a loaded rate format, as follows:

Akerson format with loaded rate:

Debt position (.75 × .11580)	.08685
Equity position (.25 × .14)	.03500
Equity build-up (.75 × .26975 × .01517)	.01046
Y_o	.11139
Periodic property tax loading (+t)	.02000
Basic rate loaded for tax expense	.13139
Expected value change (.20 × .0517)	.01034
Loaded cap rate	.12105 (rounded to 12.1%)

Capitalization: \$107,250/.12105 = \$885,997

Tax calculation: \$885,997 × .02 = \$17,720

Proof of loaded rate analysis:

Gross scheduled income		\$150,000
Less: Vacancy and collection loss (15%)		– 22,500
Effective gross income		127,500
Less: Expenses:		
Taxes	\$17,720	
Insurance	5,000	
Management (10%)	12,750	
Maintenance	2,500	
Total expenses		39,970
NOI		\$ 89,530

$\frac{NOI}{R_o}$ or $NOI \div R_o$ = \$89,530 ÷ .10105 = \$885,997

(a) ELLWOOD FORMAT

The load rate can also be constructed in the Ellwood format:

$$R_o = Y_E - M(Y_E + P\frac{1}{s_{\overline{n}|y}} - R_M) + t - \Delta_o\frac{1}{s_{\overline{n}|y}}$$

$$= .14 - .75(.14 + .26975 \times .0517 - .11580) + .02 - .20(.0517)$$

$$= .12105$$

NOI/R_o = \$107,250/.12105 = \$885,997 (rounded to \$886,000)

(b) LOADED RATE ANALYSIS AND CASH FLOW PROJECTION

Yield capitalization enables the calculation of the impact of the yearly property tax deduction within the rate structure. A fallacy of using discounted cash flow in tax analysis is that ad valorem taxes cannot be forecast without the projection of a value estimate over time. Again, the dilemma of the relationship of value to property tax arises.

The loaded rate method aids compliance with the process considered in the discounted cash flow model, by enabling an estimation of the missing data (future taxes; therefore, future NOI), as follows:

	Year		
	1	2	3
EGI	$127,500	$133,875	$140,568
Less: Property tax	17,720	—	—
Less: Other operating expenses	20,250	21,667	23,184
NOI	$ 89,530	?	?

As illustrated above, if sufficient date are not available, the cash flow cannot be generated. The yield capitalization technique allows a forecast of possible property taxes based on the forecast of future resale.

Continuing the previous example, the property is projected to appreciate by 20 percent over a 10-year period. Given the current estimated value of $885,997, the property value in 10 years would be $1,063,196 ($885,997 × 1.20). If the tax rate remains at $2.00 per $100 of assessed value, the property tax in 10 years will be $21,264. The forecast in taxes per year over the 10 years, at the desired 14 percent equity yield rate, would be as follows:

Total growth in property taxes over the 10-year holding period ($17,720 × 1.20) = $21,264

Total change or increase for period: $tn - t_1 = \Delta t$

$21,264 − $17,720 = $3,544 (future value of $183.22 per year for 10 years at 14% = $3,543, rounded to $3,544)

Change per year based on the 14 percent yield:

$$\Delta t \times \frac{1}{s_n} \text{ @ } 14\% = \text{Base tax flow per year}$$

$3,544 × .0517 = $183.22

Table 12.2 Annual Projection of Property Tax Over Holding Period

Year	Beginning Taxes (t_1)	+	Base Tax Flow (Sinking Fund)	×	s_n	=	Tax forecast
1	$17,720		$183.22		1		$17,903.22
2	17,720		183.22		2.140		18,112.10
3	17,720		183.22		3.439		18,350.22
4	17,720		183.22		4.921		18,621.68
5	17,720		183.22		6.610		18,931.14
6	17,720		183.22		8.535		19,283.92
7	17,720		183.22		10.730		19,686.09
8	17,720		183.22		13.232		20,144.56
9	17,720		183.22		16.085		20,667.23
10	17,720		183.22		19.337		21,263.07

$s_{\overline{n}|}$ = future worth of $1 per period. The factors are truncated. Table 12.2 illustrates an income or, more specifically, a tax outflow that follows the pattern of an accumulating sinking fund. The property tax growth pattern is that of the J-factor income pattern. The J pattern is used to remain consistent with the structure of the mortgage-equity yield capitalization models (both Ellwood's and Akerson's).

If the appraiser is required, or requested, or prefers to illustrate the tax forecast in the context of a discounted cash flow, the projected J pattern expenses can be used in that context. The J pattern can only be used if a flexible cash flow program is available. Most cash flow programs are designed to deal with income and expenses figures growing (declining) at compound rates.

The J pattern tax flows approximate a compounding income pattern and can be converted into an estimation of such a pattern.

The conversion from the J pattern to a compounding growth rate usable in a discounted cash flow (which is required in most computer programs) is possible by converting the J factor to a K factor, as follows:

$$K = 1 + \Delta_I J$$

where:

Δ_I = the 20 percent growth projection for the property taxes

J = the value/income adjustment for a changing cash flow (expense) for 10 years at 14 percent; that factor is .3388

$K = 1 + (.20 \times .3388)$

$= 1.06776$

The K factor table (or the formula worked through) indicates that, at 14 percent for 10 years, the compounding growth rate for the property taxes is 1.8772 percent or a factor of 1.018772. The following 10-year expense forecast for property taxes results:

Year 1	$18,054	Year 6	$19,812
2	18,391	7	20,183
3	18,736	8	20,562
4	19,088	9	20,948
5	19,447	10	21,341

The compounding projection starts about $50 higher in year 1 than the J pattern estimates, and grows to a difference of more than $500 (by year 6). The difference between J and K estimates then collapses to within $78 in year 10. The total forecasted change in property tax over the holding period can be checked by considering the loaded rates within the value structure:

$$\text{Value} \times \text{Appreciation} \text{Tax rate} = \text{Change in taxes}$$
$$V_o \times \Delta_o \times t = \Delta t$$
$$\$885{,}997 \times (.20 \times .02) = \$3{,}544$$

§ 12.3 VALUE IMPACT OF CHANGES IN PROPERTY TAX

There has been an ongoing debate as to whether expectations of increasing property tax are incorporated into current transaction prices. If the perspective is that the impact of future expenditures (in this case, property taxes) is implicit in the prices negotiated in real estate, then yield capitalization can be expanded to explicitly identify the present worth of the tax flow.

The impact of the increasing taxes over the holding period can be incorporated into the valuation model as follows:

$$R_o = Y_E - M(Y_E + P\frac{1}{S_{\overline{n}|y}} - R_M) + t - \left((1 - t)\Delta_o\frac{1}{S_{\overline{n}|y}}\right)$$
$$= .14 - .75(.14 + .26975 \times .0517 - .11580) + .02 - ((1 - .02)$$
$$(.20).0517)$$
$$= .13139 - (.010133)$$
$$= .121257$$
$$\frac{NOI}{R_o} = \$107{,}250/.121257 = \$884{,}486 \text{ (rounded to } \$884{,}500)$$

The impact on value of an increasing tax flow in the projected pattern is approximately $1,500 ($886,000 – $884,500).

The question for debate among appraisers is: Should the valuation for property taxes consider the impact of property taxes on value? This is similar to the dilemma in mortgage-equity analysis. If the impact of financing on value (which is the basis of financing) is considered, tax flows should be considered also. On the other hand, the Federal Home Loan Bank Board and other groups require cash equivalency analysis; this dilemma is the basis for alternative philosophical perspectives that will be argued through the appeals process.

§ 12.4 CONCLUSION

The issues of tax assessment and market value estimation are renewed areas of appraisal debate. Various positions will continue to be taken by individual appraisers. This chapter has offered a technique of analysis that is appropriate, regardless of the position taken.

The logic of the loaded rate technique is tied to the appraisal dilemma of calculating value and taxes simultaneously. The value of the loaded rate has been illustrated and expanded via yield capitalization as a tool for forecasting.